JURISDICTION AND JUDGMENTS IN RELATION TO EU COMPETITION LAW CLAIMS

This book sets out the way that, through enhanced private antitrust enforcement reform, private international law has a pivotal role in EU competition law disputes with an international element. The author offers a thorough analysis of the post-2003 policy of the EU favouring private law enforcement of EU competition law and its implementation under the existing provisions for jurisdiction and recognition and enforcement of foreign judgments under the Brussels I regime. The work also deals with how the jurisdiction and recognition and enforcement of judgments issues are dealt with in England under the common law rules applicable when Brussels I does not apply. The complex private international law problems in respect of cross-border class actions that have arisen in several countries, as well as judgments in relation to antitrust infringements, are also discussed. The author further examines the choice of law issues that may arise before the English courts under Rome I and Rome II. The potential problems regarding jurisdiction of arbitral tribunals and choice of law in arbitral proceedings in relation to EU competition law claims, and the jurisdiction of English courts in proceedings ancillary to arbitration claims, are dealt with accordingly.

Volume 3 in the series Studies in Private International Law

Studies in Private International Law

Volume 1*: Electronic Consumer Contracts in the Conflict of Laws*
Sophia Tang

Volume 2*: Foreign Currency Claims in the Conflict of Laws*
Vaughan Black

Volume 3*: Jurisdiction and Judgments in Relation to EU Competition Law Claims*
Mihail Danov

Jurisdiction and Judgments in Relation to EU Competition Law Claims

Mihail Danov

•HART•
PUBLISHING
OXFORD AND PORTLAND, OREGON
2011

Published in the United Kingdom by Hart Publishing Ltd
16C Worcester Place, Oxford, OX1 2JW
Telephone: +44 (0)1865 517530
Fax: +44 (0)1865 510710
E-mail: mail@hartpub.co.uk
Website: http://www.hartpub.co.uk

Published in North America (US and Canada) by
Hart Publishing
c/o International Specialized Book Services
920 NE 58th Avenue, Suite 300
Portland, OR 97213-3786
USA
Tel: +1 503 287 3093 or toll-free: (1) 800 944 6190
Fax: +1 503 280 8832
E-mail: orders@isbs.com
Website: http://www.isbs.com

British Library Cataloguing in Publication Data
Data Available

ISBN: 978-1-84113-659-2

Typeset by Compuscript Ltd, Shannon
Printed and bound in Great Britain by
TJ International Ltd, Padstow, Cornwall

SERIES EDITORS' PREFACE

Studies in Private International Law is a new series of books published by Hart Publishing under the Series Editorship of Paul Beaumont and Jonathan Harris. It builds on the success of the *Journal of Private International Law*, which is published by the same publisher and is subject to the same editorial control. The *Journal* began life in 2005. Due to its success in attracting high-quality articles and its rigorous double-blind refereeing system, it has quickly established itself as an essential reference point for anyone doing research on private international law. The circulation of the *Journal* is growing steadily and it expanded from two issues to three issues per year in 2008.

The *Journal* has helped to bring together the global private international law community by providing a dedicated forum for publishing excellent articles in English, and by running conferences at which ideas can be exchanged and young scholars are given an opportunity to cut their teeth. Successful conferences have taken place in Aberdeen (2005), Birmingham (2007) and New York (2009). The next *Journal* conference will be in Milan (2011).

As part of the same stable, the www.conflictoflaws.net website provides the private international law community with an innovative and readily accessible means of keeping up to date with developments in the subject. It is an interactive news and discussion portal, updated by a team of scholars from around the world. The creator and Chief Editor of the website is Martin George (University of Birmingham).

The one obvious gap in our activities was a book series for the publication in English of scholarly monographs, collections of essays, or other specialised works on private international law. We are delighted that this has now been rectified with the launch of 'Studies in Private International Law'. The series editors are keen to receive proposals for books in this series on any aspect of private international law. The emphasis is on quality. We are particularly interested in books that have relevance to readers in more than one country. This can be achieved by writing, for instance, about the Hague Conventions on Private International Law, or regional instruments on private international law (eg a monograph on a European Regulation), or by a comparative, historical, policy-oriented or theoretical approach to private international law.

Dr Mihail Danov has produced a book that tackles most aspects of the private international law of competition in EU and English law. The title of the book modestly focuses on the jurisdiction rules and recognition and enforcement of judgments in the context of EU competition law claims. The Brussels I Regulation is indeed the primary focus of the book. The publication is timely because the author has cogent suggestions for how Brussels I might be reformed in the forthcoming review that will fully get under way with the Commission's proposal in December 2010. The author goes further by also tackling the English rules on jurisdiction which are preserved by Article 4 of Brussels I. His preference for the flexibility of those rules in this context should be taken into account when considering whether or not to globalise the Brussels I rules to apply no matter where the defendant is domiciled in the forthcoming review of Brussels I.

However, the content of the book goes further than its title suggests, with important and extensive treatment of arbitration, and an analysis of the applicable law rules under the Rome I and Rome II Regulations, in relation to private competition claims. The book will be of primary relevance to academics and practitioners in the EU but it should have a wider resonance in the global private international law and competition law communities given the importance of EU private international law and competition law and the author's awareness of important developments elsewhere, notably in the US.

This is a thorough and well argued work on an area of law, the interface between private international law and competition law, that is of great practical importance and that has not been comprehensively analysed before.

Paul Beaumont (University of Aberdeen)
Jonathan Harris (University of Birmingham)

ACKNOWLEDGEMENTS

This book is a significantly expanded and updated version of my PhD thesis which was submitted to the University of Aberdeen in October 2007. I am particularly indebted to my PhD supervisor, Professor Dr Florian Becker, for his invaluable academic support without which this book would not have been written. In this context, I wish to thank the University of Aberdeen and their Six Century Campaign for providing their generous funding for my PhD study within the School of Law.

I would also like to thank to Professor Tibor Varady (Central European University, Budapest) and Dr Vesna Lazic (TMC Asser Institute, The Hague) for their valuable help and advice at the early stage of my research. Gratitude is extended to the Central European University for financing the early stage of my research and the Dutch Foreign Office for paying the cost for my 3-month research period at TMC Asser Institute.

I am also very grateful to my PhD examiners, Professor Paul Beaumont and Dr Jonathan Fitchen, for their challenging questions and constructive suggestions which helped me turn my PhD thesis into a book.

I want to thank to Mr Richard Hart and his team at Hart Publishing for making the publication of this book possible.

I have tried to state the law as it stood on 1 January 2010.

CONTENTS

TABLE OF CASES

United Kingdom

Australia

Belgium

Canada

Denmark

European Union

France

Germany

Italy

Netherlands

Republic of Ireland

Singapore

Sweden

Switzerland

United States of America

International

TABLE OF LEGISLATION

United Kingdom

Statutory Instruments

Austria

Belgium

European Union

Directives

Regulations

France

Germany

Italy

Lithuania

Netherlands

Spain

Portugal

Sweden

Switzerland

United States of America

International

1

Introduction

1.1 EU Competition Law

The UK's accession to the European Community, through the European Communities Act 1972, made the EC Treaties part of the law of the UK, authorised the implementation of future EU legislation by delegated legislation, and established the supremacy of EU law.[1] Thus, it is a duty of an English court, when delivering a final judgment, to override any rule of national law found to be in conflict with any directly enforceable rule derived from the EU Treaties.[2] Moreover, case law has made clear that much of the EU law is directly applicable and may also have 'direct effect'.[3] For example, the Court of Justice held that Arts 101(1) and 102 TFEU (ex Arts 81(1) and 82 TEC) produce direct effects in relations between individuals and create rights for individuals concerned, which the national courts must safeguard.[4] Although, the EU case law lays down the general principle of national procedural autonomy,[5] certain limits on that principle have been placed by the Court of Justice with regard to EU competition law claims.[6]

Articles 101 and 102 (ex Arts 81 and 82 TEC) are the main competition law provisions contained in the Treaty on the Functioning of the European Union.[7] Article 101(1) TFEU prohibits agreements between undertakings which prevent,

[1] See *R v Secretary of State for Transport, ex p Factortame (No 2)* [1991] 1 AC 603 (HL) 659 (Lord Bridge). See more on supremacy: P Craig and G de Burca, *EU Law: Text, Cases and Materials* (4th edn, OUP, Oxford 2008) 344–77; C Grabenwarter, 'National constitutional law relating to the European Union' in A von Bogdandy and J Bast (eds), *Principles of European Constitutional Law* (2nd edn, Hart Publishing and Verlag CH Beck, Oxford and Munich, 2010) 83.

[2] C Mollers, 'Pouvoir Constituant-Constitution-Constitutionalisation' in Bogdandy and Bast (n 1) 169, 193.

[3] See Case 26/62 *Van Gend en Loos v Nederlandse Administratie der Belastingen* [1963] ECR 1.

[4] Case 127/73 *BRT v SABAM* [1974] ECR 51 [16]; Case C-282/95 P *Guerin Automobiles v Commission* [1997] ECR I-1503 [39]; Case C-453/99 *Courage Ltd v Crehan* [2001] ECR I-6297 [23].

[5] Case 158/80 *Rewe-Handelsgesellschaft Nord mbH v Hauptzollamt Kiel* [1981] ECR 1805; Case C-261/95 *Palmisani* [1997] ECR I-4025 [27]; Joined Cases C-295/04-298/04 *Manfredi v Lloyd Adriatico Assicurazioni SpA* [2006] 5 CMLR 17. See also Case C-126/97 *Eco Swiss China Time Ltd v Benetton International NV* [1999] ECR I-3055 [43]–[48]. See more: F Becker, 'Application of Community law by Member States' public authorities: between autonomy and effectiveness' (2007) 44 *CML Rev* 1035.

[6] *Courage* (n 4).

[7] J Drexl, 'Competition law as part of the European Constitution' in Bogdandy and Bast (n 1) 653.

restrict or distort competition within the Member States;[8] Art 101(2) TFEU declares all such agreements void. Article 101(3) TFEU, however, exempts agreements under Art 101(1) TFEU provided that certain conditions are met. It should be clearly understood that the presence of an anti-competitive term in a contract does not necessarily invalidate the whole agreement, as the practice of the Court of Justice of the European Union[9] and the English court[10] is to sever illegal provisions from otherwise lawful agreements.[11] Article 102 TFEU prohibits conduct which amounts to abusive behaviour by a dominant undertaking in a relevant market. In spite of the fact that Art 102 does not include a provision equivalent to Art 101(2) TFEU, which automatically and retroactively nullifies any agreements prohibited by Art 101(1) TFEU, the Court of Justice has stated that an agreement in conflict with Art 102 TFEU should be automatically void as well.[12] In addition, Council Regulation 139/2004[13] was introduced, in order to permit effective control of all concentrations in terms of their effect on the structure of competition in the EU.[14] The Regulation empowers the Commission to establish whether a merger with an EU dimension is compatible with the internal market, and to prohibit it if it would significantly impeded effective competition in the internal market.[15]

It is well established that Arts 101 and 102 TFEU may be applied extra-territorially. The extra-territorial application of competition laws has been widely discussed by the courts[16] and commentators.[17] In the *Wood Pulp*

[8] The test that is adopted by the EU Court of Justice is whether it is 'possible to foresee with a sufficient degree of probability on the basis of a set of objective factors of law or of fact that agreement in question may have an influence direct or indirect, actual or potential on the pattern of trade between Member States.' See Case 56/65 *Société de la Technique Minière v Maschinenbau Ulm GmbH* [1966] ECR 235, 249.

[9] Eg *Société de la Technique Minière* (n 8); Case 319/82 *Societe de Vente de Ciments et Betons de l'Est v Kerpen and Kerepen GmbH* [1983] ECR 4173.

[10] Eg *Chemidus Wavin v Société pour la Transformation* [1977] FSR 181 (CA); *Inntepreneur Estates Ltd v Mason* [1993] 2 CMLR 293 (QBD); *Innterpreneur Estates (GL) Ltd v Boyes* [1995] ECC 16 (CA).

[11] R Whish, *Competition Law* (6th edn, OUP, Oxford, 2008) 312–14.

[12] *BRT* (n 4). See also: J Faull and A Nikpay, *The EC Law of Competition* (2nd edn, OUP, Oxford, 2007) 412–13; U Bernitz, 'The sanction of voidness under Article 82 EC and its relation to the right to damages' in A Ezrachi (ed), *Article 82 EC: Reflection on its Recent Evolution* (Hart Publishing, Oxford, 2009) 187, 188–89.

[13] Council Regulation 139/2004 of 20 January 2004 on the control of concentrations between undertakings [2004] OJ L24/1.

[14] Recital 6 of Merger Regulation (n 13).

[15] Recitals 23 and 24 of Merger Regulation (n 13).

[16] The EU approach: Joined Cases 89/85, 104/85, 114/85, 116–17/85, and 125–29/85 *Ahlstrom v Commission* [1988] ECR 5193 (*Wood Pulp* Cartel Case). Compare the US approach: (a) territorial approach: *America Banana v United Fruit* 213 US 347 (1909); (b) the 'effects' approach: *United States v Aluminum Co of America (Alcoa)* 148 F 2d 416 (2d Cir 1945); (c) the 'balancing' approach: *Timberline Lumber v Bank of America* 549 F 2d 597 (9th Cir 1976). See also Restatement of the Law (Third), The Foreign Relations Law of the United States (1987) [403].

[17] M Waelbroeck, 'The European Community Approach' in CJ Omstead (ed) *Extra-territorial Application of Laws and Responses Thereto* (International Law Association in association with ESC Publishing Limited, Oxford 1989) 74; V Pavic, *Extra-territoriality in the Matters of Antitrust* (European Press Academic Publishing, Italy, 2001); WS Dodge, 'Extraterritoriality and Conflict-of-Laws Theory:

case,[18] the Court of Justice held that the threshold for application of Art 101 TFEU is the 'implementation' of an agreement within the EU.[19] As a result, Art 101 would apply to an agreement or concerted practice entered into between non-EU undertakings outside the EU. This would be so, if the agreement or concerted practice was (or was intended to be) implemented within the EU. Following this line of reasoning, it could be concluded that Art 102 TFEU would also apply to conduct of a firm, which holds a dominant position within the EU, even if the firm in question was established outside of the EU. The extra-territorial application of EU competition laws can be further deduced from the decisions in the *Gencor/Lonrho*[20] and *GE/Honeywell*[21] cases.[22] There is 'no reason to suggest the territorial scope of application of [Arts 101 and 102 TFEU] would be any different in the case of private litigation'[23] which seems to suggest that different sets of private international law rules could be relevant in this context.[24]

1.2 Enforcement of EU Competition Law

A centralised enforcement scheme was set up by Regulation 17.[25] Pursuant to Art 9(1) of Regulation 17, only the European Commission could award an individual exemption under Art 101(3) TFEU. This was meant to ensure that Arts 101 and 102 TFEU were applied effectively and uniformly in the EU. Further Regulations such as 19/65/EEC[26] and 2821/71[27] empowered the Commission to issue block exemptions under Art 101(3) TFEU to certain categories of agreements. However, the centralised scheme was found to hamper the application

An argument for judicial unilateralism' (1998) 39 *Harvard International Law Journal* 101; J Adolphsen, 'The Conflict of laws in cartel matters in a globalised world: alternatives to the effects doctrine' (2005) *Journal of International Private Law* 156; A Jones and B Sufrin, *EC Competition Law: Text, Cases and Materials* (3rd edn, OUP, Oxford, 2008) 1356–95.

[18] *Wood Pulp* (n 16).

[19] Ibid [16].

[20] Case T-102/96 *Gencor Ltd v Commission* [1999] ECR II-753. See also Case No IV/M.619 *Gencor/Lonrho* [1997] OJ L11/30.

[21] Case T-210/01 *General Electric v Commission* [2005] ECR II-5575.

[22] Jones and Sufrin (n 17) 1377–87. See also E Fox, 'The Merger Regulation and its territorial reach' [1999] *European Competition Law Review* 334.

[23] C Withers, 'Jurisdiction and Applicable Law in Antitrust Tort Claims' (2002) *Journal of Business Law* 250, 257–58.

[24] See section 1.6 below.

[25] Council Regulation (EEC) 17 of 6 February 1962: first Regulation implementing Articles 81 and 82 of the Treaty [1962] OJ L13/204.

[26] Council Regulation (ECC) 19/65 of 2 March 1965 on the application of Article 85(3) of the Treaty to certain categories of agreements and concerted practices [1965] OJ 36/533). See also Council Regulation (EC) 1215/1999 of 10 June 1999 amending Regulation 19/65 [1999] OJ L148/1.

[27] Council Regulation (EEC) 2821/71 of 20 December 1971 on the application of Article 85(3) of the Treaty to categories of agreements, decisions and concerted practices [1971] OJ L285/46.

of EU competition rules by the courts and competition authorities.[28] This was largely due to the fact that the Commission was overloaded with administrative work, and the centralised enforcement of competition law was considered increasingly difficult in a European Union with 27 Member States.

Regulation 1/2003 replaced the centralised system with a directly applicable exception system, in which the competition authorities and Member States' courts have the power to apply not only Art 101(1) and Art 102, which had been deemed to have direct effect by virtue of the Court of Justice case law,[29] but also Art 101(3).[30] One of the important objectives of Regulation 1/2003 was to encourage private EU competition law enforcement in Europe. Regulation 1/2003 regards Arts 101(1) and (3) TFEU as forming an indivisible whole. There is a great amount of literature that is devoted to decentralised enforcement of EU competition law, dealing with the substantive and procedural framework for private actions in Europe.[31] The Regulation abolished the Commission's monopoly on exemption decisions issued under Art 101(3) TFEU and national courts were allowed to apply Art 101 in its entirety. Article 6 of Regulation 1/2003 states that national courts will have full jurisdiction to determine whether an agreement complies with EU competition law. For that reason Art 15 of Regulation 1/2003 sets out a mechanism for co-operation between national courts and the Commission. Article 16 of Regulation 1/2003 obliges national courts to avoid judgments that would conflict with a decision contemplated by the Commission. Accordingly, a national court has to consider the question of whether it would be necessary to stay its proceedings to avoid such a conflict. If the answer is affirmative, then the English court should determine whether it would be necessary to order interim measures to safeguard the interest of the parties.[32]

After the reform, private parties are supposed to play a pivotal role in aiding enforcement of Arts 101 and 102 TFEU by means of private actions for damages before national courts.[33] The Commission regards such private enforcement as

[28] Recital 3 of Council Regulation (EC) 1/2003 of 16 December 2002 on the implementation of the rules on competition laid down in Articles 81 and 82 of the Treaty [2003] OJ L1/1. See for more arguments for decentralisation Commission (EC) 'Modernisation of the Rules Implementing Articles 85 and 86 of the EC Treaty' (White Paper) Commission Programme 99/027 COM (1999) 101 final [1999] OJ C132/1.

[29] *BRT* (n 4) [14]–[16]; *Guerin Automobiles* (n 4) [39]; *Courage* (n 4) [23].

[30] See Recital 4 of Regulation 1/2003.

[31] Eg WPJ Wils, *Principles of European Antitrust Enforcement* (Hart Publishing, Oxford, 2005); M Gray, M Lester, C Darbon and others, *EU Competition Law: Procedure and Remedies* (OUP, Oxford, 2006); A Komninos, *EC Private Antitrust Enforcement: Decentralised Application of EC Competition Law by National Courts* (Hart Publishing, Oxford, 2008); J Basedow (ed), *Private Enforcement of EC Competition Law* (Kluwer Law International, The Hague, 2007).

[32] Case C234/89 *Delimitis v Henninger Brau* [1991] ECR I-935 [52]; Case C-344/98 *Masterfoods* [2000] ECR I-11369 [58]. The grant of an interim injunction is an inherent power of the national courts (eg *Cutsforth v Mansfield Inns* [1986] 1 WLR 558). This remains the case under Regulation 1/2003. See more Goyder (n 14) 473; C Kerse and N Khan, *EC Antitrust Procedure* (5th edn, Sweet & Maxwell, London, 2005) 301.

[33] See Recital 7 of Regulation 1/2003; 'Damages Actions for Breach of the EC Antitrust Rules' (White Paper) COM (2008) 165 final. See also: Case C-213/89 *R v Secretary of State ex p Factortame*

a useful and necessary adjunct to the activities of the Commission and National Competition Authorities (NCAs).[34] Enhanced private enforcement is set to maximise the amount of enforcement as a means of enforcement complementary to public enforcement.[35] It has been held by the Court of Justice that the full effectiveness of Arts 101 and 102 TFEU would be put at risk if it were not open to any individual in proceedings before a national court to claim damages for loss caused to him by a contract or by conduct liable to restrict or distort competition.[36] However, the Commission's Ashurst study[37] showed that actions for damages as a form of private EU competition law enforcement are underdeveloped in Europe. The main reason was said to stem from 'lack of clarity, either because what the legal basis actually is for such claims is unclear or because the interaction between the specific legal basis and general provisions on conditions for liability is unclear.'[38] Accordingly, the Commission published a Green Paper,[39] and later a White Paper,[40] the aims of which were to identify the appropriate incentives for private antitrust[41] damages claims and to adopt any new legislation. At the time of writing, a Directive on damages actions was being finalised.

1.3 EU Competition Law Disputes Before National Courts

Private EU competition law claims may arise in many contexts. For example, some antitrust claims could arise out of franchise agreements,[42] distribution

[1990] ECR I-2423; Joined Cases C-6 & 9/90 *Francovich v Italy* [1991] ECR I-5357; Case C-128/92 *HJ Banks v British Coal Corporation* [1994] ECR I-1209; Case C-5/94 *R v Minister of Agriculture, Fisheries and Food ex p Hedley Lomas (Ireland)* [1996] ECR I-2553; *Courage* (n 4); *Manfredi* (n 5).

[34] Case 253/00 *Munoz v Frumar* [2002] ECR I-7289 [58] (opinion of AG Geelhoed). See also Commission (EC) Staff Working Paper SEC 2005 1732 [13]–[15].

[35] Commission Staff Working Paper (n 34) [5] and [13]. See also *Van Gend Loos* (n 3) 13.

[36] *Courage* (n 4) [26] and [27]. See also Joined Cases C-264/01, C-306/01 C-354/01 and 355/01 *AOK Bundesverband v Ichthycol-Gesellschaft Cordes, Hermani & Co* [2004] ECR I-2493.

[37] A study in the conditions of claims for damages in case of infringement of EC competition rules http://ec.europa.eu/comm/competition/antitrust/others/actions_for_damages/study.html.

[38] Ibid 1.

[39] Commission (EC), 'Damages actions for breach of EC antitrust rules' (Green Paper) COM (2005) 672 final. See also: N Kroes, 'Enhancing actions for damages for breach of competition rules in Europe' Speech at the Harvard Club, New York, 22 September 2005 http://europa.eu/rapid/pressReleasesAction.do?reference=SPEECH/05/533&format=PDF&aged=1&language=EN&guiLanguage=en; N Kroes, 'The Green Paper on antitrust damages: empowering European citizens to enforce their rights' at the European Parliament Workshop on damages actions for breach of the EC antitrust rules http://ec.europa.eu/comm/competition/antitrust/actionsdamages/speech_06062006.pdf.

[40] White Paper (n 33).

[41] In spite of the fact that the term 'antitrust' is American, the Commission pattern, using 'antitrust' and 'competition' interchangeably, will be followed in this book (*cf* Green Paper (n 39)).

[42] Case 161/84 *Pronuptia de Paris GmbH v Pronuptia de Paris Irmgard Schillgallis* [1986] ECR 353.

agreements,[43] partial function joint ventures[44] licensing agreements[45] and consumer contracts.[46] In such cases, the question whether there is a breach of Arts 101 and/or 102 TFEU should be determined as a matter of EU law.[47] In spite of the fact that the Commission has been given exclusive jurisdiction to apply Regulation 139/2004 subject to review by the Court of Justice,[48] disputes as to whether restrictions are directly related and necessary to the implementation of the concentration,[49] and, if not, whether they are anti-competitive under Arts 101 and 102 TFEU should be resolved before national courts.[50] Accordingly, further private antitrust claims may arise out of commitments decisions in mergers and Arts 101 and 102 TFEU cases. Although, it is an open question whether third parties can enforce the commitments and invoke them as a basis for claiming damages,[51] in any event private antitrust claimants could base their claims on Arts 101 and 102 TFEU and use the Commission's commitment decision as prima facie evidence that the undertaking in question was bound by the commitment. However, 'since the Commission "should" not conclude whether or not there has been or still is an infringement, a commitment decision cannot be used as conclusive proof by a company claiming damages from the undertaking which made the commitment.'[52]

The Commission has pointed out the important role that should be played by national courts in enforcement of EU competition law, inter alia by emphasising the advantages of private litigation for complainants (e.g. award of damages and legal costs, interim measures) in order to direct more 'claims' to the courts.[53] The fact that the majority of agreements and practices that could give rise to antitrust concerns may involve the companies from different countries and affect

[43] Cases 56 and 58/64 *Consten and Grundig v Commission* [1966] ECR 266.

[44] Case COMP/37.730 *Re The Agreement between Deutsche Lufthansa AG and Austrian Airlines* OJ [2002] L242/25; [2003] 4 CMLR 252.

[45] *Eco Swiss* (n 5).

[46] *The Consumers Association v JJB Sports* (case number 1078/7/9/07) discussed in R Mulheron, 'Reform of collective redress in England and Wales: a perspective of need'. A research paper for submission www.civiljusticecouncil.gov.uk/files/collective_redress.pdf.

[47] *Provimi v Aventis Animal Nutrition* [2003] EWHC 961 (Comm), [2003] ECC 29 [25].

[48] Recital 17 of Merger Regulation (n 13).

[49] The Merger Regulation provides on a number of occasions that a decision declaring a concentration compatible with the internal market 'shall be deemed to cover restrictions directly related and necessary to the implementation of the concentration'. (See Arts 6(1)(b), 8(1) and 8(2) of the Merger Regulation (n 13).)

[50] See the Commission Notice on restrictions directly related and necessary to concentrations (2005/C56/03) [2].

[51] Recital 12 of the Commission's Proposal for a Council Regulation on the implementation of the rules on competition laid down in Articles 81 and 82 of the Treaty (Com (2000) 582 final) provided that the commitments could be relied upon by third parties. However, the statement was deleted from the final text of Regulation 1/2003. See more: Faull and Nikpay (n 12) p. 125.

[52] JT Lang, 'Commitment decisions under Regulation 1/2003: legal aspects of a new kind of competition decision' (2003) *European Competition Law Review* 347, 350.

[53] See Commission (EC) Notice on the handling of complaints by the Commission under Article 81 and 82 of the EC Treaty [2004] OJ C101/65 [16].

the market, businesses and consumers in several countries indicates that private international law issues would be important in such cases.

1.4 Cross-Border EU Competition Law Disputes

The question whether a national court has jurisdiction to deal with Arts 101 and 102 disputes is to be determined by the relevant jurisdictional sets of rules that are applicable in various Member States. Jurisdiction over disputes as to whether anti-competitive restrictions are directly related and necessary to the implementation of a concentration, and, if not, whether they are compatible with EU competition law will be also allocated with regard to either Art 101 or Art 102 TFEU type of infringements. As a result of the enhanced private antitrust enforcement reform, private international law will have a very important role to play if EU competition rules are to be enforced effectively in court proceedings with an international element. The importance of clear jurisdiction rules for effective private antitrust enforcement was identified in some of the opinions submitted by the respondents to the Green Paper.[54]

The architects of the decentralisation reform have largely ignored the question of how the EU policy encouraging private antitrust enforcement can be implemented under the current EU private international law framework.[55] This can be deduced from a speech of the former Commissioner Mario Monti. According to him, the 'multiple control and forum shopping before national courts should be avoided. In this respect we can fortunately rely on the rules of the Brussels [Regulation].'[56] This leaves no doubt that reliance has been placed on the Brussels I Regulation. This is a problem, however, as the Regulation contains no specific provisions to deal with jurisdiction and judgments in relation to EU competition law claims. It is further questionable whether the Brussels I Regulation can be relied upon to avoid the problem of parallel proceedings which are bound to arise in view of the various bodies responsible for the enforcement of Arts 101 and 102 TFEU.[57] Indeed, cross-border private EU competition law disputes and judgments in relation to them, nevertheless, give rise to specific private international law issues. Some examples of some potential private international law problems will be given below.

[54] Eg Freshfields' Response [54] and Linklaters' Response [12.2] http://ec.europa.eu/competition/antitrust/actionsdamages/green_paper_comments.html.

[55] Compare E de Smijter, C Stropp and D Woods (DG Comp, unit A-1), 'Green paper on damages actions for breach of the EC antitrust rules' (2006) *Competition Policy Newsletter* 1, 3.

[56] M Monti, 'Competition Law Reform', Speech made at the CBI Conference on Competition Law Reform, London, 12 June 2000 http://ec.europa.eu/comm/competition/speeches/text/sp2000_008_en.html.

[57] See S Brammer, *Co-operation between National Competition Agencies in the Enforcement of EC Competition Law* (Hart Publishing, Oxford, 2009) 25.

1.4.1 Problems Related to Jurisdiction of Courts

With regard to claims arising from contracts, it appears that jurisdictional issues would be very important because many agreements that could give rise to EU competition law concerns are concluded between companies from different countries. This point can be illustrated by providing two examples. First, an English manufacturer may grant distribution rights to a French distributor, thus, resulting in a vertical agreement. Secondly, in the event that demand for a certain product falls, English and French producers may agree to close down part of their productive capacity, which would amount to a horizontal agreement. Both contracts may contain clauses that distort competition and may give rise to disputes. For example, because the French distributor may find out that some other distributors receive goods at substantially lower prices and such agreement would result in driving him out of business. The other contract may be breached, because the English producer refused to close the agreed part of its productive capacity, arguing that the agreement is void as being in conflict with EU competition law. Which court will have jurisdiction to deal with an EU competition law claim in these situations? An English court, a French court or a court of the country of the place of performance of the obligation in question are just a few potential courts where the antitrust proceedings might be brought. Does the court, which is designated under jurisdictional rules for contracts, have jurisdiction to deal with both the question of voidness of the contract and also an EU competition law damages claim? What if parallel proceedings are brought in France and England? Does the Brussels I Regulation avoid the problem of parallel proceedings in a situation where a claim (counter-claim) that a contract (or contracts) is in conflict with EU competition law is brought before the English court and a complaint is lodged before a foreign NCA?

As to tort-based EU competition law claims, jurisdictional problems can potentially arise in a situation where the anti-competitive agreement or practice causes harm and affects the market in more than one country. Which court should have jurisdiction? The court of the defendant's (or defendants') domicile? The court of the plaintiff's home state? The court where the breach of EU competition law has occurred? If the latter alternative is adopted, then how would that place be identified in relation to EU antitrust claims? Can the plaintiff (or plaintiffs) choose which court to bring his (or their) antitrust actions before? What if there are parallel antitrust proceedings in respect of the same antitrust agreement or practice that has produced effects in more than one state? What if there are parallel antitrust proceedings between a French NCA and an English court in respect of the same agreement (or network of agreements)?

1.4.2 Problems Related to Choice of Law

Choice of law problems are bound to arise in relation to EU competition law claims brought in the European context, as Art 101 and 102 TFEU and Council

Regulation 1/2003 do not deal with all the issues that would be relevant for an antitrust suit. For example, problems may arise because neither the Treaty on the Functioning of the European Union nor the Court of Justice have fully identified the consequences of invalidating only the part of a contract which is in conflict with Arts 101 and/or 102 TFEU.[58] As a result, the applicable law should determine whether the rest of the contract would be enforceable. Further, EU law does not define the 'damage' for the purposes of a private EU competition law claim, which seems to indicate that the national law applicable to antitrust breach will determine the available remedies and the level of damage that is to be awarded.[59] Which national law would determine liability, causation and quantum in an EU competition law case where the market is, or is likely to be, affected in more than one country? A recent study has presented the various methods and models which can be used in quantifying the damage.[60] In the absence of unified practice throughout the EU, different Member States could employ different methodologies as to the quantification of antitrust damages. What if markets in several Member States have been affected? What remedies would be available for a breach of EU competition law? Can a German court (or a Scottish court or an Italian court) award exemplary or punitive antitrust damages when applying English law, if applicable under the Rome II Regulation?[61] Can an English court award treble antitrust damages when applying US federal law, if applicable under the Rome II Regulation? Can an arbitral tribunal sitting in England award treble antitrust damages?

1.4.3 Problems Related to Foreign Judgments and Foreign Arbitral Awards

The main private international law issues, which can arise in this context, relate to the scope of review and grounds for refusing recognition of foreign judgments (or foreign arbitral awards) in relation to antitrust law claims. It seems that the powers of national courts (or arbitral tribunals if at all allowed) to deal with EU competition law claims would necessitate stricter scrutiny of the foreign courts' (or arbitral tribunals') decisions in relation to such claims at the recognition and enforcement stage. This would inevitably be so, if EU competition law had a public policy character for the purposes of recognition and enforcement of a foreign judgment (and/or an arbitral award) in England.[62] Does EU competition

58 See Whish (n 11) 313. Komninos (n 31) 156–57.

59 See Commission Staff Working Paper accompanying the White Paper on damages actions for breach of EC rules SEC(2008) 404 [197]. See also Art 15(c) of Regulation 864/2007 on the law applicable to non-contractual obligations (Rome II).

60 Oxera and multi-jurisdictional team of lawyers led by Dr A Komninos, 'Quantifying antitrust damages: towards non-binding guidance for courts—Study prepared for the European Commission' http://ec.europa.eu/competition/antitrust/actionsdamages/quantification_study.pdf.

61 See Recital 32 of the Rome II Regulation.

62 *Eco Swiss* (n 5) [38]. Compare Case C-38/98 *Renault v Maxicar* [2000] ECR I-2973.

law enjoy public policy character for those purposes? Does a non-application or a wrong application of Arts 101 and 102 TFEU entitle the English court to refuse recognition of a foreign judgment in relation to an EU competition law claim? Would the answer to this question depend on whether the recognition and enforcement is sought under the Brussels I Regime or under English common law?

1.4.4 Problems Related to Jurisdiction of Arbitral Tribunals

Complex jurisdiction and choice of law problems could arise in private antitrust disputes brought before arbitral tribunals. For example, the jurisdiction problems would arise fairly easily where one of the parties argues that an EU competition law issue is not capable of settlement by arbitration. Which law determines the arbitrability of EU competition law? What law should govern the merits of an antitrust dispute? Can an arbitral tribunal sitting in England award treble antitrust damages when applying US antitrust law?

1.5 The Purpose of the Book

This book fills a gap in the literature by presenting a systematic discussion of the private international law issues that are likely to arise with regard to private EU competition law claims brought before English courts[63] or arbitral tribunals[64]

[63] The question of the basis upon which English courts may exercise jurisdiction in private EC competition law proceedings has been discussed only marginally by academics. See JJ Fawcett and P Torremans, *Intellectual Property and Private International Law* (OUP, Oxford, 1998) 423–26; Withers (n 23); BJ Rodger, 'Competition law in a Scottish forum' (2003) *Juridical Review* 247; J Hill, *International Commercial Disputes in English Courts* (3rd edn, Hart Publishing, Oxford, 2005) 154. See also CMV Clarkson and J Hill, *The Conflict of Laws* (3rd edn, OUP, Oxford, 2006) 258; J Fitchen, 'Allocating jurisdiction in private competition law claims within the EU' (2006) 13 *Maastricht Journal of European and Comparative Law* 381; L Collins and others (eds) *Dicey, Morris and Collins on the Conflict of Laws* (14th edn, Sweet & Maxwell, London, 2006) 662; J Basedow, 'Jurisdiction and choice of law in the private enforcement of EC competition law' in Basedow (n 31) 229–53; Komninos (n 31) 239–59.

[64] As far as the application of EC competition law in arbitral proceedings is concerned, it should be outlined that this problem has been examined in more detail elsewhere, eg A McClellan, 'Commercial Arbitration and European Community Law' (1989) 5 *Arbitration International* 68; ICC Publication No 480-3 *Competition and Arbitration Law,* (ICC Publishing SA, Paris, 1993); *International Commercial Arbitration in Europe—Special Supplement 1994*; The International Court of Arbitration Bulletin (Paris, 1994); J Werner, 'Application of Competition Laws by Arbitrators: The Step Too Far' (1995) 12 *Journal of International Arbitration* 21; JH Dalhuisen, 'The Arbitrability of Competition Issues' (1995) 11 *Arbitration International* 151; PJ Slot, 'The enforcement of EC competition law in arbitral proceedings' (1996) *Legal Issues of European Integration* 101–13; J Beechy, 'Arbitrability of Anti-trust/Competition Law Issues—Common Law' (1996) 12 *Arbitration International* 179; HG Gharavi, 'The proper scope of arbitration in European Community Competition Law' (1996) 11 *Tulane European and Civil Law Forum* 185; A Komninos, 'Arbitration and the modernisation of European competition law enforcement' (2001) 24 *World Competition* 211–38; N Shelkoplyas *The Application of EC Law in Arbitration Proceedings* (Europa Law Publishing, Groningen, 2003); M Blessing, *Arbitrating Antitrust and Merger*

based in England. To this end, the work[65] makes a thorough analysis of how the post-2003 policy of the European Union favouring private law enforcement of EU competition law can be implemented under the existing provisions for jurisdiction and recognition and enforcement of foreign judgments under the Brussels I regime. The book also deals with how the jurisdiction and recognition and enforcement of judgments issues are dealt with in England under English traditional rules applicable when Brussels I does not apply. The complex private international law problems in respect of cross-border class action and judgments in relation to antitrust infringements that have occurred in several countries are discussed as well. The work further examines the choice of law issues that may arise before the English courts under Rome I[66] and Rome II. The potential problems regarding jurisdiction of arbitral tribunals and choice of law in arbitral proceedings in relation to EU competition law claims and the jurisdiction of English courts in proceedings ancillary to arbitration with regard to such claims are dealt with accordingly.

1.6 The Relevant Private International Law Sets of Rules

The purpose of this chapter is to briefly outline the sets of private international law rules that would be relevant in EU competition law claims. Whilst there is a special choice of law rule applicable to EU competition law claims,[67] there are no special jurisdictional rules relevant for such claims. Accordingly, the jurisdictional

Control issues (Bär & Karrer, Zürich, and Helbing & Lichtenhahn, Basel/Geneva/Munich, 2003) http://www.baerkarrer.ch/upload/publications/4_3_14.pdf; M Dolmans and J Grierson, 'Arbitration and the Modernisation of EC Antitrust Law: New Opportunities and New Responsibilities' (2003) 14 *ICC International Court of Arbitration Bulletin* 37; R di Brozolo, 'Antitrust: A paradigm of the relations between mandatory rules and arbitration—a fresh look at the 'second look'' (2004) *International Arbitration Law Review* 23; R Nazzini, *Concurrent Proceedings in Competition Law: Procedure, Evidence and Remedies* (OUP, Oxford, 2004) 325–47; C Nisser and G Blanke, 'Reflections on the role of the European Commission as Amicus Curiae in International Arbitration Proceeding' (2006) 27 *European Competition Law Review* 174; SI Dempegiotis, 'EC competition law and international arbitration in the light of EC Regulation 1/2003' (2008) 25 *Journal of International Arbitration* 365; P Landolt, *Modernised EC Competition Law in International Arbitration* (Kluwer Law International, The Hague, 2006). See also: C-D Ehlermann and I Atanasiu (eds), *European Competition Law Annual 2000: The Modernisation of EU Competition Law* (Hart Publishing, Oxford, 2001); C-D Ehlermann and I Atanasiu (eds), *European Competition Law Annual 2001: Effective Private Enforcement of EC Antitrust Law* (Hart Publishing, Oxford, 2003).

[65] The structure of the book and some of the headings of sections (in particular the parts regarding English traditional rules) are influenced to a certain extent by the structure and headings in a book concerned with the application of private international law to intellectual property cases. See Fawcett and Torremans (n 63).

[66] Regulation (EC) 593/2008 on the law applicable to contractual obligations (Rome I).

[67] Art 6(3) of the Rome II Regulation.

rules of general application are to be used in competition law cases. There are two relevant sets of rules that must be considered. The first set of private international law rules is derived from EU law. The second set is the English traditional rules that are applicable in cases, where the EU rules do not apply. Accordingly, in this section first, the EU law sets of rules will be introduced. Then the focus will shift to the English law.

1.6.1 EU Private International Law

The most important private international law rules that operate at EU level are: the Brussels I regime (which covers the Brussels I Regulation and the Lugano Convention); and the Rome regime (which includes the Rome I Regulation and the Rome II Regulation). Whereas Brussels I is concerned with allocation of jurisdiction and the recognition and enforcement of judgments in civil and commercial matters, Rome I and Rome II deal with choice of law with regard to contractual obligations (Rome I) and non-contractual obligations (Rome II).

1.6.1.1 Brussels I—Jurisdiction and Judgments

The Brussels I regime covers the original Brussels Convention (as amended throughout the years), the Lugano Convention (signed between the states of the EEC and members of the EFTA) and the Brussels I Regulation.[68] Although, there are some minor differences between them, the structure and the basic principles are common to all of those instruments.[69] The focus in this book will be on the Brussels I Regulation,[70] since this is the fundamental instrument for determining jurisdiction in all proceedings brought on or after 1 March 2002.

It is well settled that where a claim that has an international element relates to a 'civil and commercial matter', the court has jurisdiction to entertain a claim *in personam* solely in accordance with the Brussels I Regulation, if the dispute falls within its scope.[71] Are EU competition law claims within the scope

[68] Council Regulation (EC) 44/2001 of 22 December 2000 on jurisdiction and the recognition and the enforcement of judgments in civil and commercial matters [2001] OJ L12/1. The Brussels I Regulation, which entered into force on 1 March 2002, is in practice the successor of the Brussels Convention (Civil Jurisdiction and Judgments Act 1982 sch 1). (See more PR Beaumont, 'The Brussels Convention becomes a Regulation: implications for legal basis, external competence, and contract jurisdiction' in James J Fawcett (ed) *Reform and Development of Private International Law* (OUP, Oxford, 2002). It should be mentioned that Denmark is not subject to the Brussels Regulation, but it has entered into an agreement with the EC that applies the same rules as the Brussels Regulation.

[69] See more A Briggs and P Rees, *Civil Jurisdiction and Judgments* (5th edn, Informa, London, 2009) 6–10; Hill (n 63) 6–7.

[70] Art 81 TFEU (ex Art 55 TEC) is the legal basis for new private international law initiatives; see P Beaumont, 'European Court of Justice and Jurisdiction and enforcement of judgments in civil and commercial matters' (1999) 48 ICLQ 223, 225.

[71] Art 1 of the Brussels I Regulation. See more: *Dicey, Morris and Collins on the Conflict of Laws* (n 63) 311–12.

of Brussels I? Article 1 deals with the scope of the Regulation. Although no definition is given to the concept 'civil and commercial matter', it has been clearly set by the Court of Justice that the concept 'civil and commercial matter' must be given an independent meaning in the light of 'the objectives and scheme of the [Regulation]'[72] and 'the general principles which stem from the corpus of the national legal system'.[73]

The European Commission has clearly stated that the Brussels I Regulation will be applicable to all competition cases of a civil and commercial nature.[74] A similar conclusion has been arrived at by Professor Brozolo, who holds that there is no doubt that an EU competition law claim falls within the scope of the term 'civil and commercial matter'.[75] That deduction was explicitly confirmed by the English High Court in *SanDisk*.[76] Accordingly, it can be concluded that an EU competition law claim is properly regarded as a 'civil and commercial matter' for the purposes of the Brussels I Regulation.

Article 1(2) of Brussels I, however, sets out a number of matters, which are excluded from the scope of the Brussels I Regulation, even though they are civil and commercial matters. Thus, the process of arbitration is excluded in its entirety from Brussels I.[77] Nonetheless, it is well settled that provisional measures, granted by a national court, using Art 31 of the Regulation in support of arbitration proceedings, would not be regarded as ancillary to those proceedings, but as parallel to them.[78] As a result, jurisdiction of a Member State's court to grant provisional measures in support of antitrust arbitration proceedings will be determined under the Brussels I Regulation.

Article 2 of Brussels I states that a person domiciled in a Member State must be sued in the courts of that Member State. If a person domiciled in a Member State is to be sued in the courts of a Member State other than that of his domicile, this can

[72] Case 29/76 *LTU v Eurocontrol* [1976] ECR 1541. See also *Dicey, Morris and Collins* (n 63) 314.

[73] See *Eurocontrol* (n 72) [5].

[74] See Commission Notice on the co-operation between the Commission and the courts of the EU Member States in the application of Arts 81 and 82 [2004] OJ C101/04 [3]. See also Green Paper (n 39) [2.8]; Office of Fair Trading, 'Response to the European Commission's Green Paper, Damages actions for breach of the EC antitrust rules' May 2006 http://ec.europa.eu/comm/competition/antitrust/others/actions_for_damages/130.pdf.

[75] R di Brozolo, 'Antitrust claims: why exclude them from The Hague jurisdiction and judgment convention', (2004) 25 *European Competition Law Review* 780, 783.

[76] *SanDisk Corporation v Koninklijke Philips Electronics and others* [2007] EWHC 332 (Ch); [2007] Bus LR 705. See also *Provimi* (n 47).

[77] Art 1(2)(d) of Brussels Regulation. See also Case C-190/89 *Marc Rich & Co v Societa Italiana Impianti PA* [1991] ECR I-3855. Compare Case C-185/07 *Allianz SpA v West Tankers In.* [2009] 1 Lloyd's Rep 413 (Court of Justice of the EU, Grand Chamber). Compare also *Through Transport Mutual Insurance Association v New India Assurance* [2004] EWCA Civ 1598; [2005] 1 Lloyd's Rep 67 (CA) [44]. See also *The Ivan Zagubanski* [2002] 1 Lloyd's Rep 107 (Comm); Briggs and Rees (n 69) 78–82; A. Briggs, 'The Brussels Convention' (1991) *Yearbook of European Law* 521, 527. *Cf Toepfer v Cargill* [1997] 2 Lloyd's Rep 98 (Comm); A Briggs, 'Decisions of British Courts During 1997: Private International Law' (1997) *British Yearbook of International Law* 331, 364.

[78] Case C-391/95 *Van Uden Maritime BV v Kommanditgesellschaft in Firma Deco-Line* [1998] ECR I-7091 [34]. See also *West Tankers* (n 77).

only be done by virtue of the bases of jurisdiction set out in ss 2 to 7 of Brussels I. Therefore, the national courts cannot derive jurisdiction in an action brought against a person who is domiciled in a Member State from their domestic jurisdictional and/or 'exorbitant' rules.[79]

Article 4 of Brussels I, however, states that 'if the defendant is not domiciled in a Member State, the jurisdiction of the courts of each Member State shall, subject to Articles 22 and 23, be determined by the law of that Member State.' In other words, English traditional rules, including exorbitant rules, would be applicable if an EU competition law claim is brought against a defendant who is not domiciled in a Member State. An example of such a case would be where an English plaintiff wishes to bring an action in England against New York defendants for a breach of EU competition law, arising out of a cartel agreement or abusive practice that is implemented in England. Another example would be a claim for damages made by an English distributor against a Canadian manufacturer, arising out of a contract clause that is contrary to EU competition law.

1.6.1.2 Rome—the Applicable Laws

There is a high degree of harmonisation of choice of law rules relating to contractual and non-contractual obligations in Europe. The Rome I Regulation,[80] which replaced the Rome Convention for contracts concluded after 17 December 2009, applies, in situations involving conflict of laws, to contractual obligations in civil and commercial matters. The Rome II Regulation[81] lays down the law applicable to non-contractual obligations in civil and commercial matters and applies as from 11 January 2009. In other words, for the events occurring after this date choice of law in tort in English law is not to be regulated by Part III of the Private International Law (Miscellaneous Provisions) Act 1995 as the latter part is disapplied where the rules in the Rome II Regulation apply.[82]

Rome I Regulation.[83] The Rome I Regulation is the successor of the Rome Convention of 1980,[84] adopted to establish uniform rules concerning the law applicable to contractual obligations. The parties' freedom to choose the law governing their contract is the general rule in Rome I.

In cases where there has been no choice of law, Art 4(1) states that specified types of contracts are to be governed by the law of the country in which one of the

[79] JJ Fawcett and JM Carruthers, *Cheshire, North & Fawcett Private International Law* (14th edn, OUP, Oxford, 2008) 223.

[80] Regulation (EC) 593/2008 of the European Parliament and of the Council of 17 June 2008 on the law applicable to contractual obligations (Rome I) [2008] OJ L177/6.

[81] Regulation (EC) 864/2007 of the European Parliament and of the Council of 11 July 2007 on the law applicable to non-contractual obligations (Rome II) [2007] OJ L199/40.

[82] See s 15A of the Private International Law (Miscellaneous Provisions) Act 1995.

[83] See more: R Plender and M Wilderspin, *The European Private International Law of Obligations* (3rd edn, Sweet & Maxwell, London, 2009) 3–432; F Ferrari and S Leibbe (eds), *Rome I Regulation: The Law Applicable to Contractual Obligations in Europe* (Sellier, Munich, 2009).

[84] The Contracts (Applicable law) Act 1991.

parties to the contract is habitually resident. If the contract cannot be categorised as being one of the specified types, or where its elements fall within more than one of the specified types, Art 4(2) indicates that the contract should be governed by the law of the country where the party required to effect the characteristic performance of the contract has his habitual residence. However, if the contract is manifestly more closely connected with a country other than that indicated in Art 4(1) or (2), then Art 4(3) stipulates that the law of that country is to be applicable. Art 4(4) accommodates cases in which the law applicable cannot be determined pursuant to Art 4(1) or (2) by stating that such a contract is to be governed by the law of the country with which it is most closely connected.

The Regulation has a special rule, which is intended to limit the freedom of choice of parties and to disregard it. Article 3(4) limits the evasion of EU law and would be relevant to EU competition law cases where all elements germane to the situation (apart from the choice of law made by the parties) at the time of the choice are located in one or more Member States. Freedom of choice is further limited by the rules providing protection for weaker parties (consumers and employees). Further, the choice of law made by the parties or the law otherwise applicable under the Rome I Regulation may be disregarded in cases triggering the application of mandatory rules of the forum, mandatory rules of a third country and by reason of a breach of public policy. The fact that EU competition law rules are essential for the functioning of the internal market,[85] and the importance of the 'principle of an open market economy with free competition',[86] seem to suggest that Arts 101 and 102 TFEU may often be regarded as mandatory for the purposes of Rome I.[87]

Rome II Regulation.[88] The Regulation deals with choice of law with regard to tort, unjust enrichment, *negotiorum gestio* and *culpa in contrahendo*. The general rule is that the law applicable to a non-contractual obligation arising out of a tort/delict shall be the law of the country in which the damage occurs, irrespective of the country in which the event giving rise to the damage occurred and irrespective of the country or countries in which the indirect consequences of that event occur.[89]

Article 6(3), the special rule designated to deal with non-contractual obligations arising out of restrictions of competition, is the most important choice-of-law rule in tort in the context of this book. According to Art 6(3)(a) of Rome II, the law applicable to non-contractual obligations arising out of restrictions of competition should be the law of the country where the market is, or is likely

[85] See Art 3(3) TEU-Lis and the Protocol on internal market and competition. Old Art 3(1)(g) EC provided that the activities of the Community include 'a system ensuring that competition in the internal market is not distorted.'

[86] Art 119 TFEU.

[87] M Giuliano and P Legarde, 'Report on the law applicable to contractual obligations' [1980] OJ C282/1, 28. See more ch 5 below.

[88] See more: A Dickinson, *The Rome II Regulation: The Law Applicable to Non-contractual Obligations* (OUP, Oxford, 2008); Plender and Wilderspin (n 83) 435–781.

[89] Art 4 of the Rome II Regulation.

to be, affected. In cases where the market is, or is likely to be, affected in more than one country, Art 6(3)(b) allows the claimant in certain circumstances to choose to base his or her entire claim on the law of the seised court, the *lex fori*. The important role of the law of the forum in EU competition law cases can be further deduced from the fact that considerations of public interest justify giving the courts of the Member States the possibility, in exceptional circumstances, of applying exceptions based on public policy of the forum and overriding mandatory provisions of the law of the forum.[90]

1.6.2 English Law

The English choice-of-law rules in relation to competition law disputes brought before national courts are primarily derived from the Rome I Regulation and Rome II Regulation. However, the English law would have a role to play in cases which are not within the scope of Art 1 of the Brussels I Regulation (i.e. arbitration). Further, English traditional rules on jurisdiction would apply to cases falling within the scope of Brussels I, if a defendant is not domiciled in a Member State and jurisdiction is not allocated by any of the rules which apply regardless of such domicile.[91] Accordingly, in this section, the sources of English law will be briefly examined. First, the law sources relevant for jurisdiction of English courts and recognition of foreign judgments in relation to EU antitrust claims will be briefly outlined. Secondly, the main provisions that would be of relevance to arbitral proceedings in relation to EU competition law claims will be enumerated.

1.6.2.1 English Court Proceedings—Relevant Rules

The major sources for jurisdiction of English courts are procedural in nature and can be found in statutes and statutory instruments.[92] For example, the Supreme Court Act 1981 contains special provisions dealing with the Divisions of the High Court.[93] The most important rules for purposes of determining court's jurisdiction, however, are the Civil Procedure Rules (CPR) 1998, which have largely codified the traditional rules relating to jurisdiction.[94]

English courts base their jurisdiction on the service of a claim form on the defendant. CPR 6.33 concerns service of a claim form out of jurisdiction where a permission of the court is not required. CPR 6.36 read together with para 3.1 of CPR PD 6B lists the conditions which should be satisfied for a claim form to be served out of the jurisdiction with the permission of the court. Service out of

[90] See Art 16 of the Rome II Regulation.

[91] See Art 4 of the Brussels I Regulation. See also Clarkson and Hill (n 63) 87; Komninos (n 31) 247; Whish (n 11) 301.

[92] JIH Jacob, *The Fabric of English Civil Justice* (Stevens, London, 1987).

[93] Arts 5, 6 and 7.

[94] See more: N Andrews, *English Civil Procedure: Fundamentals of the New Civil Justice System* (OUP, Oxford, 2003) 2–25.

jurisdiction, however, is regarded as being 'exorbitant' and 'extraordinary'.[95] CPR 6.37(1)(b) sets out the 'reasonable prospects of success' threshold that should be satisfied by the plaintiff, who makes an application for service of a claim form out of jurisdiction. These are the most important rules relevant for jurisdiction of English law in relation to antitrust claims.

In addition, the judicial decisions, when authoritatively reported, are also among the main sources of law relevant for jurisdiction and recognition of foreign judgments under English law.[96] The majority of case law that emerged under RSC Ord 11 and CPR 6.20, the predecessors of para 3.1 of CPR PD 6B, is to be considered, when determining the jurisdiction of an English court in EU competition law claims.[97] Indeed, it has been submitted that the 'reasonable prospects of success' test under CPR 6.37(1)(b) (and its predecessor CPR 6.21(1)(b)) is not likely to differ from the 'serious question test' test under RSC Ord 11.[98] Thus, the analysis in this book will be largely based on the relevant CPR and its para 3.1 of PD 6B, together with case law, which has emerged under RSC Order 11 and the subsequent CPR.

Finally, it should be made clear that despite an arbitration agreement, the English courts would have common jurisdiction in proceedings ancillary to arbitration proceedings, such as granting interim relief, setting aside of awards rendered by arbitral tribunals sitting in England, recognition and enforcement of foreign awards. The 1996 Act confers powers that could be exercised by the court in support and supervision of arbitration proceedings. The proceedings under the Arbitration Act 1996 are to be commenced and process is to be served on the respondent in accordance with CPR 62, which should also be mentioned as a relevant rule in the context of this book.

1.6.2.2 Arbitration and Proceedings Ancillary to Arbitration—Relevant Rules

The main source of English arbitration law is the Arbitration Act 1996, which repealed the earlier legislation. It should be pointed out that the structure and content of the 1996 Act have been influenced by the UNCITRAL Model Law,[99] which is defined as 'the cornerstone of international dispute resolution' by the

[95] *Spiliada Maritime v Cansulex* [1987] AC 460 (HL) 481 (Lord Goff).

[96] R Cross and JW Harris, *Precedent in English Law* (4th edn, OUP, Oxford 1991) 6. See also *Quinn v Leathem* [1901] AC 495 (HL) (see opinion of Lord Chancellor Hallsbury); *American Express Europe v Royal Bank of Scotland (No 2)* 1989 SLT 650 (Court of Session).

[97] E.g. *Spiliada* (n 95); *Adams v Cape Industry* [1990] Ch 433 (CA).

[98] *Ophthalmic Innovations (UK) v Ophthalmic Innovations (USA)* [2004] EWHC 2948 (ChD); [2005] ILPr 10, [39].

[99] Department Advisory Committee on Arbitration, *Report on The Arbitration Bill* (DTI, London, 1996) [4]. See also F Davidson, 'The New Arbitration Act—a Model Law?' (1997) *JBL* 101. Compare UNCITRAL Modern Law on International Commercial Arbitration. The Model Law has the force of law in Scotland in the form set out in sch 7 to the Law Reform (Miscellaneous Provisions) (Scotland) Act 1990. See more: RLC Hunter, *The Law of Arbitration in Scotland* (2nd edn, Butterworths, Edinburgh, 2002) 49.

Report on the Arbitration Bill.[100] Although English arbitration law retains a number of distinctive features, the 1996 Act brought English law more into line with modern international practice.[101] Therefore, the relevant provisions of the 1996 Act should be examined in the context of the UNCITRAL Model Law.

Further, the New York Convention[102] should be considered as well. Articles 100 to 104 of the 1996 Act give effect to the provisions of the New York Convention. The importance of the New York Convention for this book is beyond doubt, since it contains some important provisions not only about recognition and enforcement of arbitral awards, but also about validity of an arbitration agreement and arbitrability of the subject matter of the dispute.[103] Arbitrability is an important issue in the context of this book, since it will indicate which types of EU competition law claims may be settled by an arbitral tribunal based in England. Accordingly, the relevant provisions of the 1996 Act and the New York Convention will be duly examined in chapter seven of this book.

In addition, the Geneva Convention on International Commercial Arbitration[104] should be outlined among the sources that could be relevant for jurisdiction of arbitral tribunals and recognition of arbitral awards in relation to antitrust claims. The Geneva Convention, however, remains in force between its state parties which have not subsequently become parties to the New York Convention.[105] As far as the UK is concerned, it is believed that only a few states would remain in that category.[106]

Finally, it should be recalled that the Court of Justice[107] and English[108] case law will also give some hints as to the application of those sources by the arbitral tribunals and courts in EU competition cases.

Having outlined the sources of law, in the following section a brief discussion of the question how an EU competition law claim is characterised for conflict-of-laws purposes by English courts is offered.

[100] Department Advisory Committee (n 99) [347].

[101] J Hill, 'Some private international law aspects of the Arbitration Act 1996' (1997) 46 *ICLQ* 274.

[102] Convention on the Recognition and Enforcement of Foreign Arbitral Awards, New York, 1958. The New York Convention has been widely ratified by many trading nations.

[103] The condition set out in Art II(1) of the New York Convention is commonly referred to as 'arbitrability of disputes'. Moreover, it has been argued that a court may refuse to enforce an agreement to arbitrate a subject matter that is non-arbitrable in domestic law under Art II(3) as well as under Art II(1). Since awards rendered under such agreements could not be enforced under Art V(2)(a) the arbitration agreement would be 'incapable of being performed'. See Exec Doc E, 90th Cong, 2d Sess, 19 (1968); G Haight, *Convention on the Recognition and Enforcement of Foreign Awards* (1958) 27–28 quoted in *Mitsubishi Motors v Soler Chrysler-Plymouth* 473 US 614, 87 L Ed 2d 444 (1985) [473 US 660]. See also Art VI(2)(c) of the 1961 European Convention.

[104] European Convention on International Commercial Arbitration, Geneva 21 April 1961.

[105] Art 99 of the 1996 Act holds that Part II of the Arbitration Act 1950, which gave effect to the UK's treaty obligations under the Geneva Convention, continues to apply to Geneva Convention awards.

[106] Department Advisory Committee (n 99) [346].

[107] *Eco Swiss* (n 5).

[108] *ET Plus v Welter* [2005] EWHC 2115, [2006] 1 Lloyd's Rep 251 (Comm).

1.7 Characterisation of EU Competition Law Claims

The first issue that must be determined by a court faced with an EU competition law claim containing a foreign element is whether it has jurisdiction not only over parties, but also over the cause of action. Accordingly, the question of how an EU competition law claim is to be characterised for jurisdictional purposes is addressed below. Characterising the nature of the claim means identifying the rules of a particular legal system that are behind it. Those rules of law would specify the facts that should exist for a plaintiff to bring his claim under the tort head or contract head.[109] It is for national judges to carry the characterisation out.[110] Although, in most cases the classification will be made on the basis of the law of the forum,[111] the characterisation in a case involving a foreign element need not necessarily be the same as that which is made in a purely domestic case.[112] For the purpose of characterisation a wider meaning may be given to such concepts as 'contract', 'tort', 'undertaking' and 'domicile', in order to classify analogous legal relationships of a foreign type.[113]

There seem to be strong reasons why an action for breach of EU competition law must be regarded as tortious in nature for private international law purposes. Indeed, the EU legislator has clearly stated that 'the non-contractual obligations arising out of restrictions of competition in [Rome II] should cover infringements of both national and [EU] competition law.'[114] The tortious classification of actions for breach of Arts 101 and/or 102 TFEU has been adopted by the English courts with regard to EU competition law claims brought in domestic context in England. In *Application des Gaz v Falks Veritas*,[115] it was stated that 'Articles [101] and [102] are part of [English] law. They create new torts or wrongs.'[116] Commentators also have submitted that infringement of EU competition law should be regarded as a new tort.[117] With reference to the latter, it has been noted that the development of a new tort might avoid the difficulties associated with the need to characterise the Treaty on the Functioning of the European Union as

[109] C Forsyth, 'Characterisation Revised: an essay in the theory and practice of the English conflict of laws' (1998) 114 *LQR* 141, 149. See also *Letang v Cooper* [1965] 1 QB 232 (CA) 242–44 (Diplock LJ); AH Robertson, *Characterization in the Conflict of Laws* (Harvard University Press, Cambridge, 1940) 61.

[110] Ibid 152; See also *Cheshire, North & Fawcett* (n 79) 44.

[111] *Macmillan Inc v Bishposgate Trust (No 3)* [1996] 1 WLR 387 (CA) 407 (Auld LJ).

[112] *Macmillan* (n 111). See also: *Cheshire, North & Fawcett* (n 79) 44; J Fitchen, 'Choice of law in international claims based on restriction of competition: Article 6(3) of the Rome II Regulation' (2009) 5 *Journal of Private International Law* 337, 346–47.

[113] A Nussbaum, Book Reviews (1940) 40 *Columbia Law Review* 1461, 1471.

[114] See recital 22 of the Rome II Regulation. See also Dickinson (n 88) 270–71.

[115] *Application des Gaz v Falks Veritas* [1974] Ch 381 (CA).

[116] Ibid 396 (Lord Denning MR).

[117] M Staines, 'The right to sue in Ireland for violation of the EEC rules on competition' (1977) 2 *Legal Issues of Eur Integration* 53. See also Clifford A Jones, *Private Enforcement of Antitrust Law in the EU, UK and USA* (OUP, Oxford, 1999) 146.

if it were a statute.[118] More authorities in domestic context nevertheless sustain the view that an EU competition law claim for damages should be classified as a tortious claim.[119] This opinion is expressed by the English court in *Garden Cottage Foods v Milk Marketing Board*.[120] In this case, the House of Lords held that a breach of the duty imposed by Art 102 TFEU not to abuse a dominant position can be characterised in English law as a 'breach of statutory duty' for the purposes of English domestic law. Such a duty is imposed for a benefit of private individuals to whom loss or damage is caused by its breach.[121] Although Art 102 TFEU is different from Art 101 TFEU, it seems that similar characterisation will be followed for cases where a claim for a breach of Art 101 TFEU is brought by a third party against the parties to a contract that allegedly distorts competition.

In any case, it is beyond question that an EU antitrust damages action should be tortious in nature. However, although there are good reasons suggesting that a claim for breach of EU competition law should be characterised as tortious even in cases where the antitrust damages claim were brought by a contracting party after the contract had been invalidated,[122] difficulties may arise with regard to characterisation in a context of tortious claims brought by a weaker party to an anti-competitive contract. For example, the dispute about how the principle of severance of illegal provisions from otherwise lawful agreements is to affect the parties' contract could be seen as contractual in nature,[123] whereas the question of causation and quantum in a private antitrust damages claim could be regarded as tortious in nature.[124] Before the Court of Justice ruling in *Courage*,[125] an action for antitrust damages was not open in English law to those who were parties to a prohibited anti-competitive agreement,[126] so that there is no English authority directly on this point.

It has been submitted in relation to unfair competition actions that the presence of a contract will not change the tortious characterisation of such an action, but will simplify proof of unfair dealing.[127] The opposing view is that the prohibited effect of antitrust agreements or practices should be channelled by the

[118] See C Kerse, *EC Antitrust Procedure* (3rd edn, Sweet & Maxwell, London, 1994) 376.

[119] WVH Rogers (ed) *Winfield and Jolowicz on Tort* (15th edn, Sweet & Maxwell, London, 1998) 619. See also: J Steiner, 'How to make the action suit the case: domestic remedies for breach of ECC law' (1987) *European Law Review* 102, 107–08; K. M. Stanton, 'New forms of the tort of breach of statutory duty' (2004) 120 *Law Quarterly Review* 324.

[120] *Garden Cottage Foods v Milk Marketing Board* [1984] AC 130 (HL).

[121] Ibid 141 (Lord Diplock).

[122] *Provimi* (n 47); See also *Camera Care v Victor Hasselbland* [1986] ECC 373 (CA); *ET Plus* (n 108); Withers (n 23) 253; A Briggs, 'Private international law decisions' (2003) 75 *British Year Book of International Law* 511, 535.

[123] Whish (n 11) 313. See also: Komninos (n 31) 156–57; Bernitz (n 12) 190–91. See more ch 5.

[124] See more ch 5.

[125] See *Courage* (n 4) [26] and [36].

[126] See *Gibbs Mew v Gemmell* [1998] EuLR 588 (CA).

[127] C Kessedjian, 'Competition' in C McLachlan and P Nygh (eds), *Transnational Tort Litigation: Jurisdictional Principles* (Clarendon Press, Oxford, 1996) 171, 174. See also P Kaye, *Civil Jurisdiction and Enforcement of Foreign Judgments* (Professional Books, Oxford, 1987) 570.

contract.[128] Is the matter still regarded as related to contract simply because the parties have a contractual relationship and the claim may have been brought in contract? Can the plaintiff overlook the existence of a contract and base his claim solely on breach of a statutory duty by framing it solely in tort? Is an EU competition law claim still classified as tortious if there is a contractual dispute about how the principle of severance of illegal provisions from otherwise lawful agreements is to affect the parties' contract? Is it left to the plaintiff to choose whether to frame the claim in contract or in tort? These are some of the private international issues related to characterisation of EU competition law claims that need to be dealt with by an English court with regard to transnational disputes involving EU competition law claims. The characterisation questions will be answered when the EU competition law claims brought by contracting parties are examined below. It is likely that different outcomes would be reached depending on whether antitrust damages claims were brought by a contracting party under the Brussels I Regulation or English law.

[128] Case 189/97 *Kalfelis v Schroder* [1988] ECR 5565 [31] (AG Darmon). See also J Kropholler, *Europäisches Zivilprozessrecht. Kommentar zu EuGVO und Lugano- Übereinkommen* (Recht und Wirtschaft, Frankfurt, 1982) 64; C Castronovo, 'Private law remedies for antitrust violations—a point of view from Italy' in Basedow (n 31) 107, 117.

2

Jurisdiction with Regard to Contract-Based EU Competition Law Claims

2.1 Introduction

There are two possible scenarios for contract-based EU competition law disputes. The first one is where the defendant submits as a defence in an action that a contract (or a contractual provision), which the plaintiff seeks to enforce, infringes EU competition law. In such a scenario, though, the issue of jurisdiction would have been addressed before the EU competition law issue is raised.[1] Nevertheless, the defendant could bring a counter-claim for antitrust damages, based on the nullity of the contract in conflict with EU competition law. In the latter case, the jurisdictional issue that is likely to arise is related to the question of whether the court seised with the original claim will have jurisdiction over a counter-claim for EU competition law damages, which may potentially raise issues as to parallel proceedings with regard to related EU antitrust law claims brought in another Member State's courts.[2]

The second scenario is where the EU competition law claim is a central element of an action in which a plaintiff, for example, can seek nullity of an agreement that is in conflict with Art 101 TFEU. Although, the nullity referred to in Art 101(2) TFEU is absolute,[3] the defendant may argue that the conditions of Art 101(3) TFEU have been satisfied and the agreement is valid. Moreover, whilst the nullity provided for by Art 101(2) TFEU is a fundamental sanction it is not always sufficient to make good the loss caused.[4] Accordingly, a claimant may go a step further and add an EU competition law claim for damages. Further, a plaintiff may wish to add another defendant and sue, for example, a subsidiary and its parent company. The second scenario is likely to give rise to more jurisdictional

[1] J Fawcett and P Torremans, *Intellectual Property in Private International Law* (OUP, Oxford, 1998) 422.

[2] See ch 4 below.

[3] Case 22/71 *Beguelin* [1971] ECR 949.

[4] Case C-453/99 *Courage Ltd v Crehan* [2001] ECR I-6297 [54].

problems than the first one with regard to allocation of jurisdiction in EU competition law claims.

The jurisdictional analysis below will not be concerned with most of the cases that are likely to arise under the first scenario, since in those cases the jurisdiction would already have been determined at the time when the antitrust claim is raised. This chapter is mainly focused on cases where the EU competition law is brought as a principal claim as they may give rise to specific jurisdictional problems, which will be examined below. Accordingly, first, the jurisdictional rules applicable to contracts under the Brussels I Regulation will be examined in light of EU competition law claims. After that, the bases of jurisdiction under traditional rules will be considered.

2.2 Jurisdiction under the Brussels I Regulation

This section will open with a brief review of the generic rules, which would be relevant in contract-based EU competition law cases. Then, the relevant rules and their application in competition cases will be examined in detail.

2.2.1 Rules Allocating Jurisdiction in Contract-Based EU Competition Law Claims

It is clearly established that the basic jurisdictional rule is to be found in Art 2 of the Brussels Regulation.[5] This provision allows a plaintiff to bring an action against a defendant in the Member State in which the latter is domiciled.[6] Thus, a defendant can always be sued in the courts of his domicile with regard to an EU competition law claim. The major disadvantage of bringing an antitrust claim on the basis of Art 2 stems from the fact that the plaintiff will have to follow the defendant to the Member State of his domicile. Moreover, sometimes it would be more difficult for a court of the defendant's domicile to consider the economic and legal context of an agreement which was implemented and affected the plaintiff's business within the market of another Member State.[7] The court of the defendant's domicile may not be well placed to hear and determine

[5] Case 12/76 *Tessili v Dunlop* [1976] ECR 1473 [12]; Case C-220/88 *Dumez France and Tracoba v Hessische Landesbank (Helaba)* [1990] ECR I-49 [16].

[6] Art 60(1) of Brussels I provides that for the purposes of the Brussels I Regulation, a company is 'domiciled at the place where it has its: (a) statutory seat, or (b) central administration, or (c) principal place of business.' See some of the problems with interpretation of the concept of 'statutory seat' in civil law countries in M Weser, 'Bases of Judicial Jurisdiction in the Common Market Countries' (1961) 10 *American Journal of Comparative Law* 323, 329–30. Art 60(2) gives a definition of the term 'statutory seat', but this definition is applicable only for the UK and Ireland.

[7] Compare Case 23/67 *Brasserie de Haecht SA v Wilkin* [1967] ECR 407, 415.

such an EU competition law dispute. Furthermore, if the European institutions really want to create incentives for private antitrust enforcement,[8] then 'special' bases for jurisdiction should have a role to play in encouraging plaintiffs to bring their EU competition law claims in courts of a Member State other thanthose in which defendants are domiciled. Having said that it should be outlined that there are no specific difficulties in applying Art 2 in competition cases,[9] so the focus in this chapter will be on the 'special' bases for jurisdiction that allow courts which may have a closer connection with antitrust disputes to hear and determine them.

The fact that there is no special provision in the Brussels I Regulation for contracts distorting competition indicates that these contracts should be treated the same as other contracts. Accordingly, when it comes to a trial in the courts of a Member State other than the one in which a defendant is domiciled, the most important provision for allocating jurisdiction in EU competition law claims brought by any of the contracting parties will be Art 5(1). Article 5(1) states that: '[a] person domiciled in a Member State may, in another Member State, be sued … in matters relating to a contract, in the courts for the place of performance of the obligation in question.' Before dealing with specific problems in allocating jurisdiction with regard to EU competition law claims, the basic principles that underlie Art 5(1) will be briefly outlined. Its rationale is that there should be a particular close connecting factor between a dispute and the court which may be called upon to hear it.[10] The assumption is that there will be a close connection where 'in matters relating to a contract' the claim is brought 'in the courts for the place of performance of the obligation in question'. Accordingly, when a trial takes place in England, a plaintiff, who seeks to rely on this provision, has to establish a 'good arguable case' that there is a matter relating to contract.[11] There are sufficient authorities to result in a European interpretation of the concept of 'matters relating to contract', which could provide more certainty for parties.[12]

[8] As declared by Council Regulation (EC) 1/2003 of 16 December 2002 on the implementation of the rules on competition laid down in Articles 81 and 82 of the Treaty [2003] OJ L1/1; and Commission (EC), 'Damages action for breach of the EC antitrust rules' (Green Paper) COM (2005) 672 final. See also E de Smijter, C Stropp and D Woods (DG Comp, unit A-1), 'Green paper on damages actions for breach of the EC antitrust rules' 2006(1) *Competition Policy Newsletter* 1–3.

[9] See more: J Fitchen, 'Allocating jurisdiction in private competition law claims within the EU' (2006) 13 *Maastricht Journal of European and Comparative Law* 381, 388–89.

[10] *Tessili* (n 5) [13]; Case 34/82 *Peters v ZNAV* [1983] ECR 987 [11]; See also Jenard Report [1979] OJ C59/1, 22. Compare Case C-288/92 *Customs Made Commercial v Stawa Metallbau* [1994] ECR I-2913; J Hill, 'Jurisdiction in Matters Relating to a Contract' (1995) 44 *ICLQ* 591; J Hill, 'Jurisdiction in Civil and Commercial Matters: Is there a third way?' (2001) 54 *Current Legal Problems* 439, 443.

[11] *Boss Group v Boss France* [1996] 4 All ER 970 (CA) 975 (Saville LJ).

[12] Eg *Peters* (n 10); Case 9/87 *Arcado v Haviland* [1988] ECR 1539; Case C-26/91 *Jacob Handte v TMCS* [1992] ECR I-3967; Case C-51/97 *Reunion Européenne v Spliethoff's Bevrachtingskantoor* [1998] ECR I-6511. See also W Allwood, 'The scope of "matters" relating to a contract' (1988) 13 *EL Rev* 366.

The Brussels I Regulation brought into being some amendments in Art 5(1).[13] Sub-paragraph (b) was inserted. That amendment, however, affects only contracts for the sale of goods and the provision of services. In regard to them, the Regulation adopts the 'characteristic obligation' theory. The Court of Justice of the EU has held that:

> By that provision, the [EU] legislature issued, in respect of sales contracts, expressly to break with the earlier solution under which the place of performance was determined, for each of the obligations in question, in accordance with the private international rules of the court seised of the dispute. By designating autonomously as 'the place of performance' the place where the obligation which characterises the contract is to be performed, the [EU] legislature sought to centralise at its place of performance jurisdiction over disputes concerning the contractual obligations and to determine sole jurisdiction for all claims arising out of the contract.[14]

Article 5(1)(b), however, does not define either 'contract for a sale of goods' or that for a provision of services, which may give rise to some uncertainty with regard to jurisdiction of courts over antitrust claims arising out of distribution and licensing agreements.[15] The Regulation states that where sub-para (b) does not apply, sub-para (a) will apply. Sub-paragraph (a), like Art 5(1) of the Convention, confers jurisdiction to the courts for the 'place of performance of the obligation in question'. It is supposed that these two phrases will carry the same meaning under the Regulation as under the Convention.[16] The Court of Justice held that 'the obligation to be taken into account is that which corresponds to the contractual right on which the plaintiff's action is based'.[17]

Bearing in mind the fact that jurisdiction under Art 5 is an exception to the general rule under Art 2, English courts have accepted that there is a threshold requirement which the plaintiff has to satisfy before a defendant can be subject to jurisdiction on the basis of Art 5. Accordingly, the court must be satisfied that there is a serious question, which calls for a trial for its proper determination.[18]

Other provisions that may be relevant to contract-based competition cases are Arts 5(5), 6(1) and 16 of Brussels I. Article 5(5) allocates jurisdiction with regard to disputes arising out of the operations of a branch, agency or other establishment.

[13] See ch 1, section 1.6 above, for the relationship between the Brussels Convention and the Brussels I Regulation.

[14] Case C-386/05 *Color Drack GmbH v LEXX International Vertriebs GmbH* [2007] ECR I-3699.

[15] See Case C-533/07 *Falco Privatstiftung and Thomas Rabitsch v Gisela Weller-Lindhorst*—Judgment of 23 April 2009 (Court of Justice, Fourth Chamber) [19]. For the difficulties surrounding the relevant definitions, see more: JJ Fawcett and JM Carruthers, *Cheshire, North & Fawcett Private International Law* (OUP, Oxford, 2008) 238 and 239. See more: sections 2.2.2.2.2.1 and 2.2.2.2.2.2 below.

[16] *Falco Privatstiftung* (n 15) [46]–[51]. See also K Takahashi, 'Jurisdiction in matters relating to contract: Art 5(1) of the Brussels Convention and Regulation' (2002) 27 *EL Rev* 530, 531.

[17] Case 14/76 *De Bloos v Bouyer* [1976] ECR 1497 [13]. See also Case 266/85 *Shenavai v Kreischer* [1987] ECR 239 [19]; *Tessili* (n 5); C Forsyth and P Moser, 'The impact of the applicable law of contract on the law of jurisdiction under the European Convention' (1996) 45 *ICLQ* 190.

[18] *Tesam Distribution v Schuh Mode Team* [1990] ILPr 149 [23] (CA).

Article 6(1) is of relevance in EU competition law cases, where claims may be brought against two or three potential defendants.[19] Under Art 6(1):

> [A] person domiciled in a Member State may also be sued where he is one of a number of defendants, in the courts for the place where any one of them is domiciled,[20] provided the claims are so closely connected that it is expedient to hear and determine them together to avoid the risk of irreconcilable judgments resulting from separate proceedings.[21]

In addition to above outlined special rules, the jurisdictional rules contained in s 4 of c II of the Brussels I Regulation, which are to do with claims initiated by consumers, will be highlighted. Further Art 22(4), which may be relevant in EU competition law cases where the issue of validity of an intellectual property right is crucial for allocating the jurisdiction of a court in respect of an antitrust claim, will be outlined. Furthermore, the English courts may have jurisdiction under Art 23 to rule on EU competition law contract-based claims in cases where the agreement in question incorporates a jurisdictional clause.

In the following sections, the application of the special jurisdictional rules to contract-based competition law claims will be examined.

2.2.2 Application of Article 5(1) to EU Competition Law Claims

How will Art 5(1) apply with regard to EU competition law claims brought by contracting parties? The jurisdictional problems in such cases can be easily demonstrated by taking a simple example, where an English distributor (D) agrees to purchase from a French manufacturer (M) and distribute in England a fixed minimum quantity of goods at the price that is shown in the latter's price list. A prohibition on exporting is also imposed on D by M. Subsequently, the market slackens and D runs into serious difficulties in meeting the expected sales volume. D discovers that M sells its goods to other distributors in England at substantially lower prices, and declines to carry on performing his duties under the contract. D asserts that M: has abused its dominant position; has fixed the maximum level of discount D can grant from a prescribed price level; and has made the grant of reimbursement of promotional costs subject to observance of a given price level. Based on that, D can claim that the agreement impedes parallel trade within the EU and enforces resale prices maintenance, so it is void as being in conflict with EU competition law. Furthermore, D can seek EU competition law damages for loss caused to him by the contract liable to distort competition.

[19] Eg joint venture agreements.

[20] 'Article 6(1) of the Brussels and Lugano Conventions stops here.' See n 91 in *Provimi v Aventis Animal Nutrition* [2003] EWHC 961 (Comm); [2003] ECC 29 [41].

[21] 'The added wording is the same as that in what was Article 22, but is now Article 28(3) of the Regulation. Those Articles deal with staying "related actions". The new words also reflect the rationale for Article 6(1), as interpreted by the Court of Justice in Case 189/97 *Kalfelis v Schroder* [1988] ECR 5565 [31].' See n 92 in *Provimi* (n 20) [41]. See also Case C-539/03 *Roche Netherland BV and Others v Primus, Goldenberg* [2006] ECR I-6535 (Court of Justice, First Chamber) [22].

As already mentioned,[22] however, a typical claim for EU competition law damages is tortious in nature and arises solely by reason of the breach of EU competition law provisions. Accordingly, in such a scenario, the same set of facts gives rise to two claims: a contractual claim (validity of the contract), and a (contingent) tortious claim (EU competition law damages). Among the advantages of private antitrust enforcement, the Commission has outlined that 'national courts may apply civil sanctions of nullity to contractual relationships at the same time as hearing a damages claim'.[23] Is it really so if both claims are brought by a contracting party under the Brussels I Regulation? Does an action for nullity of a contract under EU competition law fall within Art 5(1)? Can a plaintiff bring under Art 5(1) a claim for voidness of a contract that distorts competition together with a claim for EU competition law damages? Would the outcome be different if the antitrust damages claim was raised in an action for enforcement of a contract?

2.2.2.1 EU Competition Law Claims Brought by Contracting Parties

It is well established that as a matter of European law, an agreement that infringes EU competition law is void and unenforceable.[24] Furthermore, under English law such an agreement is also illegal.[25] Based on that it seems that the answer to the question of whether Art 5(1) will be interpreted as covering claims arising out of void contracts is important for determining the bases for jurisdiction in competition cases. Accordingly, in this section, first, the jurisdiction under Art 5(1) will be determined with regard to an action for nullity of a contract that is allegedly in conflict with EU competition law. Secondly, the basis for jurisdiction will be defined with regard to proceedings where a declaration for an agreement is sought together with a claim for damages for breach of EU competition law.

2.2.2.1.1 A Claim for a Declaration that a Contract is Void under EU Competition Law

In the context of this book, it is important to outline that jurisdiction under Art 5(1) may be invoked by the plaintiff, even where there is a dispute between the parties over existence of the contract on which the claim is based.[26] But, do disputes over 'existence of a contract' cover a claim seeking a declaration that the contract is void and illegal under EU competition law and English law? Does a

[22] See Section 1.7 above.

[23] Commission (EC), 'Commission Staff Working Paper' (Annex to the Green paper on damages actions for breach of the EC antitrust rules) SEC(2005) 1732 [8].

[24] See Art 101(2) TFEU; Case 48/72 *Haecht v Wilkin-Janssen* [1973] ECR 77 [25]–[27].

[25] *Gibbs Mew v Gemmell* [1998] EuLR 588 (CA).

[26] Case C-38/81 *Effer v Kantner* [1982] ECR 825.

Member State court have jurisdiction under Art 5(1) over a dispute as to the validity of a contract that is allegedly in conflict with Arts 101 and 102 TFEU?

According to Lord Millett, '[i]t is a question of some difficulty whether Art 5(1) operates to confer jurisdiction on a court to pronounce on the validity of a contract except where this is necessary to enable it to adjudicate on the contractual claim itself.'[27] It was held by Lord Goff obiter that 'there must be a serious doubt whether, as a general rule, a court can have jurisdiction under Art 5(1) to rule upon the validity of a contract.'[28] A contract that is in conflict with Art 101 TFEU can produce no legal effects.[29] The nullity referred to in Art 101(2) TFEU is absolute.[30] An agreement that is null and void by virtue of this provision has no effect as between the contracting parties, and cannot be held against third parties.[31] Would the result be different in cases, where a claim is based on abuse of a dominant position? In the context of Art 102 TFEU cases, it has been submitted that a breach by a party abusing its dominant position in negotiating the terms of a contract with the other side may fall within Art 5(1) of Brussels I.[32] However, as already clarified, even though Art 102 TFEU does not include a provision equivalent to Art 101(2) TFEU, which automatically and retroactively nullifies any agreements prohibited by Art 101(1) TFEU, the Court of Justice has stated that an agreement in conflict with Art 102 TFEU should automatically be void as well.[33] Thus, a restrictive interpretation of Art 5(1) of Brussels I should be followed and only those obligations, which are created by the contract (ie voluntary obligations), will be covered by it.[34] Following this line of reasoning one may argue that contracts in breach of Arts 101 and/or 102 TFEU give rise to no legal obligations. If there were no obligation, then there would be no jurisdiction under Art 5(1) of Brussels I.[35]

A majority of the House of Lords have held that a claim for restitution of money paid under a supposed contract, which in law never existed, does not fall within Art 5(1) of Brussels I. It was said that a claim can only come within this provision

[27] *Agnew v Länsförsäkringsbolagens* [2000] UKHL 7; [2001] 1 AC 223 (HL) 264.

[28] *Kleinwort Benson v Glasgow City Council* [1999] 1 AC 153 (HL) 169 (Lord Goff). Fortunately, the rest of the House did not share his view. See *Kleinwort Benson* 172 (Lord Mustill), 174 (Lord Nicholls), 182 (Lord Clyde), 195 (Lord Hutton). See also SGA Pitel, 'Jurisdiction over Restitutionary claims' (1998) *CLJ* 19, 21. A similar approach with regard to jurisdiction in respect of the issue of validity is followed by the French Cour de Cassation. See *Société I.S.I. v Société de promotion des Centres prive audiovisuals* (1983) LXXII *Revue critique de droit international prive*, 516.

[29] Compare HG Beale and others (eds), *Chitty on Contracts* (vol 1, 29th edn, Sweet & Maxwell, London, 2004) 46.

[30] *Beguelin* (n 3).

[31] Ibid.

[32] Ibid 268.

[33] Case 172/73 *BRT v SABAM* [1974] ECR 51. See also: J Faull and A Nikpay, *The EC Law of Competition* (2nd edn, OUP, Oxford, 2007) 412–13; U Bernitz, 'The sanction of voidness under Article 82 EC and its relation to the right to damages' in A Ezrachi (ed), *Article 82 EC: Reflection on its Recent Evolution* (Hart Publishing, Oxford, 2009) 187, 188–89.

[34] BJ Rodger, 'Competition law in a Scottish forum' (2003) *Juridical Review* 247, 267. See also *Agnew* (n 27) 254 (Lord Hope); *Handte* (n 12) [15]; Case C-334/00 *Fonderie Officine Meccaniche Tacconi v Heinrich Wagner Sinto Maschinenfabrik* [2002] ECR I-7537 [23].

[35] Compare *De Bloos* (n 17) [15]; *Kleinwort Benson* (n 28) 181 (Lord Clyde).

if it is based on a particular contractual obligation.[36] Nevertheless, jurisdiction in a case of a void contract can still be determined under Art 5(1) by using the 'intended place of performance of the supposed obligation'.[37] In the *Kleinwort Benson* case, however, Lord Hutton expressly declined to accept this approach. His opinion, though, was motivated by the fact that both parties accepted before the commencement of the action that the contract was void *ab initio*.[38] If there had been a dispute over the validity of the contract in the *Kleinwort Benson* case, the opinion of Lord Hutton probably would have been different and the court at the 'intended place of performance of the supposed obligation' would have had jurisdiction to hear and determine the dispute. It has been submitted that 'it remains possible that Lord Nicholls' more expansive interpretation of the scope of Article 5(1) may be adopted'[39] in EU competition law cases. Following this line of reasoning, it can be suggested that the court at the place of performance of the contractual obligation that allegedly distorts competition would have a role to play in cases, where one party claimed that the contract ran against EU competition law and was void and the other party contended that the contract either met the conditions of Art 101(3) TFEU and was valid or was not in conflict with Art 102 TFEU.[40] That can be further supported by the practical consideration that the court appears to be well placed to determine validity[41] of an obligation with regard to its compliance with EU competition law.[42] Indeed, it has been held by the Court of Justice that the anti-competitive effects of such an agreement should be assessed within the market where it is implemented.[43]

Moreover, it is well established that 'contract' has a wider meaning for the purposes of Art 5(1) of Brussels I.[44] The position that a claim for a negative declaration that no contract existed is within the scope of Art 5(1) was adopted in *Boss Group v Boss France*.[45] In this case, the plaintiff brought an action for a negative declaration that no contract existed, asserting jurisdiction under Art 5(1) of Brussels I. It was submitted by the defendant that the proceedings should be set aside or stayed on the ground that the court did not have jurisdiction to hear the matter on the grounds of Art 5(1) of Brussels I. The court held

[36] *Kleinwort Benson* (n 28) 167 (Goff LJ).

[37] *Kleinwort Benson* [1996] QB 678 (CA) 699 (Millett LJ).

[38] *Kleinwort Benson* (HL) (n 28) 195–96.

[39] Rodger (n 34).

[40] *Cf Boss* (n 11) 975.

[41] A Briggs, 'Decisions of British courts during 1996: private international law' (1996) 67 *British Yearbook of International Law* 577, 585.

[42] Compare Commission Notice on cooperation within the Network of Competition Authorities OJ [2004] C101/43 [8].

[43] *Haecht* (n 7) 415. See the definition of geographical market in the Commission Notice on the definition of relevant market for the purposes of Community competition law ([1997] OJ C372/5 [28]–[31]). See also Case COMP/M.1672 *Volvo/Scania*; Case 27/76 *United Brands v Commission* [1978] ECR 207 [10]–[11].

[44] *Peters* (n 10). See also: Briggs (n 41) 584; A Briggs and P Rees, *Civil Jurisdiction and Judgements* (5th edn, Informa, London, 2009) 211 and 214–23.

[45] *Boss* (n 11).

that '[the] plaintiff establishes a good arguable case that there is a matter relating to contract by relying on the fact that this is what the defendant is contending against it'.[46] Nevertheless, it is submitted by Hill that 'in view of the Court of Justice's case law, *Boss Group v Boss France* … must be regarded as having been wrongfully decided.'[47] This has been justified by the fact that if the claimant argued that the contract was void, he would not be able to identify any obligation as a basis for his claim under Art 5(1) of Brussels I. Concerns about the accuracy of that judgment were also raised by Lord Millett.[48] Notwithstanding, the *Boss* judgment was confirmed by Lord Clyde in *Kleinwort Benson*[49] and Lord Hope in *Agnew*.[50]

The view that a claim for nullity of a contract under Art 101(2) TFEU is a contractual matter can find further support in the EU legislation, and Art 12(1)(e) of the Rome I Regulation in particular.[51] The Regulation expressly provides that the law applicable to a contract shall govern 'the consequences of nullity of the contract'. If the nullity of a contract is a matter relating to a contract for the choice of law purposes, it is difficult to see why it should be different in regard to jurisdiction.[52] Given the fact that for the purposes of Art 5(1), a European definition of 'matters relating to contract' is required, the incorporation of Art 12(1)(e) into an EU legal instrument is to be regarded as reflecting the European concept of 'matters relating to contract'.

In the light of the foregoing considerations, it can be concluded that an action for nullity of a contract under EU competition law falls within Art 5(1) of Brussels I. This is in line with a judgment of a Belgian Cour D'Appel that it has jurisdiction under Art 5(1) of Brussels I to examine the validity of an agreement in relation to Art 101(1) TFEU.[53] The Belgian decision was a follow-on to the judgment of the Court of Justice in *De Bloos v Bouyer*.[54] Going back to the example given above, it can be stated that jurisdiction is to be determined by using the 'place of performance of the supposed obligation', and the English court would have jurisdiction over D's claim for nullity of a contract. As a result, the court at the place of performance of the obligation, which is alleged to distort competition, will have jurisdiction to deal with the question of validity of the contract under EU

[46] Ibid 975 (Saville LJ).

[47] J Hill, *International Commercial Disputes in English Courts* (3rd edn, Hart Publishing, Oxford, 2005) 137.

[48] *Agnew* (n 27) 264.

[49] See *Kleinwort Benson* (n 28) 182.

[50] See *Agnew* (n 27) 258. See also Briggs (n 41) 583 (supporting the decision).

[51] Art 12(1)(e) of the Rome I Regulation is modelled on Art 10(1)(e) of the Rome Convention 1980. Art 10(1)(e) of the Rome Convention did not have the force of law in England. See Contracts (Applicable Law) Act 1991 s 2(2).

[52] J Riley, 'Void contracts, restitution and jurisdiction' (1996) *Lloyd's Maritime and Commercial Law Quarterly* 182, 184.

[53] Indeed, the case reached the Court of Justice again, this time in relation to the application of Art 101 TFEU. See Case 59/77 *De Bloos v Bouyer* [1978] 1 CMLR 511.

[54] *De Bloos* (n 17).

competition law. That solution would allow the best placed court to determine the validity of a contractual obligation that is alleged to distort competition.

2.2.2.1.2 A Claim for EU Competition Law Damages brought by a Contracting Party

It was clarified that the court under Art 5(1) of Brussels I can have jurisdiction over a claim seeking a declaration that a contract is void as being in conflict with EU competition law; it remains to be seen, however, whether the same court can rule on a claim for EU competition law damages. This would give rise to some difficulties with regard to EU competition law claims for damages brought by contracting parties together with a claim seeking nullity of the contract. This is due to the fact that in theory, a claim for damages could not arise from a void contract, which is incapable of generating any legal rights. As already clarified,[55] such a claim is not contractual but tortious in nature, and it arises solely by reason of the breach of EU competition law. In this section, first, the jurisdiction of courts over a counter-claim for antitrust damages brought by the other contracting party under Art 6(3) of Brussels I will be briefly examined. Then, the question whether a claim for EU competition law damages can be brought together with a claim for voidness of a contract under Art 5(1) of Brussels I will be discussed. Finally, the question of court jurisdiction under Art 5(3) of Brussels I over claims for damages and nullity of a contract that distorts competition will be analysed.

It is beyond doubt that if M sues D for damages for non-performance of the contract, Art 5(1) of Brussels I should apply.[56] The English court will have jurisdiction over a defence that a contract is void due to EU competition law. How about its jurisdiction over a counter-claim for antitrust damages made by D? Such a counter-claim would be tortious in nature and would not be based on any term of the contract, which would be eventually invalidated as being in conflict with Arts 101 and/or 102 TFEU. Nevertheless, it seems clear that the counter-claim for EU competition law damages does satisfy the requirements of Art 6(3) of Brussels I. It relates to the same distribution agreement that is alleged to distort competition. There would be a factual connection between M's claim for enforcement of a contract and D's counter-claim for antitrust damages that is based on the alleged voidness under EU competition law of the very same agreement. In view of that, it seems that again the dispute over the compliance of the agreement with Arts 101 and 102 TFEU will be at the heart of the argument. Accordingly, the requirement of Art 6(3)[57] that the claim and the counter-claim arise out of 'the same contract or facts'[58] will be easily satisfied as the application of EU competition law is largely

[55] See ch 1, section 1.7 above.

[56] Compare the reasoning of Lord Nicholls of Birkenhead in *Kleinwort Benson* (n 28) 174.

[57] See Case C-341/93 *Danvaern Production v Schuhfabriken Otterbeck* [1995] ECR I-2053 (Decision of the Full Court) [7] (opinion of the AG Leger).

[58] Case VIII ZR 110/92 *Re A Counterclaim under Italian Law* [1995] ILPr 133 (Federal Supreme Court, Germany); *Cha Cha Denmark v Commercial Textiles* [2002] ILPr 53 (Danish Supreme Court);

fact-based assessment. Moreover, there is no doubt that a claim for EU antitrust law damages would involve a separate judgment and could be distinguished from a pure defence.[59] Based on that, it can be stated that a claim for damages arising out of a contract that infringes EU competition law can be brought as a counter-claim at the court of place of performance of obligation on the basis of Art 6(3) of Brussels I.

But, what if D decides to bring a claim for EU competition law damages together with a claim for voidness of a contract under EU competition law on the basis of Art 5(1) of Brussels I? Does the court at the place of performance of the supposed obligation have jurisdiction to rule on an EU competition law damages claim brought by a contracting party under Art 5(1) of Brussels I? In this scenario, there are two EU competition law claims. On the first claim, D seeks a declaration that the contract is void by setting details of its illegality under Arts 101 and/or 102 TFEU. It was already demonstrated that such a claim would be covered by Art 5(1) of Brussels I. In addition, there is another claim for antitrust damages arising out of an EU competition law infringement. The second claim is to be determined by the court only if the primary claim is not dismissed, ie the court is satisfied that the contract is void. In spite of the fact that the claim for antitrust damages does not arise out of the void contract, but from the fact that there is a breach of statutory duty, it is based on the illegality of the contract that is in conflict with EU competition law. This appears to indicate that that the tortious claim for antitrust damages is closely related to the contractual claim seeking nullity of the contract under EU competition law.

Can the jurisdiction of the English court in these claims be justified by the objective of the Brussels I Regulation to avoid multiplicity of closely related proceedings? Articles 27 and 28 of Brussels I serve to avoid the risk of conflicting judgments where the cause of actions and parties are the same or the actions are related.[60] It should be recalled that Arts 27 and 28 of Brussels I, on the one hand, and Arts 2–6 of Brussels I, on the other hand, relate to two completely distinct procedural situations. Articles 27 and 28 of Brussels I will apply only where parallel and related actions are brought before the courts of two or more Member States.[61] As a result, those provisions will not help to answer the question of jurisdiction regarding an eventual EU competition claim, despite the fact that the actions in the given example are related.

The scenario where a claim for antitrust damages is brought together with a claim for nullity of a contract that is alleged to distort competition would raise

Case VIII ZR 263/00 *Re The Assertion of a Set-off and Counter Claim* [2003] ILPr 543 (Federal Supreme Court, Germany).

[59] *Danvaern* (n 57) [12], [15], [16] and [18] of the judgment; See also: A Briggs, 'Brussels Convention' (1995) 15 *Yearbook of European Law* 498; T Hartley, 'Article 6(3): Counterclaims' (1996) 21 *EL Rev* 166; Hill (n 47) 165.

[60] See Jenard Report (n 10).

[61] See Case 150/80 *Elefanten Schuh v Jacqmain* [1981] ECR 1671 [19] and [20]. See more about the application of Arts 27 and 28 of Brussels I with regard to EU competition law claims in ch 4 below.

particularly difficult problems in relation to the scope of the contract head (Art 5(1)) and the tort head (Art 5(3))[62] in the Brussels I Regulation. Commentators support opposing views of what should be the basis of jurisdiction where the same set of facts would give rise to claims in contract and tort. According to Kaye,[63] 'when the principal subject matter of the proceedings concerns the existence or not of liability in tort, the matter in dispute should be regarded as tortious for the purposes of application of Article 5(3), notwithstanding the existence of the incidental issue of contract.'[64] This view seems to be in line with the English jurisprudence.[65] The opposing view is held by Kropholler.[66] According to him, it is the contractual relationship which is decisive, so jurisdiction should be determined under Art 5(1). The view that the prohibited effect of antitrust agreements or practices should be channelled by the contract appears to be preferred on the Continent.[67]

In English law the existence of a contractual relationship is no barrier to a claim based on tort.[68] Accordingly, under English traditional rules, a claim for antitrust damages made by a contracting party would be regarded as tortious, notwithstanding the existence of the incidental contractual issue.[69] In *Source v TUV*, however, the Court of Appeal held that a claim, which may be brought under a contract or independently of a contract on the same facts, cannot be brought in tort under the Brussels I Regulation.[70] This ruling suggests that a broader interpretation of Art 5(1) of Brussels I would mean that the 'matters relating to a contract' could have also channelled the claim for EU competition law damages brought by a contracting party, since that claim would be directly connected with the contractual relationship that is alleged to distort competition.[71] This can be questioned, however, in the light of the subsequent narrow interpretation given to the concept of 'matters relating to a contract' in the *Kleinwort Benson* case.[72] Although *Source* was not cited in *Kleinwort Benson*, in *RZB v NBC*[73] the court questioned whether the *Source* ruling is still good law, in light of the House of

[62] The application of Art 5(3) of Brussels I in EU antitrust claims is dealt with in ch 3 below.

[63] P Kaye, *Civil Jurisdiction and Enforcement of Foreign Judgments* (Professional Books, Oxford, 1987).

[64] Ibid 570.

[65] See: *Matthews v Kuwait Bechtel Corp* [1959] 2 QB 57 (CA); *Coupland v Arabian Gulf Oil* [1983] 1 WLR 1136 (CA); *Base Metal Trading v Shamurin* [2003] EWHC 2419 (Comm); [2004] ILPr 5; a'ffd *Base Metal Trading v Shamurin* [2004] EWCA Civ 1316 (CA).

[66] J Kropholler, *Europäisches Zivilprozessrecht. Kommentar zu EuGVO und Lugano- Übereinkommen* (Recht und Wirtschaft, Frankfurt, 1982) 64.

[67] C Castronovo, 'Private law remedies for antitrust violations—a point of view from Italy' in J Basedow, *Private Enforcement of EC Competition Law* (Kluwer Law International, The Hague, 2008) 107, 117.

[68] Eg *Matthews* (n 65); *Coupland* (65); *Base Metal* (n 65).

[69] Compare *Hedley Byrne v Heller* [1964] AC 465 (HL). See also *Burke v Uvex Sports* (Record No 2003 4850P) [2005] IEHC 68; [2005] ILPr 26.

[70] *Source v TUV Rheinland Holding* [1998] QB 54 (CA) 63; See also *Kalfelis* (n 21) [17].

[71] Compare *Kalfelis* (n 21) [31] (AG Darmon).

[72] See *Cheshire, North & Fawcett* (n 15) 251. See also *Raiffeisen Zentralbank Osterreich v National Bank of Greece* [1999] 1 Lloyd's Rep 408 (QBD (Comm)).

[73] *Raiffeisen* (n 72).

Lords' judgment. If it were good law, then the EU competition law damages claim would be a matter relating to contract. There are, however, more arguments suggesting that the *Source* case will be overridden by the *Kleinwort Benson* judgment. Moreover, the judgment of the Court of Justice in the *Kalfelis* case[74] is interpreted as rejecting the proposal of AG Darmon[75] that 'an action based on tort and contract … is governed exclusively by the rules laid down for contractual matters in Article 5(1) of the [Regulation].'[76]

Furthermore, the House of Lords has interpreted the ruling in the *Kafelis* case as defining claims under Art 5(1) and (3) of Brussels I to be mutually exclusive.[77] The matter has to be characterised as either one relating to a tort, or as one relating to a contract, but not both.[78] Following the *Kalfelis* case, the Belgian Commercial Court held that a court which has jurisdiction to hear a claim does not *ipso facto* have jurisdiction also to hear other claims that are formulated within the same court proceedings or simultaneously, when both claims have a different basis, even if the factual elements are based with one another.[79]

Therefore, the current case law suggests that a claim for EU competition law damages is not covered by Art 5(1) of Brussels I. This will be so, since the EU competition law damages claims cannot be based on a particular contractual obligation.[80] As a matter of law, such a contract (or contractual clause) will be invalidated as being contrary to Arts 101 and/or 102 TFEU. Thus, D would be prevented from bringing under Art 5(1) of Brussels I a claim for nullity of a contract together with a tortious action for antitrust damages.

It seems that Art 5(3) of Brussels I should be the basis of jurisdiction for bringing a claim for EU competition law damages that are suffered by a contracting party. Can D overlook the incidental contractual issue and bring his EU competition law claim for damages under the tort head? In spite of the fact that D's claim may have been framed solely in tort, it seems that the dispute over the validity of the contract under EU competition law would be the major feature of the litigation in such a scenario. In light of that, the validity of the contract that allegedly distorts competition should not be regarded as an incidental issue but as a matter the action is principally concerned with. As already clarified, a claim seeking nullity of a contract is to be viewed as a matter relating to a contract under Art 5(1) of the Brussels I Regulation.

The Irish High Court recently held that 'the plaintiff cannot avoid the consequences of the existence of [the] contract by seeking his remedy solely in tort'.[81]

[74] *Kalfelis* (n 21).

[75] *Kleinwort Benson* (HL) (n 28) 166–67 (Lord Goff), 183–84 (Lord Clyde).

[76] *Kalfelis* (n 21) [31] (AG Darmon).

[77] See *Agnew* (n 27).

[78] *Cheshire, North & Fawcett* (n 15) 251; Briggs and Rees (n 44) 253–56.

[79] *NV Euro Boat v Sarl Team Boat* [2006] ILPr 15 [7] (Rechtbank Van Koophandel (Commercial Court) Belgium).

[80] See *Cheshire, North & Fawcett* (n 15) 251–52.

[81] *Burke* (n 69) [31]. In this case, however, the validity of the contract was not in dispute.

The Court held that the objectives of the Regulation should override the fact that the local legislation permits such action. It seems that a similar approach will be followed by the English courts when a contracting party brings under Art 5(3) of Brussels I a claim for EU competition law damages together with a claim for voidness of a contract. This result would be in accord with the French Cour de Cassation (Supreme Court) practice in claims for damages for unfair competition.[82] It was held by the French Court that if one of the claims is based on contract and the other on tort, then the court having jurisdiction under Art 5(3) of Brussels I does not have jurisdiction over claims based on contract.[83] Thus, for the purposes of the Brussels Regulation, the plaintiff cannot disregard the incidental issue of contract by bringing his claim for EU competition law damages under Art 5(3) of Brussels I.

It can be concluded that a claim for a declaration that a contract is void as being in conflict with EU competition law is regarded as covered by Art 5(1) of Brussels I. A counter-claim for damages, arising out of breach of EU competition law, falls within Art 6(3) of Brussels I. It would not be reasonable to accept that the court would have jurisdiction over the EU competition law claim for damages if the proceedings were initiated by the party who had no competition claim, but not if they were started by the opposing party. A better result would have been reached if Art 5(1) of Brussels I had channelled all EU competition law claims brought by any contracting party.

However, the current case law suggests that a claim for EU competition law damages is not covered by Art 5(1) of Brussels I. Further, it seems that a claimant would not be allowed to overlook the dispute over the validity of a contract and bring his claim for antitrust damages under Art 5(3) of Brussels I. This is an unsatisfactory outcome that contradicts the purpose of the enhanced private antitrust law reform which is supposed to create incentives for plaintiffs who have EU competition law claims. Although a plaintiff is always entitled to bring his action in its entirety before the courts of the defendant's domicile, in such a case, he will lose the advantages for bringing his claim under Art 5. The English court nonetheless may apply civil sanctions of nullity to a contractual relationship and rule on an antitrust damages claim, if it has jurisdiction under the contract and tort heads of Art 5 of Brussels I, respectively. Having clarified that, it remains to be seen how Art 5(1) of Brussels I would apply with regard to specific EU competition law claims brought by contracting parties.

2.2.2.2 EU Antitrust Law Claims arising out of Anti-Competitive Agreements

It is well established that EU competition law may apply to agreements between undertakings operating at the same level of the market, as well as agreements

[82] *Rudolph Roock Transeurope Haus-Haus Speditions v Boulnager Belgique* [2005] ILPr 21 (Cour de Cassation (France)).

[83] Ibid [4].

between traders operating at different levels in the chain of supply.[84] It is beyond doubt that an anti-competitive agreement can infringe both Arts 101 and 102 TFEU.[85]

As a general rule, resale price maintenance,[86] absolute territorial protection,[87] exclusion of parallel imports/exports,[88] restrictions of cross-supplies within a selective distribution system,[89] tie-in agreements[90] and agreements whereby a customer is required to purchase a specified type of goods only from a dominant supplier[91] may often result in EU competition law disputes.

2.2.2.2.1 EU Competition Law Claims arising out of 'Sale of Goods' Agreements

A contract may contain a clause requiring an English buyer to purchase all his supplies of a given product by a French supplier who holds a dominant position within the EU, so that the buyer would not be allowed to buy and resell competing goods.[92] Which court would have jurisdiction under Art 5(1) of Brussels I to determine whether the agreement has anti-competitive effect on inter-brand competition? Another example may be an agreement between an English buyer and a French supplier which contains a clause that makes the sale of one product conditional upon the purchase of another product (ie tied product) from the French supplier or someone designated by him.[93] Which court should determine whether the agreement has possible foreclosure effects on the market of the tied product? These questions may arise in relation to Arts 101 and/or 102 TFEU claims as well as Merger-based claims.[94]

As already mentioned, the first indent of Art 5(1)(b) of Brussels I allocates jurisdiction with regard to 'sale of goods' agreements. Application of the 'sale of goods' jurisdictional rule would not give rise to any particular problems, apart from those which were already outlined above, with regard to EU competition law claims. A private EU competition law plaintiff should bring his claim before the courts at the Member State where, under the contract, the goods were delivered

[84] R Whish, *Competition Law* (OUP, Oxford, 2008) 115.

[85] Case 85/76 *Hoffmann-La Roche v Commission* [1979] ECR 461 [116]. See also: Commission Notice, *Guidance on Vertical Restraints* [2000] OJ 291/1 [1]; Faull and Nikpay (n 33) 408; Whish (n 84) 674.

[86] Case 243/83 *Binon* [1985] ECR 201.

[87] Case C-70/93 *BMW v Auto-Leasing* [1995] ECR I-3439. See also Joined Cases 56/64 and 58/64 *Consten and Grunding v Commission* [1966] ECR 299.

[88] *Consten and Grundig* (n 87). See also Case 19/77 *Miller International Schallplatten v Commission* [1978] ECR 131.

[89] *Binon* (n 86).

[90] Eg Case T-201/04 *Microsoft Corporation v Commission* [2007] 5 CMLR 846. See also Art 82(2)(d).

[91] Eg *Hoffmann-La Roche* (n 85) [89].

[92] *Guidance on Vertical Restraints* (n 85) [138].

[93] *Guidance on Vertical Restraints* (n 85) [215].

[94] Commission Notice on restrictions directly related and necessary to concentrations [2005] OJ C-56/24 [32]–[35].

or should have been delivered. It is the parties' agreement that would indicate where the place is located and respectively which court would have jurisdiction.[95] The House of Lords appeared to favour the view that the place of delivery for jurisdictional purposes would depend on whether the sale is ex-works, or FOB or CIF contract.[96] This means that in cases where the sale is an FOB contract, the place of ultimate destination of goods may be irrelevant for jurisdictional purpose.[97] Such an interpretation could allow a dominant undertaking to avoid the possibility to be sued in a foreign forum, for example, by selling its goods on FOB terms.

Parallel antitrust proceedings involving related EU competition law claims may arise in cases where small companies are parties to contracts forming a cross-border parallel network of similar types of restrictive agreements[98] involving places of delivery in a number of Member of States. It seems that in such a scenario, an affected small or medium-sized company may bring an EU competition law under Art 5(1)(b) of Brussels I seeking a declaration that their contracts (or a contractual clause in their contracts) are in conflict with EU competition law, and thus void. If a number of small and medium-sized companies across Europe wanted to bring collective redress actions by relying on Art 5(1)(b) of Brussels I, then a number of parallel collective proceedings could be the result.[99]

2.2.2.2.2 EU Competition Law Claims arising out of Licensing Agreements or Distribution Agreements

The special Commission Regulations that are dealing with vertical restraints[100] indicate that the distribution and technology transfer agreements are likely to give rise to future private EU competition law disputes.[101] However, there are potential problems surrounding the definition of such agreements for the purposes of Art 5 of the Brussels I Regulation.

As already mentioned,[102] the Regulation does not indicate whether distribution contracts and licensing agreements amount to contracts for 'sale of goods' or 'provision of service', or whether they are contracts which belong to none

[95] *Cheshire, North & Fawcett* (n 15) 239–40.

[96] *Scottish & Newcastle International Ltd v Othon Ghalanos Ltd* [2008] UKHL 11.

[97] Ibid [49]–[55]. See also *Cheshire, North & Fawcett* (n 15) 239.

[98] Art 101(1) TFEU has been interpreted as allowing the cumulative effect of similar agreements of a number of undertakings to be taken into account in judging vertical agreements. See *Haecht* (n 7).

[99] See more: ch 4.

[100] Commission Regulation (EC) 2790/1999 of 22 December 1999 on the application of Article 81(3) of the Treaty to categories of vertical agreements and concerted practices; Commission Regulation (EC) 1400/2002 of 31 July 2002 on the application of Article 81(3) of the Treaty to categories of vertical agreements and concerted practices in the motor vehicle sector; Commission Regulation (EC) 772/2004 of 27 April 2004 on the application of Article 81(3) of the Treaty to categories of technology transfer agreements. See also *Guidance on Vertical Restraints* (n 85).

[101] See also Commission Notice on restrictions directly related and necessary to concentrations [2005] OJ C56/24 [27]–[31].

[102] See section 2.2.2 above.

of those categories.[103] There are three possible ways of classifying distribution and licensing agreements for purposes of Art 5(1). First, the contracts can be characterised according to law of the forum. Second, the applicable law can define whether the agreement amounts to 'sale of goods' or 'provision of services'. Thirdly, independent and autonomous European definitions can be given to the expressions used in Art 5(1). Considering the objectives of the Brussels Regulation, it seems that the third approach towards addressing the question must be adopted. [104] The fact that the law of jurisdiction is now contained in the Regulation has been interpreted as an indication that it is more open to the EU influence.[105]

2.2.2.2.2.1 EU Competition Law Claims arising out of Licensing Agreements

Under a typical technology transfer agreement a licensor grants to a licensee an exclusive right to exploit an intellectual property right, and consideration for this is the royalty.[106] Can such an agreement be regarded as a 'sale of goods' agreement within the meaning of Art 5(1)(b) of Brussels I? The answer to this question should be negative.[107] The inference that the expression 'sale of goods' will not be broad enough to include licensing agreements can be strengthened by reference to the Vienna Convention.[108] In view of the fact that most of the EU Member States have adopted that Convention, it has been submitted that its concept of sale of goods is representative for most of the EU countries.[109] Non-physical items such as intellectual property rights should not be regarded as goods. This can be deduced from Art 30 of the Vienna Convention, that requires the seller to 'transfer the property in the goods'. The intellectual property rights are intangible matter and cannot be transferred by a physical delivery. Accordingly, it seems to follow that a technology transfer agreement is not a 'sale of goods' contract under the Regulation.[110]

Is a contract, under which the owner of an intellectual property right grants its contractual partner the right to use the right in return for remuneration, to be regarded as a contract for the provision of services? The question was referred to the Court of Justice by the Austrian Supreme Court (*Oberster Gerichtshof*).[111] The Court pointed out that 'service' implies a continuing economic activity in return for remuneration, whilst the licensing agreement is merely a one-off act

[103] Compare the Draft Hague Convention on Jurisdiction and Foreign Judgments in Civil and Commercial Matters uses similar terms. See also P Nygh and F Pocar, 'Report—Preliminary Document No 11 of August 2000' *Hague Conference* http://hcch.e-vision.nl/upload/wop/jdgmpd11.pdf.

[104] Compare *Handte* (n 12).

[105] J Fawcett, J Harris and M Bridge, *International Sale of Goods in the Conflict of Laws* (OUP, Oxford, 2005) 87.

[106] See Art 1(1)b of Commission Regulation (EC) 772/2004.

[107] See Hill (n 47) 135; Takahashi (n 16) 534.

[108] United Nation Convention on contracts for international sales of goods, 1980 (CISG).

[109] Fawcett, Harris and Bridge (n 105) 87.

[110] Ibid 513 and 955. See also *St Albans City v International Computers* [1996] 4 All ER 481 (CA).

[111] *Falco Privatstiftung* (n 15).

and does not involve such activity.[112] As a result, licensing agreements should not be classified as a 'provision of services' contract for the purposes of Art 5(1) of Brussels I.

Based on that, it may be concluded that the jurisdiction of English courts with regard to private EU competition law claims arising out of technology transfer agreements will be determined on the basis of Art 5(1)(a) of Brussels I. But where can a contracting party bring an EU competition law claim arising out of a licensing agreement that is alleged to be in conflict with EU competition law claims? It seems that jurisdiction in EU competition law claims arising out of technology transfer agreements should be defined on a case-by-case basis. Some examples illustrating the most common scenarios will be given below.

The antitrust dispute may arise out of a 'grant-back clause' which may have been included in the contract by the licensor who obliges a licensee to grant back to the licensor an exclusive licence in respect to any new improvements. Such clauses may be used by a licensor in an attempt to exclude competitors. A grant-back clause may have been combined with other restrictions of the competition as for example allocation of markets. In such a scenario, if the licensee makes a claim seeking nullity of the contract as a whole, then the judge is required to identify the intended place of performance of the supposed obligation on which the plaintiff's action is based and jurisdiction is to be determined in accordance with this.[113] Considering the EU law definition given by Art 1 of Commission Regulation 772/2004 on Technology Transfer Agreements, the principal obligation in respect of a licensing agreement would be the granting of a licence to exploit an intellectual property right. As an indication of where such obligation would be performed, we may use the decision of the Irish court in *Olympia Production v Cameron Mackintosh*.[114] In that case, the court held that this obligation would be performed by the execution of a valid legal document by which exclusive distribution rights are granted. The Irish courts had no jurisdiction under Art 5(1) of Brussels I, since the execution of this document took place in England, or at the grantor's domicile. Thus, it seems that the court at the intended place of performance of the obligation to grant the licence would have jurisdiction in EU competition law cases where the licensee claims that the whole contract is void. If the *Cameron Mackintosh* case is followed, then that obligation would have been performed by the execution of a valid legal document by which exclusive rights are granted. The court where that obligation is performed would hear and determine the EU competition law claim.

Furthermore, there may well be competition cases, where there is no dispute about the voidness of the contract as a whole, but the dispute is about the existence

[112] *Falco Privatstiftung* (n 15) [29]–[31]. See also: Fawcett, Harris and Bridge (n 105) 513.

[113] *Shenavai* (n 17) [19]. Compare *Kleinwort* (CA) (n 37) 699 (Millett LJ). See more section 2.2.2.1.1 above.

[114] *Olympia Production v Cameron Mackintosh* [1992] ILRM 204. See also: Fawcett and Torremans (n 1) 80 and 89.

of the 'obligation in question'.[115] Thus, in an EU competition claim a licensee may allege, for example, that his royalties are substantially higher than those of other licensees, intending to drive him out of business. In such a case, it seems that the subject-matter of the proceedings would be the obligation to pay royalties. The ruling of the English Commercial Court in *Rank Film Distributors v Lanterna Editrice*[116] is that normally, the obligation to pay royalties is due in the state where the licensor resides. In that case, it was held by Saville J that, as a matter of contractual interpretation, a certain instalment of the royalties was payable in London, being the place where the licensor resides. It is very likely that this ruling will be relevant for the EU competition claim as well. Thus, if, for example, an English licensee alleges that he is paying royalties that are excessive and contrary to Arts 101 and 102 TFEU, he should sue the licensor in the court where he resides.[117]

What can be concluded is that jurisdiction in EU competition law claims arising out of technology transfer agreements will be defined on a case-by-case basis, depending on the place of performance of the supposed obligation on which the plaintiff's action is based. Jurisdiction of English courts in such claims will depend on the obligation in question that forms the subject-matter of the proceedings. It seems, however, that Art 5(1) of Brussels I would be of little use to licensees who wish to sue in their home state a licensor domiciled in another Member State and rely on a contract that is contrary to EU competition law because the execution of the legal document (being the principal obligation) by which exclusive distribution rights were granted took place at the licensor's domicile. The same would be true if a claim was made in respect of royalties that are allegedly substantially higher than those of other licensees and intended to drive the licensee out of business. The result is rather unsatisfactory, since in many cases jurisdiction in an EU competition law claim will be conferred to courts that have little connection with the substance of the claim and relevant market and thus may not be well placed to hear and determine the action. This would be particularly so in cases, where the valid legal document by which exclusive distribution rights are granted is executed in one Member State, but implemented in another.

2.2.2.2.2.2 EU Competition Law Claims arising out of Distribution Agreements

Distribution agreements are complex arrangements, which involve not only sale of a manufacturer's goods by a distributor, but also some services that are provided by the distributor in respect of those goods.[118] Not surprisingly, different opinions have been expressed with regard to questions of jurisdiction in claims

[115] *Rank Film Distributors v Lanterna Editrice* [1992] ILPr 58 (QBD (Comm)). See also: Fawcett and Torremans (n 1) 79 and 95.

[116] *Rank Film* (n 115). See also: Fawcett and Torremans (n 1) 79 and 95.

[117] See Art 5(1)(a).

[118] Fawcett, Harris and Bridge (n 105) 92. *Print Concept v GEW* [2001] EWCA Civ 352; [2002] CLC 382 [21]–[26] (CA).

arising out of such agreements. Some commentators[119] submit that it is possible to separate out different contracts and apply Art 5(1)(b) to them. According to Briggs and Rees, if the manufacturer sells goods to a distributor for resale by the latter, then the contract may be seen as one for the sale of goods.[120] On the other hand, if the distributor provides services in respect of the manufacturer's goods, it may more easily be seen as a contract for the provision of services.[121] Briggs and Rees go further, and hold that contracts for distribution should not fall within Art 5(1)(b) at all, because of the fact that the distribution agreements are complex contracts, which require complicated analyses to be made by the courts.[122] Such a result seems to be in line with the decision of the French Cour de Cassation in *Waeco International and Cardon*.[123] In this case, the French Court held that 'an exclusive distributorship agreement is neither a contract for sale nor a provision of services.'[124] But to say that Art 5(1)(b) would apply only in cases where obligations were not complex would minimise the effect of the changes made by the Brussels I Regulation. Such an outcome is not in accord with the purposes of Art 5(1)(b), which was designed to avoid complicated legal analyses that were made under the Brussels Convention,[125] to centralise litigation before the courts at 'the place of performance' and to determine sole jurisdiction for all claims arising out of the contract.[126]

In *Print Concept v GEW*,[127] the Court of Appeal held that the essential characteristic of a distributorship agreement was the 'intended supply and purchase' of the products. Based on that, it was concluded that the party who was to effect the characteristic performance for the choice of law purposes was the manufacturer, not the distributor.[128] Nevertheless, it seems difficult to characterise such contracts as sale of goods contracts, since a 'distributorship agreement lacks the true characteristic of a true sale contract such as terms relating to delivery and (often) quantity.'[129] The real commercial purpose of a distributorship contract is the penetration and promotion of the manufacturer's products within a given

119 Briggs and Rees (n 44) 242–244.
120 Ibid 242.
121 Ibid 242.
122 Ibid 243. See also: PR Beaumont, 'The Brussels Convention becomes a Regulation: implications for legal basis, external competence, and contract jurisdiction' in JJ Fawcett (ed), *Reform and Development of Private International Law* (OUP, Oxford, 2002) 9, 20.
123 *Waeco International GmbH v Cardon* [2007] ILPr 38 (French Supreme Court).
124 Ibid [6]. See also: *Nestorway Ltd v Ambaflex BV* [2006] IEHC 235, [2007] ILPr 48.
125 See *De Bloos* (n 17); *Medway Packaging v Meurer Maschinen* [1990] 2 Lloyd's Rep 112 (CA); *Boss* (n 11); *USF v Aquatechnology Hanson* [2001] 1 All ER (Comm) 856 (Comm); *Bio-Medical Resarch v Delatex* [2000] IESC 32; [2001] ILRM 51 [18] (Irish Supreme Court). See more: Fawcett and Torremans (n 1) 81–87. For summary of the case law from the other Member States, see K Hertz *Jurisdiction in Contract and Tort under the Brussels Convention* (DJOF Publishing, Copenhagen, 1998) 132–40.
126 *Color Drack* (n 14) [39]. Compare Beaumont (n 122) 20.
127 *Print Concept* (n 118).
128 Ibid [34] (Longmore LJ).
129 Fawcett, Harris and Bridge (n 105) 93, 959 and 960.

geographical market. Based on that it would be more appropriate if distribution agreements are regarded as contracts for the 'provision of services' and thus fall within Art 5(1)(b) of the Brussels I Regulation.[130]

Such a conclusion will be in line with the definition of 'service' contained in Art 4 of the Service Directive.[131] In the explanation given by the Commission in its proposal for the directive it was outlined that the definition covers a very wide range of activities including the distributive trade given as an example.[132] However, it is arguable whether the Service Regulation would be indicative when interpreting the question what constitutes 'contract for services' within the meaning of Art 5(1)(b) of Brussels I. In the *Falco Privatstiftung* case, the Court of Justice explicitly held that:

> [t]hat analysis cannot be called into question by the arguments concerning the interpretation of the concept of 'services' within the meaning of Art 50 EC or secondary [EU] legislation other than Regulation No 44/2001 and the broad logic and scheme of Article 5(1) of that Regulation.[133]

Nevertheless, the fact that Rome I also regards the distribution contracts as contracts for services[134] could be taken to mean that the EU legislator firmly believes that distribution agreements are to be considered as services in the private international law context.[135] Therefore, a distribution agreement would probably be regarded as contracts for 'provision of services' for the purposes of allocating jurisdiction[136] with regard to EU competition law claims arising out of them.

Article 5(1)(b) of Brussels I allocates jurisdiction to the place where, under the contract, the services are provided or should have been provided. It seems that in many cases Art 5(1)(b) may entitle a distributor to bring an EU competition claim before the national court where the goods are distributed.[137] Under a typical distribution agreement a distributor usually is given distribution rights for a certain territory.[138] Normally, a locally domiciled distributor is appointed for a certain territory. The obligations of the distributor are frequently specifically related to the territory over which the distribution rights have been granted, and will be performed there. In view of that, from a jurisdictional perspective, it is relatively easy to identify under Art 5(1)(b) of Brussels I the intended place of

[130] Ibid 92–93. See also: Takahashi (n 16) 533.

[131] Directive 2006/123/EC of the European Parliament of 12 December 2006 on services in the internal market. Pursuant to Art 4(1) of the Directive, 'service' is any self-employed economic activity, as provided for by Article 57 TFEU (ex Art 50 TEC), consisting of the *provision of a service against consideration*.

[132] See also Proposal for a Directive of the European Parliament and of the Council on services in the internal market COM (2004) 2 final/3 [7].

[133] *Falco Privatstiftung* (n 15) [33].

[134] Recital 17 of the Rome I Regulation.

[135] Recital 7 of the Rome I Regulation.

[136] *Cheshire, North & Fawcett* (n 15) 239.

[137] Compare Art 4(1)(f) of the Rome I Regulation.

[138] *Bio-Medical Resarch* (n 121).

performance of the obligation that is in conflict with Arts 101 and 102 TFEU. This can be illustrated by the following example: B manufacturer, domiciled in state B, grants distribution rights to distributor A, domiciled in state A. The distributor A is under an obligation to distribute the manufacturer's goods in state A. No doubt, the place where the services are provided or should have been provided is state A.[139] Accordingly, the distributor may seek a declaration that the contract is void under EU competition law in the courts in the Member State (A), for which it has been given the distribution rights. It seems clear that Art 5(1)(b) of Brussels I cannot be used by a mala fide manufacturer, who might try to initiate a claim against the distributor at another court, making it the 'court first seised', for the purpose of Arts 27 and 28 of Brussels I.[140] It can be concluded that the Brussels I Regulation provides for a well placed court to deal with EU competition claims arising out of distribution agreements. Classifying the distribution agreements as services precludes such a manufacturer from protecting itself from being sued in a Member State other than its domicile, which was possible under the old regime.[141]

But what if a distributor has distribution rights for a market which is broader than the territory of a single Member State? Is the distributor entitled to bring his EU competition law claim for nullity of the allegedly anti-competitive agreement before the courts of any country over which territory distribution rights have been granted? The answer to these questions can be derived by analogy from the Court of Justice judgment in *Color Drack*.[142] Although, the latter judgment was rendered in the context of the first indent of Art 5(1)(b) with regard to a contract involving several places delivery within a single Member State, the Court of Justice reasoning would be equally valid to cases falling within the second indent of Art 5(1)(b), involving several Member States in which the obligation is performed. Indeed, in *Rehder*,[143] the Court of Justice explicitly stated that:

> The factors on which the Court based itself in order to arrive at the interpretation set out in *Color Drack* are also valid with regard to contracts for the provision of services, including the cases where such provision is not effected in one single Member State.[144]

Accordingly, the *Color Drack* principles should be followed in a case where the distribution rights have been granted for several Member States. In such a scenario, the 'place of performance' for the purposes of allocating jurisdiction should be the place with the closest linking factor between the contract and the court having jurisdiction.[145] In other words, the closest linking factor would be at the country where the principal place of distribution of the manufacturer's goods takes place.

[139] See *Boss* (n 11). See also the example given by Fawcett and Torremans (n 1) 82.
[140] Compare Fawcett and Torremans (n 1) 82. See ch 4, section 4.2 below.
[141] See Fawcett and Torremans (n 1) 82.
[142] *Color Drack* (n 14).
[143] Case C-204/08 *Peter Rehder v Air Baltic Corporation* [2009] ILPr 44, [2010] ECR-0000, 9 July 2009.
[144] *Rehder* (n 143) [36].
[145] *Rehder* (n 143) [38].

The latter place should be determined on the basis of economic criteria. If it is not possible to determine such a place of delivery, then each country where the manufacturer's goods were distributed would have a sufficiently close link of proximity to the material elements of the dispute for the purposes of allocating jurisdiction, so that the plaintiff would be able to sue the defendant in the court of its choice.[146] It seems that in such cases the national court would have jurisdiction to determine validity of all the obligations which may give rise to EU competition law concerns—no matter whether they are performed in that particular place or not. This would be a satisfactory outcome in view of the fact that the question whether there is a breach of EU competition law is to be determined as a matter of EU law,[147] and the geographical market may be broader than the territory of a single Member State.

2.2.2.2.3 EU Competition Law Claims arising out of other Agreements

In this section the basis for jurisdiction of English courts will be discussed with regard to EU competition law claims arising out of agreements to limit or control production (*crisis cartels*) and non-aggression pacts.

2.2.2.2.3.1 EU Competition Law Claims arising out of Agreements to Limit Production

A good example of an agreement that has the effect of limiting production directly is the so-called 'crisis cartel'.[148] The parties to such a cartel may agree to close down parts of their productive capacity, in the event that demand falls so low that normal competition is thought to be impossible. Such a conduct may be justified by the disparity between the total productive capacity of the industry and the actual demand for output of those factories. For example, a big company and a medium-sized company whose factories are situated in different Member States agree to implement an X per cent reduction in capacity related to production of chemical product Y. Furthermore, the parties agree that no new capacity will be brought on-stream. This can be justified by a serious imbalance between their production capacity and existing demand.[149] Subsequently, the medium-sized company may discover that the bigger company, which has closed down its plant in a Member State X, is building a new plant located in another country where the production would be more cost-effective. Based on that, the smaller undertaking may withdraw its agrement to closing down the agreed productive capacity and claim that the agreement is intended to drive it out of the business, and is in conflict with EU competition law. Where can the medium-sized company bring an EU competition law claim under the Brussels I Regulation?

[146] *Color Drack* (n 14) [40]–[42]; *Rehder* (n 143) [40]–[46].

[147] See ch 5.

[148] J Goyder and A Albors-Llorens, *Goyder's EC Competition Law* (5th edn, OUP, Oxford, 2009) 184–87.

[149] Eg *Re Synthetic Fibres Agreement* [1985] 1 CMLR 787 (Commission (EC)).

It seems clear that due to the contractual relationship, the applicable jurisdictional provision is Art 5(1) of Brussels I. It is beyond doubt that such an agreement cannot be regarded as a contract for 'sale of goods' or 'provision of service' for jurisdictional purposes. Indeed, the jurisdiction of courts with regard to EU competition law claims arising out of it will be determined on the basis of Art 5(1)(a), as it belongs to none of the categories mentioned in Art 5(1)(b) of Brussels I. Which is the obligation that special jurisdiction under Art 5(1) of Brussels I may be founded upon in this scenario? Is it the obligation to close down the agreed productive capacity? Or is it the obligation not to bring the new capacity on-stream?

If the latter was at the heart of the plaintiff's claim, Art 5 would be of no use. This is due to the fact that the obligation not to bring new capacity on stream is an obligation 'not to do something', so the *Besix* ruling will be applicable. In this case, the Court of Justice has clearly held that in such claims, jurisdiction would be determined by application of the general criterion laid down in Art 2 of Brussels I.[150] A better outcome would be reached if the plaintiff's claim was based on the obligation to close down part of the parties' productive capacity. Indeed, it would be relatively easy to identify the relevant place, since this obligation would have to be performed at the place where the plaintiff's factory was situated. That place will often coincide with his domicile. Thus, should the contracting party allege that its obligation to close down productive capacity is in breach of EU competition law and thus void, this party would be able to sue in its home state under Art 5(1) of Brussels I. But does Art 5(1) of Brussels I confer jurisdiction in respect of only that obligation which is meant to be performed in that particular place?

If the (positive) obligation to close down the agreed productive capacity is regarded as the main one, and to allocate special jurisdiction over the whole of the claim to the court of the place where this main obligation was due to be performed,[151] then a national court will have international jurisdiction over all EU competition law claims and the plaintiff may well benefit from Art 5(1) of Brussels I by bringing an antitrust action in his home state.

However, if both obligations are regarded as of equal significance, the court has special jurisdiction only over that part of the claim which arises from the obligation that is to be performed within its territory, but not over the claim which arises from the obligation that is to be performed in another Member State.[152] In other words, in such a scenario the territorial scope of the court's jurisdiction will be limited.[153] If *Leathertext* were followed in EU competition law cases, the court's jurisdiction could be affected. A court with limited territorial jurisdiction may not be entitled to determine whether the obligation that is to be performed in another

[150] Case C-256/00 *Besix v Wasserreinigungsbau Alfred Kretzschmar* [2002] ECR I-1699.

[151] Compare *Shenavai* (n 17) [19]. See also: *Boss* (n 11); *Source* (n 70).

[152] Case C-420/97 *Leathertex v Bodetex* [1999] ECR I-6779 [40].

[153] Compare Case C-68/93 *Shevill and Others v Presse Alliance SA* [1995] ECR I-415; *Shevill and Others v Presse Alliance SA* [1996] AC 959 (HL) 983; *SanDisk Corporation v Koninklijke Philips Electronics NV* [2007] EWHC 332 (Ch); [2007] Bus LR 705 [25].

Member State is in conflict with EU competition law, as the scope of application of Arts 101 and 102 TFEU is not limited to the territory of a single Member State. Furthermore, in order to establish whether the agreement or practice affects trade between Member States within the meaning of Arts 101 and 102 TFEU, a national court must determine whether the agreement in question has 'an impact on cross-border economic activity involving at least two Member States.'[154] In other words, the foregoing problems raise the question whether it would be ultra vires for a court, whose jurisdiction is limited to the obligation that is to be performed within its territory, to rule on whether there has been an impact on at least two Member States and whether the obligation that is to be performed in another Member State is valid under EU competition law. Even if the determination of impact in another Member State were regarded as a preliminary issue for deciding whether the obligation to be performed within the territory of the court's jurisdiction is compatible with EU competition law, it is difficult to see how a national court decision that the obligation in question is in conflict with Arts 101 and 102 TFEU would not affect the obligations that are to be performed in another Member State under the very same agreement. Indeed, it is well established that an agreement (or contractual clause) that is in conflict with EU competition law can produce no legal effects, as it is automatically null and void.

2.2.2.2.3.2 EU Competition Law Claims arising out of Commercialisation Agreements

A large multinational beer producer and another beer producer, which is active in one Member State and wants to expand to a neighbouring Member State, may consult together and make a general commercialised agreement. Such long-term and complex restrictive agreements can give rise to EU competition law claims.[155] For example, parties may agree on their marketing strategies and on sharing commercial information on pricing. The market may get stagnant and the local producer (after a drop in his sales) can claim that the agreement allows exchange of sensitive commercial information, and so it is in conflict with EU competition law.[156]

It seems that the jurisdiction of courts with regard to EU competition law claims arising out of such agreements once again will be determined on the basis of Art 5(1)(a) as they belong to none of the categories mentioned in Art 5(1)(b) of Brussels I. Indeed, a contracting party bringing an EU competition claim should sue in the courts at the intended place of performance of supposed obligation. In the above example, various obligations are at issue, so the main obligation should determine the court's jurisdiction.[157] The identification of the main obligation may

[154] *Guidelines on the effect on trade concept contained in Articles 81 and 82 of the Treaty* [2004] OJ C-101/81 [21].

[155] Eg Case IV/37.614/F3 *The Community v Interbrew (Re The Belgian Beer Cartel)* [2004] 4 CMLR 2.

[156] Eg Case C-7/96P *John Deere v EC Commission* [1998] ECR I-3111.

[157] *Shenavai* (n 17) [19]. See section 2.2.2.2.3.1 above.

appear to be difficult in some competition law disputes arising out of horizontal agreements.

Nonetheless, a claimant will have to define the particular obligation in an EU competition claim that seeks nullity of that obligation. Based on its place of performance, the claim may be brought at the appropriate national court. Accordingly, if the contracting party contends that the obligation to share information on sales is in conflict with EU competition law, then the place where such obligation is to be performed must be determined. Is it performed at the place where the party sends off the telexes/emails and from where his representatives speak on the telephone? Or is it rather performed at the place where the information is received?

It is well settled that it is for the court before which the matter is brought to determine whether the place of performance is situated within its territory.[158] That place must be defined in accordance with conflict of laws rules, which would indicate the law applicable to the contractual relationship in question.[159] In England, case law supports the submission that the court at the place where the information is received will have jurisdiction to hear and determine an EU competition law claim based on an obligation to share information. That follows by analogy from what the English court has held in regard to cases involving economic loss as a result of negligent misstatement[160] and contracts.[161] It seems that in most cases, this place would coincide with the place of the defendant's domicile, so Art 5(1) would be of little use in regard to that particular obligation.

The plaintiff may seek nullity of the obligation to have implemented common marketing strategies. Those strategies may include an obligation to raise promotion prices as rapidly as possible to a certain level. That may go together with a promise not to pay for any promotion or advertising brochures for a pre-defined period of time. Where is the place of performance of all these obligations? It seems that this is the place where a marketing strategy is implemented. That place would in most cases be in the plaintiff's home state.[162] Accordingly, in such cases the plaintiff would be able to make an EU competition law claim in the courts at the place of his domicile on the basis of Art 5(1) of Brussels I.

In view of that, if the plaintiff wants the court at the place of his domicile to assume special jurisdiction over the whole of the claim, he must prove that the obligation to have common marketing strategies is the main obligation of the commercialised agreement. The obligation to share commercial information on pricing is to be regarded as an ancillary obligation, which is following the principal obligation.[163] Otherwise, as already mentioned,[164] both obligations

[158] *Tessili* (n 5) [13].
[159] Ibid.
[160] *Diamond v Bank of London & Montreal* [1979] 1 QB 333 (CA).
[161] *Entores v Miles Far East Corporation* [1955] 2 QB 327 (CA) 332–33.
[162] *Re The Belgian Beer Cartel* (n 155).
[163] Art 5(1) interpretation in *Shenavai* (n 17).
[164] See section 2.2.2.2.3.1 above.

may be regarded as of equal prominence and the jurisdiction of the court of the plaintiff's home state may be restricted to the part of the claim which arose from the obligation which was to be performed within its territory,[165] which might limit the national courts' jurisdiction to assess the impact of the agreement on cross-border economic activity involving at least two Member States and the validity of the obligation that is to be performed in another Member State. In this context, everything which was said in the preceding section would be equally valid here.

In light of the above examples, it can be concluded that the Brussels I Regulation does not satisfactorily allocate jurisdiction with regard to EU competition law claims arising out of horizontal agreements. Jurisdiction in respect of those claims will be determined on a case-by-case basis, depending on the obligation in question that forms the subject-matter of the EU competition law claims. Although, this may provide for flexibility, the complicated jurisdictional analysis above indicates that in many of those cases the primary issue would be related to the question which court has jurisdiction over an EU competition law claim without discussing whether the court seised is well placed to hear and determine the relevant EU competition law action/s.

2.2.2.3 Concluding Remarks

It can be concluded that Art 5(1) of Brussels I is not well suited to accommodate EU competition law claims brought by contracting parties. It is clear that under Art 5(1) of Brussels I the national courts have jurisdiction to determine the validity of contracts that are alleged to infringe EU competition law. The same court, however, would not have jurisdiction under Art 5(1) of Brussels I over a claim for antitrust damages brought by contracting parties together with a claim for nullity of a contract. Moreover, further problems can arise with regard to allocation of jurisdiction in EU competition claims arising out of vertical and horizontal agreements.

2.2.3 Application of Article 5(5) to EU Competition Law Claims

Article 5(5) allows, for example, an action to be brought in England against a French manufacturing company (a member of an international cartel) which markets a product (at an inflated price, in breach of EU competition law) in England through its English branch. The branch office cannot be sued as a defendant, since it is not a separate legal entity. The French manufacturing company, however, can be sued in England by virtue of Art 5(5) of Brussels I, provided that the dispute arises out of the operations of the branch.[166] If the branch markets

[165] Art 5(1) interpretation in *Leathertex* (n 152).
[166] Case 33/78 *Somafer v Saar-Ferngas* [1978] ECR 2183.

a product at an inflated price in breach of EU competition law in England this requirement will be satisfied. Practice, however, shows that in most competition cases the market would be penetrated through setting up a subsidiary or an exclusive distributor. But, can a plaintiff bring an EU competition law claim against the French mother company of an English subsidiary (or an English exclusive distributor) in England under Art 5(5) of Brussels I?

It should be mentioned that the Court of Justice has held that the grantee of an exclusive sales concession who is subject neither to the control nor to the direction of the grantor cannot be regarded as being within Art 5(5) of Brussels I.[167] This is justified by the fact that the subsidiary is a separate legal entity and lacks the authority to act on behalf of the parent company.[168] Although the subsidiary may be covered by Art 5(5) in cases where it acts as if it were a branch,[169] the Court of Justice has held that the grantee of an exclusive sales concession who is subject neither to the control nor to the direction of the grantor cannot be regarded as being within the head of Art 5(5) of Brussels I.[170] It has been submitted that the '[subsidiary] normally acts for itself and not for the parent company, and will thus be outside the scope of Art 5(5)'.[171]

Therefore, normally, the fact that a subsidiary has a separate legal personality would probably exclude it from the scope of this provision. Will it be so in EU competition law cases? If subsidiaries and exclusive distributors are regarded as not covered by Art 5(5) of Brussels I, then this provision would not be of use in many EU competition law claims, where competition within a given market is distorted through them. However, it is well established that if a subsidiary has no real freedom to determine its course of action, it is to be regarded as forming one economic unit with its parent company under the competition rules.[172] Two or more legally separate entities may be treated as a single undertaking for the purposes of Arts 101 and 102 TFEU if their relationship justifies regarding them as a single economic unit.[173] The EU competition law concept of the 'undertaking', however, can embrace a number of legal entities, as long as they act as a single economic unit, and no legal entity acts independently for any relevant purpose.[174] The legal entities that are part of one undertaking, by definition of

[167] *De Bloos* (n 17) [23].

[168] Ibid 1519 (AG Reischel).

[169] Case C-218/86 *Sar Schotte v Parfums Rothschild* [1987] ECR 4905.

[170] *De Bloos* (n 53) [23]. See also the opinion of AG Reischl in *De Bloos* (n 53) 1519.

[171] J Fawcett, 'A new approach to jurisdiction over companies in private international law' (1988) 37 *ICLQ* 645, 659. See also: WA Allwood, 'Art 5(5): Meaning of 'branch, agency or other establishment' (1988) 13 *EL Rev* 213; Case 139/80 *Blanckaert and Willems v Torst* [1981] ECR 819; *Sar Schotte* (n 169) [15].

[172] Case 48/69 *ICI v Commission* [1972] ECR 619 [134]; Case 66/86 *Ahmed Saeed Flurgreisen v Zentrale zur Bekampfung unlauteren Wettbewerbs* [1989] ECR 803 [35].

[173] Case 15/74 *Centrafarm v Sterling Drug* [1974] ECR 1183 [41]; Case C-73/95 *Viho v Commission* [1996] ECR I-5457. See also: *Provimi* (n 20) [31]. See more: Faull and Nikpay (n 33) 206–08. Compare *The Albazero* [1977] AC 774 (HL) 807 (Roskill LJ); *Adams v Cape Industries* [1990] ChD 433 (CA) 532 (Slade LJ).

[174] *Provimi* (n 20) [31]. See also section 2.2.1 above.

the concept, have no independence of mind or action or will,[175] so they are to be regarded as all one. Accordingly, the mind and will of one legal entity is, for the purposes of EU competition law, to be treated as the mind and will of the other.

Following this line of reasoning, it can be inferred that the claimant in such cases can use Art 5(5) of Brussels I to subject to jurisdiction a parent company, provided that the EU competition law claim has arisen out of the operation of the exclusive distributor or subsidiary. In such a case, some conduct by the exclusive distributor or subsidiary would be required. The implementation of the cartel agreement, on behalf of the parent, would satisfy the second requirement (ie the dispute will 'arise out of the operations of the branch'). Therefore, there might well be cases where Art 5(5) of Brussels I could be a useful provision in EU competition law claims, arising out of the operation of exclusive distributors and subsidiaries as well. Thus, for the purposes of an EU competition law claim a legally independent undertaking may be regarded as an establishment under Art 5(5) of Brussels I because of its economic dependence. Accordingly, the English court may have jurisdiction in an antitrust claim brought by a contracting party against the parent company of a subsidiary firm settled in England. This would be of great relevance in cases where a subsidiary implements a cartel agreement that is entered into by its parent and the parent's competitors. The need to bring an antitrust claim also against the parent company may arise, because the subsidiary may not have many assets.

There are, however, difficulties in invoking Art 5(5) of Brussels I as a basis for jurisdiction in EU competition law cases under the Regulation. First, the question whether the corporate veil should be lifted may give rise to a considerable debate before English courts.[176] Whilst, there are strong arguments suggesting that the corporate veil should be lifted so as to make a parent company liable for the infringement of EU competition law on the English market in view of the fact that the market was penetrated by the subsidiary, it is true that the doctrine of 'undertaking' for the purposes of Arts 101 and 102 TFEU is different from the concepts of 'persons' establishing jurisdiction under Brussels I.[177] Secondly, Art 6(3)(b) of Rome II read together with *Freeport v Arnoldsson*[178] seems to suggest that a private antitrust claimant would be better off if he had established jurisdiction under Art 6(1) of Brussels I instead of Art 5(5) of Brussels I. This would be especially so in cases where the market is affected in a number of Member States and the plaintiff wants to plead, for example, punitive damages before English courts.

175 *Viho* (n 173).

176 *Adams* (n 173).

177 Compare Cases 6 and 7/73 *Istituto Chemioterapico Italiano SpA and Commercial Solvents Corp v Commission of the European Communities* [1974] ECR 223, 263 (AG Warner).

178 Case C-98/06 *Freeport Plc v Arnoldsson* [2008] QB 634 (Court of Justice, Third Chamber).

2.2.4 Application of Article 6(1) to EU Competition Law Claims

It has already been demonstrated that under Art 5(1) of Brussels I the national courts will not have jurisdiction over a claim for antitrust damages brought by contracting parties together with a claim for nullity of a contract under Art 5(1) of Brussels I. It has further been shown that a plaintiff cannot overlook the incidental contractual issue as to validity of the agreement that is allegedly in breach of EU competition law and bring his claim for antitrust damages under the tort head. But can the plaintiff bring EU competition law claims based on tort and contract against multiple parties under Art 6(1) of Brussels I?

Under Art 6(1),

> a person domiciled in a Member State may also be sued[,] where he is one of a number of defendants, in the courts for the place where any one of them is domiciled, provided the claims are so closely connected that it is expedient to hear and determine them together to avoid the risk of irreconcilable judgments resulting from separate proceedings.

As already mentioned, this provision is specifically designed for multi-defendant cases. Its rationale is to centralise litigation against all defendants in one Member State and avoid the risk of (potentially) irreconcilable judgments if the different actions were brought in different Member States. Clearly, Art 6(1) of Brussels I contains no requirement to the effect that the actions relating to the various defendants must have the same basis.[179] Can the court with jurisdiction under Art 6(1) rule on all claims against the multiple parties, no matter whether they relate to tort or contract?

The early view expressed by the Court of Justice was that the court with jurisdiction under Art 6(1) of Brussels I could not hear and determine 'two claims in one action for compensation, directed against different defendants and based in one instance on contractual liability and in the other on liability in tort or delict ....'[180] In *Freeport and Arnoldson,* the Court of Justice took the chance to reconsider this, by holding that Art 6(1) applies in situations which involve contractual and non-contractual liability.[181] The Court of Justice went on to reaffirm that the only requirement for the application of Art 6(1) is the existence of a connection between claims.[182] Thus, it is clear that there must be a connection between the claims made against the various defendants.[183] However, as long as this connection is established, there is no 'further need to establish separately that the claims

[179] *Freeport* (n 178) [38] of the Court of Justice decision. See also Opinion of AG Mengozzi [43].

[180] *Reunion* (n 12) [50].

[181] *Freeport* (n 178) [38] of the Court of Justice decision. See also Opinion of AG Mengozzi [45].

[182] *Freeport* (n 178) [39] of the Court of Justice decision. See also Opinion of AG Mengozzi [43].

[183] See more: Jenard Report (n 10) 26. See also: *Kalfelis* (n 21); *Banque Nationale de Paris v Soc Carl Felk et Soc Serifit* [1979] Revue critique de droit international prive 444 (Cour d' Appel de Paris, 28 June 1978). See also Corte di Cassazione, 6 November 1975, dir Com Scambi int, 1976, 383 cited by AG Darmon in *Kalfelis* (n 21).

were not brought with the sole object of ousting the jurisdiction of the courts of the member state where one of the defendants is domiciled.'[184]

How is this connection to be established in EU competition law cases? It has been held by the Court of Justice that:

> [I]n order that decisions may be regarded as contradictory it is not sufficient that there be a divergence in the outcome of the dispute, but that divergence must also arise in the context of the same situation of law and fact.[185]

In other words, the risk of irreconcilable judgments applies just as much to the risk of inconsistent findings of fact as it does to the risk of inconsistent findings of law.[186] Although the risk of conflict in conclusions with regard to an EU competition law claim may be a serious matter, such conflicts, where based on different interpretations of legal provisions, may eventually be remedied through a reference to the Court of Justice, provided that a national court makes use of its power under Art 267 TFEU (ex Art 234 TEC). Contradictory findings of fact made by different judges in different European jurisdictions, however, are virtually impossible to reconcile. Different findings of fact also frequently lead to inconsistent conclusions with regard to the application of EU competition law.[187] This is largely due to the fact that the application of Arts 101 and 102 TFEU is a fact-based assessment. Conflicting views from different national courts in relation to the same factual background and the same antitrust infringement cannot be tolerated. In the *Provimi* case, the English court clearly outlined that different views of national courts may be a reason for hearing EU competition law claims together in order to avoid irreconcilable judgments.[188] The court went further and held that even though the law on competition in European countries is very similar, 'it is highly arguable that different courts would take different approaches to these issues and those different approaches could result in irreconcilable judgments.'[189] It can be concluded that a possibility of irreconcilable judgments, resulting from separate proceedings in EU competition law claims, would be enough to meet the requirements of Art 6(1) of Brussels I. Therefore, the test would be easily satisfied in a case where a private antitrust plaintiff wants to sue one party (eg subsidiary) in contract and tort and a second party (eg parent company) in tort alone.

It is important to emphasise though that Art 6(1) of Brussels I applies only if the proceedings in question are brought before the courts in the Member State, where one of the defendants is domiciled.[190] Accordingly, a claimant in an EU competition law action, who sues a defendant (domiciled in Germany) in England

[184] *Freeport* (n 178) [54].

[185] *Roche Netherland* (n 21) [26]; *Freeport* (n 178) [40]. See also: Briggs and Rees (n 44) 295.

[186] *Gascoine v Pyrah* [1994] ILPr 82 (CA) [44]; See also: *ET Plus SA v Welter* [2005] EWHC 2115 (Comm), [2006] 1 Lloyd's Rep 251 [59].

[187] Compare *Gascoine* (n 186) [45].

[188] See *Provimi* (n 20) [47].

[189] Ibid [45]–[46].

[190] *Reunion* (n 12) [44].

on the basis of Art 5(3) of Brussels I, cannot rely on Art 6(1) of the Regulation to sue a second defendant (domiciled in France) in England. Nonetheless, Art 6(1) will be particularly relevant for a plaintiff, who wishes to pursue an EU competition law claim against two defendants—a local subsidiary, which implements an anti-competitive agreement in England, and a foreign parent company. In such cases, the plaintiff would be able to proceed against both companies in either England or France.

There are good reasons explaining why a plaintiff in an EU competition law claim may desire to base his EU competition law claims on Art 6(1) of Brussels I. First, the plaintiff can consolidate his EU competition law claims based on contract and tort against multiple defendants in the same litigation before the domiciliary court of one of the defendants at his choice. Secondly, by choosing such a forum, the plaintiff may wish to consider whether punitive damages are available under that *lex fori*. If they are available, Art 6(3)(b) of Rome II seems to suggest that if he had suffered damages in several countries, then he may be awarded punitive damages even for the antitrust infringements that took place in a country where such damages are not available[191] because jurisdiction under Art 6(1) of Brussels I is international (ie it will not be restricted to the local effects of the infringement).[192] A third reason is to do with evidence, which may be kept by a foreign company. This is very important indeed, in view of the fact that the local subsidiary and the foreign parent—even if considered as two persons for the purposes of jurisdiction—are regarded as one undertaking for the purposes of Arts 101 and 102 TFEU, so that a joinder of a parent company may be crucial, in order to obtain discovery of certain documents.[193] Another reason is that the plaintiff would have a potential advantage to obtain a judgment against two defendants. This right of choice may be valuable to him, for a number of quite different reasons. The respective financial situations of the two defendants may be one reason. In addition, it may be practically easier to enforce the judgment against one defendant than against the other. Alternatively, he may prefer, for good commercial reasons, to enforce his judgment against one defendant rather than against the other.[194] For example, the plaintiffs could prefer to enforce a judgment against the party who is a competitor of his operating at the same level of distribution or production rather than against the party, who is a potential partner operating at another level of production or distribution.

[191] See more: ch 5.

[192] For distinction between international and local jurisdiction, see generally CM Schmitthoff, *The English Conflict of Laws* (3rd edn, Stevens & Sons, London, 1954) 11. The validity of such a distinction in the context of EU competition law cases was recently confirmed by the English High Court in *SanDisk* (n 153) [25].

[193] Compare *Unilever v Gillette* [1989] RPC 583 (CA) 601. See also: Fawcett and Torremans (n 1) 313.

[194] Compare *The Electric Furnace v Selas Corp of America* [1987] RPC 23 (CA) 33. See also Fawcett and Torremans (n 1) 263–64.

Therefore, Art 6(1) of Brussels I could be a relevant basis of jurisdiction in respect of EU competition law claims, given the fact that multi-defendant litigation is quite common in such claims.[195] It would be a very useful provision indeed in view of the fact that Art 6(1) of Brussels I provides a plaintiff with a choice of where to bring his EU competition law claim. If, for example, there are two defendants, one domiciled in England and the other in Germany, the plaintiff can choose whether to sue both defendants in England or both in Germany. [196]

2.2.5 Application of Section 4 of Brussels I to EU Competition Law Claims

It is beyond doubt that a consumer can bring a claim for a breach of EU competition law before a national court. This has been reaffirmed by a recent Court of Justice ruling holding that 'any individual can rely on the invalidity of an agreement or practice prohibited under [Art 101 TFEU] and, where there is a causal relationship between the latter and the harm suffered, claim compensation for that.'[197] This ruling can boost EU competition law claims brought by consumers. An illegal cartel agreement or abusive practice often, however, spreads its effects across more than one Member State, so that consumers in various Member States may be affected. Where is an antitrust claim to be brought by a consumer in such cases?

A consumer may bring his claim under s 4 of chapter II in the Brussels I Regulation, which is meant to deal with jurisdiction in respect of contracts concluded by consumers. It will be applicable where the defendant seller (or supplier) is domiciled, or deemed to be domiciled in a Member State[198] and the other party to the contract (the consumer) is acting outside his trade or profession.[199] Contracts for the supply of goods or services fall within the scope of the consumer contracts provisions of the Brussels Regulation, provided the criteria set out in Art 15 are met.[200] But, how about tortious claims for antitrust damages suffered by a consumer who has been subject to a contract that is in conflict

[195] See *Provimi* (n 20), which is further discussed in the context of follow-on tort based action in ch 3, below.

[196] JJ Fawcett, 'Multi-party Litigation in Private International Law' (1995) 44 *ICLQ* 744, 747.

[197] Joined Cases C-295/04–C-298/04 *Manfredi v Lloyd Adriaticco* [2006] 5 CMLR 17 [63]. See the judgment of the Italian Corte di Cassazione in *Compagnia Assicuratrice Unipol v Mario R* Cass civ su, 2207 of February 7, 2005, reported in M Negri Marcella, 'Il lento cammino della tutela civile antitrust: luci ed ombre di un atteso grand arrét', Commento a Cass sez un civ 4 febbraio 2005, 2207 [2005] 3 *Il Corriere giuridico* 342. See more: R Incardonna and C Poncibo, 'The Corte di Cassazione takes "*Courage*": a recent ruling opens limited rights for consumer in competition cases' (2005) 26 *European Competition Law Review* 445.

[198] Art 15 of the Brussels Regulation.

[199] See more: J Hill, *Cross-border Consumer Contracts* (OUP, Oxford, 2008) 88–97.

[200] That is, the contract must have been concluded with a person who pursues commercial or professional activities in the Member State of the consumer's domicile, or directs such activities to that Member State. The contract must fall within the scope of such activities. See more: Hill (n 199) 115–20.

with EU competition laws? Is jurisdiction in representative actions based on contract and tort under s 47B of the Competition Act 1998 to be derived by s 4 of Brussels I[201]?

The issue is a very practical one because, even though s 47B of the 1998 Act can only be used when an EU competition law infringement has been already established by the Commission (or the OFT) and any appeals have been finally determined,[202] the dispute about how the principle of severance of illegal provisions from otherwise lawful agreements is to affect the parties' contract would be contractual in nature,[203] whereas the question of causation and quantum in a private antitrust damages would be tortious in nature.[204] In other words, in such a dispute, there would be two claims: a contractual claim as to whether the whole contract is invalid or only part of it is in conflict with EU competition law, and a tortious claims for antitrust damages.[205] In view of that, one may argue that s 4 of the Brussels I Regulation would be relevant with regard to the claim arising out of contract, but would not cover the closely related tortious claim. Such a deduction could be based on the fact that Art 15 is similar to Art 5(1) as both are using the expression 'matters relating to contract', so that the *Kalfelis* ruling should be applicable by analogy.[206] It has been submitted by AG Darmon in *Shearson* that 'the Court's interpretation of "matters relating to contract" in Article 5 should be taken into account for interpreting the similar provision of Article 1[5].'[207]

However, if Art 5(1) and Art 15 are only 'similar', then can they be distinguished in some cases? The Court of Justice has clearly done that in *Engler*.[208] In this case, it was explicitly stated that Art 15 constitutes a *lex specialis* in relation to Art 5(1), in so far as the latter provision relates specifically to contracts concluded by a consumer, but does not extend to cover a situation where no contract has been concluded.[209] That said, it seems that once a contract by a consumer had been concluded, then Art 15 would be applicable with regard to all claims arising of the contract. In *Shearson*, AG Darmon went further to hold that '"centralization" of jurisdiction which seemed ... to be necessary in connection with matters relating to a contract under Article 5 is even more necessary ... where what is involved is contracts concluded by a consumer, on whom the multiplication of bases of

201 See more: M Danov, 'The Brussels I Regulation: cross-border collective redress actions and judgments' (2010) *Journal of Private International Law* forthcoming.

202 See s 47A(6) of the Competition Act 1998—amendment pending.

203 Whish (n 84) 313. See also: Bernitz (n 33) 190–91. See more ch 5.

204 See more ch 5.

205 See more ch 1.

206 See above. See also Case C-96/00 *Gabriel v Schlanck & Schick* [2002] ECR 6367 [49]; *Tacconi* (n 34) [23].

207 Case C-89/91 *Shearson Lehman Hutton* [1993] ECR I-139 [87] (AG Darmon).

208 Case C-27/02 *Petra Engler v Janus Versand GmbH* [2005] ECR I-481.

209 *Engler* (n 208) [31, 32, 40, 44 and 49]. See also: Case C-180/06 *Ilsinger v Martin Dreschers (acting as administrator in the insolvency of Schlank & Schick GmbH* [2009] ECR I-0000, 14 May 2009 [52 and 53].

jurisdiction could have a very particular adverse effect.'[210] The Court of Justice has recently held that 'the scope of Article 15(1)(c) of Regulation No 44/2001 appears … to be no longer being [sic] limited to those situations in which the parties have assumed reciprocal obligations.'[211] The rationale is for Arts 15 and 16 of Brussels I to enable the consumer to bring all claims arising out a contract before the same court 'in order to avoid, in so far as possible, creating a situation in which a number of courts had jurisdiction in respect of one and the same contract.'[212] In other words, the Court of Justice seems to endorse the one-stop adjudication doctrine in respect of claims arising out of consumer contracts.

Therefore, there are strong arguments indicating that Art 15 should be interpreted as allocating jurisdiction in an action based on contract and tort as long as the tortious claims are closely related to the claim which is based on a contract concluded by a consumer.[213] The difficulties that would be encountered with regard to contracts falling within Art 5(1)[214] would not arise in relation to collective actions arising out of consumer contracts. First, the wording of Art 15 leaves no doubt that the provision is meant to cover all claims arising out of a contract concluded by a consumer.[215] This deduction can be strengthened by reading Art 16, which determines jurisdiction in such disputes by stating that '[a] consumer may bring proceedings against the other party to a contract' without limiting such proceedings to be concerned with contractual claims only. In fact, s 4 of chapter II in Brussels I is without prejudice to Art 4 and Art 5(5) only, so that the courts' jurisdiction to hear and determine a tortious claim arising out of a consumer contract and closely related to the consumer contract in question could not be precluded by reference to Art 5(3) of Brussels I. This means that s 4 of Chapter II in the Brussels I Regulation would confer jurisdiction over contractual claims and closely related tortious claims arising out of such consumer contracts. Secondly, the jurisdiction of courts over claims related to consumer contracts is special and is meant to strengthen consumer protection in Europe. Such jurisdiction should not be limited by the narrow interpretation defining claims under Art 5(1) and (3) to be mutually exclusive as interpreted in cases that arose in the context of Art 5.[216] It has been submitted that '[c]onsumer litigation both publicizes abusive marketing practices and can play a role in deterring such

[210] *Shearson* (n 207) [108] (AG Darmon). Compare the one-stop adjudication doctrine which was recently endorsed by the House of Lords in the context of arbitration agreements, see *Premium Nafta Products Ltd v Fili Shipping* [2007] UKHL 40; [2008] 1 Lloyd's Rep 254 (HL); see also: *The Playa Larga* [1983] 2 Lloyd's Rep 171 (CA) 183; *The 'Angelic Grace'* [1995] 1 Lloyd's Rep 87 (CA) 89, which are discussed in ch 7 below.

[211] *Ilsinger* (n 209) [51].

[212] *Ilsinger* (n 209) [44].

[213] Compare *Kalfelis* (n 21) [31] (AG Darmon).

[214] See J Harris, 'Product liability and the conflict of laws' in CJ Miller and RS Goldberg, *Product Liability* (2nd edn, OUP, Oxford, 2004) 777, 792–95, 801–02.

[215] *Engler* (n 208) [34]. See more: Hill (n 199) 86–87.

[216] Eg *Kalfelis* (n 21); *Tacconi* (n 34) [23]; *Gabriel* (n 206) [49].

practices being used in the future.'[217] Thus, there are very strong legal and policy reasons indicating that Art 15 should have a broader meaning and cover tortious claims that are closely connected with consumer contracts. In view of that, the proposal of AG Darmon in *Kalfelis* that 'an action based on tort and contract … is governed exclusively by the rules laid down for contractual matters'[218] should be followed in respect of collective redress claims brought by consumers under s 4 of Chapter II of Brussels I. Such a deduction is in line also with the opinion of AG Darmon in Shearson[219] which leaves no doubt that centralising litigation would be very important in cases where there is a sufficiently close connection between a tortious claim and the claim under the contract.[220]

In view of the foregoing, it appears that an English court would have jurisdiction over a collective redress consumer action brought under s 4 of Chapter II of Brussels I if the resolution of the contractual issue is necessary for a decision on the tortious claim, or if the contractual and tortious claims brought by the consumers are closely knitted on the facts.[221] This would be clearly so in the majority of collective redress antitrust proceedings. The need for consumers to rely on special jurisdictional rules may be further justified by the Commission's initiative[222] to pave the way for private antitrust enforcement in Europe, which would be socially efficient.[223] In such cases the consumers and/or their representatives may be unwilling to bear the expenses and uncertainties of a suit at the court of the defendant's domicile, where they could think that they would be treated unfavourably by a national court which could be, for example, tempted to promote 'national champions'.[224] Accordingly, there are very strong legal and policy considerations indicating that the local consumers should be allowed to bring their collective actions in their home state by relying on Art 16 of Brussels I.[225]

But, is jurisdiction in actions brought by consumer representatives on behalf of consumers to be derived by s 4 of chapter II of Brussels I? The answer to this question would depend on whether an action is brought in the public interest by an association in respect of unlawful behaviour notwithstanding the absence of

217 Hill (n 199) 87.

218 *Kalfelis* (n 21) [31] (AG Darmon). See also: *Shearson* (n 207) [111] (AG Darmon).

219 *Shearson* (n 207) [108] (AG Darmon). See text to note 210.

220 This would be certainly so with regard to EU competition law claims which would raise a contractual claim (is the whole contract invalid, or is only part of it?) and a tortious claim (is there a breach of statutory duty and assessment of damages?). See more: the discussion regarding Art 16 of Brussels I below.

221 Analogy can be made with the judgments of English courts in the context of interpreting the scope of arbitration agreements—e.g. *The Playa Larga* (n 210) 183; *The 'Angelic Grace'* (n 210) 89; *Fili Shipping* (n 210) concerned with one-stop adjudication—discussed in ch 7 below.

222 See Council Regulation 1/2003 and the White Paper on Damages Actions (n 2).

223 See more regarding the theoretical framework which would favour rules facilitating collective redress actions in WN Landes and RA Posner, 'The private enforcement of law' (1975) 33 *Journal of Legal Studies* 1, 33. See also KW Dam, 'Class actions: efficiency, compensation, deterrence, and conflict of interest' (1975) 4 *Journal of Legal Studies* 47.

224 Danov (n 201).

225 Danov (n 201).

damage[226] or the action is brought by a representative body on behalf of identified (or identifiable) consumers for declaratory relief and antitrust damages resulting from an EU competition law infringement.

In *Henkel*,[227] an injunction was sought to prevent the continued use of unfair terms in consumers' contracts. The action was brought on behalf of the entire class of consumers.[228] In this case, the Consumers Association's right of action was justified by its own legitimate interest in protecting consumers which was shown to have been recognised by ss 28 and 29 of the Consumer Protection Law and Council Directive 93/13.[229] In view of the fact that the Consumers Association had its own legitimate interests to bring an action on behalf of the entire class of consumers in general, the Court of Justice held that such an action would not fall within s 4 of chapter II of Brussels I.[230] Thus, 'a person bringing an action who is not himself a party to one of the contracts listed in Article 15(1) is not a consumer within the meaning of Articles 15 and 16.' Similar result will be reached if the action before the court was not brought by the consumer, but by a commercial company to whom that person had assigned his rights, then s 4 chapter II of Brussels I would be the basis for jurisdiction.[231]

The *Green Paper on consumer collective redress*[232] appears to reaffirm that *Henkel* should be followed with regard to actions brought on behalf of the entire class of consumers.[233] However, it seems to this author that if the EU competition law action was brought on behalf of identified (or identifiable) consumers by a representative body,[234] then jurisdiction should be derived by s 4 of chapter II of Brussels I. This would be so, unless the consumers' substantive law rights had been assigned[235] or the Consumer Association had its own standing to bring an action on behalf of consumers in general.[236]

Although there is a view that 'it is … implicit that one of the parties to the litigation must be a consumer in order for Section 4 to apply',[237] it seems to this author that the question who is party to litigation does not arise for the purposes of allocating jurisdiction under s 4 of chapter II of Brussels I. The wording of Art 16(1) leaves no doubt that the proceedings *may* be brought by consumers, but they may also be initiated on behalf of the identified (or identifiable) consumers. The fact

[226] Case 167/00 *Verein Fur Konsumenteninformation v KH Henkel* [2003] ILPr 1 (ECJ, Sixth Chamber).
[227] Ibid.
[228] Ibid [25]. See also the opinion of AG Jacob, [10] and [12].
[229] Council Directive 93/13 of 5 April 1993 on unfair terms in consumer contracts [1993] OJ L95/29. See also: JA Jolowicz, *On Civil Procedure* (CUP, Cambridge, 2000) 131.
[230] *Henkel* (n 226) [33].
[231] *Shearson* (n 207).
[232] Green Paper on consumer collective redress, COM (2008) 794 final.
[233] Ibid [58].
[234] Eg Art 47B of the Competition Act 1998.
[235] *Shearson* (n 207).
[236] *Henkel* (n 226) [33].
[237] Hill (n 199) 97. See also: *Shearson* (n 207) [35] (AG Darmon).

that under some national laws consumers' representatives may be regarded as a party to litigation in cases where the damage is caused to consumers[238] would not affect the court's jurisdiction over a dispute that is to do with particular substantive rights of identified (or identifiable) consumers which have not been assigned to the representative body. It is well established that the right to bring an action, which may be conferred to a consumers body, 'is not a function of subjective law or rights; the claim to judicial tutelage is a means which permits a right to be enforced, but it is not the right itself.'[239]

Therefore, the question whether a representative body has a procedural right to bring a representative action is distinct from the issue of which court has jurisdiction to hear and determine a dispute which is to do with the enforcement of substantive rights of identified (or identifiable) consumers. The fact that the action was brought by a representative body would not affect the court's jurisdiction over a consumer's contract, which is determined by Arts 15 and 16 of Brussels I on the basis of whether the dispute is in respect of identified (or identifiable) contracts concluded by consumers. The only relevant tests for allocating jurisdiction under Brussels I are whether the contract is concluded by a consumer and whether the action was brought in respect of identified (or identifiable) consumer contracts.[240]

In spite of the fact that in representatives' actions, the representatives are parties to the proceedings,[241] jurisdiction over the EU competition law claims brought by consumers is derived by s 4 of chapter II of Brussels I. Such a deduction can be reinforced by the rationale of s 4 of chapter II of Brussels I which is to protect consumer interests and the Commission's objective to promote representative actions as stated in the White Paper for antitrust damages,[242] in order to protect substantive rights of identified (or identifiable) consumers who may be party to a contract that is in conflict with EU competition law. If jurisdiction in representative (or class) actions were to be derived by Art 5(1) of Brussels I, then this would be clearly seen as a disincentive, in view of the fact that the court which has jurisdiction over an EU competition law claim for nullity of a contract in so far as it is based on Art 5(1) of Brussels I, does not have jurisdiction over the claim for antitrust damages in so far as it is based on tort. Such a result would have flown in the face of EU Consumer Policy Strategy 2007–13.[243] One should not forget that the rationale behind promoting collective redress proceedings is to make

[238] See Jolowicz (n 229) 118 and 130–42.

[239] Wach, *Handbuch des Deutschen Zivilprozessrecht* (1885) quoted in E Couture, 'The nature of judicial process' (1950) 25 *Tulane Law Review* 1, 4–5. See also: *Poyser v Minors* (1881) LR 7 QBD 329 (CA) 333 (Lush LJ); Jolowicz (n 229) 84.

[240] *Henkel* (n 226).

[241] A Zuckerman, *Civil Procedure* (LexisNexis, London, 2003) 446.

[242] 'Damages actions for breach of the EC antitrust rules' (White Paper) COM (2008) 165 final.

[243] COM (2007) 99 final [5.3].

'possible litigation that would not be in the courts at all if individual actions were required.'[244]

Article 16 of Brussels I, which entitles a claimant to bring proceedings related to a consumer contract either in the place of his domicile or in the courts of the place of the seller or supplier's domicile, would be relevant for allocating jurisdiction in EU competition law claims brought by individual consumers or representative body on behalf of identified (or identifiable) consumers. There are no particular difficulties in applying these provisions to EU competition law disputes. For example, under s 4 of chapter II of Brussels I a consumer can bring an EU competition law claim against companies guilty of illegal price-fixing.[245] Consequently, it will be open for a consumer to sue a company infringing Arts 101 and 102 TFEU either in the court at the place of his domicile or in the court of the company's domicile under s 4 of chapter II of Brussels I.[246] But could Art 6(1) of Brussels I be applied in cross-border collective redress actions brought by consumers in antitrust cases?

It is tempting to say that consumers do not need Art 6(1) of Brussels I, as they can sue in their domicile.[247] However, Art 6(1) of Brussels I may be of relevance in collective redress actions brought by affected consumers across Europe. For example, consumers who have suffered damages as a result of purchasing faulty products sold by local retailers, may wish to centralise litigation by bringing collective redress proceedings against the different local retailers in contract, together with a collective redress action based in tort against the local distributor and the foreign manufacturer.[248] Section 4 of chapter II of Brussels I says nothing about actions against multiple defendants. As a result, complicated issues would arise in product liability cases where the bodies representing the consumers decide to centralise litigation by bringing a collective redress action against two or more defendants under Art 6(1) of Brussels I. The current law suggests that consumers may not rely on Art 6(1) of Brussels I. This conclusion can be deduced by analogy from the recent ruling in *Glaxosmithkline.*[249] The reading of the Court of Justice decision, together with Art 15 of Brussels I, indicates that Art 6(1) (unlike Art 4 and Art 5(5)) will not be applicable to claims brought by consumers. The issue needs to receive some attention by the legislators in the context of collective redress proceedings where more complicated actions are bound to arise and consumers may need to rely on Art 6(1) of Brussels I.

Thus, Brussels I, in its current version, notwithstanding the objective of consumer protection referred to in recital 13, does not seem well suited for centralising

[244] Dam (n 223) 49. See also: C Hodges, 'From class actions to collective redress: a resolution in approach to compensation' (2009) *Civil Justice Quarterly* 41.

[245] C Withers, 'Jurisdiction and applicable law in antitrust tort claims' (2002) *Journal of Business Law* 250, 263.

[246] Art 16 of Brussels Regulation.

[247] See Art 16 of the Brussels I Regulation. See more Danov (n 201).

[248] Compare *Watson v First Choice Holidays* [2001] EWCA Civ 972 [33].

[249] Case C-462/06 *Laboratoires Glaxosmithkline* [2008] ICR 1375.

representative actions brought on behalf of the consumers from different Members States who want to centralise those actions at their preferred location by suing more than one defendant under Art 6(1). Such an outcome is unsatisfactory, as it may result in parallel collective redress actions that give rise to common issues of fact and law.

2.2.6 Application of Article 22(4) in EU Competition Law Cases

Article 22(4) of Brussels I specifies the courts of the Member State which shall have exclusive jurisdiction in proceedings concerned with the registration or validity of intellectual property rights required to be deposited or registered. The importance of the issue of validity of intellectual property rights for competition law cases is not in doubt if the ruling of the Court of Appeal in *Intel Corporation v VIA Technologies*[250] is considered. In this case it was stated that the issues in relation to EU competition law only arise if the patents in suit are both valid and infringed. Accordingly, if in an action for enforcement of a contract that allegedly distorts competition a counter-claim[251] is brought, together with a defence that a patent is not valid, then the first question that the court should deal with is related to the validity of the intellectual property right. Moreover, unless and until it has been determined that the claim in the patents in suit is valid, the extent to which any of the patents in suit is capable of restricting competition and therefore capable of giving rise to infringements of Arts 101 and 102 EFTU is uncertain.

This gives rise to a more general question: whether an EU competition law claim and the issue of the validity of an intellectual property right should be split between the courts of different Member States? The answer to this question, however, depends on whether the courts are precluded from trying an infringement of an intellectual property right claim where its validity is at issue. There are a number of English cases which have held that the courts of a Member State are precluded from trying an intellectual property infringement action, where the validity is an issue.[252] This has been justified by outlining that the validity of intellectual property is not a merely incidental issue, but is the matter with which the action is principally concerned. Most recently, the Court of Justice held that Art 22(4) of Brussels I is 'to be interpreted as meaning that the rule of exclusive jurisdiction laid down therein concerns all proceedings related to the registration and validity of a patent, irrespective of whether the issue is raised by way of an action or a plea in objection.'[253]

[250] *Intel Corporation v VIA Technologies* [2003] EWCA Civ 1905; [2003] ECC 16 (CA).

[251] It was already clarified that a counter-claim for antitrust damages is within the scope of Art 6(3) of the Brussels I Regulation. See more: section 2.2.2.1.2 above.

[252] *Coin Controls v Suzo International* [1999] Ch 33 (ChD) 50–51; *Fort Dodge v Akzo Nobel* [1998] FSR 222 (CA). See also: JJ Fawcett, 'Special Rules of Private International Law for Special Cases: What Should We Do about Intellectual Property', in Fawcett (n 122) 143.

[253] Case C-4/03 *GAT v Luk* [2006] ECR I-6509 [31]. See also Case 2U 104/01 *GAT v Luk* [2003] ILPr 41 (Oberlandesgericht Dusseldorf).

The Court of Justice decision was severely criticised by Briggs.[254] According to him, the ruling is detached from legal and economic reality, as the only possibility for the German court is to stay its proceedings and resume after the French decision on the validity of the patent is rendered. Each day of infringement or judicially-ordered interim restraint may result in enormous sums of money being lost.[255]

Nonetheless, the Court of Justice ruling would be instructive for a competition case where an issue of validity of an intellectual property right is raised. Article 22(4) of Brussels I precludes the court that has no jurisdiction under it from ruling not only on the validity of the intellectual property right, but also on EU competition law claim issues if such a claim (or a defence) is raised. This is a rather unfortunate outcome. A more appropriate result would be for the court that has jurisdiction over the infringement action to rule on the incidental issue of the validity of the intellectual property right involved.[256] This would also confer on this court jurisdiction over a counter-claim for antitrust damages.

2.2.7 Application of Article 23 to EU Competition Law Claims

Article 23 is concerned with the situation where the parties have agreed that a court of a Member State is to have jurisdiction to settle any dispute, which has arisen or which may arise in connection with a particular legal relationship.[257] If one or more of the parties is domiciled in a Member State, the effect of a jurisdiction clause is to confer exclusive jurisdiction to the court so chosen. As a result, Arts 2, 5 and 6 can be overridden by the jurisdictional rule in Art 23 of the Brussels Regulation. However, in the context of this book, it is important to outline that a non-consumer party to a consumer contract would not be able to rely on a jurisdiction agreement unless the agreement in question was entered into after the dispute has arisen[258] or at the time of the conclusion of the contract the consumer and non-consumer party to the contract were domiciled or habitually resident in the same Member State and agreed to the jurisdiction of the courts of that Member State.[259] This would be the case irrespective of whether the jurisdictional agreement is in respect of a Member State court or a non-Member State court.[260] The rationale behind such a restrictive rule is that a consumer may be reluctant to litigate a claim abroad where he would incur higher costs and would have to manage cross-border litigation risks.[261] A consumer nonetheless may rely

[254] A Briggs, 'Jurisdiction over defences and connected claims (*Roche v Primus*; *GAT v LuK*; *Reisch v Kiesel*)' (2006) *Lloyd's Maritime and Commercial Law Quarterly* 447.

[255] Ibid.

[256] Compare Fawcett and Torremans (n 1) 235–36; Fawcett (n 252) 165–66.

[257] See generally: A Briggs, *Agreements on Jurisdiction and Choice of Law* (OUP, Oxford, 2008).

[258] Art 17(1) of the Brussels I Regulation.

[259] Art 17(3) of the Brussels I Regulation. See more: Hill (n 199) 196–200.

[260] Compare *Samengo-Turner v March & McLennan (Services) Ltd* [2007] EWCA Civ 723, [2008] ICR 18 (CA).

[261] Hill (n 199) 196–97.

on jurisdiction agreement, which allows him to bring proceedings in courts other than those indicated in s 4 of Brussels, and invoke jurisdiction of the selected forum if he wished to do so.

To invoke the exclusive jurisdiction of the selected court the party, who is relying on it, must demonstrate that the jurisdictional agreement is valid and its scope is wide enough to cover the claims in question. With regard to the second question an important issue would be whether the clause invoked before the Member State court covers EU competition law claims. The Member States before which court proceedings are brought with regard to the dispute that is to be resolved by an (allegedly) chosen court would determine the validity of the jurisdiction agreement.[262] The questions that must be considered in the context of antitrust claims are: Is it the law applicable to the jurisdiction agreement that would indicate whether the agreement is valid? Does the nullity of the main contract under EU competition law invalidate a jurisdiction clause?

One approach is to accept that a jurisdictional clause should be treated as any other contractual clauses and the invalidity of the main contract should entail the invalidity of the jurisdiction clause which is incorporated into the main contract because the greater includes the lesser.[263] It has been submitted by Harris that 'it is difficult to see why [a jurisdiction clause] need not be substantively valid according to the applicable law,[264] just as any contractual term would need to be.'[265] But, what if it was alleged that the contract (and incorporated jurisdictional clause) were void *ab initio* under the applicable substantive competition law? In such a scenario, at the jurisdictional stage, the court would need to examine whether the main contract (and incorporated jurisdictional clause) is valid under the applicable competition law.[266] This means that a judge could have to dismiss the action because the rules of jurisdiction were not satisfied after he had already decided whether the contract (and incorporated jurisdictional clause) were not valid.[267] Such an approach would be far from satisfactory.

The fact that Rome I, which specifies the law applicable to contractual obligations, explicitly states that jurisdictional agreements are excluded from its scope[268] clearly indicates that a jurisdictional clause should not be treated as any other contractual term. Whilst, the other contractual clauses set out obligations which the parties undertake towards each other, the jurisdiction agreement determines which court will have jurisdiction over any dispute that arises with regard to the obligations which the one party has undertaken to the other.[269]

[262] Briggs (n 257) 239.
[263] *Heyman v Darwins* [1942] AC 356 (HL) 371 (Lord Macmillan).
[264] Or rather, why the court need not satisfy itself to its civil standard of proof that the clause is substantively valid.
[265] J Harris, 'Jurisdiction Clause and Void Contracts' (1998) 23 *EL Rev* 279, 282.
[266] See ch 5.
[267] See also ch 7, section 7.2 below.
[268] Art 1(2)(e) of the Rome I Regulation.
[269] *Heyman* (n 263) 373–74.

The doctrine of separability seems to be favoured by the EU legislator in the context of jurisdiction agreements.[270] The Court of Justice has underlined that a distinction must be drawn between a jurisdiction clause and the substantive provisions of the contract in which it is incorporated. The court went further and held that the jurisdiction clause serves a procedural purpose, so it is to be governed by Art 23 of the Brussels Regulation.[271] As Briggs points out: '[t]he fact that the substantive obligations of the contract may be unenforceable need not mean that the associated procedural obligations should be treated as ineffective as well.'[272]

Although it has been submitted that 'English law has no statutory equivalent of the Arbitration Act 1996, s 7 for jurisdiction agreement',[273] one should not forget that the doctrine of separability was developed well before the entrance into force of the 1996 Act.[274] The doctrine of separability appears to be adopted by English common law[275] as well as Art 23 of Brussels I.[276] This was clearly confirmed by the English Court of Appeal in *Deutsche Bank AG v Asia Pacific Broadband Wireless Communications*.[277] In this case, it was held that the jurisdiction clause is to be treated as distinct from the main contract in which it is incorporated. In other words, even if it is alleged that the main contract is void, the jurisdiction clause remains valid and binds the parties to resolve their dispute at the designated Member State court. Longmore LJ went further, to state that:

> It is only if the jurisdiction clause is itself under some specific attack that a question can arise whether it is right to invoke the jurisdiction clause. Examples of this might be fraud or duress alleged in relation specifically to the jurisdiction clause. Another example might be if the signatures to the agreement were alleged to be forgeries, although no authority has so far so stated. Even in such a case someone has to decide whether the signatures were in fact forged. It might well be thought that a mere allegation to that effect could not have the effect of rendering a jurisdiction clause inapplicable.[278]

Therefore, the Art 23 solution seems to be very appropriate and in line with the parties' agreement and the purpose of the Brussels Regulation, providing more certainty to parties in law disputes. Hence, Brussels I has detached the question of validity of a jurisdictional agreement under Art 23, in order to provide for uniform application and predictability of the outcome throughout the EU.[279] For those purposes, Art 23 of Brussels I lays down three requirements for an enforceable

[270] Case C-214/89 *Powell Duffryn v Peteriet* [1992] ECR I-1745 [14]. See also: Case C-269/95 *Benincasa v Dentalkit* [1997] ECR I-3767 [73] (AG La Pergola).

[271] *Benincasa* (n 270) [24]–[25].

[272] Briggs (n 257) 242.

[273] Briggs (n 257) 79.

[274] *Harbour Assurance Co (UK) Ltd v Kansa General International Insurance Co Ltd* [1993] QB (CA); *Fili Shipping* (n 210).

[275] *Mackender v Feldia AG* [1967] 2 QB 590 (CA). See more: Briggs (n 257) 80–82.

[276] *Benincasa* (n 270).

[277] *Deutsche Bank AG and Others v Asia Pacific Broadband Wireless Communications Inc and Another* [2008] EWCA Civ 1091, [2008] 2 Lloyd's Rep 619 (CA). Compare Briggs and Rees (n 44) 194.

[278] Ibid [24].

[279] *Benincasa* (n 270) [25]. See also: Briggs (n 257) 241.

jurisdictional agreement. First, the parties must have agreed that a court or the courts of a Member State are to have jurisdiction to settle their disputes. Secondly, the dispute must arise in connection with a 'particular legal relationship'. Thirdly, the agreement fulfils the formal requirements of Art 23(1).[280] But what would be the scope of the jurisdiction clause?

It is well established that it is for the national court to determine which disputes fall within the scope of jurisdiction clauses.[281] For those purposes, a national court needs to ascertain what law governs the jurisdiction agreement, in order to determine what the scope of the agreement in question is.[282] For example, in *Provimi*, the High Court considered Swiss law, French law and German law, in order to determine whether EU competition law claims for damages were in the scope of the jurisdiction clauses governed by those laws.[283] It was concluded that under the laws of Switzerland, Germany and France, even a widely drafted jurisdiction clause did not cover claims for damages for infringement of EU competition law. That was justified by the fact that the antitrust disputes in question did not arise out of the legal relationship in connection with which the jurisdiction agreement was made, but rather out of an illegal cartel.[284] It was assumed that when the claimants concluded the contracts they did not know that there were secret cartels on price-fixing and market allocation and that the prices they would have to pay for the goods were those fixed by the secret cartel which infringed EU competition law.[285]

Although the antitrust dispute in *Provimi v Aventis* followed a Commission Decision, which found that various manufacturers had operated cartels, contrary to EU competition law, in relation to the sale of vitamins within the EU and EEA over a 10-year period, in other cases the dispute could have been within the scope of the jurisdiction agreement. Under English law, if there was a contractual dispute of how the principle of severance of illegal provisions from otherwise lawful agreements would affect the parties' contract, it would certainly be within the scope of jurisdiction agreement that stated that all disputes arising out of a contract are to be dealt by the English court. The Court of Appeal has held that a broadly drafted jurisdiction clause covers not only contractual claims, but also tortious claims which are closely connected with them.[286] Similarly, the English High Court recently found that despite the fact that claims for breach of Arts 101 and 102 TFEU do raise considerations distinct from other tortious claims, they

[280] See more: Briggs (n 257) 244–77.

[281] *Powell Duffryn* (n 270) [37]. *Benincasa* (n 270) [31].

[282] *Powell Duffryn* (n 270). See also: Briggs (n 257) 248. Compare O Kahn-Freud, 'Jurisdiction agreements: some reflections' (1977) 26 ICLQ 825, 828–29.

[283] *Provimi* (n 20).

[284] See more about the scope of the German jurisdiction clause, *Provimi* (n 20) [71].

[285] See more about the scope of the Swiss jurisdiction clause: *Provimi* (n 20) [62]–[66]. See also: Decision 16013/2001 *Re The Termination of a Distribution Contract* [2003] ILPr 633 (Multi-Member First Instance Court, Thessaloniki).

[286] *Kitetechnology v Unicor* [1992] ILPr 568 (CA).

may well be within the scope of an arbitration agreement.[287] Thus, it seems clear that there may be cases where a jurisdictional clause may cover not only the EU competition law claims based on contract, but also the tortious claims for antitrust damages. That could be a problem, as a commercial company that wanted to opt in to a collective redress action pending before a national court other than the one selected may be precluded from doing so if the defendant relied on a jurisdiction agreement.

Further problems that may arise in competition cases are to do with fact that if the parties agreed to confer exclusive jurisdiction on the courts of a non-Member State, a dominant undertaking (or undertaking which enjoys market power) 'may avoid private enforcement within the EU by appropriate choice of court clauses'.[288] How can a problem be dealt with by the English courts? Can an English court restrain foreign antitrust proceedings? Restraining foreign proceedings is a preserving measure that grants an English court a discretionary power, in certain limited circumstances, to issue an injunction restraining a party from commencing or continuing as a plaintiff with foreign proceedings.[289] It is now, however, recognised that one of the reasons for the caution with which the jurisdiction must be exercised is that 'it involves interference with the process of the foreign court concerned.'[290] The question how this power could be exercised in regard to an international antitrust dispute will be discussed below.

The relevance of anti-suit injunctions with regard to antitrust law disputes can be illustrated by the *Laker Airways* litigation that was intitiated in the District of Columbia.[291] Subsequently, an application for injunctions to restrain Laker from continuing their American action was brought in England.[292] The House of Lords discharged the injunction which was granted by the Court of Appeal. It was held that an injunction restraining the US proceedings would only be granted if British Airways and British Caledonian had shown that it had been 'unconscionable' for Laker Airways to sue them in the US.[293] In this case, however, there was only one forum in which Laker Airways could bring its antitrust actions, namely the US.

In the European context, however, even if a claimant had shown that it would be 'unconscionable' to be sued in another state, the English court would be precluded from granting an anti-suit injunction as the Member State court's

[287] *ET Plus* (n 186) [51].

[288] J Basedow, 'Jurisdiction and choice of law in the private enforcement of EC competition law' in Basedow (n 67) 229, 235.

[289] *Cheshire, North & Fawcett* (n 15) 334–41.

[290] *South Carolina v Assurantie Maatshapij* [1987] AC 24 (HL) 40. See also: T Raphael, *The Anti-Suit Injunction* (OUP, Oxford, 2008) 110–18.

[291] *Laker Airways v Pan American Airways* 559 F Supp 1124 (DDC 1983), aff'd *Laker Airways v Sabena Belgium World Airways* 731 F 2d 909 (DC Cir 1984).

[292] *British Airways Board v Laker Airways* [1983] ECC 503 (QBD (Comm)) (Parker J); [1984] 1 QB 142 (CA) 202; [1985] AC 58 (HL). See also L Collins, 'Comity in Modern Private International Law' in Fawcett (n 122) 89, 103.

[293] *Laker Airways* (HL) (n 292) 84.

jurisdiction would have as its basis the Brussels I Regulation.[294] In such cases, it is well established that an anti-suit injunction cannot be granted by the English court, even if that party is acting in bad faith with a view to frustrate the existing proceedings. The Court of Justice decision in the *Turner* case has been criticised as reducing the power of English courts to do practical justice between litigants.[295] This would be certainly so in cases where jurisdiction over an EU competition law claim is invoked under the Brussels I Regulation.

But, what if the parties agreed to confer exclusive jurisdiction on the courts of a non-Member State? It appears that there is nothing that could preclude an English court to issue an anti-suit injunction in such cases, as Art 23 of Brussels I only applies if 'the jurisdiction clause designates the court or the courts of a [Member] State'.[296] This can be deduced by analogy from the judgment of the Court of Appeal in *Samengo-Turner v March & McLennan (Services) Ltd*.[297] In this case, the claimants, who were domiciled in the United Kingdom, were employed by an English company belonging to a group of companies based in New York. The claimants gave a six-month notice to terminate their contracts of employment and disclosed that they intended to work for a competitor. The defendant relied on an exclusive New York jurisdiction clause in the bonus agreement, and brought proceedings in New York claiming that the plaintiffs should repay the bonus award. The plaintiffs applied to the English court for an interim anti-suit injunction to restrain the New York proceedings, asserting that those proceedings related to individual contracts of employment, so that they should have been brought in England under s 5 of Brussels I. The English court issued an anti-suit injunction by disregarding the exclusive New York jurisdiction clause, on the ground that s 5 allocates jurisdiction in such cases. The case of injunction was particularly strong, in view of the fact that Brussels I imposed exclusive jurisdiction of English courts in employment disputes.[298] One may argue that an English court should have discretion to issue an anti-suit injunction with respect to an EU competition law suit even if the antitrust claim is within the scope of a valid agreement conferring exclusive jurisdiction on the courts of a non-Member.[299]

However, difficulties in applying by analogy *Samengo-Turner* in EU competition law cases can arise, as there is no statute allocating exclusive jurisdiction of English courts.[300] On the one hand, it seems that an anti-suit injunction may be granted if there is a good arguable case that the defendant has included the jurisdiction clause, in order to avoid private enforcement of EU competition law in cases where

[294] Case C-159/02 *Turner v Grovit* [2004] ECR I-3565.

[295] A Briggs, 'Anti-suit injunction and utopian ideals' (2004) 120 *LQR* 529. See also J Mance, 'Exclusive Jurisdiction Agreements and European Ideals' (2004) 120 *LQR* 357.

[296] Case C-387/98 *Coreck Maritime GmbH v Handelsveem BV* [2000] ECR I-9337 [17 and 19].

[297] *Samengo-Turner* (n 260).

[298] Ibid [37, 44, 45 and 46].

[299] Briggs (n 257) 295.

[300] *Samengo-Turner* (n 260) [41]. See also: *OT Africa Line v Magic Sportwear Corp* [2005] 2 Lloyd's Rep 170.

jurisdiction should have been derived by the Brussels I Regulation. This could be so, if, for example, all the elements of the dispute are connected with the European Union. Such an approach could be reinforced by the fundamental character of EU competition law and its public policy character[301] as non-application may affect the 'proper functioning of the internal market'.[302] On the other hand, one may say that 'the principle of legal certainty is secured by agreement in advance, and by its strict enforcement, and is greater than that which results from the judicial interpretation of a statute.'[303] It remains to be seen which approach will be adopted by the English courts. Even if the English court decided not to ignore a jurisdiction agreement and refused to grant an anti-suit injunction in an EU competition law case, it seems that the English court could deny recognition and enforcement a foreign judgment which misapplies or ignores Arts 101 and 102 TFEU.[304]

2.2.8 Application of Article 31 to EU Competition Law Claims

In this section, the basis for jurisdiction to grant provisional measures[305] in support of foreign EU competition law proceedings will be highlighted. It should be outlined that 'applications for provisional measures (such as cease and desist orders) are key to the enforcement of the competition rules.'[306] Can a plaintiff in an EU competition law claim seek an injunction under Brussels I, if antitrust proceedings are taking place outside of England?[307]

Article 31 of Brussels I permits application to be made to a court of a Member State, which does not have jurisdiction in relation to the substance of the matter, for such provisional measures that are intended to preserve a factual or legal situation.[308] Furthermore, Section 25 of the 1982 Act empowered the High Court to grant provisional measures in support of any legal[309] or arbitral[310] proceedings which have been (or will be) commenced abroad.[311] The court will have jurisdiction to grant provisional measures irrespective of the domicile of the defendant[312]

[301] See more: ch 5.

[302] Compare C-281/02 *Owusu v Jackson* [2005] ECR I-1383 [34].

[303] Briggs (n 257) 293.

[304] See more: ch 6.

[305] Case C-391/95 *Van Uden Maritime BV v Kommanditgesellschaft in Firma Deco-Line* [1998] ECR I-7091; Case C-99/96 *Mietz v Intership Yachting Sneek* [1999] ECR I-2277. See also *Spray Network Telenor* [2004] ILPr 586 (Supreme Court, Netherlands).

[306] HM Gilliams, 'Modernisation: From Policy to Practice' (2003) 28 *Eur LR* 450, 468.

[307] It is well established that '[w]here England is the forum for the trial of the claim, the court has jurisdiction to grant the full range of provisional measures available under English law in relation to those proceedings.' See Hill (n 47) 329.

[308] Case C-261/90 *Reichert v Dresdner Bank* [1992] ECR I-2149 [34]; Case C-104/03 *St Paul Dairy Industries v Unibel Exser BVBA* [2005] ILPr 31 [13]; See also *Van Uden* (n 305) [28].

[309] See also sections 2.3.2.1.3 and 3.3.2.1.3 below.

[310] See ch 8 below.

[311] *Credit Suisse Fides Trust v Cuoghi* [1998] QB 818 (CA) 825 (Millett LJ).

[312] In cases where the defendant is domiciled in England, service of a claim form abroad is possible without the leave of the court: CPR 6.19. For service of a claim form out of the jurisdiction where the

and the basis on which the foreign court exercised jurisdiction. This jurisdiction is intended to avoid causing loss to the parties as a result of the long delays inherent in any international proceedings.[313] However, the Court of Justice has held that:

> [T]he granting of provisional or protective measures on the basis of article [31] is conditional on, inter alia, the existence of a real connecting link between the subject matter of the measures sought and the territorial jurisdiction of the contracting state of the court before which those measures are sought.[314]

After applying this test in an EU competition law case,[315] where an application was made by the plaintiff seeking to restrain the defendants from commencing any action without 14 days' written notice to the plaintiff (based on any patent before any court, administrative body or other body) in the European Economic Area, the English court found that it had no jurisdiction. More specifically, the court concluded that there was no connection between the subject matter of the measure sought and the territorial jurisdiction of the Member State court because the defendants had no assets within England, nor were the person/s the subject of the order within England, so that compliance could not be secured as necessary.

Another issue that may arise is to do with the question whether the court will grant measures of a kind[316] which the foreign court cannot or will not itself grant. The answer given by the English Court of Appeal is that such relief may be granted. Thus a court in one jurisdiction may render whatever assistance it properly can to a court in another in respect of assets located or persons resident within the territory of the former.[317]

Consequently, it seems that Art 31 and s 25 of the 1982 Act would be particularly useful provisions in EU competition law claims, where the grant of an injunction is a normal remedy. They would allow the English court, which lacks jurisdiction as to the substantive claim, to grant injunctive relief preventing EU competition law infringement in England pending the determination of the substantive dispute in another Member State.[318] This would be relevant, for example, to a case, where an anti-competitive agreement or conduct has affected the market in Germany, France and England, but the plaintiff decided to rely on Art 6(1) and pursue his action Germany.

permission of the court is required, CPR 6.20(2) and CPR 6.20(4) (considered in sections 2.3.2.1.3 and 3.3.2.1.3 below) will be applicable. See also: *X v Y* [1990] 1 QB 220 (Comm).

313 *St Paul Dairy* (n 308) [12].

314 *Van Uden* (n 305) [40].

315 *SanDisk* (n 153) [52 and 55].

316 Eg a *Mareva* injunction (now called 'Freezing order'), which was established as an exceptional remedy to prevent a foreign defendant from defeating any ultimate judgment by removing his assets from the jurisdiction. It was extended in 1990 by restraining defendants from dealing with their assets both inside and outside the jurisdiction. See *Babanaft International v Bassatne* [1990] Ch 13 (CA).

317 *Credit Suisse* (n 311) 827.

318 Compare *Kitetechnology* (n 286).

2.3 Jurisdiction under English Traditional Rules

In cases where the defendant is not domiciled within the EU, the traditional English rules would apply. Under those rules the court may have jurisdiction with regard to EU competition law claims in three situations: first, if the defendant is present in England; secondly, if the defendant submits to the court's jurisdiction; thirdly, if a permission to serve a claim form out of jurisdiction is granted by the court. In this part of the book the traditional rules and their application in EU competition law claims brought by the contracting parties will be examined.

2.3.1 Service of a Claim Form within the Jurisdiction

The English courts have jurisdiction over an action *in personam* in the situation, where there has been a service of a claim form on a defendant present within the jurisdiction.[319] This basis of jurisdiction is not concerned with the nature of the cause of action and there seem to be no special difficulties in respect of serving a claim form on a defendant with regard to EU competition law claims. Nonetheless, due to the tortious nature of a typical EU competition law claim,[320] the rules on service of a claim form within the jurisdiction are best discussed in detail in the context of tort-based EU competition law claims as being more relevant for antitrust law disputes.[321]

2.3.2 Service of a Claim Form out of the Jurisdiction

Where the defendant company has no presence in the forum, a plaintiff may bring an EU competition law claim against a defendant by service of a claim form out of the jurisdiction. In such cases, the service must take effect in accordance with English traditional rules. The court will not give permission for service of a claim form out of jurisdiction, unless satisfied that England is 'the proper place in which to bring the claim'.[322] There are three requirements that must be satisfied by a plaintiff, who wants to sue an absent defendant in England. First, he has to show that one of the grounds of paragraph 3.1 of Practice Direction B to Part 6 of the CPR (old CPR 6.20) is applicable.[323] Secondly, the plaintiff needs to demonstrate

[319] CPR 6 and CPR 7.5 read with Art 4 of Brussels I. See more: L Collins and others (eds) *Dicey, Morris and Collins on the Conflict of Laws* (14th edn, Sweet & Maxwell, London, 2006) 306; A Zuckerman, 'New provision for service: a great improvement threaten by discretion' (2009) *Civil Justice Quarterly* 1; Briggs and Rees (n 44) 410, 545–56.

[320] See more: ch 1, section 1.7 above. See also the Rome II Regulation.

[321] See more: ch 3, section 3.3 below.

[322] CPR 6.37(3).

[323] The court has no inherent power to allow service of process out of jurisdiction in cases not falling within the scope of the CPR. See *Re Busfield* (1886) 32 ChD 123 (CA); *Re Anglo African Steamship* (1886) 32 ChD 348 (CA).

that the claim has reasonable prospects of success.[324] Finally, the court must be persuaded to exercise its discretion to permit service of a claim form out of the jurisdiction. The onus is on the plaintiff to show that England is a clearly appropriate forum for trial.[325] Accordingly the requirements for service out of jurisdiction with regard to EU competition claims under the traditional English rules will be examined below.

2.3.2.1 The Grounds of Para 3.1 of CPR PD 6B

Paragraph 3.1 of CPR PD 6B lists the grounds on which a 'claimant may serve a claim form out of the jurisdiction with the permission of the court under rule 6.36.' The grounds listed are neither concerned with the type of contract involved nor the obligation the breach of which is relied upon by the plaintiff.[326] Therefore, contract grounds of para 3.1 of CPR PD 6B would be also relevant to cases where it is alleged that an agreement is in conflict with Arts 101 and/or 102 TFEU. That said, it should be noted that jurisdiction based on a service of a claim form out of jurisdiction with the permission of the courts is regarded as being 'exorbitant' and 'extraordinary'.[327] Accordingly, the exorbitance of jurisdiction sought to be invoked is an important factor to be placed in the balance against granting leave.[328] There may be special difficulties in applying the grounds listed in para 3.1 of CPR PD 6B to an agreement in conflict with EU competition law, because in such cases the issue of validity of the contract will be the primary issue that should be determined by the court. These difficulties will be examined below in the light of the relevant civil procedure rules. As far as contract-based EU competition law claims are concerned, the following rules seem to be relevant: contract grounds, multiple defendants ground and injunctions ground. Accordingly, in this sub-section, these rules will be discussed with regard to EU competition law claims.

2.3.2.1.1 EU Competition Law Claims and Contract Grounds

Paragraph 3.1 of CPR PD 6B contains three separate grounds that may be relevant with regard to contractual disputes: para 3.1(6), para 3.1(7) and para 3.1(8). It would be sufficient if the claimant can bring his case within any one of those grounds.[329] The aim of this section is to clarify which of the contract grounds will be applicable in EU competition law claims brought by contracting parties. Accordingly, the first question that will be examined is whether a plaintiff can seek service out of jurisdiction when he argues that the contract is invalid under EU competition law. Then, the possibilities for seeking a declaration that a contract is

[324] CPR 6.37(1)(b).
[325] See *Spiliada Maritime v Cansulex* [1987] AC 460 (HL) 480 (Lord Goff). See also CPR 6.37(3).
[326] Fawcett and Torremans (n 1) 97.
[327] *Spiliada* (n 325) 481 (Lord Goff).
[328] *Amin Rasheed Shipping v Kuwait Insurance* [1984] AC 50 (HL) 68; See also PB Carter, 'Private International Law' (1990) 61 *British Yearbook of International Law* 395, 396.
[329] *Wansborough Paper v Laughland* [1920] WN 344 (CA).

invalidated together with a claim for antitrust damages will be discussed in light of contract grounds.

It is well established that a claim for a declaration that a contract had been rescinded for misrepresentation[330] would be a claim 'in respect of a contract' within the meaning of para 3.1. The same is true for a claim that a contract had been discharged by frustration.[331] But what if the plaintiff's case is that there never has been a contract, or alternatively the contract is void *ab initio*? The question of jurisdiction in regard to a contract which has never been entered into was addressed under the old RSC Ord 11 in *Finnish Marine Insurance v Protective National Insurance.*[332] In this case the judge recognised the distinction between the case where there has been a contract, which later has been discharged by an accepted repudiation, frustration or rescission, and a 'contract' which has never been entered into.[333] Based on that distinction, the previous edition of Dicey and Moris stated that the permission for service out of jurisdiction would not be granted if the claimant seeks a declaration that he is not bound by the contract.[334] Thus, following the old case law, if the claimant was seeking a declaration that the contract is void, then the court would have no jurisdiction under traditional English rules.

The uncertainty surrounding an action for a declaration that no contract exists was considered and remedied in the old CPR 6.20,[335] on which para 3.1 of CPR PD 6B is modelled. More specifically, para 3.1(8) makes it clear that permission to serve out may be given in cases where the claimant seeks such a declaration. Accordingly, a claim form may be served out of the jurisdiction if the claim is made for a declaration that the contract is void under EU competition law. There is little doubt that a dispute over the voidness of a contract would be the primary issue in such a case. As a matter of fact, this would be as much a dispute 'in regard to contract' as would a dispute over the performance of a contract.

It should be stressed, however, that para 3.1(8) refers specifically to para 3.1(6), but makes no reference to para 3.1(7). By virtue of the latter provision, the English court may exercise jurisdiction over a defendant where the claim is made in respect of a breach of a contract committed within the jurisdiction. It seems that this rule would be of little use in claims based on EU competition law, because the nullity in such cases is absolute. In an action seeking a nullity of an anti-competitive agreement, the plaintiff bases his claim on the invalidity of the contract. If there is no contract, no breach can take place within the jurisdiction. In cases covered by para 3.1(7), permission for service out of jurisdiction would not be granted unless

[330] *Insurance Corporation of Ireland v Strombus International Insurance* [1985] 2 Lloyd's Rep 138 (CA) 142.

[331] *BP Exploration (Libya) v Hunt* [1976] 1 WLR 788 (Comm) 795 (Kerr J).

[332] *Finnish Marine Insurance v Protective National Insurance* [1990] 1 QB 1078 (Comm).

[333] Ibid 1084 (Hamilton QC); see also *Heyman* (n 263) 366 (Lord Simon), 384 (Lord Wright).

[334] L Collins and others (eds) *Dicey and Morris on the Conflict of Laws* (13th edn, Sweet & Maxwell, London, 2000) 319. See also L Collins and others (eds) *Dicey and Morris on the Conflict of Laws: second cumulative supplement to thirteenth edition* (Sweet & Maxwell, London, 2002) [S11-188].

[335] *Dicey, Morris and Collins* (n 319) 377.

the court was satisfied that the contract existed and a breach took place within the jurisdiction. Accordingly, an EU competition law claim should not be made on the ground of para 3.1(7), since this provision requires a preliminary determination that there is a contract and that it is breached within the jurisdiction.

Thus, the English court will have jurisdiction on the ground of para 3.1(8) only in cases where, if the contract had been found to exist, it would comply with the conditions set out in para 3.1(6). As a result, para 3.1(8) must be read and interpreted together with para 3.1(6). According to the latter, a claim form may be served out of the jurisdiction with the permission of the court, if 'a claim is made in respect of the contract' in the following cases:

(a) *Where the contract 'was made within the jurisdiction'*. It has been submitted that the place where the contract was concluded for the purposes of para 3.1(6)(a) will be determined in accordance with English contract law rules.[336] There are no particular difficulties in applying this provision to an EU competition law claim for a declaration that a contract is void. If the parties enter into negotiations by correspondence from different countries, then the contract is made where the letter of acceptance is posted.[337] In commercial transactions, however, communication by 'instantaneous' means of communication such as telephone, telex, fax and electronic mail is very common these days. According to *Entores v Miles Far East Corporation*,[338] a contract concluded by telephone or telex is made when and where the notification of acceptance is received by the offeror.[339] It has been suggested that the court should bring contracts concluded by emails into line with those concluded by telephone, telex and fax.[340]

(b) *Where the 'contract was made by or through an agent trading or residing within the jurisdiction on behalf of a principal trading or residing out of the jurisdiction'*. It has been underlined that the clause says 'by *or through*' an agent, not just 'by' an agent. Based on that it has been submitted that the case would be within the clause, even if the agent has been limited to obtaining orders and transmitting them to his principal for acceptance or rejection.[341] Likewise, there are no particular difficulties in applying this provision to an EU competition law claim for nullity of the agreement.

(c) *Where the contract 'is governed by English law'.* Under para 3.1(6)(c), a claim form may be served out of the jurisdiction with the permission of the court, if 'a claim is made in respect of a contract where the contract is governed by

336 CMV Clarkson and J Hill, *The Conflict of Laws* (3rd edn, OUP, Oxford, 2006) 92.

337 *Wansborough* (n 329); *Benaim v Debono* [1924] AC 514 (PC) 520; *Clarke v Harper and Robinson* [1938] NIr 162; *Williams v Society of Lloyd's* [1994] 1 VR 274.

338 See *Entores* (n 161).

339 See also: *Brinkibon v Stahag* [1983] 2 AC 34 (HL) 42.

340 Hill (n 47) 215.

341 *Dicey, Morris and Collins* (n 319) 377; See also: *National Mortgage v Gosselin* [1922] 38 TLR 832 (CA).

English law'. It is common for vertical agreements, which may sometimes give rise to anti-competitive concerns, to contain a choice of law clause. The Rome I Regulation is to be applied[342] to determine whether a contract by its terms or by implication is governed by English law for the jurisdictional purposes.[343] Choice-of-law rules, however, cannot restrict the application of the provisions which cannot be derogated within the meaning of Art 3(3) of Rome I and the overriding mandatory provisions of the forum under Art 9(2) of Rome I. There is no doubt that EU competition law is part of English law. That is well settled after the *Van Gend en Loos* case,[344] where it was held that the EU legal order is an integrated system, where EU law is an integral part of each Member State's legal system. It is well established that the threshold for application of EU competition law is the 'implementation' of an agreement within the EU.[345] The end result is that EU competition law must be applied to the subject-matter before the court regardless of any choice of law by the parties.[346] Does the fact that dispute in question raises the compatibility of the contract with Arts 101 and 102 TFEU mean that a contract is governed by English law for the purposes of para 3.1(6)(c) CPR PD 6B?

The problems are to do with the fact that if the mandatory provisions were applicable, then different laws could govern different parts of the contract.[347] In view of that, one still may argue that even if the overriding mandatory provisions were potentially applicable, the contract for the jurisdictional purposes should not be regarded as 'governed by English law', but by the law which regulates its 'general obligation'.[348] This may be reinforced by the proposition that:

> … the whole theory which lies at the root of private international law … is that the law of one country, and one country alone, can be the proper or governing law of the contract; so that … although the law of the country A is the proper law or governing law of contract, and the law of country B may be referred to in order to determine the method and incidents of performance of the contract, this is because the law of country A itself requires or concedes that the methods and incidents of performance should depend upon the law in force at the locality of performance, that is, country B.[349]

[342] *Bank of Baroda v Vysya Bank* [1994] 2 Lloyd's Report 87 (QBD (Comm)); *Egon Oldendorff v Liberia Corp* [1995] 2 Lloyd's Rep 64 (Comm). See more: ch 5 below.

[343] *Dicey, Morris and Collins on the Conflict of Laws* (n 319) 378; see also JJ Fawcett, 'The interrelationship of jurisdiction and choice of law in private international law' (1991) 44 *Current Legal Problems* 39.

[344] Case 26/62 *Van Gend en Loos* [1963] ECR 1, 12. See also *R v Secretary of State for Transport ex p Factortame (No 2)* [1991] 1 AC 603 (HL) 659 (Lord Bridge).

[345] Joined Cases 89/85, 104/85, 114/85, 116–117/85, and 125–129/85 *Ahlstrom v Commission* [1988] ECR 5193 (the *Wood Pulp* cartel case) [16].

[346] See ch 5 below.

[347] WLM Reese, 'Dépeçage: A Common phenomenon in Choice of Law' [1973] 73 *Columbia Law Review* 58.

[348] *Dicey, Morris and Collins on the Conflict of Laws* (n 334) [32-049]; P Nygh, *Autonomy in International Contracts* (OUP, Oxford, 1999) 133–34.

[349] *Wanganui-Rangitikei Electric Board v Australian Mutual Provident Society* (1933) 50 CLR 581, 604.

Although this statement is derived from an old authority, it seems that the view treating only one law as governing law of a contract would work well in the context of para 3.1(6)(c), which seems to be based on the assumption that one law governs the whole contract.[350] But what is the law which governs the contract for the purposes of establishing jurisdiction under English traditional rules in EU competition law cases where different laws could govern different parts of the contract?

Is it the law selected by the parties (or determined under the Rome I Regulation)? Is it the law of the forum in which overriding mandatory provisions are at stake? If the law selected by the parties (or determined under the Rome I Regulation), then the English court would have to decline jurisdiction and leave the question of compatibility of contract with Arts 101 and/or 102 TFEU to be decided by a non-EU court. This would be unfortunate, as an antitrust claim would raise a question of the effect on an anti-competitive contract or practice on English public policy, which is an important factor that may make England the natural forum where the dispute should be tried.[351]

A better solution would be to regard the law of the forum in which overriding mandatory provisions are at stake as the governing law for jurisdictional purposes, if the dispute before the court is to do with that part of the contract.[352] On the one hand, such an interpretation may encourage claimants to raise an EU competition law claim in purely contractual disputes, in order to have their disputes litigated in England. On the other hand, it has been clarified that EU competition laws are not only regarded as overriding mandatory provisions, but also reflect English public policy which is not an issue that is capable of fair resolution in any foreign court.[353] The unique character of EU competition laws appears to reinforce the view that an English court should accept jurisdiction to the extent that it relates to the part of the validity of the contract under Arts 101 and 102 TFEU as being the part of the contract that is governed by English law by virtue of the overriding mandatory provisions.[354]

Therefore, there are strong arguments suggesting that EU competition law as part of English law would be applicable to the case before the court, when a claim for declaration that the contract is invalidated is launched. Due to the mandatory character of EU competition law, this would be relevant as to whether the agreement does distort competition, even if the law of a non-Member State

[350] See *Armar Shipping Co Ltd v Caisse Algerienne d'Assurance et de Reassurance, The Armar* [1981] 1 WLR 207, 216.

[351] See *Novus Aviation Ltd v Onur Air Tasimacilik A/S* [2009] EWCA Civ 122; [2009] 1 Lloyd's Rep 576 (CA) [78]. See also Briggs and Rees (n 44) 528.

[352] *Cheshire, North & Fawcett* (n 15) 381.

[353] Compare *El du Pont de Nemours v Agnew* [1987] 2 Lloyd's Rep 585 (CA) 594. See also *Novus Aviation* (n 351) [78].

[354] *Cheshire, North & Fawcett* (n 15) 381.

is applicable to the contract. Consequently, the fact that the question of English public policy is involved should be enough to satisfy the terms of para 3.1(6)(c) with regard to EU competition law claims, provided that there is a 'good arguable case' that the contract was in conflict with Arts 101 and 102 TFEU, which would be applicable as being a mandatory provision that expresses European public policy, which is part of English public policy as well.

(d) *Where the contract 'contains a term to the effect that the High Court shall have jurisdiction to hear and determine any action in respect of the contract.'* It is common for distribution and technology transfer agreements to contain a choice of jurisdiction clause. It has been submitted that cases are rare in which para 3.1(6)(d) would be the only available ground of jurisdiction.[355] This would be particularly true with regard to EU competition law claims, where the contested issue will involve application of English law and will raise an argument of English public policy.[356] Moreover, it has been submitted that 'in most cases [para 3.1(6)(d)] will be displaced by Article 23 of the Brussels I Regulation, under which the claimant may serve a foreign defendant out of jurisdiction without the court's permission.'[357] Accordingly, the jurisdictional clause and its implications in connection with the jurisdiction of the English courts with regard to EU competition law claims is dealt with more fully in the context of Art 23 of Brussels I.[358]

It can be concluded that para 3.1(8) would confer jurisdiction on an English court in cases where there is a dispute as to the validity of whether or not a contract is in conflict with EU competition law. The next question that is bound to arise is: will the court, on the ground of para 3.1(8), have jurisdiction over a claim for antitrust damages (provided it has decided that the contract is void)? In this context, it should be outlined that it is well established that under English law a claimant can sue in contract or in tort.[359] If that is so, what will be the basis for jurisdiction in a claim for EU competition law damages brought against a non-EC defendant?

It was pointed out earlier that the action for antitrust damages is tortious in nature and arises solely by reason of the breach of EU competition law, which is regarded as a breach of a statutory duty.[360] Therefore, the service of the claim form out of the jurisdiction in an action for EU competition law damages is not to be allowed on the ground of para 3.1(8), but rather on the ground of para 3.1(9) which is concerned with tort claims.[361] This outcome will be in accord with the result reached with regard to an antitrust damages claim brought by a

355 *Dicey, Morris and Collins* (n 319) p 537.
356 See the discussion above.
357 Hill (n 47) 217. See also Art 4 of the Brussels I Regulation.
358 See section 2.2.7 above.
359 *Matthews* (n 65).
360 See section 1.7 above.
361 See section 3.3.2.1.1 below.

contracting party under the Brussels I Regulation.[362] The difference, however, is that for the purposes of para 3.1, a claim for EU competition law damages made by a contracting party would be regarded as tortious in nature, notwithstanding the existence of the incidental contractual issue.[363] That is a different approach to the one adopted under Brussels I, where the existence of a contractual relationship would not be a barrier to a claim based on tort in England.[364] Thus, torts and contracts are regarded as 'overlapping categories' under the traditional English rules.[365]

Therefore, para 3.1(8) will give to a plaintiff a somewhat limiting effect on his rights against the defendant, as compared with his more extensive rights if he sues in tort. In the former case, a claimant may seek only the nullity of a contract that is alleged to distort competition. A judgment declaring a nullity of an agreement under EU competition law will not always be sufficient to make good the loss caused. If, the claim was framed solely in tort, then the plaintiff would be allowed to overlook the incidental contractual issue and seek antitrust damages and nullity of an agreement that distorts competition. Nonetheless, if the voidness of a contract is the only remedy that is sought by a plaintiff, then he should bring his EU competition law claim on the ground of para 3.1(9).

2.3.2.1.2 EU Competition Law Claims and Multiple Defendants Ground

Horizontal agreements between companies operating at the same level of production or distribution may often involve three or more companies with different market shares. Those agreements may generate efficiency gains. They may, however, also affect trade between Member States.[366] This is particularly true for agreements on production, purchasing or commercialisation. Accordingly, a smaller undertaking may want to bring an EU competition law claim arising out of such agreement against two or three potential defendants. What is the basis for bringing such a claim under English traditional rules?

Paragraph 3.1(3) would be of relevance in EU competition law actions brought against multiple defendants. This rule provides that service of a claim form out of the jurisdiction is permissible with the leave of the court where a claim is made against someone on whom the claim form has been or will be served (otherwise than in reliance on this paragraph). Under the old Ord 11(1)(c), there was a precondition that another defendant must have already been served within or outside the jurisdiction.[367] This is not required for allowing service of a claim form on a defendant out of the jurisdiction on the ground of para 3.1(3).

[362] See section 2.2.2.1.2 above.
[363] See section 3.3.2 below, concerning jurisdiction of English courts on the ground of para 3.1(9).
[364] *Hedley* (n 69); See also *Burke* (n 69).
[365] Hill (n 47) 125.
[366] See Commission (EC) Guidelines on the applicability of Art 81 EC to horizontal cooperation agreements [25]–[26].
[367] *Kuwait Oil Tanker v Al-Bader* [1997] 1 WLR 1410 (CA).

In order to bring an EU competition law claim under the multiple defendants ground, however, the plaintiff needs to satisfy two other cumulative conditions. First, it must be demonstrated that there is a real issue between the claimant and that person: 'A real issue no doubt means what it says, that is, it must be a real and not a fanciful issue.'[368] The requirement for a real issue prevents a plaintiff from bringing a claim against a 'dummy' defendant, who is subject to jurisdiction, solely in order to join a defendant who is outside the jurisdiction.[369] Indeed, that condition is intended to ensure that the claim is brought bona fide against the defendant in the jurisdiction, and not merely in order to bring in the foreign defendant as a necessary or proper party.[370]

Secondly, a safeguard for the second defendant is provided by the requirement that this person is a necessary and proper party to the action against the first defendant. In determining whether a defendant is a necessary and proper party the courts are very much influenced by English procedural rules on joinder of parties. The Court of Appeal in *United Film Distribution v Chhabria*[371] answered the question of who is a 'necessary or proper party' to the claim in light of the joint venture agreement. In this case the court identified the persons who may be joined, in general terms, by looking at CPR 19.2(2). It was held that where claims against a number of defendants arise out of the same series of transactions and involve common questions of fact, each defendant is to be regarded as a necessary or proper party for the purposes of para 3.1(3).[372] It seems that the same test will apply in cases where a smaller undertaking wants to bring an EU competition law claim arising out of multi-party agreements on production, purchasing or commercialisation, which may give rise to EU competition law concerns.

Thus, it seems that multiple defendants ground will be useful with regard to EU competition law claims brought against two or three potential defendants, who may, for example, be parties to a joint venture agreement.

2.3.2.1.3 EU Competition Law Claims and Injunction Grounds

Paragraph 3.1(2) provides that service of a claim form out of the jurisdiction is permissible with the leave of the court where 'a claim is made for an injunction ordering the defendant to do or refrain from doing an act within the jurisdiction.' To come within the sub-rule, the injunction sought has to be part of the substantive relief to which the claimant's cause of action entitles him.[373] Moreover, where a claimant applies to the court for an injunction against a foreign defendant the application for

[368] *Booth v Phillips* [2004] EWHC 1437; [2004] WLR 3292 (Comm).

[369] Fawcett (n 196). See also: *Multinational Gas* [1983] Ch 258 (CA); JJ Fawcett, 'Jurisdiction over Foreign Companies' (1984) 100 *LQR* 17.

[370] *Konamaneni v Rolls-Royce* [2001] EWHC Ch 470; [2002] 1 All ER 979 (ChD) [44].

[371] *United Film Distribution v Chhabria* [2001] EWCA Civ 416; [2001] 2 All ER (Comm) 865 (CA).

[372] Ibid [38]–[42].

[373] *Siskina v Distos* [1979] AC 210 (HL) 256 (Lord Diplock). See also *Rosler v Hilbery* [1925] Ch 250 (CA); K Lipstein, 'Conflict of laws—jurisdiction—Mareva injunction as basis for sevice abroad—R.S.C., Ord 11, r. 1 (1) (i)' (1978) 37 *CLJ* 241.

an injunction 'cannot stand on its own. It is dependent upon there being a pre-existing cause of action against the defendant.'[374] Thus, the claimant must be able to bring a substantive claim within one of the other grounds of para 3.1.

Paragraph 3.1(2) could be relevant, for example, in an EU competition law claim made by a contracting party against an undertaking that is infringing EU competition law. Accordingly, an injunction may be sought to restrain a defendant from imposing significantly different terms in relation to the supply of a particular product to buyers whether as regards price quantity, credit terms or otherwise. Thus, it seems that para 3.1(2) is wide enough to cover a claim based on substantive EU competition law, when it is made for an injunction to restrain the defendants from committing future breaches of the statutory duty not to infringe EU competition law for example, by selling a product at an inflated price or selling tied products in England.[375]

However, according to Lord Diplock, the High Court would be entitled to grant an interlocutory injunction only if it had to enforce a plaintiff's right by a final judgment.[376] This has been followed in *Mercedes Benz*,[377] which appears to indicate that a freezing order could not be issued under para 3.1(2).[378] Notwithstanding, it has been argued that:

> [T]he reformulation of the rule now appearing as Ground 2 has removed such limitation, and that court may grant permission to serve a claim form out of jurisdiction if a claim is made for an injunction even if not in relation to substantive rights, so reversing the effect of *Mercedes Benz*.[379]

In any case, even if *Siskina* and *Mercedes Benz* are still regarded as good authorities, their effects have been minimised by s 25(3) of the 1982 Act, which gave the High Court wider power to grant interim relief with regard to proceedings taking place abroad.[380] Thus, a freezing order could be certainly issued if the claim was based on para 3.1(5).[381]

More specifically, para 3.1(5) would allow permission for a service out to be given where the claim is made for an interim remedy under s 25 of the Civil Jurisdiction and Judgments Act 1982. Section 25(1) and (3) of the 1982 Act entitles the High Court to grant interim relief in aid of legal proceedings in other countries, regardless of where the proceedings are pursued and whether the proceedings are in the scope of the Brussels I Regulation. Accordingly, the 'High Court has the power to grant an interim relief in aid of substantive proceedings

[374] *Siskina* (n 373). See also Hill (n 47) 331.

[375] See *Cheshire, North & Fawcett* (n 15) 374.

[376] *Siskina* (n 373) 256 (Lord Diplock). It should be noted though that Lord Diplock's opinion was made in the context of the old RSC Ord 11 r 1(1)(b).

[377] *Mercedes Benz v Leiduck* [1996] 1 AC 284 (PC).

[378] Ibid. See also: *Cheshire, North & Fawcett* (n 15) 374.

[379] See Briggs and Rees (n 44) 498.

[380] *Dicey, Morris and Collins* (n 319) 375; *Cheshire, North & Fawcett* (n 15) 378; Hill (n 47) 331. See also CPR PD 6B para 3.1(5).

[381] *Cheshire, North & Fawcett* (n 15) 374 and 378.

elsewhere of whatever kind and wherever taking place.'[382] It should be outlined though that at the centre of the powers conferred by para 3.1(2) is a proposed action which will decide upon and give effect to rights.[383] Therefore, para 3.1(5) appears to have broader scope than para 3.1(2).

It can be concluded that the injunction grounds would have a role to play and would be particularly useful in some EU competition law claims. For example, in such claims, a contracting party may ask inter alia for an injunction restraining the defendants from selling a given product to the plaintiff at an inflated price that has been agreed by the defendant and his competitors in an agreement contrary to EU competition law.

2.3.2.2 The Claim must have Reasonable Prospects of Success

According to Collins J (as he then was), the answer to the question whether there will be 'reasonable prospects of success' under CPR 6.21(1)(b), which is now CPR 6.37(1)(b), is not likely to differ from that under the old RSC Ord 11.[384] Accordingly, the plaintiff will have to establish that there is 'a substantial question of fact or law or both, arising on the facts disclosed by the affidavits, which the plaintiff *bona fide* desires to try.'[385] This is a lesser standard of proof than the 'good arguable case' standard,[386] which requires a higher standard of probability of winning and is applicable when the plaintiff tries to establish that the ground of para 3.1 is satisfied.[387] As a result, when considering the merits of the plaintiff's claim, the lesser standard of 'reasonable prospects for success' is to be applied. However, in some case, in order to establish that a particular ground is satisfied, it may be necessary to go into the merits of the case with regard to certain grounds of para 3.1.[388] Should the merits of the claim be gone into again when establishing that the claim has reasonable prospects of success? It has been submitted that the answer to this question would vary depending on the ground on which an EU competition law claim is based.[389] Thus, the relevant standards of proof need to be examined with regard to the grounds of para 3.1 that will be commonly used by a contracting party who wants to bring an EU competition law claim:

[382] *Credit Suisse* (n 311) 825 (Millett LJ). See also the Civil Jurisdiction and Judgments Act 1982 (Interim Relief) Order 1997 (SI 1997/302); *Dicey, Morris and Collins* (n 319) 374–375. Before 1982, the court could not have granted interlocutory relief when the substantive proceedings were taking place abroad: See *Siskina* (n 373). See also section 2.2.7 above.

[383] *Mercedes Benz* (n 377) 302.

[384] *Opthalmic Innovations (UK) v Opthalmic Innovations (USA)* [2004] EWHC 2948 (ChD); [2005] ILPr 10 [39].

[385] *Seaconsar v Bank Markazi* [1994] 1 AC 438 (CA) 452.

[386] '[A] good arguable case reflects that … one side has a much better argument on the material available.' *Canada Trust v Stolzenberg (No 2)* [1998] 1 WLR 547 (CA) 556. See more: *Cheshire, North & Fawcett* (n 15) 397–99; Briggs and Rees (n 44) 525–26.

[387] *Seaconsar* (n 385) 454.

[388] See Fawcett and Torremans (n 1) 101; *Cheshire, North & Fawcett* (n 15) 398.

[389] See more: *Cheshire, North & Fawcett* (n 15) 398.

Contract grounds. The position with regard to para 3.1(8) will depend on the standard of proof under para 3.1(6), which seems to be quite complex,[390] because the plaintiff must demonstrate that if the contract was found to exist, it would comply with the conditions set out in para 3.1(6). Under para 3.1(6)(a), the plaintiff has to establish a 'good arguable case' that if there had been a contract, then such a contract would have been made within the jurisdiction. In order to come within sub-paragraph (b), (c) or (d), the plaintiff must establish a 'good arguable case' that if the relevant contract had not been void as being in conflict with EU competition law, then it would satisfy the terms of these sub-paragraphs. But, once that is done, a separate issue arises as to the merits of the plaintiff's claim for a declaration that the contract is in breach of EU competition law and thus void.[391] It seems that the lesser burden will fall on the plaintiff with regard to this.[392]

Multiple defendants ground. Paragraph 3.1(3) lays down several requirements that need to be satisfied by a private antitrust plaintiff who wants to serve a claim form out of jurisdiction. First, a claimant needs to establish that there is a 'real issue' to be tried in relation to the first defendant. This is a merits threshold test.[393] Its rationale is to ensure that the claim against the first defendant is bona fide and is not merely brought in order to obtain jurisdiction over the foreign defendant.[394] Secondly, the claimant must also establish that there is a good arguable case that the second defendant, who is out of the jurisdiction, is a necessary or proper party.[395] In this context, the court would be required to identify the common questions of law and fact which arise in the EU competition law claim against the first and second defendant, who is a necessary or proper party.[396] Once that is done, the merits will then be gone into in order to determine whether the allegation that a contract is in breach of Arts 101 and 102 TFEU and thus void under EU competition law does merit consideration at a trial (or alternatively does raise real issues, which the plaintiff may reasonably ask the court to try).[397]

Injunction grounds. It seems that no review into the merits would be necessary for an EU competition law claim, in order to come within the terms of para 3.1(2) and para 3.1(5). In such a claim, the 'court … is not called upon to try the action or express the premature opinion on its merits',[398] and where there are conflicting

390 *Seaconsar* (n 385) 454–55. See also: *Cheshire, North & Fawcett* (n 15) 397.

391 See *Cheshire, North & Fawcett* (n 15) 397.

392 *Cf Seaconsar* (n 385) 454–55. See also *DR Insurance v Central National Insurance* [1996] 1 Lloyd's Rep 74 (QBD (Comm)) 80.

393 *De Molestina v Ponton* [2002] 1 Lloyd's Rep 271 [3.7].

394 *Konamaneni* (n 370) [44]. See more *Cheshire, North & Fawcett* (n 15) 375.

395 *Carvill America Inc RK v Camperdown UK Ltd* [2005] EWCA Civ 645; [2005] 2 Lloyd's Rep 457 [45]. See more *Cheshire, North & Fawcett* (n 15) 376–77.

396 See *Barings v Coopers & Lybrand* [1997] ILPr 12 (ChD) [32] aff'd *Barings v Coopers & Lybrand* [1997] ILPr 576 (CA) 585. See also: *Chhabria* (n 371).

397 Compare *Barings* (ChD) (n 396) [32]. See *Cheshire, North & Fawcett* (n 15) 398.

398 *Bradley Lomas Electrolok Ltd and Another v Colt Ventilation East Asia Pte Ltd and Others* [2000] 1 SLR 673; [1999] SGCA 89 [17] (Court of Appeal, Singapore).

statements as to material facts, any such opinion must necessarily be based on insufficient materials.[399] Once the terms of para 3.1(2) and para 3.1(5) have been satisfied, then the court should go into the merits in order to determine as to whether the claim has reasonable prospects of success.[400] In this context, the court should assess whether the claim for an injunction is 'well founded as a matter of arguable fact and law.'[401]

It may be briefly concluded that the question of whether there is 'reasonable prospects of success' under CPR 6.37(1)(b) (which replaced the old CPR 6.21(1)) is not likely to differ from that under RSC Ord 11. Besides the complexity arising from different standards of proof with regard to the relevant grounds of para 3.1, it seems that establishing that there are reasonable prospects for success would not raise any particular problems in competition claims seeking declaration that the contract is in conflict with Arts 101 and 102 TFEU and thus void under EU competition law.

2.3.2.3 The Exercise of Discretion

Jurisdiction based on a service of a claim form out of jurisdiction is a discretionary form of jurisdiction. The courts may, rather than must, allow service of a claim form out of the jurisdiction. As already outlined, party to a contract that runs against EU competition law may seek a declaration that such an anti-competitive contract is void on the ground of para 3.1(8). Accordingly, the criteria for exercising discretion with regard to EU competition law will be briefly examined below.

The criterion for the exercise of discretion on whether service of a claim form out of jurisdiction should be permitted is that of *forum conveniens.*[402] The circumstances specified under the different grounds of para 3.1 are of great variety, and those circumstances would affect the court's willingness to exercise the discretion in favour of allowing service out of the jurisdiction.[403] The burden of proof is on the plaintiff to show that England is an appropriate forum for trial and that it is clearly so.[404] The same factors of appropriateness, such as those of convenience of expense, the applicable law, the place where the parties reside

[399] *Chenische Fabrik Vormals Sandoz v Badische Anilin und Soda Fabricks* [1904] 90 LT 733 (HL) 735 (Lord Davey). It has been submitted by Fawcett and Torremans that '[Lord Davey's] view has been accepted implicitly by the House of Lords in the *Seaconsar* case [(n 385) 455]'. See Fawcett and Torremans (n 1) 102.

[400] *Cheshire, North & Fawcett* (n 15) 398.

[401] Briggs and Rees (n 44) 498.

[402] *Spiliada* (n 325). PB Carter, 'Private International Law—Decisions of British Courts during 1985–1986' (1986) 57 *British Yearbook of International Law* 429; JG Collier, 'Staying of action and forum non conveniens. English law goes Scotch' (1987) *CLJ* 33.

[403] *Spiliada* (n 325) 481.

[404] Ibid. See also JJ Fawcett, 'Trial in England or Abroad: The underlying policy considerations' (1989) 9 *OJLS* 205; A Briggs, 'Forum non conveniens—the last word?' (1987) *Llolyd's Maritime and Commercial Law Quarterly* 1.

or carry on business, will apply to contract-based EU competition law cases as to any other dispute.[405] There may well be additional connecting factors, which are special to EU competition law claims. One such factor may be the territory over which an infringing agreement was implemented. If goods were sold at an inflated price by a manufacturer's subsidiary to a distributor in England, then this may be seen as an important factor that would result in granting leave for service out of jurisdiction. This could be strengthened by the unique public interest in the enforcement of EU competition law.[406] A court from outside the EU will not be able to seek a preliminary reference from the Court of Justice[407] or to assistance from the Commission.[408] Having said that, some of the connecting factors in regard to the grounds that would be relevant in competition cases will be examined below:

The contract grounds. As already mentioned, para 3.1(8) refers specifically to para 3.1(6). As a result, the criteria for the exercise of discretion should be deduced from the criteria relevant for para 3.1(6). It seems that in antitrust cases, the fact that EU competition law would apply to the contract as being mandatory and prevailing the principle of party autonomy might be a significant factor for service out of the jurisdiction.[409] This can be justified by the fact that Arts 101 and 102 TFEU are fundamental for the functioning of the internal market within the EU and as such are forming part of the English public policy.[410] The primary question in an EU competition claim seeking nullity of a contract is the effect of this contract as a matter of European and English public policy. That is a question that could not be answered correctly by a non-EU judge.[411] This fact will be of very great importance for the exercise of discretion under para 3.1(6)(c) in cases where EU competition law is at stake (ie cases where an allegedly anti-competitive agreement has been implemented within the EU[412]).

If the parties have agreed on a trial in England, the discretion usually would be exercised in favour of holding the parties to their commitment.[413] There would have to be very strong reasons not to allow service out of the jurisdiction under para 3.1(6)(d). On the other hand, the mere fact that the contract was concluded in England has not been regarded as a critical factor

405 See more: section 3.3.2.3 below.
406 See more: chs 5 and 6 below.
407 See Art 267 TFEU (ex Art 234 TEC).
408 See Art 15 of Regulation 1/2003.
409 See ch 5 and section 2.3.2.1.1 above.
410 See more: chs 5 and 6 below.
411 See *du Pont* (n 353) 595; *Mitsubishi Corp v Aristidis I Alafouzos* [1988] 1 Lloyd's Rep 191 (QBD Comm) 196. See also *BP Exploration* (n 298); *Cheshire, North & Fawcett* (n 15) 401.
412 *Wood Pulp* cartel case (n 345) [16].
413 *Unterweser Reederei v Zapata* [1968] 2 Lloyd's Rep 158 (CA); *Citi-March v Neptune Orient Lines* [1997] 1 Lloyd's Rep 72 (QBD (Comm)).

in determination of appropriate forum.[414] Although, in a case that comes within the para 3.1(6)(a), the fact the allegedly anti-competitive contract is concluded in England could not in itself constitute much of a connection with England, it is difficult, to imagine EU competition law claims where para 3.1(6)(a) would be the only available ground of jurisdiction. Indeed, in such normally English law (Arts 101 and/or 102 TFEU) will be at stake which, as already noted, would be a strong factor for the exercise of discretion on the ground of para 3.1(6)(c).

The multi-defendant ground. Permission for service of a claim form out of the jurisdiction in cases where jurisdiction is based on the multi-defendant ground may not be easily given in cases where there is no territorial connection between a claim and the jurisdiction of English courts.[415] This would clearly be so in cases where an allegedly anti-competitive agreement has not been implemented in England. Nevertheless, as already mentioned,[416] in a recent joint venture case[417] permission to serve out was given, since claims arise out of the same facts, transactions and arrangements. The latter test would be easily satisfied in EU competition law claim arising out of a joint venture agreement, especially when implemented in England. The need to consolidate proceedings in England may be another very strong argument for exercising discretion in favour of allowing service of a claim form out of jurisdiction.[418] This is would certainly be an important factor that is to be considered in EU competition law cases.

The injunction grounds. In cases where the jurisdiction is based on the injunction grounds, one important consideration is that a plaintiff seeks to restrain a foreign defendant from committing breach of EU competition law in England. In cases where jurisdiction is based on the injunction grounds, important considerations could be whether a foreign court would have be unable or unwilling to grant the relief sought and whether 'the English court is the only avenue for recourse.'[419] In this context, an English court could consider whether there is any link between the subject matter of the injunction sought and the jurisdiction of the English court,[420] so that the sought injunction can be effectively enforced in England.

414 *Bank of Baroda* (n 342) 95.
415 *Multinational Gas* (n 369).
416 See section 2.3.2.1.2 above.
417 *Chhabria* (n 371).
418 *Petroleo Brasiliero SA v Mellitus Shipping Inc (The Baltic Flame)* [2001] EWCA Civ 418, [2001] 2 Lloyd's Rep 203 (CA) [21]–[22]. See more *Cheshire, North & Fawcett* (n 15) 377.
419 *Channel Tunnel Group Ltd v Balfour Beatty Construction Ltd* [1993] AC 334 (HL) 368 (Lord Mustill).
420 Analogy can be made with the application of Art 31 from Brussels I by the Court of Justice in *Van Uden* (n 305) [40] and the English High Court in *SanDisk* (n 153).

2.4 Some Conclusions

It has been shown above that as a result of the decentralised enforcement of EU competition law, the English courts must deal with complex jurisdictional issues with regard to antitrust claims brought by contracting parties. In this context, an important issue which needs to be addressed at EU level is whether the court, which has jurisdiction to apply civil sanctions of nullity to contractual relationship, will also have jurisdiction to hear the antitrust damages claim. The current law suggests that if jurisdiction is based on the contract ground of the Brussels I Regulation, the court cannot go forward and award damages after it has been determined that the contract is void. Although, there are good reasons to suggest that EU competition law damages should be regarded as covered by Art 5(1) of Brussels I, this is far from certain. Moreover, it seems clear that under Brussels I, certain plaintiffs cannot overlook the existence of a contract and base a claim solely on breach of statutory duty by framing it solely in tort.

In addition, Art 5(1) of Brussels I is not well suited to deal with private antitrust claims brought by contracting parties. There is some uncertainty over the question how distribution contracts will be classified for jurisdictional purposes. There are good arguments for suggesting that those contracts should be classified as 'provision of services', which will ultimately result in more certainty for contracting parties who decide to bring EU competition law claims. On the other hand, jurisdiction with regard to technology transfer agreements will be allocated on a case-by-case basis, which is an unsatisfactory solution that may give rise to uncertainties for a plaintiff who wants to bring an antitrust claim. Indeed, the plaintiff will often have to follow the defendant and bring his EU competition law claim at the court of the defendant's domicile.

Under English traditional rules, a claim for EU competition law damages made by a contracting party would be regarded as tortious despite the existence of the incidental contractual issue. Such a claim may be brought under the tort ground of para 3.1, but not on the basis of the contract grounds. Nevertheless, on the ground of para 3.1(8) the plaintiff would be allowed to seek a declaration that a contract is invalidated by EU competition law. Thus, it may be that the plaintiff who sues in a contract will have a somewhat limiting effect on his rights against the defendant as compared with his more extensive rights if he sues in tort. However, if the voidness of a contract, which is in conflict with EU competition law, is the only remedy that is sought by a plaintiff then he may well ask for service of a claim form out of the jurisdiction on the ground of para 3.1(8). The discretion will be easily satisfied in cases where the agreement that allegedly distorts competition was implemented in England. This can be strengthened by the fact that application of EU competition law will raise an argument in relation to English public policy, and that is not an issue that is capable of fair resolution in any foreign court.

3

Jurisdiction in Tort-Based EU Competition Law Claims

3.1 Introduction

As already indicated,[1] an antitrust claim brought by a third party, or even by a contracting party after the parties' agreement was invalidated under EU competition law, is to be characterised as tortious in nature for jurisdictional purposes. Moreover, under the English traditional rules a claim for EU competition law damages made by a contracting party would be regarded as tortious despite the existence of an incidental contractual issue as to the validity of the contract under EU competition law. This clearly indicates the importance of the tort heads under the Brussels I Regulation and para 3.1 of CPR PD 6B for the purposes of allocating jurisdiction in EU competition law claims.

Furthermore, in a case where two or more companies took part in a cartel (upheld the cartel prices, and so caused loss), each infringing entity could be regarded as a tortfeasor.[2] In other words, each undertaking that implemented the cartel so as to cause losses may be found liable for damages for breach of EU competition rules. As a result, there will be not only standard cases, where a single plaintiff brings an EU competition law claim for damages against a single defendant, but also a number of multi-plaintiff and multi-defendant cases, involving groups of companies. This is due to the fact that different persons or companies may be affected by an anti-competitive agreement or conduct.

The purpose of this chapter is to clarify the basis for jurisdiction with regard to tortious EU competition law claims. Accordingly, first, the bases for jurisdiction will be examined with regard to such claims brought under the Brussels I Regulation. Secondly, the questions of jurisdiction will be highlighted with regard to EU competition law tort-based claims brought on the basis of traditional English rules.

[1] See ch 1, section 1.7 above.
[2] See *Provimi v Aventis Animal Nutrition* [2003] EWHC 961 (Comm); [2003] ECC 29 [38].

3.2 Jurisdiction under the Brussels I Regulation

This section will open with a brief review of the Brussels I Regulation's provisions, which would be relevant in tort based EU competition claims. After that, Arts 5(3) and 6(1) of Brussels I and their application with regard to EU competition law cases will be examined.

3.2.1 Rules Allocating Jurisdiction in Tort-Based EU Competition Law Claims

As already mentioned, there is no special provision dealing solely with an action for a breach of EU competition rules, but a number of bases of jurisdiction of general application are available for use in such cases.

Clearly, Art 2 of Brussels I can apply in tort based EU competition law claims, so each company that is infringing Art 101 TFEU may be sued in the courts of the Member State, where they are domiciled. There are two major advantages to the plaintiff in using Art 2 of Brussels I with regard to EU competition law claims. First, it can be used to consolidate in one Member State a number of claims arising out of infringements of EU competition rules that are committed in different states. Thus, for example, a plaintiff can sue in England an English-domiciled defendant following his anti-competitive conduct in Germany, France and Italy. That is based on the assumption that it is the same 'undertaking' responsible for each infringement.[3] Secondly, when jurisdiction is based on Art 2 of Brussels I, there is no need to go into the merits of the case at the jurisdictional stage of the proceedings.[4] At the same time, however, there are some disadvantages in bringing a claim under Art 2 of Brussels I. As already mentioned,[5] the major disadvantage stems from the fact that the plaintiff will have to follow the defendant to the Member State of his domicile. The court there may not be well placed to hear and determine an EU competition law claim which affected the market in the plaintiff's home state. In addition, it would be very common for a plaintiff to wish to bring an EU competition law claim against two or more defendants, domiciled in different states. If, as is natural, the plaintiff wishes to sue all the defendants together in a single action in one Member State, resort will have to be made to other provisions in Brussels I.[6]

[3] The important role that Art 2 plays in centralising litigation has been acknowledged by AG Darmon. See Case C-68/93 *Shevill v Presse Alliance* [1995] ECR I-415 [79] (AG Darmon).

[4] On the contrary, under Art 5(3) the plaintiff must establish a 'good arguable case' in the sense that there is a serious question which calls for trial for its proper determination. See *Molnlycke AB v Procter & Gamble Ltd (No 4)* [1992] 1 WLR 1112 (CA) 1120.

[5] See ch 2, section 2.1.1 above.

[6] See Art 6(1) of the Brussels I Regulation.

Article 2 of Brussels I does not give rise to any specific difficulties in competition cases, so the analysis below will only be concerned with the special jurisdictional rules. As already mentioned, those rules give a plaintiff an alternative forum, where he may sue a defendant. Such other provisions that would be relevant in EU competition law based on tortious claims are Art 5(3), which confers special jurisdiction 'in matters relating to tort, delict or quasi-delict on the courts for the place where the harmful event occurred or may occur', and Art 6(1), which as already mentioned, may be of relevance in EU competition law contract and tort-based claims brought against two or three potential defendants. In this section, Arts 5(3) and 6(1) and their application with regard to EU competition will be discussed in detail below. First, however, it should be stressed that both provisions are based on the existence of a particularly close relationship between a dispute and the court, which may be called to hear and determine the issue.[7]

3.2.2 Article 5(3) and its Application to Tort-Based EU Competition Law Claims

The expression 'matters relating to tort' used by Art 5(3) is not to be interpreted solely by reference to national law and must be regarded as an autonomous concept, which needs to be construed by reference to the objectives of Brussels I.[8] It has been held by the Court of Justice that this concept 'covers all actions which seek to establish the liability of a defendant and which are not related to a "contract" within the meaning of Article 5(1).'[9] But is an action for a breach of EU competition law within that concept? How will jurisdiction be allocated in tort-based EU competition law claims?

3.2.2.1 EU Competition Law Claims and the Scope of Art 5(3)

In an action for obtaining leave to serve a claim form on a defendant out of the jurisdiction at common law, the English court has accepted that an EU competition law place where indirect economic loss to tclaim is tortious in nature.[10] Certainly, the same characterisation will be made under the Brussels I Regulation with regard to an antitrust claim brought by a third party or by a contracting party if there is no dispute over the invalidity of the contract. There can be no real doubt that a claim for a breach of EU competition law falls within the tort

[7] Case 12/76 *Tessili v Dunlop* [1976] ECR 1473; Case C-220/88 *Dumez France and Tracoba v Hessische Landesbank (Helaba)* [1990] ECR I-49 [79]–[80]. See also: Recital (12) of the Brussels I Regulation.

[8] Case 189/97 *Kalfelis v Schroder* [1988] ECR 5565; Case C 51/97 *Réunion Européenne v Spliethoff's Bevrachtingskantoor* [1998] ECR I-6511.

[9] *Kalfelis* (n 8) 5585.

[10] *Camera Care v Victor Hasselbland* [1986] ECC 373 (CA) [25]–[27]. See also: *Garden Cottage Foods v Milk Marketing Board* [1984] AC 130 (HL).

head of the Brussels Regulation.[11] That has been accepted without discussion by the English High Court in *Provimi*[12] and *SanDisk*.[13]

But will the jurisdiction of the English court be affected, if a defendant denies that there is a breach of EU competition law? The review of the relevant Court of Justice case law indicates that the fact that a defendant contests the factors constituting the alleged tort does not deprive a national court of its jurisdiction under Art 5(3) of Brussels I.[14] If the trial takes place in England, however, the denial of a breach of EU competition law would raise the question of whether such a denial should be treated as being merely a denial of liability under the threshold requirement,[15] or as a denial of the terms of Art 5(3) of Brussels I.[16] In the *Grupo Torras* case,[17] the defendant denied that there was any conspiracy, which would justify proceedings under Art 5(3) of Brussels I. Nevertheless, it was held that there was a serious case for arguing that there was such a conspiracy.[18] If a similar approach is followed with regard to antitrust claims, then a denial of the existence of the elements constituting the breach of EU competition law cannot deprive the court of its jurisdiction under Art 5(3) of Brussels I. In other words, a denial of a breach of EU competition law is to be regarded as a denial of liability, rather than as a denial of the terms of Art 5(3) of Brussels I.

Finally, it must be considered whether an action to prevent possible future breaches of EU competition law would also fall within Art 5(3) of Brussels I. It would not be uncommon for a plaintiff to seek protection against a threatened breach of EU competition law. Actions for threatened wrongs are covered by the words 'or may occur' in Art 5(3) of the Regulation, which were added to the provision of the Brussels Convention. Accordingly, the tort head of Brussels I is intended to confer jurisdiction on the courts in respect of impending or threatened torts. It is now well established that the application of Art 5(3) of Brussels I is not conditional on the actual occurrence of damage.[19] In view of that, it is beyond doubt that Art 5(3) of Brussels I can be used by the plaintiff to prevent a threatened breach of EU competition rules.

[11] JJ Fawcett and P Torremans, *Intellectual Property in Private International Law* (OUP, Oxford, 1998) 423; See also: J Fitchen, 'Allocating jurisdiction in private competition law claims within the EU' (2006) 13 *Maastricht Journal of European and Comparative Law* 381; C Withers, 'Jurisdiction and applicable law in antitrust tort claims' (2002) *Journal of Business Law* 250, 260.

[12] *Provimi* (n 2).

[13] *SanDisk Corp v Koninklijke Philips Electronics NV* [2007] EWHC 332 (Ch); [2007] Bus LR 705.

[14] *Shevill* (n 3) [111] (AG Darmon). See in relation to the existence of a contract: Case C-38/81 *Effer v Kantner* [1982] ECR 825; *Tesam Distribution v Schuh Mode Team* [1990] ILPr 149 [23] (CA).

[15] As already mentioned, with Art 5 there is threshold requirement, which the plaintiff has to satisfy before the plaintiff is subjected to jurisdiction. See ch 2, section 2.1.1 above.

[16] See *Seaconsar v Bank Markazi* [1994] 1 AC 438 (CA) 454. See also Fawcett and Torremans (n 11) 151.

[17] *Grupo Torras v Al-Sabah (No 1)* [1995] 1 Lloyd's Rep 374 (Comm).

[18] Ibid 450 (Mance J). Compare: *Tesam* (n 14) 154.

[19] Case C-167/00 *Verein fur Konsumenteninformation v Karl Heinz Henkel* [2002] ECR I-8111[48]; Case C-18/02 *Danmarks Rederiforening v LO Landsorganisationen I Sverige* [2004] ILPr 197 [27].

It follows from the foregoing considerations that Art 5(3) of Brussels I covers not only applications for a declaration that the defendant has committed a breach of statutory duty 'not to distort competition', but also EU competition law claims for damages. Moreover, Art 5(3) confers jurisdiction in an action seeking to prevent future breaches of EU competition law. Having clarified the scope of Art 5(3) with regard to EU competition law claims, it remains to be seen how Art 5(3) of Brussels I will apply in such claims.

3.2.2.2 The Place where the Harmful Event Occurred with regard to EU Competition Law Claims

There might well be competition cases where the defendant acts in one place and the claimant suffers injury in another. If an alleged illicit agreement was concluded in France and then implemented in England, is the place of harmful event in France or England? Under Art 5(3) of Brussels I, the court at the place where harmful event occurred is an appropriate forum for deciding a tortious claim. This is so on grounds of proximity, the efficacious conduct of proceedings and ease of taking evidence.[20] But, how will the expression 'place where the harmful event occurred' be defined with regard to cross-border EU competition law claims?

The place of the harmful event has been interpreted by the Court of Justice to encompass both the place of the event giving rise to the damage and the place where the damage occurred.[21] The wide interpretation of Art 5(3) of Brussels I is explained with two important considerations. First, the expression 'place where the damage occurred' was added as an alternative, because in a significant number of cases, the place of event giving rise to the damage would be the same as the place of the defendant's domicile.[22] Secondly, the special jurisdiction is justified on the basis of a particularly close connecting factor between a dispute and the court, which may be called to hear it with a view to the efficacious conduct of the proceedings. Both the place of the event giving rise to the damage and the place where the damage occurred can constitute a significant connecting factor.[23] There is no reason to suggest that a more restrictive interpretation would apply in EU competition law cases. The same definition should be applicable to claims where the damage is physical or pecuniary.[24]

Therefore, it seems that as far as the jurisdiction of Member State courts in a tort-based competition law cases is concerned, the place of the event giving rise to

[20] See to that effect: Case C-21/76 *Handelskwekerij Bier v Mines de Potasse D'Alsace* [1976] ECR 1735 [11] and [17]; *Dumez* (n 7) [17]; *Shevill* (n 3) [19]; Case C-364/93 *Marinari v Lloyds Bank* [1995] ECR I-2719 [10]; *Henkel* (n 19) [46].

[21] *Bier* (n 20).

[22] Ibid [20].

[23] Ibid [21].

[24] *Shevill* (n 3) [23] and [33]. See also JJ Fawcett and JM Carruthers, *Cheshire, North & Fawcett Private International Law* (14th edn, OUP, Oxford, 2008) 253. Compare *Shevill* (n 3) 425–26 (AG Darmon).

damages and the place where the damage occurred would be relevant connecting factors. However, it has been submitted that:

> The [*Bier* rule] works well enough where one is dealing with physical damage to person or property. It works less well where one is dealing with damage to the personality of the victim. It works least well where the consequence of the harmful event takes the form of pure financial loss rather than damage, that is to say, financial depletion which is neither proceeded nor caused nor accompanied by any obvious impact on physical things or on personality.[25]

What is the nature of damage or loss suffered by a private antitrust claimant? The damage in most competition law cases will be financial or economic which would result from an EU competition law infringement.[26] It has been put forward that it is for the Member States to define damage for the purposes of a private antitrust law claim.[27] That is justified by the submission that the damage for that purpose is not defined by EU law and the Court of Justice. However, the Court of Justice recently held that a person, who is injured by a contract or by conduct liable to restrict or distort competition, must be able to seek compensation for actual loss and loss of profit plus interest.[28] Although, this ruling does not fully and explicitly clarify the issue, one may go a step further and suggest that such loss would constitute the damage for the purposes of an EU competition law claim brought under Art 5(3) of Brussels I. It seems that a private antitrust claimant would normally seek financial compensation for damage caused by anti-competitive practice or conduct that is liable to distort competition.[29] Hence, a causal connexion between the loss as defined in *Manfredi* and the infringement of Arts 101 and 102 TFEU which gives rise to that antitrust damage must be considered by the court when determining jurisdiction under the tort head of the Brussels I Regulation.[30] Could the difficulties in applying *Bier* in competition law case, where damages is financial, be tackled if the antitrust damages were regarded as occurring in the Member State/s where the market is affected? Where is the place of the event giving rise to damage for the purposes of allocating jurisdiction in EU competition law claims under Art 5(3)?

[25] A Briggs and P Rees, *Civil Jurisdiction and Judgments* (Informa, London, 2009) 267–68.

[26] Withers (n 11) 255; A Komninos, *EC Private Antitrust Enforcement: Decentralised Application of EC Competition Law by National Courts* (Hart Publishing, Oxford, 2008) 210–11. In England, the breach of EU competition law is classified as a breach of statutory duty (ie strict liability), so that there would be recovery for pure economic loss. See more: KM Stanton, 'New forms of the tort of breach of statutory duty' (2004) 120 *LQR* 324, 332, 333 and 334. See also: Oxera and multi-jurisdictional team of lawyers led by Dr A Komninos, *Quantifying antitrust damages: towards non-binding guidance for courts—Study prepared for the European Commission* http://ec.europa.eu/competition/antitrust/actionsdamages/quantification_study.pdf.

[27] Fitchen (n 11) 396.

[28] Joined Cases C-295/04–C-298/04 *Manfredi v Lloyd Adriaticco* [2006] 5 CMLR 17 [100].

[29] *Manfredi* (n 28) 267.

[30] Compare: *Bier* (n 20) [16].

3.2.2.2.1 The Place of the Event Giving Rise to EU Competition Law Damage

It has been submitted by Fawcett and Torremans that in an Art 101 TFEU case, the place of the event giving rise to damage for the purposes of allocating jurisdiction will be where the prohibited agreement was entered into, or the prohibited decision made or the prohibited concerted practices adopted.[31] There is no case law cited to support such a deduction. In a different context, however, the Court of Justice has held that an infringement of Art 101 TFEU consists of conduct made up of two elements: the formation of the 'agreement, decision or concerted practice', and implementation thereof.[32] If the event giving rise to antitrust damage was regarded as covering both—the place where the prohibited agreement was entered into (the prohibited decision made or the prohibited concerted practices adopted) and the place where that agreement was implemented (if different), then a plaintiff would be entitled to sue the defendant in any of those courts. Both places could be classified as the place of the event giving rise to the damage.

Allowing a claimant to bring an EU competition law claim at the court at the place where the prohibited agreement was entered would be in accord with what has been decided by the Court of Justice[33] with regard to defamation, and by the English court[34] in respect of negligent misstatement. In these judgments, it was held that the place where the harmful event giving rise to the damage occurred is where the misstatement (defamation) is made, rather than where it was received. However, proving where an anti-competitive agreement was entered into (or a prohibited concerted practice adopted) may not be easy to identify. Such agreements or concerted practices are meant to be secret and, sometime, involve series of meetings which may take place worldwide through long periods of time; the agreement may be oral and may amount to a simple understanding.[35] Nevertheless, the *Domicrest* approach was followed by the English High Court in *SanDisk* in the context of an alleged infringement of Art 102 TFEU.[36] In this case, the plaintiff alleged that the defendant had abused its dominant position in the market for the licensing of patents essential to the production, sale and importation into the EEA of MP3 players and MP3-compliant memory cards. SanDisk relied on a written offer of a licence made by the defendant in respect of the European Economic Area (EEA). Commentators have submitted that in claims based on Art 102 TFEU, the place of the event giving rise to the damage is where the actions constituting an abuse of a dominant position took place.[37]

[31] Fawcett and Torremans (n 11) 424.

[32] Joined cases 89, 104, 114, 117 and 125 to 129/85 *Ashlstrom Osakeyhtio v Commission ('Wood Pulp')* [1988] ECR 5193 [16].

[33] *Shevill* (n 3) [24] and [33].

[34] *Domicrest v Swiss Bank* [1999] QB 548 (QBD).

[35] J Faull and A Nikpay, *The EC Law of Competition* (2nd edn, OUP, Oxford, 2007) 195–217.

[36] *SanDisk* (n 13) [22].

[37] Fawcett and Torremans (n 11) 424. See also the judgment of 3 October 1978 rendered by the Oberlandesgericht Hamm 9 U 228/77, cited by Fawcett and Torremans (n 11) 424.

The *SanDisk* judgment, however, shows that the questions concerning the identity of the act which constitutes an abuse of a dominant position and where it should be located are very important. In *SanDisk*, the court assumed that the offer of an objectionable licence was to be characterised as an abuse of a dominant position.[38] In this context, the court held that it had no substantive jurisdiction to hear and determine the dispute as the event which constituted the abuse of dominant position did not take place in England. It was held that 'a tortious act is not complete until a statement has been both made and understood, the relevant location is that where the statement was made.'[39] In doing that, the court ignored the fact that 'claims for breach of articles [101 and 102 TFEU] do raise considerations distinct from those of the other tortious claims.'[40]

In particular, EU competition law rules are fundamental legal provisions that enjoy a public policy character in each Member State, which are directly derived from the Treaty on Functioning of the European Union, so that the scope of application of Arts 101 and 102 TFEU is not limited to the territory of a single Member State. Accordingly, the questions 'what is the act which constitutes an abuse of a dominant position?' and 'where does it take place?' should have been addressed under EU law. It seems to this author that Art 102 TFEU should be interpreted as suggesting that an offer of a licence would be regarded as prima facie evidence that the defendant's conduct could constitute abuse of dominant position, but not as an abuse in itself.[41] An offer of a licence should not be regarded in itself as abuse because a conduct would only be regarded as being caught by Art 102 TFEU if it harms competition within a particular market.[42] In other words, the tortious act is not completed until the abusive practice is implanted within a particular market. Thus, for jurisdictional purposes, such abuse takes place in the Member State/s where the licence was implemented (or intended to be implemented), so that the market in this country would be affected (or among those affected) by the abuse.

If the *SanDisk* approach were followed, in many cases a private antitrust claimant would have to follow the defendant and bring his claim before the court at the place of the defendant's domicile that may, sometimes, have little connection with the place where the competition was or is restricted. This would be particularly so in cases, where an offer with abusive terms is made in one Member State, but the abusive conduct has the effect of foreclosing the market and distorting the competition in another state (or in cases where the agreement is concluded in one Member State but implemented in another state). This would be a rather unfortunate outcome.[43]

38 *SanDisk* (n 13) [22].
39 Ibid.
40 *ET Plus v Welter* [2005] EWHC 2115 (Comm), [2006] 1 Lloyd's Rep 251 [51].
41 Compare: *SanDisk* (n 13) [22].
42 Faull and Nikpay (n 35) 354 and 360–62.
43 Withers (n 11) 260–61.

A better and more appropriate result was reached in *Provimi*. Here, the pleading alleged that the defendants agreed to 'implement' the cartels, with the consequence that the claimant was prevented from buying the products at a price that was lower than the cartel prices.[44] The High Court clearly stated that the 'action in "implementing" the cartel could cause the loss that the claimants allege.'[45] Unfortunately, the issue of the place where the harmful event occurred was not specifically addressed in *Provimi*.

In the light of the *Shevill* case,[46] however, it seems to be much harder to adopt a special definition of the place of the harmful event for EU competition law claims. That hurdle can be tackled, if the place where the anti-competitive agreement or the abusive practice is implemented (or likely to be implemented) is regarded as the place of the event giving rise to damage for the purposes of allocating jurisdiction in EU competition law claims under Art 5(3) of Brussels I. That would be in accord with the ruling in the *Wood Pulp* case, where the Court of Justice stressed that: '[t]he decisive factor is ... the place where [the agreement] is implemented.'[47] It is clear that adopting the place where the anti-competitive agreement or the abusive practice is implemented as the place of the event giving rise to damage for the purposes of allocating jurisdiction in EU competition law claims will better serve the purposes of Art 5(3) of Brussels I.[48] The market in such a Member State would often be affected (or among those affected), which would provide for proximity, the efficacious conduct of proceedings and ease of taking evidence in EU competition cases.[49] It is beyond doubt that the court within the Member State where the agreement or abusive practice is implemented would have a close connection with the substance of the dispute and would be well placed to deal with the case.[50] However, it is not quite clear whether this approach will be adopted with regard to EU competition law claims. It is a fairly safe prediction that the issue of the place of the event giving rise to damage for the purposes of EU competition law claims will be raised during the course of any litigation following the Commission's incentives that are meant to encourage such claims within the EU.

3.2.2.2.2 The Place Where the EU Competition Law Damage Occurred or may Occur

As already clarified, the damage for the purposes of a private EU competition claim is financial,[51] so there would be potential jurisdictional problems in cases

44 See *Provimi* (n 2) [17].
45 Ibid [38].
46 See *Shevill* (n 3) [23].
47 *Wood Pulp* (n 32) [16].
48 Withers (n 11) 261.
49 Commission Notice on cooperation within the Network of Competition Authorities [2004] OJ C-101/43 [8].
50 Ibid.
51 See section 3.2.2.2 above. See more: Withers (n 11) 255; Komninos (n 26) 210–11 See also: *Shevill* (n 3) [29] which determines the place where the damage occurs for the purposes of an international defamation through the press.

arising out of anti-competitive behaviour.[52] More specifically, the localisation of the defendant's wrongful act and the claimant's damage would be difficult, since they may occur in more than one state. In view of that, before focusing on peculiarities of an action for a breach of competition law, the rulings that have emerged from cases involving economic loss will be briefly examined.

In the *Dumez* case,[53] the Court of Justice held that the place where the damage occurred can be understood only as 'the place where the casual event, giving rise to delictual or quasi-delictual liability, directly produced the harmful effects in relation to the person who is the immediate victim.'[54] In the subsequent case of *Marinari,*[55] the Court of Justice held that Art 5(3) of Brussels I cannot be construed so extensively as to encompass any place where the adverse consequences can be felt of an event which has already caused damage actually arising elsewhere.

The question where the damage occurred with regard to an EU competition law claim has been discussed by commentators and national courts as well. It is submitted that damage caused by a breach of competition law rules occurs in the place where the direct economic loss to the plaintiff was sustained, for example where business is lost.[56] According to Hill, the place where the defendant's conduct produces a decline in the claimant's sales is to be regarded as relevant in competition cases.[57] Similarly, in a case where a claimant alleges to have suffered loss arising out of the purchase of goods or services at an inflated price, the relevant direct and immediate damage must be regarded as having occurred at the place where the goods or services are purchased.[58]

It has been submitted that limiting jurisdiction to the courts at the place where the harmful event directly produced its effects may be difficult to reconcile with the principle of 'effectiveness' of EU competition law.[59] It has been suggested that if the profitability of a subsidiary is affected by an illegal cartel, then the foreign parent company that entered the market by setting up a subsidiary is also affected. Rightly so, but then it seems that the direct financial loss would have occurred within the Member State where the market was affected, as that is the place where the subsidiary is set to operate. Moreover, it is difficult to see how the principle of effectiveness could justify a broader interpretation of direct damage for the purposes of an EU competition law claim. A narrow interpretation of 'direct economic loss' for the purposes of allocating jurisdiction under Art 5(3) will not

52 See Withers (n 11); See also BJ Rodger, 'Competition law in a Scottish forum' (2003) *Juridical Review* 247.

53 See *Dumez* (n 7).

54 Ibid [20].

55 See *Marinari* (n 20) [14]–[15].

56 Fawcett and Torremans (n 11) 424.

57 J Hill, *International Commercial Disputes in English Courts* (3rd edn, Hart Publishing, Oxford, 2005) 154. See also: *Cheshire, North & Fawcett* (n 24) 256.

58 For example in *Provimi* (n 2), the court stated that if the tort alleged is established, then the 'harmful event', that is the damage to the claimants, occurred or may have occurred in England in a case when the claimant concerned is domiciled in England.

59 Fitchen (n 11) 398.

render practically impossible or excessively difficult the exercise of rights of EU law.[60] Indeed, the EU competition law claim could be brought at the place where the anti-competitive agreement or practice had been implemented (being the event giving rise to the damage) and/or where the subsidiary suffered antitrust damage (being the place where the damage occurred). Alternatively, jurisdiction may be based on Art 2 of Brussels I. Furthermore, one should not forget that Art 5 of Brussels I is an exception to the general rule under Art 2 and as such should be narrowly interpreted. In addition, one may argue that the principle of effectiveness would be of relevance where the conflict is between a Member State's domestic legal system and the EU rules governing the matter,[61] but could not be used to remedy the Court of Justice interpretation of an EU legal instrument.

Problems, however, could arise if a court, when interpretating the place where the damage occurred, did not take account of where the direct antitrust damage occurs. This is what happened in *SanDisk*. In this case, the court refused to accept jurisdiction, as the UK subsidiaries of SanDisk did not derive a trading income from the sale of MP3 players.[62] However, it seems arguable that the fact that SanDisk UK Ltd was set up to provide services to support the marketing, distribution and promotion of MP3 players meant that its business within the English market could have been directly affected by the abusive conduct. Nevertheless, the court held that:

> '... SanDisk is in fact trading in the UK with a very substantial proportion of the available market in MP3 players. On the assumption that it is legitimate to consider the damage arising in these unusual circumstances to arise from any general inhibition on trade within England and Wales caused by the fact that SanDisk does not enjoy a lawful licence, I cannot see where the damage accrues other than to SanDisk in Delaware.[63]

A more appropriate outcome could have been reached if the court identified where the direct damage occurs in competition cases. In this context, the court could have enquired whether the market in England was affected by the (allegedly) abusive conduct and whether the sales and/or business were lost in England. Notwithstanding that a financial or economic loss occurred in Delaware, the direct antitrust damage, which occurs in the country where the market is affected, should have been regarded as the 'jurisdictionally significant element.'[64]

Nevertheless, it is believed that the problems would not persist in view of the fact that a European definition of the 'country where the damage occurs or threatens to occur' is provided by the Rome II Regulation on the law applicable

[60] This is the condition for an application of the effectiveness principle. *Manfredi* (n 28) [62]. See also Case C-261/95 *Palmisani* [1995] ECR I-4025 [27]; Case C-453/99 *Courage and Crehan* [2001] ECR I-6297 [29]. For the principle of effectiveness, see more: F Becker, 'Application of Community law by Member States' public authorities: between autonomy and effectiveness' (2007) 44 CMLR 1035.

[61] Ibid.

[62] *SanDisk* (n 13) [26].

[63] *SanDisk* (n 13) [30].

[64] See the analysis of *Shevill* (n 3) as made by Briggs and Rees (n 25) 274. See also Recitals 16 and 17 and Arts 2 and 4(1) of Rome II.

to non-contractual obligations. According to this, the place where the damage occurs or threatens to occur in EU competition law cases is the country where the market is, or is likely to be, affected.[65] The Rome II Regulation provides for such a definition for the applicable law purposes. If this was so for the choice of law purposes, it is difficult to see why it should be different for jurisdictional purposes. Such a deduction seems logical, given that the EU legislator has clearly indicated that provisions of Rome II should be consistent with Brussels I.[66] Indeed, given the fact that Rome II proceeds also on the basis of direct damage,[67] one may go a step further and argue that direct damage for jurisdictional purposes occurs in the country were the market is affected.[68]

Thus, the place where the market is affected, being the place where the damage occurs in EU competition law cases, should be regarded as an important connecting factor for the purposes of allocating jurisdiction under Art 5(3) of Brussels I. Using the place where the market is affected as such a connecting factor would confer jurisdiction to courts that in many cases are well placed to hear and determine an EU competition law claim and have a close connection with the substance of the claim and the relevant market. This can be illustrated by a brief review of the Member States' case law with regard to competition law cases as well as unfair competitive practices which are regarded by commentators[69] to be applicable by analogy for the purposes of allocating jurisdiction in EU competition law cases.

Foreclosing the market. The Tribunale di Monza in *Candy v Schell and Stoecker Reinshangen*[70] discussed the question in respect of tortious claims based on the defendant's anti-competitive conduct. The plaintiff, an Italian company, alleged that the German undertaking engaged in unfair competitive practices in Germany, with the intention of eliminating the Italian company from the German market. It was held that, for the purpose of Art 5(3) of Brussels I, the place where the damage occurred meant the place where the harmful circumstances came about, and that this consisted in the loss of business sustained by the plaintiff as a result of the unlawful conduct of the defendants. Since the damage had occurred in Germany, the Italian court had no jurisdiction. Thus the court rejected a definition of the place where indirect economic loss to the plaintiff was sustained.[71]

65 See Art 6(3) and Recitals 21–23 of the Rome II Regulation.

66 Recital 7 of the Rome II Regulation.

67 As regards Rome II, see Arts 2 and 4(1) together with Recitals 16 and 17 see more: J Fitchen, 'Choice of Law in international claims based on restrictions of competition: Art 6(3) of the Rome II Regulation' (2009) 5 *Journal of Private International Law* 337, 367. See also T Petch, 'The Rome II Regulation: an update' (2006) 21 *Journal of International Banking Law and Regulation* 449, 454. As regards Brussels I, see *Marinari* (n 20) and *Dumez* (n 7), discussed above.

68 See Recital 21 of Rome II and Arts 4(1) and 6(3) of Rome II.

69 See Fawcett and Torremans (n 11) 424–25; Hill (n 57) 154.

70 *Candy v Schell and Stoecker Reinshangen* Foro pad 1979, I, 225 cited and discussed in Fawcett and Torremans (n 11) 424–25.

71 Fawcett and Torremans (n 11) 425.

The place where the direct economic loss is sustained with regard to unfair competition claims was further clarified in *Saba Molnlycke v Procter & Gamble.*[72] In this case, an unfair competition action was brought for compensation for the decline in sales of the plaintiff's products in Norway. It was said by the Court that the 'harmful event' in Art 5(3) of Brussels I can refer to damage caused by unfair competition. Thus, the court held that the damage (decline in sales) has been sustained in Norway. This was so in relation to causation as well as to the effect. The court went further, stating that in a case of unfair competition, the decline in sales is to be considered as the immediate and directly damaging effect.[73] Although this was decided in the context of unfair competitive practices claims, it seems that similar consideration should apply in EU competition law claims.[74] Such a solution would be in accord with the fact that for private international law purposes, the place where the damage occurs in EU competition law cases would be the country where the market is affected. This would confer jurisdiction on a court that is well placed to hear and determine an EU competition law claim, because such a court would have a close connection with the substance of the dispute and indeed the relevant market. Such an outcome would certainly be better than the one adopted in *SanDisk*, and would be in accord with the purpose of Art 5(3) of Brussels I.

Agreement to inflate prices. In an Art 101 TFEU case, the place where the damage occurred would be the place or places where the illicit agreement to collude is implemented.[75] That would confer jurisdiction to courts at that place or those places. Therefore, the place where the infringing entity upholds the cartel prices and (arguably) causes loss seems to be the appropriate solution in an EU competition law claim that arises out of anti-competitive agreements, which inflate prices. This would mean that a private antitrust claimant should have a choice where to bring his EU competition law. This would be especially so in follow-on actions. However, there are some specific difficulties that may arise with regard to the other EU competition law claims brought before the court where damages occurred.

3.2.2.2.3 Territorial Scope of a Member State's Court Jurisdiction under Art 5(3) of Brussels I

In a recent EU competition law case, the English High Court held that '[t]he jurisdiction based upon the place of the harmful event will be international, while the jurisdiction based upon the relevant harm will be restricted to England and

[72] *Saba Molnlycke AS v Procter & Gamble Scandinavia Inc* [1997] ILPr 704 [12] (Agder Lagmannsrett (Court of Appeal), Tonsberg).

[73] Ibid.

[74] See also: Hill (n 57) 154.

[75] *Provimi* (n 2).

Wales.'[76] In other words, the courts in a Member State where damage was felt would only have jurisdiction for the damage that occurred in that state. This may be a problem, as it is well established that 'the cause of action [for EU competition law damages] is a mixture of E[U] law and English "domestic" law'.[77] First as a matter of EU law it must be shown that an entity is in breach of Arts 101 and 102 TFEU.[78] What is a breach of Arts 101 and 102 TFEU for those purposes should be determined with regard to European law.[79] Secondly, it must be shown, as a matter of English law, that an entity, which is recognised by English law, is liable in damages to this particular claimant for that breach.[80]

If *Shevill* were followed in EU competition law cases, potential jurisdictional problems would be bound to arise in stand-alone antitrust actions brought before the courts in the Member State where the damage occurred, as in such a scenario the territorial scope of the court's jurisdiction would be limited, which might affect the court's ability to determine whether there is a breach of EU competition law. The problems are to do with the fact that '[t]he requirement that there must be an effect on trade "between Member States" implies that there must be an impact on cross-border economic activity involving at least two Member States.'[81] Does a Member State court with territorial jurisdiction limited to England and Wales have jurisdiction to determine whether there is a breach of EU competition law in view of the fact that the scope of application of Arts 101 and 102 TFEU is not limited to the territory of a single Member State?

In other words, the question is whether it would be ultra vires for a court, whose jurisdiction is limited to the infringement that occurred within its territory, to rule on whether there has been an impact on at least two Member States. One answer to this question might be that the territorial scope of the court's jurisdiction is limited. This can be strengthened by reading Arts 101 and 102 TFEU, together with Art 1 of Regulation 1/2003, which states that:

1. Agreements, decisions and concerted practices caught by Article 101(1) of the Treaty which do not satisfy the conditions of Article 101(3) of the Treaty shall be prohibited, no prior decision to that effect being required
2. Agreements, decisions and concerted practices caught by Article 101(1) of the Treaty which satisfy the conditions of Article 101(3) of the Treaty shall not be prohibited, no prior decision to that effect being required.
3. The abuse of a dominant position referred to in Article 102 of the Treaty shall be prohibited, no prior decision to that effect being required.

[76] *SanDisk* (n 13) [25]. See also: *Shevill* (n 3).

[77] *Provimi* (n 2) [25].

[78] *Provimi* (n 2) [25].

[79] According to the ECJ, a breach of Art 101 TFEU, for example, consists of conduct made up by two elements: (a) formation of the agreement, decision or concerted practice; (b) implementation thereof; eg *Wood Pulp* (n 32) [16].

[80] *Provimi* (n 2) [25].

[81] Guidelines on the effect on trade concept contained in Articles 81 and 82 of the Treaty [2004] OJ C101/81 [21].

The latter provision leaves no doubt that a Member State court's findings of an antitrust infringement could not be limited to the territory of a single Member State. Thus, one may argue that a Member State court could not have jurisdiction to determine whether there is a breach of EU competition law as its scope of application is not limited to the territory of a single Member State. This may be problematic in view of the fact that Rome II regards the place where the damage occurs as an important connecting factor with regard to the issue of the applicable law.

A better solution would be provided if the question whether there is an EU competition law infringement within the territory of the court's jurisdiction were regarded as a preliminary issue for deciding on whether the plaintiff suffered antitrust damages in England and Wales. If that were the case, then the court at the place of damage arising out of a breach of EU competition law would only have jurisdiction to deal with the damages that occurred there. However, as already mentioned, Art 1 of Regulation 1/2003 seems to suggest that the effect of a Member State's judgment finding an EU competition law infringement, which is the basis for awarding antitrust damages at the place of the relevant harm, could not be limited to the territory of a single Member State. It seems that the issue whether there is an Art 101 and/or 102 TFEU infringement would be *res judicata*. In fact, such a decision would be easily recognised and enforced under Brussels I.

The foregoing problems would not arise if EU competition law cases were not treated like defamation cases and the *Shevill* case were not followed in Art 101 and 102 TFEU cases. Indeed, the *Shevill* case could be easily distinguished as the basis for an action for defamatory damages is English 'domestic' law, whereas an action for EU antitrust damages is based on EU law that needs to be applied consistently in the EU.

3.2.2.2.4 Multiple Locality EU Competition Law Cases

Breaches of EU competition law committed in different Member States may also arise. The application of Art 5(3) of Brussels I in the context of proceedings for restrictions on ability of competitors to compete may also give rise to jurisdictional problems.[82] For example, the plaintiff's ability to enter into or compete as a player within a relevant market can have effect in a number of places. A plaintiff's ability to compete in England, France and Germany may have been affected if a cartel agreement was implemented within the markets in those countries. As a result, a claimant may find a basis of jurisdiction in each or any of those Member States because the defendant's conduct may have produced a decline in the plaintiff's sales there. Although it is not clear whether the fact that a court of a Member State has jurisdiction under Art 5(3) of Brussels I on the basis of an act of breach committed within that state also means that it has jurisdiction in relation to the separate acts of breach committed in other Member States, Art 5(3) of Brussels I may be a useful basis for jurisdiction in follow-on collective redress actions. For

[82] Withers (n 11) 261–62.

example, if those affected by a cross-border EU competition law infringement wanted to sue in their home state for the local effects of an antitrust breach, then the basis for each of their collective redress actions would be Art 5(3) of Brussels I. This clearly suggests that if each foreign class decided to rely on special jurisdiction rules and sue at their home state for the local effects of the breach, the parallel collective redress proceedings would be an issue.[83] This gives rise to the question: can a plaintiff consolidate the litigation in one Member State, basing jurisdiction on Art 5(3) of Brussels I?

As already outlined, it may be argued that there is a territorial limitation on jurisdiction and the Member State's court, whose jurisdiction is based on a local breach, will have jurisdiction only in respect of acts committed within the territory of that state.[84] There is support for this in *Shevill* (a defamation case) and *SanDisk* (a competition law case). In *SanDisk*, the court held that jurisdiction based upon the relevant harm is restricted to the damage which occurred in England and Wales.[85] As a result, there is little doubt that it would be advantageous for the plaintiff to bring his entire claim before the courts of the defendant's domicile under Art 2[86] or before the courts of the place of the harmful event under Art 5(3) of Brussels. If that were so, then, in some cases, the antitrust claimant would lose the advantage of bringing his claim before the courts at his home state (being the place where the damage occurred) and would have to bring the claim in another Member State. This would be a rather unfortunate result, especially in the light of the Commission's objective to encourage private EU competition law claims.

The EU competition law concept of 'undertaking', read together with Art 6(1)[87] of the Brussels I Regulation could be helpful for remedying that result in antitrust cases, where the claims are brought against the subsidiaries of a cartel member or a dominant company. Accordingly, in the *Provimi* case, the High Court accepted jurisdiction in an EU competition law claim brought by a German plaintiff even though the damage was suffered in Germany rather than in England. The High Court ruled that it had jurisdiction to hear claims by European companies against the UK subsidiary of a cartel member, even if no contractual relationship existed between the two parties, if the subsidiary helped operate the cartel in the UK.[88] It was crucial for this ruling that under the EU competition law, subsidiary and parent company were part of the 'same economic unit'[89] and that by implementing the cartel, the subsidiary could have caused the loss alleged by the claimants.

[83] The issue of parallel antitrust proceedings is dealt with in ch 4 below.

[84] J Basedow, 'Jurisdiction and choice of law in the private enforcement of EC competition law' in J Basedow (ed), *Private Enforcement of EC Competition Law* (Kluwer Law International, The Hague, 2007) 229, 234.

[85] *SanDisk* (n 13) [25]. See also: *Shevill* (n 3) [30 and 33].

[86] Withers (n 11) 262.

[87] The Art 6(1) and its application in tort-based EC competition law claims is examined in section 3.2.3 below.

[88] *Provimi* (n 2) [38].

[89] Case C-73/95 *Viho v Commission* [1996] ECR I-5457.

Consequently, by using the concept of 'undertaking' and Art 6(1) of Brussels I, the English court decided to have jurisdiction in relation to acts of breach committed abroad. Accordingly, a better result will be reached in such claims if they are based on Art 6(1) of Brussels I. The implications of the multiple defendants head for EU competition claims will be discussed in detail below. For the purposes of this sub-section it should be noted that the ruling in the *Provimi* case could clear the way for victims of an international cartel to bring an action for damages in the UK, even where such damages were suffered in a different Member State, on the basis that the English company, as part of an 'undertaking' that implemented a pan-European cartel, contributed to those damages.

In spite of that, the decision in the *Provimi* case has been criticised for 'translat[ing] the widest application of the undertaking concept into a parasitic private law claim.'[90] One should, however, differentiate between a plaintiff who brings a parasitic private claim and a plaintiff in a private EU competition law claim, who takes a legitimate advantage from bringing his claim in one Member State rather than another.[91] Moreover, adopting the EU competition law concept of 'undertaking' with regard to such claims makes it much easier for claimants to centralise litigation in their preferred jurisdiction, thereby avoiding multiple lawsuits in a number of Member States.

3.2.3 Article 6(1) and its Application to Tort-based EU Competition Law Claims

As already mentioned[92], Art 6(1) of Brussels I is specifically designed for multi-defendant cases. Article 6(1) will be particularly relevant for a plaintiff who wishes to pursue an EU competition law claim against two defendants who are joint tortfeasors as being parties to an agreement in breach of EU competition law. For example, if one of those companies is domiciled in England and the other one is a French-domiciled company, then the plaintiff would be able to proceed against both companies in either England or France. Accordingly, Art 6(1) of Brussels I could be a relevant basis of jurisdiction in respect of EU competition law claims, given the fact that multi-defendant litigation is quite common in such claims.

The importance of Art 6(1) of Brussels I as a basis for jurisdiction in cases where the market in several countries is affected can be further strengthened by Art 6(3)(b) of Rome II, which suggests that in such cases the *lex fori* would determine the assessment of damages (including the availability of punitive antitrust damages). The relevance of Art 6(1) in follow-on tort-based antitrust claims can be illustrated by the English High Court judgment in the *Provimi* case. In this case a follow-on action for EU competition law damages was brought by the plaintiffs

[90] Fitchen (n 11) 395.
[91] See more ch 5, section 5.3.2.3 below.
[92] See more ch 2, section 2.2.4 above.

against the UK subsidiaries of cartel members. The claimants also sued two Swiss companies, relying on Art 6(1) of the Lugano Convention.[93] The English High Court held that the claimants could invoke Art 6(1) of the Lugano Convention and sue those defendants in the English courts.[94] It was mentioned that if the *Provimi* case were followed it would become much easier for claimants to centralise litigation in their preferred jurisdiction, thereby avoiding multiple lawsuits in a number of Member States.

It was already demonstrated[95] that a possibility of irreconcilable judgments, resulting from separate proceedings in EU competition law claims, would be enough to meet the requirements of Art 6(1) of Brussels I. The requirements will be easily satisfied, where practically identical EU competition law actions arising out of the same alleged infringements of EU competition law are brought against various defendants, based on multiple infringements taking place in different Member States. Further, the connection requirement would be clearly met in a situation where the defendants to EU competition law claims are joint tortfeasors. This will be so, when an action is brought against the participants in an illegal cartel. It would not be difficult to show with regard to such claims that all companies who 'implemented' the cartel infringed EU competition law. By taking part in the cartel and upholding the cartel prices each entity would have been contributing to the loss of the plaintiff. Based on that it can be argued that the joinder of the defendants may avoid the risk of inconsistent findings of facts in different courts, which will result in irreconcilable judgments against the different members of the same cartel.

To rely on Art 6(1) a plaintiff has to show that there is a 'real issue' as to whether the first defendant committed a breach of statutory duty not to infringe EU competition law. Accordingly, in the *Provimi* case, the High Court concluded that there was a 'real issue' as between the German company and the two English companies.[96] Based on that, it was concluded by the Court that antitrust claims by the German company were not artificial or advanced solely so that the company could take advantage of Art 6(1) of Brussels I and bring proceedings in England against a non-UK domiciled company. Such a deduction would be in accord with what has been decided by the French Cour de Cassation in the context of a recent case[97] concerned with alleged unfair competition conduct where similar considerations had to be considered. It was held that the jurisdiction is justified on the basis of Art 6(1) of Brussels I, where claims against a number of defendants arise out of tort (in the absence of any contractual link); relate to the same facts and

[93] Art 6(1) of the Lugano Convention states: 'A person domiciled in a Contracting State may also be sued[,] where he is one of a number of defendants, in the courts where any one of them is domiciled.'

[94] *Provimi* (n 2) [40]–[48] and [102].

[95] See section 2.2.4 above.

[96] *Provimi* (n 2) [40].

[97] *Hodder-Dargaud v Egmont International Holdings* [2003] ILPr 42 (Cour de Cassation (France)).

have the same objectives and legal basis; and there is no intention on the part of the claimant to deny the defendants natural justice (ie the claim is not parasitic).

Therefore, the requirements of Art 6(1) of Brussels I will be easily satisfied in cases where the defendants are joint tortfeasors or there are various defendants as a result of multiple infringements taking place in different states.

3.2.4 Conclusion

As to the jurisdiction of English courts under the Brussels I Regulation, it can be concluded that Art 5(3) in its current version does not deal particularly well with EU competition law claims. The fact that the doctrine of 'undertaking' for the purposes of Arts 101 and 102 TFEU is different from the concepts of 'persons' for the purposes of establishing jurisdiction seems to suggest that in cases where the market was penetrated by the subsidiary, a private antitrust claimant should rather try to establish jurisdiction under Art 6(1) instead of Art 5(3) of Brussels I. This would be especially so in cases where the market is affected in a number of Member States as the law of the forum may be an important factor once the issue of damages is discussed.[98]

3.3 Jurisdiction under English Traditional Rules

As discussed above, agreements between undertakings restricting competition may take place in markets which are world-wide. In the case of an anti-competitive agreement or concerted practice, the basis for the 'conspiratorial conduct' causing harm in one market may have been agreed between individuals in a distant location.[99] Thus, it is clear that there might well be cases where the defendant is not domiciled within the EU. Based on Art 4 of Brussels I, English traditional rules will be applicable with regard to such claims. In this section, those rules will be examined in respect of tort-based EU competition law claims.

3.3.1 Service of a Claim Form within the Jurisdiction

As already mentioned,[100] the English court has a jurisdiction to entertain a claim *in personam* against a defendant who is present in England and duly served with process there.[101] It should be emphasised that in EU competition law claims,

[98] See Art 6(3)(b) of the Rome II Regulation. See more ch 5.

[99] See also: *Wood Pulp* (n 32).

[100] See ch 2, section 2.3.1 above.

[101] See more: L Collins and others (eds) *Dicey, Morris and Collins on the Conflict of Laws* (14th edn, Sweet & Maxwell, London, 2006) 306; A Zuckerman, 'New provision for service: a great improvement threaten by discretion' (2009) *Civil Justice Quarterly* 1; Briggs and Rees (n 25) 410, 545–56.

the main concern will be the service of a claim form on commercial companies. Depending on the way in which the foreign company is connected for business purposes with the forum, different requirements and jurisdictional rules will be applicable. Section 1139 of the Companies Act 2006 and CPR 6 together with PD 6A are the relevant rules for service of a claim form to a company in England.[102] Accordingly, those rules will be briefly introduced.

Normally, the presence of a corporation in England at the time of service is enough to give the court jurisdiction. There would be no difficulty, if the company is registered in England under the Companies Act.[103] An 'overseas company' (ie a company incorporated outside the UK[104]), which has a branch in England, is required to register certain information with the Registrar of Companies.[105] That includes, inter alia, the names and addresses of all persons resident in Great Britain authorised to accept on the company's behalf service of process in respect of the business of the branch.[106] Accordingly, process may be served on such a person in respect of the carrying on of the business of the branch.[107] If the company fails to provide the required information, the company may be served by the claim form being left at or posted to any 'place of business'[108] 'established'[109] by the company in England.[110] In a case where the circumstances give rise to a basis of jurisdiction both under the Companies Act 2006 and by virtue of the CPR, the claimant is free to choose on which method of service to rely on.[111] The result is that the English court will easily have a basis for jurisdiction in any case where a foreign company has a business presence in England.

How do those rules apply with regard to an EU competition law claim? A common scenario, in competition cases, is where there is a foreign corporate member of a cartel within the jurisdiction. That member implements the cartel agreement either on its own or through subsidiaries established for that purpose. The plaintiff wishes to sue that company in England. Normally, there would be no difficulties in cases, where the defendant himself has implemented the cartel agreement by marketing the product at an inflated price. Difficulties, however,

[102] See JJ Fawcett, 'A new approach to jurisdiction over companies in private international law' (1988) 37 *ICLQ* 645. See also P Rogerson, 'English court's jurisdiction over companies: How important is service of the claim form in England?' (2000) 3 *Company Financial and Insolvency Law Review* 272; Briggs and Rees (n 25) 410, 545–56.

[103] See s 1139 of the Companies Act 2006. See also: *Dicey, Morris and Collins on the Conflict of Laws* (n 101) 350.

[104] Companies Act 2006 s 1044.

[105] Companies Act 2006 s 1046.

[106] Companies Act 2006 s 1139 read together with s 1046 implementing the 11th Company Law Directive 89/666/89.

[107] Companies Act 2006 s 1139(2)(a). See also NE Enonchong, 'Service of process in England on overseas companies and Article 5(5) of the Brussels Convention' (1999) 48 *ICLQ* 921.

[108] *South India Shipping Corporation v Export-Import Bank of Korea* [1985] 1 WLR 585 (CA).

[109] *Re Oriel* [1986] 1 WLR 180 (CA) 184 (Oliver LJ).

[110] Companies Act 2006 s 1139(2)(b). See also: *Rome v Punjab National Bank (No 2)* [1990] 1 All ER 58 (CA).

[111] See CPR 6.3(2). See more: *Cheshire, North & Fawcett* (n 24) 367–68; Briggs and Rees (n 25) 555.

are bound to arise in cases where a defendant has sought to implement the agreement within the English market by setting up a subsidiary or an exclusive distributor that markets the product at an inflated price. A typical example would be that of a manufacturer, who organises subsidiaries in other states or countries to sell and service the manufacturer's products. The subsidiary is not a branch, and so provisions concerning branches cannot be easily transferred. Moreover, it is doubtful whether the foreign defendant can be regarded as having established a place of business in Great Britain when it carries on business here by means of a subsidiary company. This is largely due to the fact that the subsidiary is a separate legal entity and in many cases lacks the authority to act on behalf of the parent company. Thus, the parent–subsidiary relationship could give rise to a complex jurisdictional problem in EU competition cases. It seems that in antitrust claims, economic realities of the parent–subsidiary relationship must be considered.

A good example where the commercial and economic realities were used to override the fact that the foreign parent and its local subsidiary were regarded as separate legal entities for the jurisdictional purposes is the US case of *Bulova Watch v Hattori*.[112] This case presents a classic problem in adjudicating a claim against a multinational corporation using subsidiaries to penetrate the market. In the light of that, it was difficult to see how the parent company would satisfy the New York jurisdictional requirement for doing business within the forum.[113] The court held that '[the] subsidiaries almost by definition are doing for their parent what their parent would otherwise have to do on its own'.[114] Thus, the court allowed jurisdiction against the parent company. Would the same approach be followed by an English court?

The English courts have demonstrated a different approach to the one displayed by the *Bulova* case; normally if a foreign company sets up a subsidiary company in England, there will be no jurisdiction over the parent in most cases.[115] As already mentioned, however, subsidiary and parent company are parts of the same economic unit under the EU competition law concept of 'undertaking'.[116] As a result, EU competition law denies the narrow legalistic approach of whether a subsidiary can bind a parent contractually and adopts the notion of the 'single economic unit'. That notion looks at the economic reality of the relationship between parent and subsidiary and the control that the former has over the latter. Accordingly, acts of subsidiaries are attributed to the parent. As a result, the court has jurisdiction over the parent to the same extent as it would have over the

[112] *Bulova Watch v Hattori* 508 F Supp 1322 (1981).

[113] New York Civil Procedure Law and Practice 301; E Scoles and P Hay, *Conflict of Laws* (West Publishing, St Paul, Minn, 1982) 292 ff and 325 ff.

[114] *Bulova* (n 112) 1342.

[115] JJ Fawcett, 'Jurisdiction and subsidiaries' (1985) *JBL* 16. See also *Adams and others v Cape Industries Plc* [1990] Ch 433 (CA).

[116] See *Provimi* (n 2).

subsidiary.[117] Consequently, the end result of adopting the 'single economic unit' notion is making a foreign parent subject to jurisdiction by virtue of service of a claim form on its English subsidiary. In such cases, the presence of a subsidiary in the forum should be a sufficient basis for jurisdiction over an EU competition law claim. This would allow the English court to accept jurisdiction over antitrust claims brought against a foreign parent company which carries on business in England through a subsidiary.

The wide application of the undertaking concept into a private EU competition law claim has been criticised.[118] Indeed, as already mentioned,[119] the question whether the corporate veil should be lifted may give rise to a considerable debate before English courts.[120] Whilst there are strong arguments suggesting that the corporate veil should be lifted so as to make a parent company liable for the infringement of EU competition law on the English market in view of the fact that the market was penetrated by the subsidiary, it is true that the doctrine of 'undertaking' for the purposes of Arts 101 and 102 TFEU is different from the concept of 'persons',[121] for the purposes of establishing jurisdiction. However, the wider interpretation may be adopted by the English courts in EU antitrust cases. This was indicated by the High Court in the *Provimi* case for the purposes of allocating jurisdiction in EU competition law claims under the Brussels I Regulation. It remains to be seen what approach will be adopted by the Court of Appeal in an appropriate case under the English traditional rules. Although, there are advantages to the plaintiff in serving a claim form within the jurisdiction wherever possible, he will frequently be unable to do so. In such cases, the plaintiff will have to seek the court's permission in order for a claim form to be served out of the jurisdiction.

3.3.2 Service of a Claim Form out of the Jurisdiction

As already outlined,[122] a judge faced with a question of leave to serve proceedings out of jurisdiction has to be satisfied that, first, there is a good arguable case that one of the grounds of para 3.1 of CPR PD 6B (old CPR 6.20) is applicable;[123] secondly, the claim has reasonable prospects for success;[124] thirdly, the discretion should be exercised to allow service of a claim form out of the jurisdiction.[125]

[117] Charles I Wellborn, 'Subsidiary corporations in New York: When is mere ownership enough to establish jurisdiction over the parent' (1973) 22 *Buffalo Law Review* 682, 688. See also Fawcett (n 88) 664.

[118] Fitchen (n 11) 395. See more: section 3.2.2.2.2 above.

[119] See also ch 2, section 2.2.3 above.

[120] *Adams* (n 115).

[121] CPR 2.3.

[122] Section 2.3.2 above.

[123] CPR 6.37(1)(a).

[124] CPR 6.37(1)(b).

[125] *Seaconsar* (n 16) 448 (Lord Goff). See also: CPR 6.37(3).

3.3.2.1 The Grounds of para 3.1 of PD 6B

Four of the grounds under para 3.1 of CPR PD 6B could be relevant in respect of EU competition law claims: the tort ground (para 3.1(9)); the multi-defendant ground (para 3.1(3)); and the injunction grounds (para 3.1(2) and para 3.1(5)). Accordingly, the application of these heads will be examined in the light of EU competition law claims.

3.3.2.1.1 EU Competition Law Claims and Tort Ground

Paragraph 3.1(9) provides that service of a claim form out of the jurisdiction is permissible with the leave of the court, when a claim is made in tort: 'where damage was sustained within the jurisdiction; or damage sustained resulted from an act committed within the jurisdiction.' Although, this ground is phrased in the past tense, and may be interpreted as not covering threatened wrongs, the English High Court has underlined that under the tort ground 'it makes no difference whether or not the damage has occurred or is merely threatened.'[126] Such a result is in line with Art 5(3) of the Brussels I Regulation and with the nature of EU competition law.[127]

It should be emphasised that a two-stage test must be satisfied, if a plaintiff wants to bring an EU competition law claim on the basis of para 3.1(9). First, he must show that the claim is founded on tort. To decide whether or not the action is 'founded on a tort' within the meaning of para 3.1(9), 'the court will apply exclusively English law'.[128] There is little doubt that an antitrust claim is to be regarded as founded on a tort within the wording of para 3.1(9). Moreover, as already outlined,[129] a claim for antitrust damages made by a contracting party would be regarded as tortious, notwithstanding the existence of the incidental contractual issue as to the validity of a contract under EU competition law. A tortious classification of an EU competition claim has been adopted by the English Court of Appeal in a case involving the application of the tort ground of para 3.1.[130] Thus, the first stage would be easily satisfied in respect of an EU competition law claim.

Secondly, the court must be satisfied that either the damage was sustained within the jurisdiction or the damage resulted from an act committed within the jurisdiction. Paragraph 3.1(9) is drafted in a way to ensure that English law is

[126] *Beecham Group v Norton Healthcare* [1997] FSR 81 (Ch D) 97–98; *Bastone & Firminger v Nasima Enterprises (Nigeria)* [1996] CLC 1902 (QBD).

[127] It is not certain though whether the above-cited High Court ruling will be followed with regard to EU competition law claims. Notwithstanding, a plaintiff who wishes to prevent a breach of EU competition law can always use the injunction heads. See section 3.3.2.1.3 below.

[128] *Metall und Rohstoff v Donaldson Lufkin* [1990] 1 QB 391 (CA) 443 (Slade LJ). Arguably, this would not be good law once Rome II Regulation had entered into force. Nevertheless, an EU antitrust claim will certainly be regarded as founded on a tort within the wording of para 3.1(9). Compare Rome II Regulation [22] and [23].

[129] See section 2.3.2.1.1 above.

[130] *Camera Care* (n 10).

consistent with Art 5(3) of the Brussels Regulation.[131] This suggests that case law with regard to Art 5(3) would be considered as of, at least, persuasive authority when the court is considering the second stage of the test.[132] Having said that, the possibilities of establishing jurisdiction under para 3.1(9) will be examined.

3.3.2.1.1.1 Act Committed within the Jurisdiction

The first way in which a plaintiff can obtain leave to serve a claim form outside the jurisdiction is where the tort has been committed in England. In EU competition law claims, the relevant act certainly is the breach of Arts 101 and 102 TFEU. What will be required, therefore, is for such a breach to have been committed in England. There should be evidence of commission of a breach of EU competition law within the jurisdiction. What would constitute such a breach? The question was discussed by the Court of Appeal in the context of the old RSC Ord 11 r 1(1)(h), which required that, in order to obtain leave to serve out of the jurisdiction a writ alleging a tort, the plaintiff must prove that the tort was committed within the jurisdiction.[133] More specifically, in *Camera Care*, the plaintiff brought a follow-on action after the Court of Justice had established that the defendant participated in a concerted practice, aimed at redirecting parallel imports into the UK and at preventing any imports into the UK of the defendants' cameras intended for the plaintiff. The Court of Appeal did not allow service out of the jurisdiction because there was no evidence that the first defendants had committed any act within the jurisdiction in pursuance of the 'concerted practice' or of a conspiracy to injure the plaintiff's business, or any act which could or might amount to a breach of statutory duty.[134] Fox LJ went further to state that:

> The fact that in the European proceedings there was found to be a concerted practice ... to prevent, limit or discourage exports of Hasselblad equipment does not itself provide an indication of a tort in the United Kingdom. All the relevant acts could have been done in Sweden.[135]

If this were followed, then it would make it very difficult for a plaintiff to furnish evidence that a breach of EU competition law has been committed in England. *Provimi*,[136] however, seems to indicate that evidence that there is implementation of an infringing agreement in England would suffice for the purposes of service of a claim form out of jurisdiction under para 3.1(9).[137] Such a result is in line with Art 5(3) of the Brussels I Regulation.

[131] *ABCI v Banque Franco-Tunisienne* [2003] EWCA Civ 205; [2003] 2 Lloyd's Rep 146 (CA) [41]–[43]. Compare: *Bier* (n 20). See more: Briggs and Rees (n 25) 515–16.

[132] Hill (n 57) 218.

[133] *Camera Care* (n 10).

[134] *Camera Care* (n 10) [38] (Sir Roger Ormrod).

[135] *Camera Care* (n 10) [27] (Fox LJ).

[136] *Provimi* (n 2).

[137] *Provimi* (n 2) [23].

It appears that the question where the breach of EU competition law is committed for the purposes of para 3.1(9) raises concerns similar to those discussed in regard to the connecting factor 'place of event giving rise to damages' in the sense of Art 5(3).[138] Accordingly, it would be welcomed if the implementation of the infringing agreement is regarded as the relevant act, for the purposes of service out of jurisdiction under para 3.1(9).[139] It is clear that such a solution would make the English court an appropriate forum, having a closer connection with the substance of the dispute and indeed the relevant market. This will ensure proximity, efficacious conduct of proceedings and ease of taking evidence in competition cases.

What if antitrust damage has resulted from acts in breach of EU competition law committed partly within and partly without the jurisdiction? This will often be the case where an anti-competitive agreement has been implemented in several other countries. In such cases it will be appropriate for the English court to accept jurisdiction over an EU competition law claim, even if not all acts have been committed within the jurisdiction.[140] The English court though would not accept jurisdiction if some relatively minor or insignificant acts have been committed within the jurisdiction[141] and the alleged anticompetitive price-fixing activity is in significant part foreign.[142]

3.3.2.1.1.2 Damage Sustained within the Jurisdiction

The second way in which a plaintiff can obtain leave to serve a claim form outside the jurisdiction is a case where the damage caused by a violation of EU competition law is sustained in England. As already outlined,[143] in EU competition cases the damage will be financial and there may well be cases which involve financial damages incurred in more than one state. It is well established that generally for the purpose of para 3.1(9), the damage caused must be direct rather than indirect.[144] According to the High Court a mere effect on the plaintiff's financial position in England, for example because it is a parent company to a company damaged by a tort abroad, is not sufficient. In the *Beecham* case, the plaintiff claimed that the tortious manufacturing in Slovenia of a pharmaceutical product for importation into the United Kingdom will have the inevitable consequence of causing the claimant direct damage here. The court held that the direct damage was caused by the sale in England of the product by the English importer, not the wrongful interference by the Slovenian manufacturer and supplier, so the case was not covered by para 3.1(9).[145] Although this is not a competition case, it is

[138] See section 3.2.2.2.1 above.
[139] *Provimi* (n 2) [23].
[140] Compare *Provimi* (n 2) and *Metall und Rohstoff* (n 128) 437.
[141] Compare *Camera Care* (n 10).
[142] For a common law approach, see *Empagran v F Hoffmann-LaRoche* 159 L Ed 2d 226 (2004) (Sup Ct (US)). See more, ch 4 below.
[143] See section 3.2.2.2 above.
[144] *Beecham* (n 126) 97–98; *Bastone* (n 126).
[145] *Beecham* (n 126). It was possible though, to bring the case within the multi-defendant head.

likely that a similar approach would be followed with regard to EU competition law claims. Therefore, the antitrust damage would occur within the jurisdiction, if England was the country where the market was affected by an antitrust infringement. In other words, an English court will have jurisdiction in respect of EU antitrust claims if the business is lost or, alternatively, if the decline of sales has incurred in England.[146] Consequently, the damage for the purpose of para 3.1(9) is to be defined in exactly the same way as it is in relation to Art 5(3).[147] This would also be in accordance with the definition of Rome II, which provides that the place where the damage occurs or threatens to occur is the country where the market is, or is likely to be, affected.

For the purposes of para 3.1(9) it is enough that 'some significant damage has been sustained in England'.[148] It would not be necessary for all antitrust damages to have been sustained within the jurisdiction. Accordingly, the fact that some significant damage has been sustained in England would confer jurisdiction on the English court to EU competition law cases involving multiple breaches committed in different jurisdictions. It is not clear, however, whether an English court that has jurisdiction with regard to the damage committed in England would also have jurisdiction in relation to other damage sustained abroad.[149] Jurisdiction based on a service of a claim form out of jurisdiction with the permission of the courts is regarded as being an 'exorbitant' or 'extraordinary',[150] so it should be interpreted restrictively.[151] This may preclude English courts from exercising jurisdiction for a breach committed by the same cartel members abroad. There would be further difficulties when an English court comes to exercise the *forum conveniens* discretion. It would be very hard for the plaintiff to establish that England is a clearly appropriate forum for trial if the substance of the action was concerned with an anti-competitive agreement implemented, or damage sustained, abroad.[152] As a result, it is doubtful whether the ruling of the *Provimi* case would be followed in cases falling within para 3.1(9). Nonetheless, it will be welcomed if the Court of Justice case law with regard to Art 5(3) is regarded by English courts as being of, at least, persuasive authority when they are called upon to interpret para 3.1(9). This can be strengthened by the fact that similar jurisdiction problems are bound to arise with regard to EU competition law claims brought under para 3.1(9) and Art 5(3). Developing similar jurisdiction, EU and traditional, rules with regard to such claims will be in accord with the purpose of

[146] Fawcett and Torremans (n 11) 426; Hill (n 57) 154; *Cheshire, North & Fawcett* (n 24) 256. See also: *Saba Molnlycke* (n 72).

[147] See also: CMV Clarkson and Jonathan Hill, *The Conflict of Laws* (3rd edn, OUP, Oxford, 2006) 94. See also: *ABCI* (n 131) [41]–[43].

[148] *Metall und Rohstoff* (n 128) 437.

[149] Compare: *Provimi* (n 2).

[150] *Spiliada Maritime v Cansulex* [1987] AC 460 (HL) 481 (Lord Goff).

[151] Compare: *Siskina v Distos* [1979] AC 210 (HL).

[152] See ch 4 below.

enhanced private antitrust enforcement in Europe and will make England a more attractive forum for litigating EU competition law claims.

3.3.2.1.2 EU Competition Law Claims and Multiple Defendants Ground

As has been mentioned,[153] where a claim is brought against a person on whom the claim form has been or will be served (the first defendant), permission may be granted to serve process on a person out of the jurisdiction (the second defendant), provided that certain conditions are met.[154] There may well be EU competition law claims where a plaintiff will seek to bring the proceedings against more than one defendant. Typically, the two defendants will be a foreign company and an English company that are parties to an anti-competitive agreement. Paragraph 3.1(3) seems to deal satisfactorily with such a scenario and its requirements will be easily satisfied. Indeed, the English defendant will have been duly served within the jurisdiction and the foreign defendant seems to be a necessary or proper party to that EU competition law action.

As previously submitted,[155] the requirement that there should be a real issue between the claimant and those served, or to be served, within the jurisdiction is intended to ensure that the claim was brought bona fide against a defendant in the jurisdiction, and not merely in order to bring in a foreign defendant as a necessary or a proper party.[156] In EU competition law claims, the 'necessary and proper party' requirement would be easily satisfied, if the claims arise out of the same agreement that is alleged to be in conflict with EU competition law. Thus, other parties to the same agreement may be added if there is an issue as to the validity of the agreement. In these cases it would be desirable to add such a party, so that the court may resolve whether the agreement is in conflict with Arts 101 and/or 102 TFEU. Furthermore, in a claim against a subsidiary implementing a cartel agreement, it would be desirable to add the parent company as a necessary and a proper party, so that the court can resolve all the matters in dispute in proceedings, including the relationship between the parent and the subsidiary. Many EU competition law claims may arise out of the same illicit agreement, and the nature of those claims would be identical. Moreover, such claims will involve common questions of fact and law.[157]

3.3.2.1.3 EU Competition Law Claims and Injunction Grounds

It has also been discussed[158] that under para 3.1(2), service of a claim form out of the jurisdiction is permissible with the leave of the court, where 'an injunction

[153] See ch 2, section 2.3.2.1.2 above.
[154] See para 3.1(3).
[155] See ch 2, section 2.3.2.1.2 above.
[156] CPR 19.2(2) is relevant for identifying who is 'necessary or proper party' for the purposes of para 3.1(3). See more ch 2, section 2.3.2.1.2 above. See also *Konamaneni v Rolls-Royce* [2001] EWHC Ch 470; [2002] 1 All ER 979 (ChD) [44].
[157] See ch 2, section 2.3.2.1.2 above, where multi-defendants head is discussed in more details in regard to contract-linked competition cases.
[158] See ch 2, section 2.3.2.1.3 above. See also ch 2, section 2.2.7 above.

is sought ordering the defendant to do or refrain from doing anything within the jurisdiction (whether or not damages are also claimed in respect of a failure to do or doing of that thing).' Accordingly, a claimant may seek an injunction restraining foreign companies from implementing in England an agreement that is in conflict with EU competition law. Such a claim could be often brought together with a tortious claim for breach of Arts 101 and 102 TFEU on the ground of para 3.1(9). Moreover, as already mentioned in the context of contract-based claims, para 3.1(5) broadens the scope of para 3.1(2) entitling the English court to grant interim relief in aid of legal proceedings in other countries if the claim is made for an interim remedy under s 25 of the 1982 Act. Paragraph 3.1(5) could also be relevant in tort-based competition cases.

Furthermore, the injunction grounds could be useful in the case of threatened wrongs, where a permanent injunction is sought.[159] For example, a claimant can bring an action claiming an injunction restraining a defendant from offering a given product to the claimant at unreasonable conditions which allegedly constitutes an abusive practice in conflict with Art 102 TFEU.

3.3.2.2 The Claim must have Reasonable Prospects of Success

As has been previously submitted,[160] when considering the merits of the plaintiff's claim, the lesser standard of 'reasonable prospects for success' is to be applied.[161] However, in some cases, in order to establish that a particular ground is satisfied, it may be necessary to go into the merits of the case with regard to certain grounds of para 3.1.[162] It was noted earlier[163] that the answer to the question of whether the court should go into the merits of the claim again when establishing that the claim has reasonable prospects of success would vary, depending on the ground on which an EU competition law claim is based.[164] In this sub-section, the relevant standards of proof will be examined with regard to tort-based EU competition law claims.

An important question in the context of para 3.1(9) is whether the claim is founded on an EU competition law infringement which took place in the jurisdiction. It was previously noted that breaches of Arts 101 and/or 102 TFEU are to be categorised as a tort for establishing jurisdiction on the ground of para 3.1(9).[165] In *Viskovice Horni v Korner*,[166] it was submitted that the standard of proof for

[159] Compare *James North & Sons v North Cape Textiles* [1984] 1 WLR 1428 (CA). See *Cheshire, North & Fawcett* (n 24) 374.

[160] See ch 2, section 2.3.2.2 above.

[161] *Seaconsar* (n 16) 452, 454 and 455; *Opthalmic Innovations (UK) v Opthalmic Innovations (USA)* [2004] EWHC 2948 (ChD); [2005] ILPr 10 [39]. See more: *Cheshire, North & Fawcett* (n 24) 397; Briggs and Rees (n 25) 525–26.

[162] See Fawcett and Torremans (n 11) 101; *Cheshire, North & Fawcett* (n 24) 397–99.

[163] Ch 2, section 2.3.2.2 above.

[164] See more: *Cheshire, North & Fawcett* (n 24) 398.

[165] *Camera Care* (n 10) [36].

[166] *Viskovice Horni v Korner* [1951] AC 869 (HL). It seems that in *Seaconsar* (n 16), Lord Goff approved the judgment rendered in *Viskovice Horni* (n 166). See Fawcett and Torremans (n 11) 257.

establishing a tort is a lesser one than that for establishing that the negligence occurred within the jurisdiction.[167] This should apply by analogy to EU competition law claims, because the question of whether an agreement or abusive practice is in conflict with Arts 101 and/or 102 TFEU will be subject to further investigation at a trial. Accordingly, if a service is sought with regard to implementation of a cartel agreement or abusive practice in England that is allegedly illegal, then the court will not be concerned to enter into the question of a breach of EU competition law, 'provided that the affidavits disclose a case which appears to merit consideration at a trial.'[168] In such a claim, however, the English court will require cogent evidence pointing to a strong probability that the EU competition law infringement occurred within the jurisdiction before it will allow service out of the jurisdiction.[169] The higher burden (ie the 'good arguable case' standard) as to the issue whether the breach of Arts 101 and 102 TFEU occurred in England is justified by the fact that this question may never arise at the trial. Moreover, even if it does arise and if it proved that the breach of EU competition law took place in another country, the jurisdiction of an English court that was wrongfully assumed would not be divested.[170] It seems that establishing that a breach of EU competition law has been committed in England can raise issues which go to the merits of the case and, in such circumstances, the standard of proof required of the plaintiff is, presumably, that of a 'good arguable case'.[171]

As regards the multiple defendants ground, as already discussed,[172] first, the claimant needs to establish that there is a 'real issue' to be tried in relation to the first defendant which is a merits threshold test.[173] Secondly, the claimant must also establish that there is a good arguable case that the second defendant, who is out of the jurisdiction, is a necessary or proper party.[174] Then, the merits will be gone into in order as to whether the allegation that there is a breach of Arts 101 and 102 TFEU does merit consideration at a trial (or alternatively does raise real issues, which the plaintiff may reasonably ask the court to try).[175]

It has already been pointed out[176] with regard to injunction grounds that it would not be necessary for the court to go into the merits, expressing a premature opinion, in order to establish that the terms of this ground are met.[177] Once the terms of

[167] *Viskovice Horni* (n 166) 889 (Lord Tucker).

[168] *Viskovice Horni* (n 166) 889 applied by analogy.

[169] Ibid.

[170] Ibid.

[171] *Seaconsar* (n 16). See also *Camera Care* (n 10).

[172] See ch 2, section 2.3.2.1.2 above.

[173] *De Molestina v Ponton* [2002] 1 Lloyd's Rep 271 [3.7].

[174] *Carvill America Incorporated RK v Camperdown UK Ltd* [2005] EWCA Civ 645; [2005] 2 Lloyd's Rep 457 [45]. See more, *Cheshire, North & Fawcett* (n 24) 376–77.

[175] *United Film Distribution v Chhabria* [2001] EWCA Civ 416; [2001] 2 All ER (Comm) 865 (CA) [38]–[42]. See also ch 2, section 2.3.2.1.2 above. See more: *Cheshire, North & Fawcett* (n 24) 397–99.

[176] See ch 2, section 2.3.2.1.3 above.

[177] *Chenische Fabrik Vormals Sandoz v Badische Anilin und Soda Fabricks* [1904] 90 LT 733 (HL) 735 (Lord Davey).

paras 3.1(2) and 3.1(5) have been satisfied, then the court should go into the merits in order to determine whether the claim has reasonable prospects of success.[178]

3.3.2.3 *The Exercise of the Discretion*[179]

As already mentioned,[180] jurisdiction based on service of a claim form out of jurisdiction with the permission of the courts is a discretionary form of jurisdiction and the criterion is that of *forum conveniens.* As a result, 'the basic question facing the court is …: should trial take place in England or abroad?'[181] Here the exercise of the *forum conveniens* discretion will be examined with regard to tort-based EU competition law claims. The exercise of that discretion presupposes that there are at least two alternative forums. An application for leave under CPR 6.36 is made ex parte, which entails full and fair disclosure of all material facts.[182] When exercising this discretion the court needs to identify the forum 'where the case may be tried suitably for the interests of parties and for the ends of justice'.[183] If the answer indicates that the trial should take place in England, then it is proper to allow service of the claim form out of the jurisdiction. The burden of proof is on the plaintiff to show that England is the appropriate forum for trial, and that this is clearly so.[184] Ascertaining which is the appropriate forum involves looking at the connecting factors. The connection that parties have with the alternative forums can be an important connecting factor as well.[185]

When deciding whether a claim form should be served abroad, the court should consider not only factors affecting convenience or expense, but also other factors such as the law governing the relevant transaction.[186] As already mentioned,[187] the primary issue in an EU competition claim relates to European and English public policy. That is a question that could not be answered correctly by a non-EU judge.[188] This fact will be of very great importance for the exercise of discretion under para 3.1(9) in cases where EU competition law is at stake (ie cases where an allegedly anti-competitive agreement has been implemented within the EU[189]).

[178] *Cheshire, North & Fawcett* (n 24) 398. See also: Briggs and Rees (n 25) 498.

[179] See generally: *Cheshire, North & Fawcett* (n 24) 399–412.

[180] See ch 2, section 2.3.2.3 above.

[181] J Fawcett, 'Trial in England or Abroad: The Underlying Policy Considerations' (1989) 9 *OJLS* 205. See CPR 6.37(3).

[182] See *Brinks Mat v Elcombe* [1988] 1 WLR 1350 (CA) 1356–57; *Opthalmic Innovations* (n 161) [45]. See also *Konamaneni* (n 156). Compare: *Beecham* (n 126) 89; see also *BP Exploration (Libya) v Hunt* [1976] 1 WLR 788 (Comm) 798–99.

[183] *Spiliada* (n 150) 482.

[184] CPR 6.37(3). See *Spiliada* (n 150) 481. See also *Konamaneni* (n 156) [175].

[185] Eg *The Abidin Daver* [1984] AC 398 (HL) 409. See more: *Cheshire, North & Fawcett* (n 24) 400.

[186] *Seaconsar* (n 16) 478; See also *Black Clawson International v Papierwerke Waldhof-Aschaffenburg* [1981] 2 Lloyd's Rep 446 (QBD) 457. See also Rome II Regulation.

[187] Ch 2, section 2.3.2.3 above.

[188] See *El du Pont de Nemours v Agnew* [1987] 2 Lloyd's Rep 585 (CA) 595; *Mitsubishi Corp v Aristidis I Alafouzos* [1988] 1 Lloyd's Rep 191 (QBD (Comm)) 196. See also: *BP Exploration* (n 182); *Cheshire, North & Fawcett* (n 24) 401.

[189] *Wood Pulp* (n 32) [16].

The English court nonetheless would not be allowed to be drawn into making comparisons between the two different systems of administering justice used by the English courts and the alternative forums.[190] If substantial injustice will be done abroad, however, the court may well exercise its discretion in favour of allowing service out of the jurisdiction. In such a case the strong connections with the alternative forum abroad could be neglected.[191] Accordingly, in EU competition law claims, the claimant could argue that trial abroad will deprive him of some advantage that will be obtained from trial in England. For example, as it has been touched upon, the court from outside the EU will not be able to seek a preliminary reference from the Court of Justice and assistance from the Commission under Art 15 of Regulation 1/2003. Further, the fact that damages may be awarded on a higher scale[192] and the possibility of a more complete procedure of discovery in English courts could well be treated as advantages for the plaintiff in an EU competition law claim.

There may well be additional connecting factors, which are special to competition cases. One such factor may be the territory over which the infringing agreement was implemented. If a cartel agreement is implemented in England, then this may well constitute an important factor that would result in granting leave for service out of the jurisdiction. It has often been said that 'the jurisdiction in which a tort has been committed is prima facie the natural forum for the determination of the dispute.'[193] What emerges from this is that if the events constituting the breach of EU competition law occurred in England, then this is, prima facie the natural forum for trial. Thus, in a case where the cartel agreement is implemented in England, the English court will be the natural forum for trial.

The above-mentioned factors will be of relevance to the exercise of the court's discretion with regard to EU competition law claims brought under the multi-defendant ground.[194] Sometimes it would be desirable to add another defendant, so that the court may resolve the pending EU competition law issue. This will be so if the antitrust claims arise out of the same agreement or abusive practice that is in conflict with Arts 101 TFEU and/or 102 TFEU.

Finally, it should be mentioned that if the injunction was sought to restrain breaches of EU competition law in England, then the leave to serve the claim form out of jurisdiction would be granted. Indeed, as already mentioned,[195] in cases where jurisdiction is based on the injunction grounds, important considerations could be whether a foreign court would be unable or unwilling to grant the

[190] *Aratra Potato v Egyptian Navigation Co (The 'El Amria')* [1981] 2 Lloyd's Rep 119 (CA) 127 (Brandon LJ); see also: *Amin Rasheed Shipping v Kuwait Insurance* [1984] AC 50 (HL) 72.

[191] *Spiliada* (n 150) 482.

[192] Compare *Spiliada* (n 150) 482–84.

[193] *Cordoba Shipping v National State Bank (The Albaforth)* [1984] 2 Lloyd's Rep 91 (CA) 94 (Ackner LJ), 96 (Goff LJ). Applied in *Metall und Rohstoff* (n 128); overruled on a different point in *Lonrho plc v Fayed* [1991] 3 WLR 181 (HL).

[194] See *Multinational Gas* [1983] Ch 258 (CA).

[195] See ch 2, section 2.3.2.3.

relief sought and whether 'the English court is the only avenue for recourse'.[196] In this context, an English court could consider whether there is any link between the subject matter of the injunction sought and the jurisdiction of the English court,[197] so that the sought injunction can be effectively enforced in England.

It should be noted that it is open for plaintiffs in EU competition law claims to base jurisdiction on more than one ground of para 3.1. For example, the plaintiff may seek service under the tort ground and the injunction ground. It is beyond doubt that in such cases the court will allow service out of jurisdiction with regard to the grounds whose requirements have been met.

3.4 Conclusions

It has been shown that English courts will have to deal with the potentially complicated jurisdictional problems of any dispute involving tort-based EU competition law claims. The tortious classification of EU competition law claims suggests that Art 5(3) and para 3.1(9) are the most important provisions which will be addressed by the English courts when dealing with such claims. Research shows that similar problems will arise with regard to allocating jurisdiction in EU competition law claims under EC rules and under English traditional rules.

It can be concluded that allowing a claimant to bring an EU competition law claim before the court at the place where the prohibited agreement was entered into would confer jurisdiction to courts that in many cases would have little connection with the substance of the claim and the relevant market. This would be particularly so in cases where the agreement is concluded in one Member State but implemented in another. Based on that, it can be suggested that the place where the agreement is implemented (or intended to be implemented) is to be regarded as the place of the event giving rise to damage for the purposes of allocating jurisdiction in EU competition law claims under Art 5(3). Such an outcome will be in accord with what the Court of Justice has decided with regard to the exterritorial application of EU competition laws by the Commission in the *Wood Pulp* case. Moreover, this will provide for proximity, the efficacious conduct of proceedings and the ease of taking evidence in EU competition cases. Furthermore, the analysis above shows that the place where the agreement is implemented (being the place of the event giving rise to antitrust damage) will often overlap with the place where the harmful event directly produced its effects (being the place where the antitrust damage occurs). It is beyond doubt that the

[196] *Channel Tunnel Group Ltd v Balfour Beatty Construction Ltd* [1993] AC 334 (HL) 368 (Lord Mustill).

[197] Analogy can be made with the application of Art 31 from Brussels I by the Court of Justice in Case C-391/95 *Van Uden Maritime BV v Kommanditgesellschaft in Firma Deco-Line* [1998] ECR I-7091 [40] and the English High Court in *SanDisk* (n 13).

court at that place would have a close connection with the substance and indeed the relevant market.

EU competition law damage for the purpose of para 3.1(9) should be defined in exactly the same way as it is in relation to Art 5(3). Such damage will be financial, and there may well be cases which involve financial damages incurred in more than one state. It is well established that generally for jurisdictional purposes, the EU competition damage caused must be direct and not indirect. A mere effect on the plaintiff's financial position in England, for example because it is a parent company to a company damaged by a breach of EU competition law abroad, is not sufficient.

Therefore, the EU competition law damage would occur within the jurisdiction if there is direct economic loss in England. As a result, an English court will have jurisdiction in respect of EU antitrust claims if the business is lost or, alternatively, if the decline of sales has occurred in England. The position again is the same under EC and English rules.

Having said that, it will be welcomed if the Court of Justice case law with regard to Art 5(3) is regarded by English courts as of, at least, persuasive authority when they are called upon to interpret para 3.1(9). This can be strengthened by the fact that similar jurisdiction problems are bound to arise with regard to EU competition law claims brought under para 3.1(9) and Art 5(3). Establishing similar jurisdiction over such claims under EC law and English traditional rules will be in accord with the purpose of enhanced antitrust private enforcement in Europe, and will make England a more attractive forum for litigating EU competition law claims.

4

Avoiding Parallel EU Competition Law Proceedings

4.1 Introduction

The decentralisation reform means that there would be multiple enforcers of Arts 101 and 102 TFEU.[1] The analysis of jurisdictional rules in the foregoing chapters should have demonstrated that the EU competition law claims in respect of the same breach of the same antitrust provision could be brought before the courts in several countries. In view of that, there is little doubt that one of the major challenges that Member State courts would face in this context is how to avoid the problem of parallel EU competition law proceedings[2] and ensure that a well-placed court will hear and determine an EU competition law claim.

Parallel proceedings in general should be avoided, as they may potentially result in irreconcilable judgments, 'injustice, delay and increased expense'.[3] Parallel EU competition law proceedings in particular must be avoided, because 'multiple private litigation regarding the same agreement or network of agreements before national courts of different Member States can lead to inconsistent outcomes.'[4] Such inconsistent outcomes would fly in the face of the EU legislator's objective to ensure the uniform and coherent application of EU competition law.[5] Regulation 1/2003 cannot be of use in this context because it deals only with parallel proceedings between: national courts and the Commission; and National Competition Authorities (NCAs) and the Commission. It says nothing about parallel proceedings between different national courts which should be dealt with under Brussels I or English traditional rules in cases where Brussels I does not apply.

[1] Commission (EC), 'Modernisation of the Rules implementing Articles 85 and 86 of the EC Treaty' (White Paper) Programme 99/027 [101].

[2] See S Brammer, *Co-operation between National Competition Agencies in the Enforcement of EC Competition Law* (Hart Publishing, Oxford, 2009) 25.

[3] C McLachlan, Lis Pendens *in International Litigation* (Martinus Nijhoff Publishers, Leiden/ Boston, 2009) 23.

[4] Brammer (n 2) 27.

[5] See Recitals 1 and 22 of Regulation 1/2003 and Arts 15 and 16 of Regulation 1/2003. See also: White Paper on Modernisation (n 1) [101]; Commission (EC), 'Report on the functioning of Regulation 1/2003' COM (2009) 2006 final [34].

One way to avoid parallel EU competition law proceedings before national courts is to have a special basis for jurisdiction which requires a substantial connection between the breach of Arts 101 and 102 TFEU and effects of the anti-competitive agreement or conduct within the territory of the Member State where the action is brought and in respect of which the EU antitrust law claim is brought. As it was already clarified, this is not an option adopted by the EU and UK legislators because EU competition law infringements would often directly and substantially affect the markets in several countries and/or regions. Furthermore, private antitrust claims in respect of such infringements may arise in various contexts.[6] The fact that Brussels I has no specific rule for allocation of EU competition law cases, which would guarantee that a case is allocated to an appropriate forum that is appropriate and well placed to deal with the case,[7] suggests that parallel antitrust actions are bound to arise in the European context as EU competition law court proceedings may be brought in several Member States.[8]

Parallel proceedings before national courts could only be avoided by allowing an inappropriate court (ie a court that is not well placed to deal with an EU competition law case) to decline jurisdiction. In other words, the question of whether English courts can refuse to exercise jurisdiction in an EU competition law claim is bound to arise. Declining jurisdiction, however, should be distinguished from the situation, where the court dismisses the action because the rules of jurisdiction are not satisfied.[9] It is well settled that under the Brussels I Regulation and English traditional rules there are several situations in which the English court could stay or decline jurisdiction.[10] Thus, in this section the conditions for staying and declining jurisdiction in EU competition law claims under the EU rules and English common law will be examined.

[6] EU competition law may be the basis of a primary action or a defence in respect of various agreements or practices (eg claims could arise out of franchise agreements, distribution agreements, partial function joint ventures, licensing agreements, consumer contracts).

[7] For example, an NCA 'can be considered to be well placed to deal with a case if the following three cumulative conditions are met: 1. the agreement or practice has substantial direct actual or foreseeable effects on competition within its territory, is implemented within or originates from its territory; 2. the authority is able to effectively bring to an end the entire infringement, i.e. it can adopt a cease-and-desist order the effect of which will be sufficient to bring an end to the infringement and it can, where appropriate, sanction the infringement adequately; 3. it can gather, possibly with the assistance of other authorities, the evidence required to prove the infringement.' See Commission (EC), 'Cooperation within the Network of Competition Authorities' (Notice) [2004] OJ C101/43 [8]. See more: Brammer (n 2) 155–61.

[8] Eg Commission (EC), 'Damages actions for breach of the EC antitrust rules' (White Paper) COM (2008) 165 final [2.1].

[9] See J Fawcett (ed), *Declining Jurisdiction in Private International Law* (Clarendon Press, Oxford, 1999) 2; See also P Nygh, 'Declining jurisdiction under the Brussels I Regulation 2001 and the preliminary draft Hague Judgements Convention: a comparison' in Fawcett (ed), *Reform and Development of Private International Law* (OUP, Oxford, 2002) 303.

[10] Fawcett, *Declining Jurisdiction* (n 9) 2.

4.2 Declining Jurisdiction and Staying Proceedings under the EU Rules

Under Brussels I there are circumstances in which, although a national court has jurisdiction, it is provided that proceedings must be stayed or jurisdiction must be declined. Arts 27 and 28 of Brussels I are 'intended to prevent parallel proceedings before the courts of different [Member States] and to avoid conflicts between decisions which might result therefrom.'[11]

Article 27 of Brussels I deals with the problem of *lis pendens*.[12] This is concerned with the situation where proceedings involving the same cause of action and between the same parties are brought in the courts of different Member States. Sub-section (1) states that the court second seised must stay its proceedings. Sub-section (2) provides that where the jurisdiction of the court first seised is established, 'any court other than the court first seized shall decline jurisdiction in favour of that court.' The Court of Justice held that the court second seised with the dispute is not entitled to examine the jurisdiction of the court first seised, even if the court first seised has not decided the question of its jurisdiction within a reasonable time.[13]

Article 28 of Brussels I has to do with a situation where related actions are pending in the courts of different Member States. The court second seised may, as a matter of discretion, stay its proceedings. Article 28(2) goes further and gives an additional discretion to the court. Based on that provision, the court may decide to decline jurisdiction, as opposed to merely staying its proceedings if the court first seised has jurisdiction over the actions in question and its law permits the consolidation thereof. It should be clearly noted, however, that this is not a *forum conveniens* discretion: '[T]he question: "which court would be the more convenient or the more appropriate?" does not arise'.[14] A stay should be granted, in order to avoid irreconcilable judgments. Indeed, Arts 27 and 28 always give priority to the court first seised.[15]

That said, the question is whether Arts 27 and 28 of Brussels I avoid the problem of parallel proceedings in a situation where a claim (or counter-claim) that a contract (or contracts) violates EU competition law is brought before the English court and a complaint is lodged before a foreign NCA. The fact that Arts 5 and 6 of Regulation 1/2003 state that the NCAs and national courts have the power to apply Arts 101 and 102 TFEU in individual cases seems to indicate that there

[11] *Gubisch Maschinen-fabrik v Palumbo* [1987] ECR 4861 [8].

[12] Latin for 'a pending lawsuit'. See also McLachlan (n 3).

[13] Case C-116/02 *Erich Gasser v MISAT* [2003] ECR I-14693 [42] and [54]. See for criticism of this ruling, TC Hartley, 'The European Union and the Systematic Dismantling of the Common Law of Conflict of Laws' (2005) 54 *ICLQ* 813, 820–21.

[14] *The 'Linda'* [1988] 1 Lloyd's Rep 175 (QBD (Admlty)) 179 (Sheen J).

[15] P Herzog, 'Brussels or Lugano, Should you race to the Courthouse or race for a judgement?' (1995) 43 *American Journal of Comparative Law* 379, 381–84.

is a risk of irreconcilable decisions handed over on the same EU competition law issue by a court in one Member States and an NCA in another Member State. Regulation 1/2003 itself does not deal with this problem.[16] The White Paper on modernisation, however, seems to indicate that an NCA decision is enforceable only within the territory on which the authority in question operates.[17] Nevertheless, the issue of irreconcilable decision may arise as there are strong arguments suggesting that a foreign NCA decision could be recognised by the OFT or another NCA if a request is made by the Member State which adopted the decision.[18] Furthermore, the EU legislators seem to consider adoption of a rule to the effect that a Member State court cannot take decisions running counter to a final decision of an NCA in the European Competition Network (ECN) finding an infringement of Arts 101 and 102 TFEU.[19] Is an action brought, for example, before the French Competition Authority (*Conseil de la Concurrence*) to be regarded as an action brought before a Member State court? In other words, is an NCA to be regarded as a 'court' for those purposes, or do Arts 27 and 28 of Brussels I refer merely to national courts?

The problems may arise as Art 35 of Regulation 1/2003 provides for the possibility that the administrative public authority may be an NCA in some Member States. More specifically, it is clear that either administrative authorities[20] or courts[21] may be designated as NCAs for the purposes of applying Arts 101 and 102 TFEU in the different Member States.[22] If an administrative public authority is designated, a definitional problem may arise because different Member States may have adopted different 'models of administrative adjudication'.[23] For example, it is submitted that 'the most important characteristic of the French system of administrative adjudication is the location of the administrative courts/tribunals within the executive branch ....'[24] That such public bodies are not part of the judiciary, taken together with the fact that 'the common features of administrative-public enforcement are the verticality of the dispute, which remains one between the state and private individuals ...'[25] might suggest that a narrow interpretation of Arts 27 and 28 may be adopted in some Member States. A broader interpretation may be adopted in other Member States. For example, '[i]n the UK model, ... administrative tribunals are best understood ... as species of courts.'[26]

16 Compare: Arts 13 and 15(3) of Council Regulation 1/2003.

17 White Paper on Modernisation (n 1) [60]. See A Komninos, *EC Private Antitrust Enforcement: Decentralised Application of EC Competition Law by National Courts* (Hart Publishing, Oxford, 2008) 77; Brammer (n 2) 426–36.

18 Brammer (n 2) 428–29.

19 White Paper on Damages actions (n 8) [2.3].

20 Eg Bulgaria, Czech Republic, France, Italy, Romania, the UK.

21 Eg Austria and Ireland.

22 Eg Bulgaria, Czech Republic, France, Italy, Romania, the UK.

23 See more: P Cane, *Administrative Tribunals and Adjudication* (Hart Publishing, Oxford, 2009).

24 Cane (n 23) 89.

25 Komninos (n 17) 6.

26 Cane (n 23) 72.

Thus, it seems that different Member State may have different views on whether an NCA, as administrative public authority, is to be regarded as a court within the meaning of Arts 27 and 28 of Brussels I. This clearly suggests that an autonomous definition should be adopted for the purposes of Brussels I.

Indeed, the autonomous interpretation of the scope of Brussels I has been already adopted by the Court of Justice[27] in the context of Art 1 of Brussels, which states that the 'Regulation shall apply in civil and commercial matters whatever the nature of the court or tribunal.' It has been submitted that '[Brussels I] also applies to civil or commercial matters brought before administrative tribunals.'[28] Accordingly, in order to determine whether an NCA is to be regarded as a court for the purposes of Arts 27 and 28 of Brussels I, an important factor would be whether the designated authority under Art 35 of Regulation 1/2003 is exercising judicial functions in 'civil and commercial matter'.[29] It was already concluded that an EU competition law action brought before Member State courts is properly regarded as a 'civil and commercial matter' for the purposes of the Brussels I Regulation.[30] Hence, Art 1 of Brussels, read together with the Jenard and Schlosser Reports, leaves no doubt that the context in which the decision of the NCA is made would be more important than the constitutional status of the public authority before which the proceedings are brought. In view of that, there are strong arguments suggesting that all NCAs should be regarded as 'courts' for the purposes of Arts 27 and 28 of Brussels I as long as they are bodies exercising judicial functions in civil and commercial matters. Therefore, it seems that proceedings in which NCAs seek to determine whether an undertaking (or undertakings) has committed an infringement of Arts 101 and 102 TFEU should be within the scope of Brussels I.

The autonomous approach with regard to interpretation of Brussels I would serve to avoid the risk of irreconcilable decisions handed over on the same antitrust issue in different Member States. Furthermore, a broad interpretation of Arts 27 and 28 of Brussels would serve to avoid the inconsistency that would have followed if a complaint against a decision of an NCA, constituted as an administrative authority, had been lodged and those proceeding were pending before national courts. For example, in the case of the UK, such complaint against a decision finding an EU competition law infringement could be brought before the Competition Appeal Tribunal (CAT).[31] Decisions of CATs could be further

[27] Case 29/76 *Lufttransportunternehmen GmbH & Co KG v Organisation Européenne pour la Securité de la Navigation Aerienne (Eurocontrol)* [1976] ECR 1541 [4].

[28] Jenard Report OJ [1979] C59/1, 9; Schlosser Report OJ [1979] C59/71 [23].

[29] Compare: *Eurocontrol* (n 27) [4].

[30] See more: ch 1, section 1.6.1.1 above.

[31] See ss 46 and 47 of the Competition Act 1998. The 1998 Act goes further and lists the 'appealable decisions'. Sch 4 of the Enterprise Act 2002 permits most decisions of the CAT to be enforceable by registration at the High Court in England and Wales. By virtue of those provisions, the decision becomes enforceable in the same way as a judgment of the High Court. See also: R Whish, *Competition Law* (6th edn, OUP, Oxford, 2008) 426–36; ch 6 below.

appealed before the Court of Appeal. In so far as the Competition Act does not provide for an appeal, there remains the possibility that a claim for judicial review may be brought before the Administrative Court of the Queen's Bench Division under CPR 54. In other words, for the purposes of Brussels I, the question would be not whether the action is pending before a court (or whether the action is pending before an administrative body), but what is the subject matter of the proceedings, and whether the proceedings relate to civil or commercial matter. If the proceedings sought to determine whether there was an infringement of Arts 101 and 102 TFEU, then the dispute would be within the scope of Brussels I and thus Arts 27 and 28 of Brussels I would be relevant.[32]

4.2.1 *Lis Pendens* Doctrine and its Application to EU Competition Law Claims

The effect of Art 27 of Brussels I is that any court other than the court first seized must, depending on the circumstances, either stay its proceedings or decline jurisdiction. One condition that could cause particular problems in connection with antitrust claims is to do with the requirement, 'proceedings to be brought before the *courts* of different Member States'. It should be noted that the Court of Justice has held that Art 27 of Brussels I requires the parallel proceedings to involve three elements: the proceedings must have the same subject-matter (or the same object), as well as the same cause of action and the same parties.[33] In view of that it seems that the phrase 'same cause of action' in Art 27 should be regarded as a European concept which is not to be interpreted according to the criteria of national law.[34] There are two tests that have to be satisfied in this respect. First, do the actions have as their basis the same facts and rule of law?[35] Secondly, do these actions have the same object (ie whether the claims in the parallel proceedings seek to achieve the same outcome)?[36] Briggs and Rees suggest that another way of

[32] See also: ch 6, section 6.2.1 below, in which it is submitted that a decision (or part of a decision) of an NCA in the European Competition Network, which imposes fines on undertakings that have infringed Arts 101 and 102 TFEU, would not be within the scope of Brussels I that should not apply to a decision (or part of a decision), in which a public authority has acted in exercise of its powers. However, a decision (or part of a decision) of an NCA in the ECN, which establishes an infringement of Arts 101 and 102 TFEU, should be within the scope of Brussels I. See *Eurocontrol* (n 27) [4]–[5].

[33] *Gubisch* (n 11) [14].

[34] A Briggs and P Rees, *Civil Jurisdiction and Judgements* (5th edn, Informa, London, 2009) 314; J Fawcett and JM Carruthers (eds), *Cheshire, North & Fawcett Private International Law* (14th edn, OUP, Oxford, 2008) 305. See also: *Royal & Sun Alliance Insurance v MK Digital FZE (Cyprus)* [2005] EWHC 1408 (Comm) ILPr 51 (QBD (Comm)) [66]; (reversed without reference to this point) [2006] EWCA Civ 629; [2006] 2 Lloyd's Rep 110 (CA).

[35] Case C-406/92 *Tatry* [1994] ECR I-5439 [39]; Case C-39/02 *Mærsk Olie & Gas A/S v Firma M. de Haan en W de Boer* [2004] ECR I-9657 [38] (Court of Justice, Third Chamber).

[36] *Tatry* (n 35) [41]–[43]; Case C-111/01 *Gantner Electronic GmbH v Basch Exploitatie Maatschappij BV* [2003] ECR I-4207 [25] (Court of Justice, Fifth Chamber). See also: *Gubisch* (n 11); Case C-351/89 *Overseas Union Insurance Ltd v New Hampshire Insurance Co* [1991] ECR I-3317; Case C-406/92 [1994] ECR I-5439. See more: *Cheshire, North & Fawcett* (n 34) 305–10; Briggs and Rees (n 34) 314–16.

testing the matter is to ask 'whether a decision in the one set of proceedings would have been a conclusive answer to the question raised in the other'.[37] In a recent case, the Oberlandesgericht Köln (Regional Court of Appeal, Cologne) examined the question whether the test for the 'same cause of action' is met in regard to proceedings in Salzburg District Court in Austria, where the claim was alleged restraint of trade and the German proceedings, where the subject matter of the proceedings was the question whether an undertaking of any geographical origin was permitted to offer, advertise and conduct sport betting in Germany.[38] The Court held that these sets of proceedings do not have the 'same cause of action' within the meaning of Art 27.

The question is whether Art 27 of Brussels I would operate satisfactory in EU competition cases. Is the cause of action and subject matter the same if, for example, the English proceedings involve a breach of EU competition law in England, and the Swedish proceedings involve a breach in Sweden? Linked to this is the question of whether the acts of an EU competition law breach on which the proceedings are based have to be the same. It seems that the subject matter of the two sets of proceedings would not be the same, where the English action is concerned with selling a product at an inflated price within the English market, whereas Swedish proceedings are concerned with the issue of a circular by the same manufacturer that forbids the English dealer to re-export the product to Sweden. This would be so because even if the parallel claims had the same object, seeking declaration that the conduct is in breach of the same EU competition rule, such claims would not satisfy the requirements of Art 27 as the parallel antitrust claims would not be based on the same facts.

Is the cause of action and subject matter the same in a case, where the two sets of proceeding are concerned with selling a product at an inflated price respectively within the French and the English markets? In the *Provimi* case, it was held that the nature of the claims is identical, where all claims are private law claims for damages arising out of the same alleged infringements of EU competition law. Thus, the claims were regarded to be related for the purpose of Art 6(1) of Brussels I. The decision would no doubt be the same for the purpose of Art 28 of Brussels I,[39] which is meant to avoid the risk of irreconcilable decisions in connection with related EU competition law claims, and seems to be the appropriate provision that should be used in this context.

The 'cause of action' requirement for the purposes of Art 27 obviously would be met in the situation where both sets of proceedings are for nullity of a contract that is in conflict with EU competition law. But what if a complaint is lodged before the French Competition Authority (ie *Conseil de la Concurrence*) by a company X which is party to a contract with a dominant undertaking Y

[37] Briggs and Rees (n 34) 315.

[38] Case 6U 135/03 *Re a Claim by a German Lottery Company* [2005] ILPr 35 (Cologne Court of Appeal).

[39] See section 4.2.1.2 above.

and subsequently Y brings proceedings for enforcement of the same contract in England, where a defence of nullity is raised by X together with a counter-claim for damages? In such a scenario, there would be proceedings for enforcement of a contract in England, where a defence of nullity is raised together with a counter-claim for damages; and another set of proceedings before French competition authority which are brought to put an end of an EU antitrust law infringement resulting from the implementation of the same contract in France and England. Would Art 27 be applicable in such a scenario (assuming that the NCA, being a body exercising judicial functions, is regarded as a 'court' for present purposes and that it applies the Brussels I Regulation)?

It seems that it would be impracticable for an English court to try the validity of the contract issue until the French national authority had ruled on the EU competition law infringement issue. Before hearing determining whether the contract is valid under Art 101 and/or 102 TFEU, the English court could determine neither whether the contract should be performed nor whether there is an antitrust breach (and/or whether any antitrust damage has occurred). However, it seems that the conditions of Art 27 of Brussels I would not be easily satisfied. The Court of Justice has held that:

> [I]n order to determine whether there is lis pendens in relation to two disputes, account cannot be taken of the defence submissions, whatever their nature, and in particular of defence submissions alleging set-off, on which a defendant might subsequently rely when the court is definitively seised in accordance with its national law[40]

This ruling, however, has been made in respect of defence submissions and a set-off defence in particular. This can be justified by the fact that such a defence could not result in a separate judgment. A counter-claim[41] that a contract (or part of contract) is void as being in conflict with Arts 101 and 102 TFEU would indicate that the court should make a separate judgment as to whether there is an antitrust law infringement which may result in inconsistent application of EU competition law and may potentially run counter to the decision of a foreign NCA, so that an English court would have to stay its proceedings in relation to the EU competition law claim.

However, even if *Gantner Electronic* was distinguished and the submission that the contract was in conflict with EU competition law was taken into account in order to determine whether there was *lis pendens* between the two disputes, the English court would not be precluded under Art 27 of Brussels from trying the enforcement of the contract claim. The latter claim could be seen as related to EU competition law proceedings for the purposes of Art 28, but the actions would not be identical within the meaning of Art 27. Furthermore, the 'same parties' requirement of Art 27 of Brussels I could not be satisfied, either. The company X

[40] *Gantner Electronic* (n 36) [31].

[41] Case C-341/93 *Danvaern Production A/S v Schuhfabriken Otterbeck GmbH & Co.* [1995] ECR I-2053.

that lodged the complaint before the French Competition Authority is not party to the administrative proceedings in France which are conducted between the foreign NCA and the dominant undertaking Y.

Indeed, the 'same parties' requirement would give rise to further difficulties in most competition scenarios.[42] For example, proceedings in France as to the validity of the agreement between a company and its French distributor would have little effect on the proceedings against its German distributor in Germany on a virtually identical contract. There is little doubt that German proceedings would not be stayed. Moreover, 'a judgment in France as to the validity of the agreement with one's French distributor will not have effect when suing its German distributor in Germany on a virtually identical contract.'[43] This is doubtless problematic, as one distribution system may be regarded as an illegal vertical restraint and in one Member State but not in another.

The problems increase if the Court of Justice definition on the concept of 'the same parties' in case of multi-party litigation is considered in connection with EU competition law claims. According to it, 'the second court seized is required to decline jurisdiction only to the extent to which the parties to the proceedings before it are also parties to the action previously commenced; it does not prevent proceedings from continuing between the same parties.'[44] Accordingly, if in the court first seised A and B sue X claiming damages arising out of contract contrary to EU competition law, and in the court second seised X sues A, B and C for enforcement of the same contract, Art 27 of Brussels I will not operate in respect of the action brought against C.

In the light of the foregoing considerations, it can be concluded that Art 27 of the Brussels I Regulation does not deal satisfactorily with a significant number of the issues that are to arise in relation to EU competition law claims. It remains to be seen whether those problems can be solved by Art 28 of Brussels I, which is meant to avoid the risk of irreconcilable decisions in connection with related EU competition law claims.

4.2.2 Related EU Competition Law Actions

As already mentioned, Art 28 of Brussels I is designed to deal with those situations, which do not fall within the strict confines of Art 27 of Brussels I. In other words, if antitrust actions are not identical within the meaning of Art 27, but related, then Art 28 may be applied. The latter provision contains no requirement about the same cause of action or same parties in the two proceedings. The only

[42] See section 4.2.1.3.1, concerning the specific difficulties that would arise in collective redress proceedings.

[43] V Korah, *An Introductory Guide to EC Competition Law and Practice* (9th edn, Hart Publishing, Oxford, 2007) 221. See also: J Bourgeois and C Humpe, 'The Commission's Draft 'New Regulation 17'' (2002) 23 *European Competition Law Review* 43, 46–47; Brammer (n 2) 27.

[44] *Tatry* (n 35) [36].

question which needs to be answered affirmatively, in order for a Member State court to rely on Art 28 is whether actions are related. The answer to this question should be provided in a broad commonsense manner, bearing in mind the objective of Art 28, namely to improve co-ordination of the exercise of judicial functions within the EU and to avoid conflicting and contradictory decisions,[45] thus facilitating the proper administration of justice in the EU[46] and coherent and uniform application of Arts 101 and 102 TFEU.

In the context of EU competition law claims, the court should determine two issues: are the antitrust actions related; and if so, whether to exercise its discretionary power? In order to answer the question whether the actions are related, two factors should be considered. First, the degree of risk of irreconcilable judgments should be the major factor considered by the court. What has already been said, in the context of Art 6(1) of Brussels I, about the risk of irreconcilable judgments in EU competition law claims is equally valid here.[47] It is beyond doubt that there is a risk of irreconcilable judgments if a cartel agreement (or abusive practice) has been implemented in two different states and actions related to that cartel agreement (or abusive practice) are pending in those states. The same can be said, where there are separate actions in connection with a contract that is alleged to distort competition: for enforcement of a contract in one Member State; and a claim for nullity of the same contract in another Member State. A finding that a contract is void under EU competition law would be irreconcilable with a finding that the contract should be enforced. Secondly the court should determine whether it is expedient to hear and determine the two actions together. It seems that no particular difficulties in competition cases could arise out of this requirement.

It has been submitted that Art 28 of Brussels I provides a national court with power to temporarily stay proceedings allowing another court to determine issues that may be relevant for the proceedings before it.[48] When the court in competition cases is considering whether or not to decline jurisdiction, the risk of irreconcilable judgments should be the major factor as well. Another very important factor that would be relevant for EU competition law claims is to do with the public interest of uniform and coherent application of EU competition law which is meant to be promoted by Regulation 1/2003.

Therefore, it seems that most of the issues arising out of the narrow scope of Art 27 could be tackled by the Member State courts under Art 28 of Brussels of Brussels I. There is, however, one major problem that could not be dealt with by the courts under the current version of the Brussels I Regulation which appears

[45] Ibid [32], [52]; see also [28] (AG Tesauro).

[46] *Sarrio v Kuwait Investment Authority* [1999] 1 AC 32 (HL) 39 (Lord Saville). See also: A. Briggs, 'Private International Law' (1997) *British Yearbook of International Law* 331, 339–42; J Harris, 'Related Actions and the Brussels Convention' (1998) *Lloyd's Maritime and Commercial Law Quarterly* 145.

[47] See ch 2, section 2.2.4 above.

[48] Nygh (n 9) 320.

to assume that the court first seised is always an appropriate forum. A plaintiff, who has an intention of delaying settlement of a future substantive antitrust law dispute, may deliberately commence pre-emptive proceedings before a court which is not well placed to deal with an EU competition law case or has no jurisdiction.[49] This risk was overlooked by the Court of Justice, which held that the court second seised must stay proceedings until the court first seised has declared that it has no jurisdiction.[50] This is not a satisfactory outcome, as it could result in delay.

Furthermore, it may often be the case that the court first seised is not well placed to hear and determine an EU competition law case because an anti-competitive agreement or practice, which has been implemented in a number of Member States, does not affect the market in the Member State where the action is brought. It is unfortunate that jurisdiction in such cases would depend on the question who is faster in lodging his claim. A more satisfactory result would have been reached if the court first seised was entitled to decline jurisdiction in cases where agreement or practice has no substantial direct (actual or foreseeable) effects on competition within the Member State.[51] The advantages of an approach which links the court's jurisdiction with the effects on competition within a country's territory could be demonstrated by the US Supreme Court ruling in the *Empagran* case.[52] In this case, it was held that despite the fact that the alleged anti-competitive price-fixing activity has caused some domestic antitrust injury, the US courts should dismiss the class action brought by foreign purchasers of vitamins as to the lack of subject-matter jurisdiction. This was justified by the fact that the foreign anti-competitive conduct has played a significant role and the foreign injury is independent of domestic effects.[53]

The problem is that the American experience is impossible to follow in the European context, because the Brussels I Regulation precludes a court of a Member State from declining the jurisdiction conferred on it by the Regulation. This will be so, even if the jurisdiction of no other Member State was in issue or

[49] *Erich Gasser* (n 13) [68] (AG Philip Leger). See also: Hartley (n 13); P de Vareilles-Sommieres (ed), *Forum Shopping in the European Judicial Area* (Hart Publishing, Oxford, 2007).

[50] *Erich Gasser* (n 13) [42] and [54]. See for criticism of this ruling, Hartley (n 13) 820.

[51] Compare the European approach in respect of allocation of cases between the NCAs. See Commission (EC), 'Cooperation within the Network of Competition Authorities' (Notice) [2004] OJ C-101/43 [8].

[52] See *F Hoffmann-La Roche Ltd v Empagran* (2004) 542 US 155, 167; 124 SCt 2359 (Sup Ct (US)). Although, the *Empagran* case did not entirely and absolutely eliminate the problem of forum shopping, it may be used as an example how the problem of forum shopping could be dealt with in some cases.

[53] *Empagran* (n 52) 542 US 169. Given the fact that the claimants' alternative argument that the foreign injury was not in fact independent of the domestic effects was not addressed by the Court of Appeals, the issue was left undecided by the US Supreme Court and remanded to the Court of Appeals. See *Empagran* (n 52) 542 US 175. As result, it has been claimed that '[i]t is not the case … that the *Empagran* shuts the door on claims based on foreign harm completely; rather it leaves it swinging in the wind, and whether claims can be successfully pursued may rest on the ingenuity of the law presenting the case to link the foreign injury to domestic action.' See M Furse, *Competition Law of the EC and UK* (6th edn, OUP, Oxford, 2008) 79.

the proceedings had no connecting factors to any other Member State.[54] It has been submitted that including a discretionary power for a national court to stay or dismiss an antitrust action when the natural forum is in another Member State would be 'anathema to civil lawyers'.[55] It is true that in the civil law countries, it is for the legal system to determine whether the judge has jurisdiction or not. Under the civil law doctrine, if the court has jurisdiction, it must rule and cannot decline to exercise jurisdiction as this may result in a denial of justice.

That said, the increasing importance of the principle of mutual trust between the legal systems within the EU may suggest that the time is ripe for a change in the attitude. A provision, which would allow a Member State to decline jurisdiction in a case where an allegedly anti-competitive agreement or practice has no substantial direct (actual or foreseeable) effects on competition within the Member State **if and only if** there is another Member State court well placed to hear and determine the case, could (and should) be considered by the EU legislator. In other words, a Member State court could be allowed to decline jurisdiction: (1) if it is a court which is not well placed to hear and determine an EU competition law case; and (2) there is another Member State court (or even an NCA, assuming that a broader interpretation of court was adopted) that is well placed to deal with the case in question. Such a provision would ensure that a Member State court which is well placed to deal with a case would not be allowed to decline jurisdiction even if it is alleged that there is another Member State court which is better placed to hear and determine the EU antitrust claims. Thus, this would be a mechanism which is meant to guarantee that each EU competition law case would be allocated to a forum which is well placed to deal with it. This is indeed something that is already done in Europe in the context of allocation of EU competition cases between NCAs (which are bodies exercising judicial functions as well) in the European Competition Network.[56] The introduction of such a rule would further promote the principle of mutual trust between the legal systems within the EU and safeguard the coherent application of EU competition law.

Overall, it seems that under the current version of Brussels I there are particular issues and problems that need to be considered by the EU legislator in the context of parallel antitrust proceedings. More specifically, it is not quite clear whether an NCA, being in most Members States' administrative authorities, would be regarded as a 'court' for those purposes. It would be advisable for it to be stated

[54] Case-281/02 *Owusu v Jackson* [2005] ECR I-1383. For criticism of this judgment, see Hartley (n 13); E Peel, '*Forum non-conveniens* and European Ideals' (2005) *Lloyd's Maritime and Commercial Law Quarterly* 363, 366–67; A Briggs, '*Forum non conveniens* and ideal Europeans' (2005) *Lloyd's Maritime and Commercial Law Quarterly* 378; compare: L Collins, '*Forum Non Conveniens* and the Brussels Convention' (1990) 106 *LQR* 535; J Harris, 'Stays of proceedings and the Brussels Convention' (2005) 54 *ICLQ* 933.

[55] JJ Fawcett, 'Forum shopping—some questions answered' (1984) 35 *Northern Ireland Legal Quarterly* 141, 147.

[56] See Commission (EC), on 'Cooperation within the Network of Competition Authorities' (Notice) [2004] OJ C101/43 [8]. See more: Brammer (n 2) 155–161.

clearly that a 'national competition authority when determining whether there is an infringement of Arts 101 and 102 TFEU is regarded as a "court" (ie body exercising judicial functions) for the purposes of Articles 27 and 28 of Brussels I'. The foregoing analysis demonstrated that Art 27 of Brussels is not well suited to dealing with parallel proceedings in relation to EU competition law claims. Article 28 of Brussels I, though, may be of relevance in a significant number of EU competition law claims. The assumption in Art 28, however, is that the court first seised is always well placed to hear and determine an EU competition law claim. This is far from true in EU competition law cases, where an anti-competitive agreement or practice may have been implemented in a number of Member States. A more satisfactory result would be reached if any court (no matter whether first or second seised) was entitled to stay its proceedings or decline jurisdiction should there be a more appropriate forum.

4.2.3 Specific Issues: Collective Redress Proceedings in the European Context[57]

The debate in England as to whether to maintain the opt-in regime, to introduce the opt-out regime or instead to have them both,[58] is in line with the variety of collective redress regimes adopted in Europe,[59] where some Member States have chosen the opt-out model,[60] while others have preferred to apply the opt-in

[57] See more: M Danov, 'The Brussels I Regulation: cross-border collective redress proceedings and judgments' (2010) 6 *Journal of Private International Law* forthcoming.

[58] See R Mulheron, *The Class Action in Common Law Legal Systems: A Comparative Perspective* (Hart Publishing, Oxford, 2004); C Hodges, *The Reform of Class and Representative Actions in European Legal Systems* (Hart Publishing, Oxford, 2008); Office of Fair Trading, 'Private actions in competition law: effective redress for consumers and business—Recommendations from the Office of Fair Trading', OFT916 resp; Civil Justice Council, 'Improving access to justice through collective actions—developing a more effective and efficient procedure for collective actions', *Final Report* www.civiljusticecouncil.gov.uk/files/Improving_Access_to_Justice_through_Collective_Actions.pdf; C Hodges, 'From class actions to collective redress: a resolution in approach to compensation' (2009) *Civil Justice Quarterly* 41.

[59] R Mulheron, 'Reform of collective redress in England and Wales: a perspective of need'. A research paper for submission www.civiljusticecouncil.gov.uk/files/collective_redress.pdf.

[60] Eg Portugal (Law No 83/95 of 31 August, Right of Proceeding Participation and Popular Action; see H Antunes www.globalclassactions.stanford.edu/PDF/Portugal_Legislation.pdf and D Fairgrieve and G Howells, 'Collective redress procedures—European Debates' (2009) 58 *ICLQ* 379, 386–87); an opt-out regime is also adopted in Spain, (see PG de Cabiedesthe, 'Spanish Regulation on Collective Redress Actions' www.globalclassactions.stanford.edu/PDF/Spain_Legislation.pdf); Denmark adopts the opt-in regime as the main model, but an opt-out model may be permitted by the court in respect of low-value claims (see Fairgrieve and Howells (n 60) 384–85); in the Netherlands, an opt-out regime has been adopted with regard to settlements (see I Tsankova www.globalclassactions.stanford.edu/PDF/Netherlands_National_Report.pdf and Fairgrieve and Howells (n 60) 388–89). See also 'Ashurst Study on the conditions of claims for damages in case of infringement of EC competition rules' http://ec.europa.eu/competition/antitrust/actionsdamages/comparative_report_clean_en.pdf; Mulheron (n 59) 102–06; C Hodges, 'Global Class Actions Project Summary of European Union Developments' www.globalclassactions.stanford.edu/PDF/EU_Legislation.pdf.

model.[61] The White Paper on damages actions for breach of the EU antitrust rules also appears to favour the co-existence of both forms of representative action brought on behalf of identifiable victims (ie the opt-out system) and opt-in collective actions.[62] The co-existence of both regimes in Europe would complicate the private international law problems that would be bound to arise with regard to parallel collective redress actions. The fact that the Brussels I Regulation contains no rule dealing with the cross-border implications of the collective redress proceedings will give rise to the question of whether the court in a Member State where the opt-out regime is in force would have jurisdiction over class members who are domiciled abroad and have not opted out from the collective redress action. The inherent problem lies with the uncertainty about the parties to the pending proceedings brought under the opt-out model, which may result in parallel anti-trust actions if the appropriate legislative intervention is not made at EU level.

4.2.3.1 Uncertainties Regarding Identifiable Parties to Collective Redress Proceedings under an Opt-Out Regime

The problems stem from the fact that in such cases a group notice, which sets a period for opting out, may be published by the media and/or a press conference and/or the internet.[63] Can a defendant seek a stay of collective redress proceedings brought in England by the members of a plaintiff class who have not opted out from the collective redress proceedings abroad?[64]

The main issue that needs to be determined in this context is how the plaintiff's class right of 'fair trial and hearing', as embodied in Art 6(1) of the ECHR, would be safeguarded by the Member States' courts. Under Brussels I, the general jurisdiction rule is based on the defendant's domicile. As a result, a Member States' court that had implemented an opt-out regime should have jurisdiction over a plaintiff class domiciled abroad if, for example, the collective redress action was based on Art 2 of Brussels I. The jurisdictional rules set out in the Regulation contain no requirement for an adequate notice to be served to all the members of the plaintiff's class, so that one may argue that this would not arise as an issue

[61] Eg France (see V Magnier, 'French Legislation' www.globalclassactions.stanford.edu/PDF/France_Legislation.pdf and Fairgrieve and Howells (n 60) 389–92); Italy (Art 140 of Consumer Code—in force 30 June 2008;—see I Silvestri www.globalclassactions.stanford.edu/PDF/Italian_Collective_Action_for_Damages.pdf and Fairgrieve and Howells (n 60) 392–93. See also: Ashurst Study (n 60).

[62] White Paper on Damages actions (n 8) [2.1].

[63] See Mulheron (n 59) 98 (discussing the Portuguese regime); Final Report (n 58) 250–51.

[64] Similar problems have been discussed in the American context by the US courts (*Phillips Petroleum Co v Shutts* 472 US 797, 105 SCt 2965 (1985) (Supreme Court of the United States); *International Shoe Co v Washington* 326 US 310, 66 SCt 154 (1945) (Supreme Court of the United States) and commentators (GC Lilly, 'Modelling class actions: the representative suit as an analytical tool' (2003) 81 *Nebraska Law Review* 1008; DL Bassett, 'US class actions go global: transnational class actions and personal jurisdiction' (2003–2004) 72 *Fordham Law Review* 41; J Walker, 'Crossborder class actions: a view from across the border' (2004) *Michigan State Law Review* 755) in respect of the US type of class actions.

at the jurisdictional stage. The issue, however, would be bound to arise at the recognition and enforcement stage.[65] In other words, if a Member State's court operating in an opt-out regime aimed at rendering a judgment that is binding on all members of the plaintiff's class and enforceable in the other Member States, the issue of making a due process notice would have to be carefully considered by the courts and legislators. In this context, the following questions need to be addressed: What would be considered an adequate notice which would be consistent with the plaintiff's class right of 'fair trial and hearing' as embodied in Art 6(1) of the ECHR? How would such a notice be served to the foreign members of the plaintiff class?

The Service Regulation[66] is meant to be used in deciding the adequacy of a notice in the European context. However, what is specific to an opt-out class action is that there are members of the plaintiff's class that are identified, and other members who may only be identifiable, but not identified. The Regulation would be relevant when determining the adequacy of notices served to identified parties, but not when deciding on the adequacy of public notices made to identifiable parties. This can be clearly deduced when Art 1(2) of the Regulation is considered together with the Request for service of documents form in Annex I of the Service Regulation which requires the name of the addressee to be specified. What would be an adequate public notice for those purposes? Is a public notice to German consumers adequate if made through an English newspaper and/or specially designated web site in different European languages? These questions would certainly need to be considered by the EU legislators as well as national legislators. An amendment in the Service Regulation may well be considered. Given the fact that consumers in Europe read and speak in 23 official languages, it is very important to specify how an adequate public notice may be made in the European context.

A liberal interpretation of the requirement for adequacy of a public notice may be justified by the principle of mutual trust that appears to be prevalent in Europe. The advantage of such a liberal regime, when interpreting the adequacy of a public notice, is that the entire plaintiff class, together with the defendant, would be bound by the *res judicata* effect of the class judgment.[67] However, the obvious drawback of a more liberal interpretation is that 'the granting of access to the courts in one State leads to denial of access in another State because of mechanical rules on *lis pendens* and related actions'.[68] In other words, if the opt-out regime were adopted in England, then the English collective redress proceedings might also bind members of the plaintiff class who were domiciled abroad

[65] See ch 6.

[66] Regulation (EC) 1393/2007 on the service in the Member States of judicial and extrajudicial in civil or commercial matters (service of documents), and repealing Council Regulation 1348/2000).

[67] *Shutts* (n 64). The problems that would arise at the recognition and enforcement stage are examined in detail in ch 6.

[68] J Fawcett, 'The impact of Art 6(1) of the ECHR on private international law' (2007) 56 *ICLQ* 1, 7.

and wished to sue the defendant at their home state, for example, on the basis of Art 16 of Brussels I. For example, a plaintiff class domiciled in Germany might well prefer to bring their collective redress action before the German courts.[69] Would a German court accept jurisdiction over a collective redress action brought by a plaintiff class who have neither opted out nor opted in to English proceedings, if England were to adopt the opt-out regime in respect of the class actions as recommended by the CJC?

It seems that the Civil Procedure Rules may need some amendments in order to deal with the cross-border collective redress actions. In this respect, the EU legislator and/or English legislator may refer to the legal systems that have tackled this jurisdictional problem. Thus, a provision holding that 'class members domiciled in another Member State may participate in collective redress proceedings only if they opt in' could be considered.[70] The adoption of the opt-in regime in respect of a plaintiff's class domiciled in another Member State, however, would not solve all jurisdictional problems. More specifically, this will inevitably lead to parallel collective redress proceedings, pending before different Member State courts, in respect of the same infringement raising similar issues of fact and law. This raises the question of whether Brussels I can deal satisfactorily with parallel cross-border collective redress actions.

4.2.3.2 A Need for a Specific Rule to Deal with Collective Redress Proceedings Brought under an Opt-Out Regime

Article 27 will be of no use in the context of parallel collective redress proceedings as the 'same parties' requirement contained within it will not be easily satisfied in such scenarios.[71] For example, a class action in the Netherlands in respect of a consumer contract with a Dutch distributor of gadgets would have little (or no) effect on the collective redress antitrust proceedings in Italy on a virtually identical contract, which gives rise to the 'same cause of action',[72] against the Italian distributor of gadgets.[73] There is little doubt that Italian proceedings would not be stayed, as the 'same parties' requirement could not be satisfied. Similarly, it seems that several collective redress actions in two or more different Member States may be brought, for example, in cases concerning a cross-border EU competition law infringement. This may not only lead to irreconcilable judgments regarding related actions, but may also give rise to problems at the recognition stage.[74]

[69] M. Danov, 'Awarding exemplary (or punitive) antitrust damages in EC competition cases with an international element—the Rome II Regulation and the Commission's White Paper on damages' (2008) 29 *European Competition Law Review* 430. See also ch 5 below.

[70] Compare Walker (n 64) 768. Walker outlines that such provisions exist in the legislation of British Columbia, New Jersey, New York, Pennsylvania, Connecticut, Missouri and New Hampshire. See also the petitioner's contention in *Shutts* (n 64) 2975.

[71] See section 4.2.1.1 above.

[72] See more: section 4.2.1.1 above.

[73] Compare section 4.2.1.1 above.

[74] See ch 6 below.

Furthermore, a specific issue that would be bound to arise in Europe is to do with the identity of the parties to the parallel collective redress actions brought under opt-out regimes in several Member States. For example, if England were to adopt the opt-out regime and the collective redress opt-out actions, involving the same cause of action in respect of the same infringement by the same defendant, were brought in England and, for example, in Portugal, it would not be clear which of the identifiable parties to the parallel opt-out proceedings would be bound by the English and Portuguese actions, respectively, unless the class members had opted in to one of the class actions. Article 27 would be of little use in the latter context.

The problems would not be easily dealt with under Art 28 either. Although Art 28 may entitle the Member States' courts to consolidate related collective redress actions if the second seised court decides to do so, there is no rule guaranteeing that the collective actions will be dealt with by an appropriate forum for resolution of the claims of all or the majority of the class members. This clearly confirms the need for a rule that entitles a Member State court to decline jurisdiction if there is another court that is better placed to hear and determine the EU competition law action.[75]

4.3 Declining Jurisdiction and Staying Proceedings under the English Traditional Rules[76]

As already explained, the traditional rules on jurisdiction apply in EU competition cases in the situation where neither the special jurisdictional rules nor the rules of general application contained in the Brussels I Regulation apply.[77] In such a case, even if an English court has jurisdiction, following the service of a claim form, the defendant may apply to the court to exercise its discretion to stay the proceedings on the ground, which is usually called *forum non conveniens.* In common law jurisdictions, the doctrine of *forum non conveniens* fulfils a number of roles. It is the antidote to excessively wide bases of jurisdictions. It is concerned to avoid contradictory judgments, prevents parallel proceedings and provides flexibility.[78] Thus, the doctrine of *forum non conveniens* has a role to play in competition cases where there is a risk of contradictory judgments and forum shopping.

This doctrine has long been recognised in Scots law,[79] and it has been recognised in England as well.[80] Under the law of Scotland the courts, when acceding to

[75] See more on the proposal and its justification in section 4.2.1.2 above.

[76] See more: PR Beaumont, 'Great Britain' in Fawcett, *Declining Jurisdiction* (n 9) 207.

[77] See ch 1.

[78] Fawcett, *Declining Jurisdiction* (n 9) 19–21.

[79] *Sim v Robinow* [1892] 19 R 665 (Court of Session) 668; *Société du Gaz de Paris v Société Anonyme de Navigation 'Les Armateurs Francais'* [1926] SC (HL) 13 (HL).

[80] *The Abidin Daver* [1984] AC 398 (HL) 411.

a plea of *forum non conveniens,* do not stay the proceedings in the Scottish Court, but decline jurisdiction by dismissing the action.[81] In England, though, the action will not be dismissed, but stayed. Under English law,

> a stay will only be granted on the ground of *forum non conveniens* where the court is satisfied that there is some other available forum, having competent jurisdiction, which is the appropriate forum for trial of the action, i.e. in which the case may be tried more suitably for the interests of all the parties and the ends of justice.[82]

In general, the burden of proof rests on the defendant to persuade the court to exercise its discretion to grant a stay.[83] The defendant must not only show that England is not the natural or appropriate forum for the trial, but also to establish that there is another available forum which is *clearly or distinctly more appropriate than the English forum.*[84]

The application of the doctrine of *forum non-conveniens* in EU competition law can be demonstrated by an example where an anti-competitive agreement concluded between non-EU undertakings (eg producers established in the US or Canada) is implemented by selling their products at an inflated price to their Australian and English distributors. The producers may have formed an association for the joint promotion of their exports only, so that their agreement would not violate US antitrust legislation under the Webb Pomerene Act 1918. Through such an association the producers are able to exchange information on the marketing of their products abroad and agree on export prices. The English distributors want to seek damages for the loss caused by the agreement that is in breach of EU competition law. The fact that products were marketed within the EU means that EU competition law will be applicable.[85] It seems that on those facts, the English court will have jurisdiction over a claim brought by the English distributor on the basis of the fact that damage was sustained within the jurisdiction. Can the North American producers rely on the *forum non conveniens* doctrine and argue that New York is clearly a more appropriate forum?

In EU competition cases the relevant market may be geographically worldwide. There could be cases where no particular forum can be described as the natural forum for the trial of the action. Accordingly, in competition cases there can be pointers to a number of different jurisdictions, something which is quite common in commercial disputes as well.[86] The following relevant factors

[81] *Haji-Ioannou v Frangos* [1999] 2 Lloyd's Rep 337 (CA) 347. See also: A Anton and PR Beaumont, *Private International Law* (2nd edn, W Green, Edinburgh, 1990) 213; L Collins and others (eds) *Dicey, Morris and Collins on the Conflict of Laws* (14th edn, Sweet & Maxwell, London, 2006) 465–66.

[82] *Spiliada Maritime v Cansulex* [1987] AC 460 (HL) 476.

[83] *Société du Gaz* (n 79) 21 (Lord Sumner).

[84] *Spiliada* (n 82) 477. See also *Konamaneni v Rolls-Royce* [2001] EWHC Ch 470; [2002] 1 All ER 979 (ChD) [58].

[85] Joined cases 89, 104, 114, 117 and 125 to 129/85 *Ashlstrom Osakeyhtio v Commission ('Wood Pulp')* [1988] ECR 5193 [11]–[18].

[86] See *European Asian Bank v Punjab and Sind Bank* [1982] 2 Lloyd's Rep 356 (CA).

can be appropriate in EU competition law disputes. First, in several cases[87] the applicable law has been a very significant factor in determining the appropriate forum. In the example above the applicable law is English law which includes Arts 101 and 102 TFEU. Moreover, in such cases European public policy (that forms part of English public policy) is at stake. As already mentioned,[88] the effect of an anti-competitive agreement on English public policy is not an issue that is capable of fair resolution in any foreign court.[89] Nevertheless, the English court may decline to exercise jurisdiction in a case where the anti-competitive activity is in significant part foreign. This will be in accord with the common law approach revealed by the US court that declined to exercise jurisdiction in a case where the anti-competitive price-fixing activity was in significant part foreign. In this case, the court went further and held: 'why should American law supplant, for example, Canada's or Great Britain's or Japan's own determination about how best to protect Canadian or British or Japanese customers from anticompetitive conduct engaged in significant part by Canadian or British or Japanese or other foreign companies?'[90] This is likely to be followed in an appropriate case by English courts, where 'judicial chauvinism has been replaced by judicial comity'.[91]

In addition, a 'real and close connection between the forum and the dispute' can be a significant factor in EU competition cases. This factor may be linked to the convenience of the parties in that it focuses on the place, where the parties' dispute is centred. Other factors that might be considered in competition cases are: *lis pendens*; convenience of witnesses; convenience of the parties; and related proceedings. Thus, in the example above, England is the country which has the closest connections with the subject matter of the action. Indeed, the products, which are bought at an inflated price, are mainly marketed in England. This connection with England can be strengthened by the fact the plaintiff is domiciled there.[92] Thus, the English court would not decline to exercise jurisdiction over the EU competition law claims brought by the English distributors and the proceedings will not be stayed.

Notwithstanding, if a defendant does satisfy the above-mentioned test, then the proceedings will be stayed unless a claimant establishes that there are circumstances by reason of which justice requires that a stay should nevertheless not

[87] See *Spiliada* (n 82); *Banco Atlantico v British Bank for the Middle East* [1990] 2 Lloyd's Rep 504 (CA); *El du Pont de Nemours v Agnew* [1987] 2 Lloyd's Rep 585 (CA).

[88] See more: ch 2, section 2.3.2.3 above. See also *Hartford Fire v California* 509 US 797–99, 125 L Ed 2d 612, 113 S Ct 2891 (1993) (Sup Ct (US)).

[89] The applicable law could, nevertheless, give rise to the question whether the English court seised with an antitrust claim should ever decline to exercise jurisdiction on grounds of international comity (comity of courts). See L Collins, 'Comity in Modern Private International Law' in Fawcett *Reform and development of Private International Law* (n 9) 89. See also *Re Insurance Antitrust Litigation* 938 F2d 919, 933 (US Court of Appeals, Ninth Circuit, Cal).

[90] *Empagran* (n 52) at 165; See also E Wind, 'Remedies and Sanctions in Article 82 of the EC Treaty' (2005) 26 *European Competition Law Review*, 659, 667. See also ch 5 on the issue of applicable law.

[91] *Abidin Daver* (n 80) 411 (Lord Diplock).

[92] Compare *Morrison v Panic Link* [1993] SLT 602 (IH (Ex Div)) 604.

be granted.[93] In such a case, the burden of proof shifts to the claimant to justify coming to England.[94] In this respect, it should be mentioned that in a competition case the English courts may be preferred, since unlike the civil law systems of the other Member States, the English law of civil procedure has rules of document discovery and witness statements. Further, the English courts have a reputation for awarding higher damages in comparison with civil law jurisdictions. In the *Connelly* case,[95] however, Lord Goff held that there was a general principle that if a clearly more appropriate forum overseas has been identified, then the plaintiff will have to take that forum as he finds it. This would be so, even if it is in certain respects less advantageous to him than the English forum. He may, for example, have to accept lower damages,[96] or do without the more generous English system of discovery. The same must apply to the system of court procedure, including the rules of evidence, applicable in the foreign forum. Only if the plaintiff can establish that substantial justice cannot be done in the appropriate forum, will the courts refuse to grant a stay.[97]

All this indicates that the *forum non conveniens* doctrine could be a useful tool in allocating jurisdiction in a case where an anti-competitive agreement is implemented in a number of Member States. In such a case, the English court could have granted a stay, if satisfied that there was some other available forum in which the EU competition law dispute would have been tried more suitably for the interests of all the parties and the ends of justice. Unfortunately, as submitted in the previous sub-section, the application of the doctrine of *forum non-conveniens* is prevented by the Brussels I Regulation. Thus, if an English court is the court first seised with an EU competition law claim against a non-EC undertaking, then the English court will not be entitled to stay the proceedings even if the French court is more appropriate to rule on that particular claim.[98]

4.4 Concluding Remarks

The wide bases for jurisdiction with regard to EU competition law claims under the Brussels I Regulation together with the fact that Arts 101 and 102 TFEU infringements would potentially affect claimants across Europe indicate that the parallel antitrust proceedings are bound to arise in the European context. How to deal with the problem under the Brussels I Regulation? The Brussels I Regulation in its current version does not deal satisfactorily with the problem

[93] *Spiliada* (n 82) 478; see also *Connelly v RTZ* [1997] I.L.Pr. 805 (HL) [27].
[94] *Abidin Daver* (n 80) 411 (Lord Diplock); see also *Spiliada* (n 82) 478.
[95] See *Connelly* (n 93).
[96] *Cf Herceg Novi (owners) v Ming Galaxy (owners)* [1998] 4 All ER 238 (CA).
[97] *Connelly* (n 93).
[98] See Arts 27 and 28 of the Brussels I Regulation. See also Harris (n 54).

of parallel antitrust proceedings as the existing special jurisdictional rules in Arts 2, 5 and 6 are not capable of putting an end to the multiplications of courts able to hear antitrust claims related to one and the same contract. It is unfortunate that jurisdiction in such cases would depend on the question of who is faster in lodging his claim first. Greater difficulties in competition cases (and collective redress proceedings) may arise if the 'same parties' requirement of Art 27 of Brussels I is considered. This is doubtless problematic and would give rise to further difficulties at recognition and enforcement stage.

In these circumstances, it would be more appropriate if the Brussels I Regulation envisaged the possibility of a Member State court not allowing a trial in an EU competition law case where the well placed forum to deal with the case was elsewhere. This would allow the administration of justice within the EU to be conducted in a more efficient way. This would have been achieved if any court (no matter whether first seised or second seised) were entitled to stay its proceedings or decline jurisdiction should there be a more appropriate forum. The problem is that it is difficult to implement this in the European context because Brussels I precludes a court of a Member State from declining the jurisdiction conferred on it by the Regulation.

5

The Applicable Law in Competition Law Actions Brought before English Courts

5.1 Introduction

Once a court has established that it has jurisdiction to hear and determine an EU competition law claim, it must decide which law is applicable for these purposes. Would this be important at all, if a claim is brought for an alleged breach of Art 101 TFEU (ex Art 81 TEC) and/or Art 102 TFEU (ex Art 82 TEC)? Is it not EU competition law that always would take precedence? One may argue that, according to the principle of supremacy, EU law would always be applicable.[1] It is well settled after the *Van Gend en Loos* case[2] that the EU legal order is an integrated system, where EU law is an integral part of each Member State's legal system. Therefore, it is a duty of an English court to apply Arts 101 and 102 TFEU to agreements and practices which may affect trade between Member States.[3] This can be a significant factor suggesting that choice-of-law issues may be irrelevant or less important in relation to EU competition law claims with an international element. But what if EU law is silent on the issue (eg awards of punitive antitrust damages) that is in dispute? What if the contract is most closely related to a non-EU country, or if the parties have chosen that their contract should be governed by a non-EU country's laws?

There are complex choice-of-law problems which may arise with regard to both tortious and contractual antitrust claims. As already mentioned, there are two sets of private international law rules that need to be examined in order to determine what law would govern competition law issues in dispute. The Rome I Regulation would apply in situations involving a conflict of laws with regard to contractual obligations that may restrict competition. The Rome II Regulation would apply in tortious claims arising out of restriction of competition.

[1] Case 6/64 *Costa v ENEL* [1964] ECR 585. See *R v Secretary of State for Transport ex p Factortame (No 2)* [1991] 1 AC 603 (HL) 659 (Lord Bridge).
[2] Case 26/62 *Van Gend en Loos* [1963] ECR 1, 12. See also: *Factortame* (n 1) 659 (Lord Bridge).
[3] See Recital 8 and Art 3 of Council Regulation 1/2003.

In this chapter, the applicable law in relation to EU competition law claims arising out of anti-competitive agreements and practices will be examined.

5.2 Applicable Law: Actions for Nullity of Contracts Distorting Competition

The most common antitrust disputes that may arise in the context of Rome I are to do with the validity of a contract (or of any term of a contract) that is alleged to be void[4] and illegal[5] as being in conflict with EU competition law. Very interesting practical and theoretical issues would arise as to the incidental application of competition law in the context of a claim in contract. These issues are to be determined by the law which would govern the agreement under the Rome I Regulation[6] because, as already noted, an EU competition law claim would fall within the scope of the term 'civil and commercial matter'.[7]

5.2.1 Freedom of Choice and its Limitations under Arts 3 and 6 of Rome I

Article 3(1) of Rome I adopts as a basic principle that 'the contract shall be governed by the law chosen by the parties'. The choice can be expressly or impliedly made.[8] Are there any limits to the principle of freedom of choice and party autonomy in relation to contracts raising EU competition law concerns?

The Rome Convention was criticised for 'not deal[ing] with the question of how to treat the emerging mandatory rules of the European [Union] to contracts which only have contacts with the [EU]'.[9] This problem has been rectified by Art 3(4) of Rome I, which states that:

> Where all other elements relevant to the situation at the time of the choice are located in one or more Member States, the parties' choice of applicable law other than that of a Member State shall not prejudice the application of provisions of [EU] law, where appropriate as implemented in the Member State of the forum, which cannot be derogated from by agreement.

This provision is meant to limit the parties' freedom to choose competition laws governing the validity of their agreement in cases where all the elements of the

[4] See Art 101(2) TFEU; Case 48/72 *Haecht v Wilkin-Janssen* [1973] ECR 77 [25]–[27].

[5] *Gibbs Mew v Gemmell* [1998] EuLR 588 (CA).

[6] See Art 10 of the Rome I Regulation. See also R Plender and M Wilderspin, *The European Private International Law of Obligations* (3rd edn, Sweet & Maxwell, London, 2009) 421–25.

[7] See ch 1, section 1.6.1.1 above.

[8] M Giuliano and P Legarde, 'Report on the law applicable to contractual obligations' [1980] OJ C-282/1. See also: *Egon Oldendorff v Liberia Corporation* [1995] 2 Lloyd's Rep 64 (Comm).

[9] O Lando, 'The EEC Convention on the law applicable to contractual obligations' (1987) 24 *CML Rev* 159, 181.

contract are connected with only one or more Member State at the time when the choice is made. There is little doubt that EU competition law rules, which are essential for the functioning of the internal market, would be regarded as mandatory provisions which cannot be derogated from.[10] Therefore, Arts 101 and 102 TFEU will prevail over the rules of the selected foreign law, so that the English court would be entitled to set aside the foreign law chosen by the parties to the extent that is necessary in order for it to apply the EU mandatory rules. The provision, however, would have no role to play in cases where the contract that is alleged to distort competition is substantially connected with another country and indeed implemented in the foreign country.[11] In other words, if a European producer and a US producer (or even two European manufacturers) of gadgets have chosen the law of New York as applicable to their agreement that is to be performed in the US (ie implemented in the US), then, if it is alleged that the agreement is anti-competitive, Art 3(4) of Rome I would have no role to play, as not all the elements are connected with the EU.

Furthermore, the fact that neither the Treaty on the Functioning of the European Union nor the Court of Justice have identified what are the consequences of invalidating only part of contract which is in conflict with Arts 101 and/or 102 TFEU leaves no doubt that the chosen law should determine whether the rest of the contract would be enforceable.[12] This clearly indicates that the application of EU competition law rules that form part of each Member State's law would not preclude the parties to choose the law applicable to the rest of their contract, including the question how the principle of severance of illegal provisions from otherwise lawful agreements would apply under the general law of contract.[13] Such a deduction can be strengthened by the last sentence of Art 3(1) of Rome I which provides that: 'By their choice the parties can select the law applicable to the whole or a part only of the contract.' Therefore, Art 3(4) of Rome I would indicate that EU competition law would be relevant only with regard to the issue whether the contractual clause/s of the agreement is/are valid.

[10] J Drexl, 'Competition law as part of the European Constitution' in A von Bogdandy and J Bast (eds), *Principles of European Constitutional Law* (2nd edn, Hart Publishing and Verlag CH Beck, Oxford and Munich, 2009) 659, 662–69. See also: Art 119 TFEU; the Protocol on the Internal Market and Competition annexed to the Treaty on European Union. Compare: Art 3(1)(g) TEC; Case 6/72 *Continental Can v Commission* [1973] ECR 215 [23]; Case T-34/92 *Fiatagri and New Holland Ford* [1994] ECR II-905; Case C-126/97 *Eco Swiss China Time v Benetton International ('Eco Swiss')* [1999] ECR I-3055 [36]; Case C-453/99 *Courage v Crehan* [2001] ECR I-6297 [20]. See more: sections 5.2.3.1 and 6.2.1 below.

[11] Joined Cases 89/85, 104/85, 114/85, 116–17/85, and 125–29/85 *Ahlstrom v Commission* [1988] ECR 5193 (*Wood Pulp* cartel case) [16]. See also: MP Broberg. 'The European Commission's extraterritorial powers in merger control the Court of First Instance's judgment in *Gencor v. Commission*' (2000) 49 *ICLQ* 172, 177.

[12] See Art 12(1)(e) of the Rome I Regulation. See also: A Komninos, *EC Private Antitrust Enforcement: Decentralised Application of EC Competition Law by National Courts* (Hart Publishing, Oxford, 2008) 156–57; R Whish, *Competition Law* (6th edn, OUP, Oxford, 2008) 313.

[13] Eg Case 56/65 *Société Technique Miniere v Maschinenbau* [1966] ECR 235; Case 319/82 *Société de Vente de Ciments et Betons de l'Est v Kerpen and Kerepen GmbH* [1983] ECR 4173.

If the contractual clause/s were not valid, then the chosen law would determine whether the rest of the contract would be enforceable. In other words, the application of the mandatory (EU competition law) provisions could result in different laws being applicable to the different parts of the parties' contract.[14]

The effect of Art 3(4) is that it will limit the parties' freedom of choice, in order to preclude evasion of EU competition law[15] in cases where all the relevant elements are connected with the EU. The principle of freedom of choice and party autonomy would be further limited in another type of contract that may often give rise to competition law concerns, namely the consumer contracts.[16] Article 6(2) of Rome I is set to provide special protection for consumers who would normally be in a weaker bargaining position.[17] In order to protect consumers in Europe, the Rome I Regulation has adopted the 'preferential law approach', which does not derogate the choice of law made by the parties, but the mandatory provisions of the law of the country of consumers' habitual residence will prevail to the extent that they provide better protection to consumers than the chosen law.[18]

Article 6(2) of Rome I, however, may not be easily applied in respect of consumers' claims based on competition law infringements, as what would be a higher degree of protection seems to depend on the consumer's claim. The difficulties can be demonstrated by taking a simple example, where consumers in the USA, the UK and France have been buying a given product tied in package with gadgets. If the consumer contracts included a clause selecting the law of New York as governing law, then the US federal antitrust should determine the validity of the contract unless EU competition laws offered greater protection to the parties. Let us assume that such an agreement forecloses competition on the EU market for gadgets (ie tied market) and is invalid under EU competition law, but valid under US Federal antitrust law.[19] If the European consumers had brought a class action in England seeking invalidity of the contracts for gadgets, the effect

[14] JJ Fawcett and JM Carruthers, *Cheshire, North & Fawcett Private International Law* (14th edn, OUP, Oxford, 2008) 690–92.

[15] Compare JJ Fawcett, 'Evasion of law and mandatory rules in private international law' (1990) 49 *CLJ* 44.

[16] For a detailed discussion of the application of choice-of-law rules in consumer contracts generally, see J Hill, *Cross-Border Consumer Contracts* (OUP, Oxford, 2008) 322–71.

[17] P Nygh, *Autonomy in International Contracts* (OUP, Oxford, 1999) 139.

[18] See Art 6(2) of the Rome I Regulation. See more: F Ragno, 'The law applicable to consumer contracts under the Rome I Regulation' in F Ferrari and S Leibbe (eds), *Rome I Regulation: The Law Applicable to Contractual Obligations in Europe* (Sellier, Munich, 2009) 127, 150–54. See also: CGJ Morse, 'Consumer contracts, employment contracts and the Rome Convention' (1992) 41 *ICLQ* 1, 8; Nygh (n 17) 156–59; Hill (n 16) 327–29.

[19] The choice of law of the State of New York means that anti-competitive elements of the contract question should be determined by the US Federal Antitrust Law. Indeed, Art I, s 8, cl 3 of the US Constitution states that: 'The Congress shall have power to regulate commerce with foreign nations, and among the several states, and with Indian tribes.' Further, for the purposes of allocating jurisdiction within the US, the US Code, Title 28, Pt IV, c 85, para 1337(a) clearly states that '[t]he district courts shall have original jurisdiction of any civil action or proceeding arising under any Act of Congress regulating commerce or protecting trade and commerce against restraints and monopolies ....'

of Art 6(2) of Rome I would be to invalidate the consumer contracts even if the contracts for sale of gadgets were valid under the US antitrust law, but invalid under EU competition law. However, if the consumers claimed that the defendant should have delivered the tied products, then the defendant could not refuse to deliver the tied products by claiming that the contract is invalid under EU law. In such a scenario, the defendant would not be entitled to claim that EU competition law provisions, being mandatory rules which cannot be derogated from, would be always applicable. Therefore, the answer to the question whether competition law provides a higher level of protection for consumers would largely depend on what the consumers claim to be entitled to.

5.2.2 Competition Law Disputes: The Applicable Law in the Absence of Choice

Article 4 of Rome I is set to determine which national law would govern the contract in the absence of choice made by the parties. This provision is largely based on Art 4 of the Rome Convention. The wording of Art 4(1) and (2) leaves no doubt that an important connecting factor for choice-of-law purposes is the habitual residence of the party who effects the characteristic performance. Article 4(3) and (4) goes further, to indicate that the connection of a contract with the country in question is another crucial factor that would indicate the applicable law in absence of choice.[20] Accordingly, there are several concepts which need to be examined, in order to determine the law governing the validity of an (allegedly) anti-competitive agreement (or anti-competitive term) in absence of choice under Art 4 of Rome I.

5.2.2.1 Characteristic Performance

Although, the Rome I Regulation does not define the concept of characteristic performance, it is well established that the EU legislator has referred to the 'performance for which the payment is due'.[21] Article 4(1) of Rome I has identified the party that is to effect the characteristic performance with regard to some of the most common types of contracts that may inter alia give rise to competition law disputes. In such cases, the relevant connecting factor would be the habitual residence of the party identified as effecting the characteristic performance for the choice-of-law purposes. For example, a contract for the sale of goods shall be governed by the law of the country where the seller has his habitual residence;[22] a contract for the provision of services shall be governed by the law of the country

[20] See Art 4(3) and (4) of the Rome I Regulation.

[21] See the Giuliano and Lagarde Report (n 8) 20; *Cheshire, North & Fawcett* (n 14) 712–15; C Forsyth and P Morse, 'The impact of the applicable law of contract on the law of jurisdiction under the European conventions' (1996) 45 *ICLQ* 190, 193–94.

[22] See Art 4(1)(a) of the Rome I Regulation.

where the service provider has his habitual residence;[23] a franchise contract shall be governed by the law of the country where the franchisee has his habitual residence;[24] a distribution contract shall be governed by the law of the country where the distributor has his habitual residence.[25] However, some of the most common agreements (eg technology transfer agreements) which may give rise to antitrust law disputes are not mentioned in Art 4(1) of Rome I. The characteristic performance for such types of contracts would need to be identified on a case-by-case basis, in order to identify the party who is to effect the characteristic performance for the choice-of-law purposes.[26]

What would the characteristic performance be in competition law disputes relating to a typical technology transfer agreement? As previously mentioned,[27] under such an agreement a licensor grants to a licensee an exclusive right to exploit an intellectual property right and consideration for this is the royalty (ie payment of money). The definition of characteristic performance in terms of the performance for which payment is due suggests that the granting of a licence to exploit an intellectual property right is to be regarded as characteristic performance for the purposes of the Rome I Regulation.[28] Therefore, if Art 4(2) were applied with regard to technology transfer agreements, then the law of the country where the licensor had his habitual residence would have governed the validity of an (allegedly) anti-competitive agreement (or anti-competitive term). Thus, in cases that are not mentioned in Art 4(1), the habitual residence of the party in question would need to be identified.

5.2.2.2 Habitual Residence

As already noted, once the party who effects the characteristic performance has been identified, the court should identify the applicable law by making reference to the habitual residence of the party in question.[29] Article 19 provides a definition of the concept of habitual residence, which is meant to promote unified court practice under Rome I. To this end, Art 19(1) of Rome I specifies that the place of central administration is to be regarded as the habitual residence of companies and other bodies, corporate or unincorporated. The 'place of central administration' as a connecting factor has been also used by Art 60 of Brussels I, which defines the concept of domicile for the purposes of the Regulation. The case law that emerged under the Brussels I Regulation should doubtless be followed when

[23] See Art 4(1)(b) of the Rome I Regulation.

[24] See Art 4(1)(e) of the Rome I Regulation.

[25] See Art 4(1)(f) of the Rome I Regulation.

[26] See Art 4(2) of the Rome I Regulation. See more: P Torremans, 'Licences and assignments of intellectual property rights under the Rome I Regulation (2009) *Journal of Private International Law* 397, 404–12.

[27] See ch 3, section 3.3.1.2.1.1.

[28] Torremans (n 26) 405–06. See also: JJ Fawcett and P Torremans, *Intellectual Property and Private International Law* (OUP, Oxford, 1998) 560.

[29] Eg Arts 4(2) and 6(1) of Rome I. See also: *Cheshire, North & Fawcett* (n 14) 715–17.

defining the 'central administration' concept for the purposes of Rome I. The 'administration' has been defined as the part of the business which ensures that all runs smoothly in the company.[30] The place of central administration would be easily identified in EU competition law disputes which involved major organisations because the location of the company secretary's office could be regarded as a good pointer in such cases.[31]

The provision goes further to determine that the habitual residence of a natural person acting in the course of his business activity would be his principal place of business. The English courts have defined the latter concept in the context of allocating jurisdiction under the Brussels Convention.[32] According to Leggatt LJ, the principal place of business 'means … "chief" or "most important". The principal place of business is not necessarily the place where most of the business is carried out.'[33] Identifying that place would not give rise to any particular difficulties with regard to EU competition law claims.

The Rome Convention was criticised because it contained no provision to allow for the law of the country of habitual residence of the relevant party's subsidiary establishment to govern the contract, if the characteristic performance was performed by that establishment.[34] The Rome I Regulation has addressed this by providing that:

> Where the contract is concluded in the course of the operations of a branch, agency or any other establishment, or if, under the contract, performance is the responsibility of such a branch, agency or establishment, the place where the branch, agency or any other establishment is located shall be treated as the place of habitual residence.

Although the fact that a subsidiary has a separate legal personality would normally exclude it from the scope of this provision,[35] as already established, the legal personality will not be a decisive factor in EU competition law claims, where economic matters will prevail.[36] Therefore, Art 19(2) of Rome I would have an important role to play with regard to EU competition law claims. More specifically, the provision would allow for the law of the country of habitual residence of the relevant party's subsidiary establishment to govern the contract in competition cases where the contract is concluded in the course of the operations of the establishment in question, or if, under the contract, performance is the responsibility of such a subsidiary establishment.

[30] *King v Crown Energy Trading* [2003] EWHC 163 (Comm) [12]. See more: *Cheshire, North & Fawcett* (n 14) 212.

[31] *Crown Energy* Trading (n 30) [13].

[32] Plender and Wilderspin (n 6) 192–94.

[33] *The 'Rewia'* [1991] 2 Lloyd's Rep 325 (CA) 334. See more: *Cheshire, North & Fawcett* (n 14) 213.

[34] L Collins, 'Contractual obligations—the EEC preliminary draft convention on private international law' (1976) 35 *ICLQ* 25, 46.

[35] See ch 2, section 2.2.3 where the concept of 'branch, agency or any other establishment' has been discussed in the context of Art 5(5) of Brussels I.

[36] Ibid.

Nevertheless, the habitual residence of the party who is to effect the characteristic performance may often be an inappropriate connecting factor in competition law disputes. For example, in a technology transfer agreement case, if the habitual residence of the licensor was in New York, then Art 4(2) would have suggested that the validity of the agreement (or its clauses) would need to be determined by the Sherman Act.[37] Would this be so if the licensing agreement was implemented by the licensee in the European Union? What if it had been established that the contract that is alleged to distort competition is 'manifestly more closely connected' with another country?[38]

5.2.2.3 'Manifestly More Closely Connected' and 'Most Closely Connected' Tests

Article 4(3) of Rome I states that the national court should apply the 'manifestly more closely connected' test in cases where the contract is more closely connected with a country other than one indicated in Art 4(1) and (2) of Rome II. The wording of Art 4(3) of Rome I is largely based on Art 4(5) of the Rome Convention, so that there should not be any difficulties in this context. The 'more closely connected' test was applied in *Definitely Maybe (Touring) Ltd v Marek Lieberberg Konzertagentur GmbH*.[39] In this case, the habitual residence of the party who was to effect the characteristic performance was in England. The place of characteristic performance was in Germany, where the pop group Oasis had to perform. Both parties were to perform their contractual obligations in Germany. The English court held that Germany was 'more closely connected' than England with the contract in question, so German law was applied instead of English law.

However, it should be noted that Art 4(3) of Rome I is more restrictive than Art 4(5) of the Rome Convention. Art 4(3) requires the contract to be 'manifestly more closely connected'. The inclusion of the word 'manifestly' leaves no doubt that the EU legislator intended to signify that Art 4(3) is meant to be relied upon in exceptional cases where the contract is evidently or obviously more closely connected with the law of another country. In other words, the amendment inserted into Rome I appears to indicate that Art 4(1) and (2) of Rome I would not be that easily disregarded in each and every case where the place of performance of the characteristic performance is different from the place of the habitual residence of the party who is to effect it.[40] The paragraphs in question 'should … only be disregarded in circumstances which [manifestly] demonstrate the existence of the connecting factors justifying [this].'[41] This would normally happen only in 'very

[37] See Section 5.2.2.1 above.

[38] Art 4(3) of the Rome I Regulation.

[39] *Definitely Maybe (Touring) Ltd v Marek Lieberberg Konzertagentur GmbH* [2001] 1 WLR 1745.

[40] L Collins and others (eds) *Dicey, Morris and Collins on the Conflict of Laws* (14th edn, Sweet & Maxwell, London, 2006) [32]–[127].

[41] *Samcrete Egypt Engineers and Contractors SAE v Land Rover Exports Ltd* [2001] EWCA Civ 2019; [2002] CLC 533 (CA) [45]. See also: *Ennstone Building Products Ltd v Stanger Ltd* [2002] EWCA Civ 916; [2002] 1 WLR 3059 (CA) [41]; *Iran Continental Shelf Oil Co v IRI International Corp* [2002] EWCA

special circumstances'[42] when the law of the country of the habitual residence of the party who is to effect the characteristic performance has no real significance as a connecting factor.[43] No particular difficulties would arise in competition cases where the parties to an agreement that is alleged to distort competition have their habitual residence in more than one Member State and the place of performance of the agreement is mainly in the European Union. In such cases, it would always be EU competition law, which forms part of each Member State's legal order, that would determine the validity of the contract in question.

But what if the party who is to effect the characteristic performance is habitually resident in a state in the US? For example, it was already clarified that in competition law disputes as to the validity of a technology transfer agreement, the Sherman Act may be applicable, if the habitual residence of the licensor was in New York. However, if the agreement were anti-competitive, then the exploitation of technology within the EU would not have significantly and adversely affected consumers within the US. It has been submitted that a licensing agreement is most closely connected with the protecting country which is also the country where the technology is to be exploited.[44] There are strong arguments suggesting that Art 4(3) will certainly be of relevance in cases where the licence was to be exploited within the European Union. In other words, EU competition law, which forms part of each Member State's legal order, would determine the validity of an allegedly anti-competitive licensing agreement (or allegedly anti-competitive clause contained in such an agreement) provided that the licensed technology was to be exploited in the EU. However, the choice-of-law problem may arise, for example, if the technology transfer agreement implemented within the European Union precluded parallel imports of the licensed technology within the US. Can a Member State court apply US Federal antitrust law,[45] if it has been established that the contract is most closely connected with the US?[46]

Further, conflicts of laws may arise if an antitrust dispute arises out of distribution contracts which were concluded with respect to an area which is wider than the territory of a single Member State (eg south-eastern Europe; Commonwealth countries; or the UK and the US). In such a scenario, the characteristic performance may be performed in a number of countries. Would the habitual residence of the main distributor be an appropriate connecting factor in cases where his habitual residence is in a Member State, whilst the goods are largely distributed in a non-Member State (eg the USA or Turkey)? Would

Civ 1024; [2004] 2 CLC 696 [81]–[82]; *Opthalmic Innovations (UK) v Opthalmic Innovations (USA)* [2004] EWHC 2948 (ChD); [2005] ILPr 10 [49]. See more: *Cheshire, North & Fawcett* (n 14) 718–22.

[42] *Caledonia Subsea v Micoperi* 2002 SLT 1022 [3] (Lord Marnoch).

[43] *Caledonia Subsea* (n 42) [6] (Lord Cameron).

[44] Torremans (n 26) 412–15. See also Fawcett and Torremans (n 27) 566–70.

[45] Although, the USA is composed of states, it is the US Federal Antitrust Law that would be relevant in view of that fact the US Congress has the power to regulate commerce with foreign nations, and among the several states. See Art I, s 8, cl 3 of the US Constitution.

[46] See section 5.2.3 below.

the US or Turkish antitrust law determine the validity of the agreement if the contract were manifestly more closely connected with the US or Turkey and the contract have to be or have been performed there?

Similar problems would arise in EU competition cases where the characteristic performance cannot be determined. The concept of characteristic performance would not be easily applied in competition law disputes relating to not full-function joint ventures (eg joint ventures limited to research and development,[47] production or sales); crisis cartels; agreements on companies' marketing strategies and on sharing commercial information.[48] In some cases, it would be 'difficult, if not impossible, to determine what is the characteristic performance'.[49] For example, as a result of an economic and/or financial crisis a Turkish company, a US company, a French company and an English company whose factories are situated in Turkey, the US, France and the UK may agree to implement an X per cent reduction in capacity related to production of chemical product Y. In such a case, it seems that the four parties' obligations, which are equally characteristic, are to be performed at different places. But which law would govern the validity of the agreement in question? Is it for the US Federal antitrust law, or for EU competition law, or for Turkish competition law to determine whether the contract is valid?

The Regulation provides for this by providing in Art 4(4) that, the applicable law in such scenarios would be the law of the country with which it is most closely connected. The *Wood Pulp* case indicates that the fact that the agreement is implemented within the EU taken together with the public policy character of Arts 101 and 102 TFEU would mean that EU competition law will be applicable in such a dispute. However, for example, the US federal law may have an equally strong claim. The fact that competition law provisions are fundamental for safeguarding countries' public interests leaves no doubt that national courts may not easily answer the question of which country's competition laws would govern the validity of the contract in question. Can the court make a conflict of-laws analysis when deciding which competition laws are applicable?

5.2.3 Article 9 and its Application in Competition Law Cases

Article 9(1) of the Rome I Regulation seems to indicate that in competition law disputes due consideration must be given to the 'overriding mandatory provisions' of the relevant countries. The provision states that:

> Overriding mandatory provisions are provisions the respect for which is regarded as crucial by a country for safeguarding its public interests, such as its political, social or economic organisation, to such an extent that they are applicable to any situation falling

[47] It has been submitted that '[a] joint-venture contract is probably the most problematic type of contract, especially when joint research and development is envisaged.' Torremans (n 26) 406.

[48] F Alese, *Federal Antitrust and EC competition law analysis* (Ashgate, London, 2008) 131–44.

[49] *Caledonia Subsea* (n 42) [21] (Lord President Cullen).

within their scope, irrespective of the law otherwise applicable to the contract under this Regulation.

A distinction should be made between the provisions, 'which cannot be derogated within the meaning' of Arts 3 and 6 of Rome I, and 'overriding mandatory provisions' within the meaning of Art 9 of the Regulation.[50] The first set will be relevant only in cases where all the elements of the contract are connected with one or more Member State(s) at the time when the choice is made. The second set of mandatory provisions would be applicable to any situation falling within their scope. This rule is meant to preserve the rules, which are regarded by the forum as overriding mandatory provisions or *lois de police*.[51]

5.2.3.1 EU Competition Laws—Overriding Mandatory Provisions for the Purposes of Rome I

Articles 101 and 102 TFEU are to be regarded as overriding mandatory provisions within the meaning of Art 9(1) of Rome I. Arguments to that effect can be derived from EU law and English law. Such a deduction can be reinforced by making reference to the Giuliano and Lagarde Report which indicates that the 'overriding mandatory provisions' would cover inter alia the EU rules on cartels, competition, restrictive practices and abuse of dominant position.[52] Fawcett and Torremans seem to accept that 'rules of competition law are always mandatory'.[53] The Court of Justice has consistently held that Art 101 TFEU (ex Art 81 TEC), 'constitutes a fundamental provision, which is essential for the accomplishment of the tasks entrusted to the [EU] and, in particular, for the functioning of the internal market.'[54] The CFI has also held that 'Article [101 TFEU] lays down a fundamental prohibition of agreements, which are anti-competitive in character. That provision, adopted as a matter of public policy, is therefore binding on the applicant undertaking irrespective of any binding decision adopted by the Commission on this point.'[55]

Arguments strengthening the deduction that Arts 101 and 102 TFEU should be regarded as 'overriding mandatory provisions' could also stem from the Treaty on the Functioning of the European Union and English law and the Regulations implementing the EU competition law provisions. According to Art 119 TFEU, EU and Member States' economic policies should be 'conducted in accordance with the principle of an open market economy and free competition.' Further, the Protocol on the Internal Market and Competition annexed to the Treaty on European Union states that 'the internal market as set out in Art 3 of the Treaty

[50] See more: J Harris, 'Mandatory rules and public policy under the Rome I Regulation' in Ferrari and Leibbe (n 18) 268, 292–97 and 334–41.

[51] Giuliano and Lagarde Report (n 8) 28. See also the French version of Rome I.

[52] Ibid.

[53] Fawcett and Torremans (n 28) 582.

[54] *Eco Swiss* (n 10) [36]; *Crehan* (n 10) [20]. See also: *Continental Can* (n 10) [23].

[55] *Fiatagri* (n 10) [39].

on European Union includes a system ensuring that competition is not distorted.' Thus, Arts 101 and 102 TFEU should be regarded as mandatory provisions, which are essential for the functioning of the internal market and EU legal order.[56]

Nonetheless, one may argue that similar arguments could also be used to infer a public policy character for many EU provisions (eg Art 16 TFEU (ex Art 28 TEC)). The importance of Art 101 TFEU could be deduced from its sub-s (2), which stipulates that agreements concluded in breach of the prohibition contained in Art 101(1) are automatically void. The Court of Justice has held that in such cases nullity is retroactive, irrespective of whether or not any statement to that effect is made by the body responsible for deciding the matter.[57] In spite of the fact that Art 102 TFEU does not include a provision equivalent to Art 101(2), which prescribes that any agreements prohibited by Art 101(1) shall be automatically void, the Court of Justice has stated that a similar consequence applies to any breach of Art 102 TFEU.[58] The retroactive nullity of an agreement that distorts competition re-affirms the fundamental character of EU competition law.[59]

Indeed, the unique public interest in the enforcement of competition law, however, is further reflected in the Enterprise Act 2002 that introduced criminal sanctions for individuals who have engaged in hard-core cartels.[60] Thus, there are very strong arguments suggesting that the definition of 'overriding mandatory provisions' covers EU competition law rules which form part of the individual Member States' public policy.

5.2.3.2 'Overriding Mandatory Provisions' for the Purposes of Art 9 and 'Public Policy' of the Forum under Art 21

It has been submitted that an important difference between 'overriding mandatory provisions' and the public policy exception that could be derived from the Rome I Regulation is that whereas a court may take account of a third state's mandatory provisions,[61] there is no support for enforcing the public policy of a third country.[62] However, the examples from above not only suggest that Arts 101 and 102 TFEU will be regarded as overriding mandatory provisions, but also indicate that the EU competition law rules may trigger the public policy exception of Art 21 of Rome I. The Court of Justice has clearly held that Arts 101 and 102 TFEU would have a 'public policy' character for the purposes of recognition and enforcement of foreign judgments and arbitral awards in relation to EU

[56] See Drexl (n 10) 662–69. See also: old Art 3(1)(g) TEC; *Eco Swiss* (n 10); and ch 6, section 6.2.1 below.

[57] *Haecht* (n 4) [25]–[27]. See also: *Eco Swiss* (n 10) [36] (AG Saggio).

[58] Case 172/73 *BRT v SABAM* [1974] ECR 51.

[59] See more: ch 6 below.

[60] ss 188–202 provide for a criminal offence for individuals who dishonestly engage in cartel agreements ('the criminal offence').

[61] See Art 9(3) of the Rome I Regulation.

[62] Nygh (n 17) 207. Compare: Art 21 of the Rome I Regulation.

competition law claims.[63] What is the relationship between overriding mandatory provisions and public policy for the purposes of Rome I, and how would this be relevant in EU competition law cases? The question of interrelationship between mandatory provisions and public policy has been discussed by academics.[64] It is well established that mandatory rules are an expression of public policy.[65] It has been submitted that:

> The generally accepted dividing line between the two is that public policy operates negatively in that it involves the disapplication of the relevant applicable law,[66] while mandatory rules operate positively in that they are superimposed onto the applicable law of the contract.[67]

The practical implications of such a distinction can be demonstrated by making reference to *Duarte v Black and Decker Corp*.[68] In this case, Mr Duarte sought a declaration that a restrictive covenant contained in his contract of employment with Black and Decker Corporation was void and unenforceable. The parties had expressly chosen the law of Maryland to govern their contract. In spite of the choice-of-law agreement, Art 6(2) of the Rome Convention stated that a choice of law made by the parties could not deprive an employee of the protection afforded to him by the mandatory rules of the law which would be applicable in the absence of choice. In the circumstances, English law would have been applicable to the covenant if the parties had not chosen the law of Maryland. The English High Court found that English law must not apply in preference to Maryland law in deciding whether the covenants are enforceable, because the English law of restrictive covenants in employment contracts does not consist of mandatory rules.[69] If there were overriding mandatory provisions in English law, the Court would have applied them without making reference to Maryland law. Given the fact that under English law, the law of restrictive covenants in employment contracts is based on public policy considerations, the English Court had to apply Maryland law, as the English law would have been potentially applicable only if the covenants were enforceable under Maryland law.[70]

The dividing line between overriding mandatory provisions and public policy would be artificial with regard to antitrust law claims, as competition laws are considered to reflect the public policy of different countries and at the same time

[63] *Eco Swiss* (n 10) [38]; Case C-38/98 *Renault v Maxicar* [2000] ECR I-2973. See also: HP Meidans, 'Public policy and *ordre public* in the private international law of the EC/EU: Traditional positions of the Member States and modern trends' (2005) 30 *EL Rev* 95; J-P Beraudo, 'Egregious error of law as grounds for setting aside an arbitral award' (2006) 23 *Journal of International Arbitration* 351.

[64] Nygh (n 17) 206–08; A Chong, 'The public policy and mandatory rules of third countries in international contracts' (2006) 2 *Journal of Private International Law* 27, 32–35.

[65] Nygh (n 17) 206; Chong (n 64) 32.

[66] Art 16 of the Rome Convention is given as an example. See also: Art 21 of the Rome I Regulation.

[67] Chong (n 64) 32. See also: Harris (n 50) 297–98.

[68] *Duarte v Black and Decker Corporation* [2007] EWHC 2720 (QB).

[69] Ibid [55].

[70] Ibid [104].

they consist of overriding mandatory provisions. It appears that in antitrust cases, public policy will often be used to reinforce the operation of overriding mandatory provisions.[71]

5.2.3.3 Application of Art 9 in Competition Cases

As already clarified,[72] Arts 101 and 102 TFEU would apply to an agreement or concerted practice entered into between non-EU undertakings outside the EU. This would be so, if an agreement were 'implemented' within the EU[73] and had appreciable effect on competition or inter-state trade within the EU.[74] There is 'no reason to suggest that the territorial scope of application of [EU competition law] would be any different in the case of private litigation.'[75] Therefore, another specific features of a big majority of the antitrust law provisions is that they enjoy extraterritorial effect. For example, the Sherman Act has been applied to extraterritorial conduct.[76] This may be problematic as different regulations may be applicable to a given legal relationship in different countries.[77] Does it mean that the applicable antitrust laws would depend on where the action is brought?

The fact that Art 9(1) and (2) cover the directly applicable rules of EU competition law[78] seems to suggest that an English court by virtue of Art 9(2) would always apply Arts 101 and 102 TFEU as being mandatory rules of the forum. Indeed, the extra-territorial application of antitrust laws, which has been widely discussed by the courts[79] and commentators,[80] seems to indicate that EU competition law would cover non-EU anti-competitive conduct, in order to remedy a distortion of competition within the EU. In other words, if an agreement were

[71] Compare: Nygh (n 17) 207.

[72] See ch 1 and section 5.2.1 above.

[73] *Wood Pulp* (n 11).

[74] See Case 5/69 *Volk v Vervaecke* [1969] ECR 295. See also The Commission's *Notice on Agreements of Minor Importance* OJ [2001] C368/13. See more: Whish (n 12) 137–47.

[75] C Withers, 'Jurisdiction and Applicable Law in Antitrust Tort Claims' (2002) *Journal of Business Law* 250, 257–58.

[76] *Timberline Lumber Co v Bank of America, NT & SA* 549 F2d 597 at 609 (9th Cir 1976). See also: *Continental Ore Co v Union Carbide & Carbon Corp* (1962) 370 US 268; *United States v Aluminum Co of America (Alcoa)* 148 F2d 416 (2d Cir 1945).

[77] See: CM Schmitthoff, *The English Conflict of Laws* (3rd edn, Steven & Sons, London, 1954) 11.

[78] See Lando (n 9) 207. See also Withers (n 75) 270.

[79] The EU approach: *Wood Pulp* (n 11); compare the US approach: (a) territorial approach *America Banana v United Fruit* 213 US 347 (1909); (b) the 'effects' approach *United States v Aluminum Co of America (Alcoa)* 148 F2d 416 (2d Cir 1945); (c) the 'balancing' approach *Timberline Lumber* (n 71). See also: Restatement of the Law (Third), The Foreign Relations Law of the United States (1987) [403].

[80] M Waelbroeck, 'The European Community Approach' in CJ Omstead (ed) *Extra-territorial Application of Laws and Responses Thereto* (International Law Association in association with ESC Publishing, Oxford, 1989) 74; WS Dodge, 'Extraterritoriality and Conflict-of-Laws Theory: An argument for judicial unilateralism' (1998) 39 *Harvard International Law Journal* 101; JP Griffin, 'Extraterritoriality in U.S. and EU antitrust enforcement' (1999–2000) *Antitrust Law Journal* 159; V Pavic, *Extra-territoriality in the Matters of Antitrust* (European Press Academic Publishing, Italy, 2001); J Adolphsen, 'The Conflict of laws in cartel matters in a globalised world: alternatives to the effects doctrine' (2005) *Journal of International Private Law* 156.

'implemented' within the EU and had appreciable effect on competition or inter-state trade within the EU, then the wording of Art 9(1) and (2) of Rome I suggests that an English court could not refuse to apply EU competition law, even if the parties selected New York law to govern their contract. However, as already clarified with regard to Art 3(4),[81] the fact that neither the Treaty on the Functioning of the European Union nor the Court of Justice have identified what are the consequences of invalidating only part of a contract which is in conflict with Arts 101 and/or 102 TFEU suggests that the law under Rome I should determine whether the rest of the contract would be enforceable.[82]

The implications of Art 9(1) and (2) on the law applicable to validity of an (allegedly) anti-competitive agreement can be demonstrated by taking as an example a dispute between an English manufacturer and one of its US distributors as to the anti-competitive effects of a contract, which forms part of a large network of similar agreements. If the network of similar agreements had been implemented only in the US, where the English company exported all of its output, then (if New York law were to be applicable under Rome I) there would not be ground for triggering the Rome I mandatory rules exception as the *Wood Pulp* test would not be satisfied. However, if the English companies had sold some of its outputs in both US and EU markets (i.e. some of the agreements were implemented in the EU), then Arts 101 and 102 TFEU would be applicable as overriding mandatory provisions within the meaning of Art 9(1) and (2) of Rome I.[83]

But, what if the contract in question is manifestly more closely connected with the US? What if US antitrust law had a stronger claim to govern the issue of validity of the agreement? Can the English court to make a conflict-of-laws analysis, in order to decide which set of overriding mandatory provisions should apply in competition cases where applicable US laws and English laws provide different mandatory provisions to govern the antitrust issues in the dispute? These are important omissions, as not all foreign nations have adopted antitrust law similar to EU competition laws.[84] It has been submitted by Withers that:

> [I]t is difficult to discern any compelling policy interest in favour of the application of English and European antitrust laws to disputes involving anti-competitive activities taking place outside Europe, sufficient to justify their treatment as mandatory rules of the forum. It is therefore, suggested that they should not be regarded as imposing on the courts a duty to apply those laws when a choice of law rule selects the antitrust laws of a foreign jurisdiction as applicable to the activity taking place in that jurisdiction.[85]

[81] See section 5.2.1 above.

[82] See Art 12(1)(e) of the Rome I Regulation. See also: Komninos (n 12) 156–57; Whish (n 12) 313.

[83] Compare: MJ Trebilcock and EM Iacobucci, 'National treatment and extraterritoriality: defining the domains of trade and antitrust policy' in RA Epstein and MS Greve (eds), *Competition Laws in Conflict: Antitrust Jurisdiction in the Global Economy* (AEI Press, Washington, 2004) 152, 161–62.

[84] See *F Hoffmann-La Roche Ltd v Empagran* (2004) 542 US 155, 167; 124 SCt 2359, 2368.

[85] Withers (n 75) 268.

Although, the quoted statement is made in the context of tortious antitrust claims, it appears that the arguments would be valid for any claim that would involve the application of the overriding mandatory rules of the forum. The statement is based on the assumption that the 'place of the performance' would be the main factor that would entitle the court to exercise its discretion and apply another country's overriding mandatory provisions. A similar approach can be found in the subsequently adopted Art 9(3) of the Rome I Regulation which requires the Member State judges to consider whether to give effect to the 'overriding mandatory provisions of the law of the country where the obligations arising out of the contract have to be or have been performed, in so far as those overriding mandatory provisions render the performance of the contract unlawful.'[86] Indeed, normally the English courts would not enforce a contract where its performance is unlawful by the antitrust laws at the place where the contract must be performed.[87] This proposition is 'based on the principle that it is contrary to the comity of nations that the Court of one country should seek to enforce the performance of something in another country which is forbidden by the law of that country.'[88] It also seems to be consistent with the EC/US Antitrust Co-operation Agreement 1991.[89] Accordingly, the Rome I Regulation would take account of the foreign country regulatory interests, if the application of the foreign overriding mandatory antitrust provisions made unlawful the performance of the contract in question.[90] However, if the foreign conduct had been permitted, encouraged or otherwise approved by the foreign antitrust laws, but had been forbidden by EU competition law, then Art 9(3) of Rome I suggests that the foreign antitrust law would not be given effect provided that competition within the EU market was affected. For example, in a case where a certain manufacturer had precluded a US licensee to export the licensed technology to the EU, it would be EU competition law that would determine the validity of such an agreement (or a contractual clause in it)[91] even if the contract were valid under the applicable non-EU antitrust law.

[86] Compare European Commission (EC) 'Proposal for a European Community Regulation on the law applicable to contractual obligations' COM (2005) 650 final, Art 8(3). See also A Dickinson, 'Third-country mandatory rules in the law applicable to contractual obligations: so long, farewell, auf wiedersehen, adieu?' (2007) 3 *Journal of Private International Law* 53.

[87] Compare *R v International Trustee for Bondholders AG* [1937] AC 500 (HL) 519 (Lord Wright). See also *Ralli Bros v Cia Naviera Sota y Aznar* [1920] 2 KB 287; Nygh (n 17) 224–25; A Briggs, *Agreements on Jurisdiction and Choice of Law* (OUP, Oxford, 2008) 395.

[88] *International Trustee for Bondholders* (n 58) 519 (Lord Wright). See also: L Collins, 'Comity in modern private international law' in JJ Fawcett (ed), *Reform and Development of Private International Law* (OUP, Oxford, 2002) 89, 99.

[89] Agreement between the Government of the United States of America and the Commission of the European Communities Regarding the Application of their Competition Laws (1991) 30 *International Legal Materials* 1491. See more: JP Griffin, 'EC/US Antitrust Cooperation Agreement: Impact on Transnational Business' (1992–1993) 24 *Law and Policy in International Business* 1051; AD Ham, 'International cooperation in the antitrust field and in particular the agreement between the United States of America and the Commission of the European Communities' (1993) 30 *CML Rev* 571.

[90] See Harris (n 50) 320–21.

[91] Compare Griffin (n 80) 186–87.

The question of what competition law (mandatory antitrust provisions) should apply, where applicable antitrust laws implement different economic policies and regulate their commercial affairs differently with regard to the antitrust issues in dispute, does not arise under Rome I. It would be more appropriate if Art 9(3) provided for a conflict-of-law analysis, which would have guaranteed that EU competition law would not be applicable unless the dispute is sufficiently closely connected with the European Union.[92] Under Rome I the applicable law would depend on whether the contract was implemented within the EU, which is not a conflict-of-laws test but the one introduced by *Wood Pulp*, and does not guarantee that the dispute is sufficiently closely connected with the EU.

5.3 Applicable Law: Tortious Competition Law Actions

As already clarified,[93] a typical claim for antitrust damages would be tortious in nature. Recital 22 makes clear that Art 6(3) of Rome II is meant to cover infringement of both national and EU competition law. The detail that Recital 23 defines 'the concept of restriction of competition' by referring to acts prohibited by Arts 101 and 102 TFEU or by the law of a Member State does not mean that Art 6(3) of Rome II is not capable of encompassing similar conduct that is prohibited by the antitrust legislation of a non-Member State.[94] Indeed, it has been submitted that 'the language of art. 6(3)(a) itself suggests that its scope is not so restricted since the choice of law rule that it contains designates as applicable law "the law of the country" (as opposed to "Member State") where the market is affected.'[95] Thus, the universal application under Art 3 of the Rome II Regulation and the wording of Art 6(3) of Rome II leave no doubt that in cases where the anti-competitive conduct had no appreciable effect on competition or inter-state trade within the EU, then antitrust laws of the country (including non-Member State laws) in which the market is affected are to be applicable.

Recital 23 rather reflects the fact that EU competition laws or Member States' antitrust laws would normally be applied by the Member States' courts as overriding mandatory provisions of the law of the forum.[96] In spite of that, Art 6(3) of Rome II would have an important role to play in private EU antitrust damage actions, because a claim for damages arising out of an EU competition law infringement is a mixture of EU law and 'domestic law'.[97] It has been suggested that to determine the question of whether there is a breach of Arts 101 and 102

[92] A Mills, *The Confluence of Public and Private International Law* (CUP, Cambridge, 2009) 290.

[93] See ch 1.

[94] See A Dickinson, *The Rome II Regulation: The Law Applicable to Non-contractual Obligations* (OUP, Oxford, 2008) 408.

[95] Plender and Wilderspin (n 6) 614 and 619.

[96] See Art 16 of the Rome II Regulation. See more section 5.3.3 below.

[97] *Provimi v Aventis Animal Nutrition* [2003] EWHC 961 (Comm); [2003] ECC 29 [25].

TFEU, the national courts should apply EU law, taking into account the body of law developed by the Court of First Instance and the Court of Justice.[98] However, EU law does not determine all issues that would be relevant for a private antitrust damages claim brought before a Member State court, so that the relationship between EU competition law and domestic law need to be addressed in the context of EU competition law damage cases. For those purposed, it would be important to specify as to which elements of a tort based EU competition law claim are left to be determined by the applicable domestic law that should be identified by Rome II.

5.3.1 EU Antitrust Damage Actions: the Relationship between EU Competition Law and Domestic Law

The issues that are not dealt with at the EU level should be governed by domestic laws, which would be determined by applying conflict-of-laws analyses. An important distinction that may be made in this context is to do with matters of substance and matters of procedure.[99] For example, Art 2 of Regulation 1/2003 stipulates that the burden of proving an infringement of Arts 101(1) and 102 TFEU rests on the party or the authority alleging the infringement. However, Regulation 1/2003 does not set the standard of proof.[100] In fact, Recital 5 of the Regulation states that:

> [T]his Regulation affects neither national rules on the standard of proof nor obligations of competition authorities and courts of the Member States to ascertain the relevant facts of a case, provided that such rules and obligations are compatible with general principles of [EU] law.

This text could be interpreted as leaving the domestic legal system of each Member State to determine what the 'required legal standard' of proof is.[101] However, it is not clear which national law should be used by a national court, in order to subject the national law in question to the principal of effectiveness. Is the standard of proof an issue that is governed by *lex fori* or *lex causae*?

Moreover, EU law does not set out the principles that would apply, in order to establish the factual causal connection between the EU competition law infringement and the antitrust damages. Further, Arts 101 and 102 TFEU do not define the 'damage' for the purposes of a private EU competition law claim. Given the fact that the problems are not dealt with at EU level, the principal of national procedural autonomy might suggest not only that it is for a national domestic system

[98] Ibid. See also: KM Stanton, 'New forms of the tort of breach of statutory duty' (2004) *LQR* 324, 332; T Rosenkranz and E Rohde, 'The law applicable to non-contractual obligations arising out of acts of unfair competition and acts restricting free competition under Article 6 Rome II Regulation' (2008) *Nederlands Internationaal Privaatrecht* 435–39.

[99] See more: Komninos (n 12) 141–238.

[100] J Faull and A Nikpay, *The EC Law of Competition* (2nd edn, OUP, Oxford, 2007) 95.

[101] Faull and Nikpay (n 100) 95.

to deal with the issue of damages, but also that in cross-border competition law claims it would be for private international law to decide what is the national law applicable to the issue of antitrust damage. Different Member States may adopt different solutions with regard to appropriate measure of damages in an EU competition law claim. An important question in this context would be whether to characterise the relevant aspects of the assessment of antitrust damages as issues relating to tort (or delict), to be governed by *lex causae*, or to regard them as questions of procedure, to be governed by *lex fori*.

The English conflict of laws make an important distinction between the vested right, which is governed by *lex causae,* and the right's enforcement, which is governed by *lex fori*.[102] It appears that the distinction between substance and procedure may be also important in the context of Rome II, as Art 1(3) clearly states that the Regulation does not apply to evidence and procedure. Such an approach appears to be in line with the principle of English system of private international law that 'a person suing in this country must take the law as he finds it'.[103] However, it has been submitted that the principle is difficult to apply in practice, as 'substance and procedure cannot be relegated to clear cut categories'.[104] Particular difficulties in EU competition law cases would arise with regard to the following questions: Are the burden of proof and standard of proof matters to be determined by the applicable substantive laws or procedural laws? Is assessment of damages for breach of Arts 101 and 102 TFEU to be done by Member States' courts on the basis of *lex causae* or *lex fori*?

5.3.1.1 Burden of Proof and Standard of Proof

The fact that EU law is part of the law of each and every Member State's law would suggest that the question of which national law determines the burden of proof in EU competition law cases is purely academic, as Regulation 1/2003 stipulates that the burden of proving an infringement of Arts 101(1) and 102 TFEU rests on the party or the authority alleging the infringement.[105] But which national law does determine the standard of proof? As already mentioned, this question is not dealt with at EU level, so that its answer, which is of huge practical importance, is to be determined by private international law.[106]

[102] Schmitthoff (n 77) 395. See also: A Scott, 'Substance and procedure and choice of law in torts' (2007) *Lloyd's Maritime and Commercial Law Quarterly* 44; M Illmer, 'Neutrality matters—some thoughts about the Rome Regulations and the so-called dichotomy of substance and procedure in European private international law' (2009) *Civil Justice Quarterly* 237.

[103] *De la Vega v Vianna* (1830) 1 B & Ad 284, 288 (Tenterden CJ). See also: E Spiro, 'Forum Regit Processum (Procedure is governed by the *lex fori*)' (1969) *ICLQ* 949, 952; *Cheshire, North & Fawcett* (n 14) 75–76.

[104] S Szaszy, 'The basic connecting factor in international cases in the domain of civil procedure' (1966) 15 *ICLQ* 436, 455.

[105] See Art 2 of Regulation 1/2003.

[106] See Recital 5 of Regulation 1/2003.

It is an open question whether standard of proof is a matter that affects procedure or substance for private international law purposes. Although, Art 1(3) of Rome II indicates that Member States' courts should apply its own law in order to decide matters of evidence and/or procedure relevant to the infringement of Arts 101 and 102 TFEU, Art 22(1) of Rome II suggests that the law applicable to non-contractual obligations arising out of restrictions of competition shall apply to the extent it contains rules which determine the burden of proof. In other words, the burden of proof is to be regarded as a matter of substance for the purposes of Rome II. However, the fact that Art 22 of Rome II says nothing about the standard of proof appears to indicate that the matter is to be regarded as evidence and procedure within the meaning of Art 1(3) of Rome II. Accordingly, the question 'whether certain evidence proves a certain fact … is to be determined by the law of the country where the question arises.'[107] The answer to this question in many cases would be pre-determined by establishing jurisdiction in the plaintiff's preferred forum.[108]

However, it should not be forgotten that national rules must be compatible with general principles of EU law and the principle of effectiveness in particular.[109] In other words, when determining the required legal standard of proof the Member States must not make 'practically impossible or excessively difficult the exercise of rights conferred by [EU] law'.[110] In view of that, it has been submitted that 'the standard of proof cannot be set at such a high level that the application of [EU competition law] becomes impossible or unduly difficult.'[111] Therefore, the standard of proof in private EU competition law actions would be determined by *lex fori* subject to the general principles of EU law.

5.3.1.2 Remoteness of Damages and Assessment of Damages

The Court of Justice has recently held that a person who is injured by anti-competitive practice or conduct, must be able to seek compensation for actual loss and loss of profit plus interest.[112] However, depending on the applicable law there could be different amounted of damages awarded as, for example, different countries may have different rules with regard to remoteness of damages or availability of exemplary or punitive antitrust damages. A recent study has presented the various methods and models which can be used in quantifying the antitrust damage.[113]

[107] *Bain v Whitehaven Rly Co* (1850) 3 HL Cas 1, 19. See also: *Cheshire, North & Fawcett* (n 14) 83.

[108] Illmer (n 102) 242.

[109] Faull and Nikpay (n 100) 95; Komninos (n 12) 226–27. See also: F Becker, 'Application of Community law by Member States' public authorities: between autonomy and effectiveness' (2007) 44 *CML Rev* 1035.

[110] Joined Cases C-295/04–C-298/04 *Manfredi v. Lloyd Adriaticco* [2006] 5 CMLR 17 [62]. See also Becker (n 109).

[111] Faull and Nikpay (n 100) 95. See more: Komninos (n 12) 226–27.

[112] *Manfredi* (n 110) [26].

[113] Oxera and multi-jurisdictional team of lawyers led by Dr A Komninos, 'Quantifying antitrust damages: towards non-binding guidance for courts – Study prepared for the European Commission' http://ec.europa.eu/competition/antitrust/actionsdamages/quantification_study.pdf.

In the absence of unified practice throughout the EU, different Member States could employ different methodology as to quantification of antitrust damages.

In a private EU competition law damages claim, 'the claimant must prove not only that the relevant [provision] has been broken, but also that the breach in question has caused him a relevant loss.'[114] Which law would determine liability, causation and quantum in a private antitrust damages claim with an international element? As already mentioned, Arts 101 and 102 TFEU do not indicate how the defendant's liability is to be determined and how the assessment of antitrust damages is to be made by national courts. This appears to be a very serious omission in view of the fact that '… even where nations agree about primary conduct, say, price fixing, they disagree dramatically about appropriate remedies.'[115] It has been submitted that '[t]he principle of national procedural autonomy means that in considering the issues of causation and quantum, it is appropriate first to apply the ordinary domestic rules applicable to claims of breach of statutory duty.'[116] Which domestic rules are to be applied in a cross-border EU competition law claim?

Article 15(a) and (b) of Rome II leaves no doubt that the question whether the plaintiff would be entitled to recover the pleaded loss is to be decided according to the applicable national law. This means that the applicable law would not only indicate the relevant national rules for remoteness of damages,[117] but also the availability of any rules that could limit the defendant's liability. An important defence that may be raised in the latter context is the so-called 'passing-on defence'.[118] In competition cases, such a defence could be a significant substantive law barrier.[119] Even more private international law issues should be considered by a private antitrust claimant in the context of the issue of assessment of antitrust damage. Article 15(c) leaves no doubt that the law applicable to non-contractual obligations governs 'the assessment of damages or remedy claimed'.[120] Although,

[114] *Devenish Nutrition Ltd v Sanofi-Aventis SA* [2007] EWHC 2394; [2008] 2 WLR 637 (Ch) [18]; a'ffd *Devenish Nutrition Ltd v Sanofi-Aventis SA* [2008] EWCA Civ 1086; [2009] 3 WLR 198 (CA).

[115] *Empagran* (n 84) 542 US 167.

[116] D Beard, 'Damages in competition law litigation' in T Ward and K Smith, *Competition Litigation in the UK* (Sweet & Maxwell, London, 2005) 257, 270.

[117] Compare: *D'Almeida Araujo Lda v Frederick Becker & Co Ltd* [1953] 2 QB 329.

[118] 'That defence is that the claimant had in fact not made any loss because they were able to pass on the loss to their own customers, the final consumers.' See D Sheehan, 'Competition law meets restitution for wrongs' (2009) 125 *LQR* 225.

[119] R Mulheron, 'Reform of collective redress in England and Wales: a perspective of need', research paper for submission to the Civil Council of England and Wales www.civiljusticecouncil.gov.uk/files/collective_redress.pdf. See also: Beard (n 116) 271–272; M Hellwig, 'Private damage claims and the passing-on defense in horizontal price-fixing cases – an economist's perspective' in J Basedow (ed), *Private Enforcement of EC Competition Law* (Kluwer Law International, The Hague, 2007) 121; *Devenish* (CA) (n 114) [99], [114 and 130].

[120] Under English law (eg *Boys v Chaplin* [1971] AC 356) and Scottish law (eg *McElroy v McAllister* 1949 SC 110) the questions as to the quantification of damages were classified as procedural. See *Harding v Wealands* [2006] UKHL 32 (HL) [66]–[67]. This has changed after the entrance into force of the Rome II Regulation. See more: PR Beaumont and Z Tang, ' Classification of Delictual Damages—*Harding v Wealands* and the Rome II Regulation' (2008) 12 *Edinburgh Law Review* 131, 135.

it seems that in the context of assessment of damages the EU is moving towards non-binding guidance for the courts, the question what remedies would be available in tort-based EU competition law actions is left to be dealt with by domestic legal orders of individual Member States. Therefore, the applicable national law would have a very important role in the context of the determination of a defendant's liability. This law should be determined in accordance with Art 6(3) of Rome II, which will be discussed below.[121]

5.3.1.3 Conclusions Regarding Applicable Domestic Laws in EU Competition Law Claims

Although, the question of whether there is a breach of Arts 101 and 102 TFEU is to be determined as a matter of EU law, it appears that Member States' domestic laws would be relevant to determine such issues as for example the standard of proof. Furthermore, national orders should determine the relevant rules for remoteness of damages;[122] the available remedies for breach of EU competition law (eg whether punitive (or exemplary) damages,[123] which may be subject to considerations of public policy[124] and the possibility that the award of such damages infringes an English statute,[125] would be available); and assessment of damages.[126] The fact that these questions have been left to be determined by the Member States' national orders indicates that it is for the choice-of-law rules to determine which law would govern the issues in question.[127]

Therefore, choice-of-law problems would arise particularly sharply in situations where the conduct, causing anti-competitive harm within England is agreed between companies in a distant location affecting markets in more than one country. The Rome II Regulation has a vital role play in such cases as the applicable law would indicate the scope of the defendant's liability and respectively what a plaintiff would be entitled to recover in a private antitrust damages claim.

[121] See section 5.3.2 below.

[122] *D'Almeida* (n 117).

[123] Compare: *SA Consortium Textiles v Sun and Sand Agencies Ltd* [1978] QB 279; *Waterhouse v Australian Broadcasting Corp* (1989) ACTR 1, 19; *Devenish* (HC) (n 114). See also M Danov, 'Awarding exemplary (or punitive) antitrust damages in EC competition cases with an international element—the Rome II Regulation and the Commission's White Paper on damages' (2008) 29 *ECL Rev* 430.

[124] Recital 32 of the Rome II Regulation.

[125] Section 5(2) of the Protection of Trading Interests Act 1980. K Huntley, 'The Protection of Trading Interests Act 1980: Some jurisdictional aspects of enforcement of antitrust laws' (1981) 30 *ICLQ* 213; DL Jones, 'Protection of Trading Interests Act 1980' (1981) 40 *CLJ* 41; AV Lowe, 'Blocking extraterritorial jurisdiction: the British Protection of Trading Interests Act, 1980' (1981) 75 *American Journal of International Law* 257; MA Blythe, 'The extraterritorial impact of the anti-trust laws: Protecting British Trading Interests' (1983) 31 *American Journal of International Law* 99; L Collins, 'Blocking and Clawback Statutes: The United Kingdom Approach' (1986) *JBL* 372 and 452; *Cheshire, North & Fawcett* (n 14) 561–63.

[126] 'Quantifying antitrust damages: towards non-binding guidance for courts' (n 113). See also: Beaumont and Tang (n 120); Stanton (n 98) 338–39.

[127] Compare: CGJ Morse, 'Torts in private international law: a new statutory framework' (1996) 45 *ICLQ* 888, 895.

5.3.2 Article 6(3) of Rome II and its Application in EU Competition Law Cases

Article 6(3) of the Rome II Regulation concerns the law applicable to acts distorting competition. The analysis should not be made without due consideration of Art 4(1), which as a general rule in the Rome II Regulation is the *lex loci damni,* as provided in Art 4(1):[128]

> Unless otherwise provided for in this Regulation, the law applicable to a non-contractual obligation arising out of a tort/delict shall be the law of the country in which the damage occurs irrespective of the country in which the event giving rise to the damage occurred and irrespective of the country or countries in which the indirect consequences of that event occur.

Recital 21, which explicitly states that 'Article 6 is not an exception to the general rule in Article 4(1) but rather a clarification of it', seems to indicate that Art 6(3) is designated as a special rule that is applicable in EU competition law cases (ie *lex specialis derogate legi generali*). Article 6(3) of Rome II contains two sub-sections which are to be used by national courts, in order to determine the law applicable to non-contractual obligations arising out of restrictions of competition. Under Art 6(3)(a) of Rome II, the law applicable to such acts should be the 'law of the country where the market is, or is likely to be, affected.' Article 6(3)(a), being a clarification of the general rule, leaves no doubt that the law of the country in which the market is affected is to be regarded as the place where the direct damage occurred for the purposes of private antitrust damages claims.[129]

Article 6(3)(b) of Rome II provides that in competition law cases where the market is, or is likely to be, affected in more than one country, the claimant would be able in certain circumstances to choose to base his or her claim on the law of the court seised (ie *lex fori*). This sub-section could be seen as further clarifying the general rule in view of the fact that Art 4(1) is meant to strike a balance between the interests of the person claimed to be liable for competition law infringement and the person sustaining the antitrust damage.[130] Thus, Rome II takes account of the fact that in competition law cases the defendant would normally enjoy market (and bargaining) power, whilst the plaintiff (or members of the plaintiff's class), who brought a private antitrust claim would be in a weaker position (eg consumers or a small (or medium sized) commercial company which has less market power than the defendant). Article 6(4) of Rome II, which limits parties' freedom

[128] See Recital 18 of the Rome II Regulation.

[129] See also M Helner, 'Unfair Competition and acts restricting free competition—a commentary on Article 6 of the Rome II Regulation' (2007) 9 *Yearbook of Private International Law* 50, 51. Compare Dickinson (n 94) 397.

[130] See Recital 16 of the Rome II Regulation. Compare Dickinson (n 94) 397.

of choice in cases relating to non-contractual obligations arising out of restriction of competition, is just another reflection of the same policy.[131]

It has been submitted that Art 6(3)(a) should be regarded as the general rule in competition law claims and Art 6(3)(b) as a special rule which would be applicable law if the market is affect in several countries.[132] The distinction has been justified by the legislative history of the provision and the fact that Art 6(3)(b) was inserted quite late by the EU legislature.[133] The language of the Rome II Regulation, however, does not support such interpretation. The relationship, general rule (Art 6(3)(a) of Rome II) and special rule (Art 6(3)(b) of Rome II), would have meant that Art 6(3)(b) would override Art 6(3)(a) in cases where its requirements had been satisfied. This is not the intention of the EU legislator. In fact, Art 6(3)(b) of Rome II states that: '... the person seeking compensation for damage ... may instead choose to base his or her claim on the law of the court seised', provided that certain requirements have been satisfied. Therefore, it seems to this author that Art 6(3)(b) is an exception to Art 6(3)(a) of Rome II—the latter rule being clearly the special rule for competition law claims.[134] In other words, the exception of Art 6(3)(b) is meant to confirm that the special rule of Art 6(3)(a) will apply in EU competition law cases not excepted (ie *exceptio probat regulam in casibus non exceptis*).

5.3.2.1 Article 6(3)(a)—the Law of the Country where the Market is Affected

As already mentioned, for the purposes of Art 6(3)(a) of Rome II, the 'country where the market is affected' must be determined by a national court, so that the applicable substantive law may be ascertained. It has been submitted that such a connecting factor could give rise to some complexities in private EU competition law claims.[135] In support of such an argument, Dickinson states that:

> The requirement for individual litigants, and their legal advisers, to undertake legal-economic analysis ... in order to determine the law applicable to a non-contractual obligation is one of the least satisfactory aspects of the Rome II Regulation, and seems likely significantly to increase costs in cases of this kind.[136]

[131] ThM de Boer, 'Party autonomy and its limitations in the Rome II Regulation' (2007) *Yearbook of Private International Law* 19, 24–25. See more section 5.4 below.

[132] E. R. Pineau, 'Conflict of laws comes to the rescue of competition law: the new Rome II Regulation' (2009) 5 *Journal of Private International Law* 311, 318. See also: J. Fitchen, 'Choice of law in international claims based on restriction of competition: Art 6(3) of the Rome II Regulation' (2009) 5 *Journal of Private International Law* 337, 357. Although, Fitchen seems to regard Art 6(3)(a) as a general rule applicable in competition claims (See Fitchen (n 132) 355, 357 and 364), he sometimes refers to Art 6(3)(b) as a special rule (See Fitchen (n 127) 357) and more often refers to it as an exception to Art 6(3)(a) (See Fitchen (n 132) 353, 355, 356, 357, 358, 364, 365 and 366).

[133] Pineau (n 132) 317–318.

[134] See Recital 21 of Rome II. Compare: Art 4(1) of Rome II.

[135] Helner (n 129) 59; Dickinson (n 94) 419–23; Plender and Wilderspin (n 6) 619–20.

[136] Dickinson (n 94) 422.

In spite of the criticism, it should be recognised that Art 6(3) of Rome II would work reasonably well in follow-on actions in which the work of defining the relevant geographic market would have been already completed by national competition authorities or the Commission.[137] In such cases, the individual litigants (and their legal advisers) bringing follow-on damages actions would be able to rely on the geographical market analysis and the other relevant legal-economic analyses undertaken by a national competition authority or the Commission.

However, it should be noted that the connecting factor for choice-of-law purposes—'the country where the market is affected'—is different from the concept of 'relevant geographic market' for substantive law purposes.[138] Indeed, it seems to this author that a distinction should be made between the connecting factor employed to identify the applicable law, which is to be determined for the purposes of Art 6(3) of Rome II, and applying the concept of 'relevant geographic market' which is derived by national law (or EU competition law, for that matter). More specifically, as a matter of substantive EU competition law the market definition would play an important role in providing the framework within which a national court should determine whether the defendant, or the defendants, have market power, so that they could limit the output, raise prices and deprive consumers of choice by entering into agreements that restrict competition or abusing their dominant position.[139] It is well established that:

> [T]he approach to defining the relevant market differs according to whether Article 8[1] or Article 8[2] of the Treaty is to be applied. For the purposes of Article 8[2], the proper definition of the relevant market is a necessary precondition for any judgment as to allegedly anti-competitive behaviour, since, before an abuse of a dominant position is ascertained, it is necessary to establish the existence of a dominant position in a given market, which presupposes that such a market has already been defined. On the other hand, for the purposes of applying Article 8[1], the reason for defining the relevant market, if at all, is to determine whether the agreement, the decision by an association of undertakings or the concerted practice at issue is liable to affect trade between Member States and has as its object or effect the prevention, restriction or distortion of competition within the Common Market.[140]

Thus, in a case where a parent company had, jointly with its subsidiaries, partitioned a Member State market, it naturally followed that the transactions from the Member State in question to all the other Member States were capable of being affected, so that the application of Art 101 TFEU in such a case would not require a national court first to define the geographic market.[141] However, this could not be followed for the choice-of-law purposes as the applicable national law

[137] See Helner (n 129) 60; Plender and Wilderspin (n 6) 620.

[138] See also: Fitchen (n 132) 363. Compare: Helner (n 129) 60; Dickinson (n 94) 419–23.

[139] See Commission (EC), 'The Definition of the Relevant Market for the Purposes of Community Competition Law' (Notice) [1997] OJ C372/5. See also Faull and Nikpay (n 100) 40–85.

[140] Case T-62/98 *Volkswagen v Commission* [2000] 5 CMLR 853 [230] (Court of First Instance).

[141] Ibid [231].

(or EU competition law for that matter) could not be identified unless the 'affected market' has been identified by a national court.

Therefore, the connecting factor for choice-of-law purposes—'the country where the market is affected'—would involve an enquiry into the material available, in order to determine whether there is a sufficient degree of probability that the implementation of the agreement or practice could have an actual effect on the market in the country in question.[142] This is not the same as defining the geographic market which involves a hypothetical enquiry into demand-side substitution and supply-side substitution that is meant to define the appropriate boundaries for the purposes of starting an analysis of competition required by the applicable substantive law.[143] In other words, given the fact that 'the country where the market is affected' is a connecting factor which links an antitrust damages claim to a defined legal system, at the stage when the applicable law is to be identified, the court is not supposed to define the relevant market, but rather to make an enquiry into the material available, in order to see which country's market (countries' markets) may be affected by the (alleged) infringement. Once this had been done, then the applicable national law would be identified. If an English court established that an (allegedly) anti-competitive agreement or practice is capable of appreciably affecting the trade between Member States,[144] then EU competition law, which forms part of law of each Member State, will be applicable[145] and the 'relevant market' analysis is to be made.

Thus, for choice-of-law purposes, the national court should specify a country in which the market may be affected by the (allegedly) anti-competitive agreement and/or conduct by making a factual assessment of the available material, in order to determine the position and the importance of the defendant's company (or defendants' companies) on the national market in question. The stronger the market position of the defendant/s, the more likely it is that an anti-competitive agreement or practice is capable of affecting the market in the identified country (or countries).[146]

The fact that Art 6(3)(b) of Rome II is an exception to Art 6(3)(a) leaves no doubt that despite the fact that the latter provision refers to the 'law of the country where the market is, or is likely to be, affected', Art 6(3)(a) should be interpreted as covering also the laws of several countries where the market is, or is likely to be, affected. In other words, Art 6(3)(a) of Rome II should apply in competition

[142] Compare: the 'may affect' test defining the jurisdictional reach of Arts 81 and 82 EC. See Commission (EC) 'The effect on trade concept contained in Articles 81 and 82 of the Treaty' (Guidelines) [2004] OJ C101/81 [23].

[143] Eg the 'small but significant non-transitory increase in price' test is to be employed for those purposes. See Faull and Nikpay (n 100) 49–50. See also: Fitchen (n 132) 360–61; Plender and Wilderspin (n 6) 620.

[144] Commission Guidelines (n 142) [12]. See also: Joined Cases 56/64 and 58/64 *Consten and Grundig v Commission* [1966] ECR 429; Joined Cases 6/73 and 7/73 *Commercial Solvents* [1974] ECR 223.

[145] See also: Art 3 of Regulation 1/2003.

[146] Compare Commission Guidelines (n 142) [45].

cases where the markets in several countries are affected but the conditions of Art 6(3)(b) of Rome II are not satisfied. For example, the Art 6(3)(a) provision will apply in cases where the forum's international jurisdiction to award antitrust damages is derived from other jurisdictional rules as, for example, Art 5(3) or Art 23 of Brussels I. As another example, Art 6(3)(a) would be relevant if the market in the Member State where the actions was brought is only insignificantly affected.[147]

In such cases, the English court would not be entitled to base the assessment of EU competition law damages only on the *lex fori*, as Art 6(3)(a) of Rome II requires a national court to apply the law of each country where the market is affected. This may give rise to difficulties as 'the laws of all the countries concerned will have to be applied on a distributive basis, applying what is known as "Mosaikbetrachtung" in German law'.[148] The 'mosaic principle' has been criticised by Dickinson[149] on the ground that it could drive costs up in such cases, as each applicable foreign law should be proved. According to him, this may result in Member States' courts being tempted to define the geographic area of the relevant market more restrictively.[150] It is difficult to see how this could happen, as in practice the question of the relevant market is one of fact which should be proved by the plaintiff in order to establish a breach of the applicable substantive law. Given the fact that EU competition law is part of the Member States' domestic orders, it seems to this author that no significant difficulties would arise in EU competition cases. In fact, if an infringement of Arts 101 and 102 TFEU had been established and if the plaintiff had proved that the decline of the plaintiff's sales had been incurred in several countries as a direct result of the defendant's anti-competitive conduct, then it is hard to understand why a court would need to define the geographic area of the relevant market more restrictively for the choice of law purposes at the stage when the damage should be assessed. Furthermore, in a follow-on action the relevant market would already have been defined by a national competition authority or the Commission which had established the EU competition law infringement.

It has been further submitted that the 'mosaic principle' would mean that 'the claimant must either decline to proceed with parts of his [competition law] claim or, at least before the English courts, potentially face the additional costs of pleading and establishing the multiple laws in accordance with particular *Mosaikbetrachtung* adopted by that court.'[151] This may be a problem in some competition law cases, but this would certainly not be an issue in EU competition cases brought before English courts (or another Member State court). There are

[147] Compare Commission (EC) 'Agreements of minor importance which do not appreciably restrict competition under Article 81(1) of the Treaty' (Notice) [2001] OJ C368/13.

[148] See Commission (EC), 'Proposal for a Regulation of the European Parliament and the Council on the law applicable to non-contractual obligations' COM (2003) 427 final.

[149] Dickinson (n 94) 422–23.

[150] Ibid.

[151] Fitchen (n 132) 358. See also: Dickinson (n 94) 422–23.

three main reasons for that. First, it is for EU law to determine whether there is a breach of Arts 101 and 102 TFEU. As a result, there would not be additional costs of pleading and establishing the EU competition laws which form part of the legal orders of all Member States, and England in particular.

Secondly, even though EU competition law provisions do not indicate how the defendant's liability is to be determined and how the assessment of antitrust damages is to be made by national courts, the question of identifying the applicable laws for those purposes would only arise after the EU competition law infringement had been established. Once that is done, it would be highly unlikely for a private antitrust claimant to decline to proceed with parts of his claim for damages being faced with the additional costs of pleading and establishing different laws.

Thirdly, the difficulties that would arise in determining the defendant's liability and assessing antitrust damages in EU competition law cases would not be specific for actions brought in a cross-border context, but indeed similar to those encountered in domestic context.[152] Such a private antitrust claimant nonetheless may rely on the Court of Justice ruling suggesting that a person who is injured by a contract, or by conduct liable to restrict or distort competition, must be able to seek compensation for actual loss and loss of profit plus interest.[153] Indeed, the awarded damages must be compatible with general principles of EU law and the principle of effectiveness in particular. Although, it would be unfair that different damages are awarded by the various Member States' courts for the same breach of the very same EU provision, a different level of redress would come to no surprise in view of the fact that the EU has opted for a private international law solution. One should not forget that the purpose of Rome II is the unification of choice-of-law, not the harmonisation of the Member States' remedies in tortious actions based on EU competition law.[154]

Further, the fact that Rome II contains another provision, Art 6(3)(b), which may be relied upon by a private antitrust claimant, leaves no doubt that the EU legislator, being aware of the potential problems attached to the use of the mosaic principle in cross-border EU competition law cases, has envisaged the use of the *lex fori* with regard to all parts of the claim as an alternative available in cases where the market is affected in more than one country. Accordingly, private antitrust claimants and their lawyers, who are not willing to face the additional costs of pleading and establishing the multiple laws, should consider basing the relevant EU antitrust damages claim on the *lex fori* under Art 6(3)(b) of Rome II.

152 See 'Quantifying antitrust damages' (n 113). See also: Komninos (n 12) 207–11. It has been submitted that '[t]he assessment of damages in competition related claims is a complex process with which Member States have not yet had much experience.' See Plender and Wilderspin (n 6) 631–32. See also The European Commission's invitation to tender for the provision of a study on the quantification of the harm suffered by victims of competition law infringements (COMP/2008/A5/10).

153 *Manfredi* (n 110) [26].

154 Council of the European Union, 'The Hague Programme: strengthening freedom, security and justice in the European Union' http://ec.europa.eu/justice_home/doc_centre/doc/hague_programme_en.pdf.

5.3.2.2 *Article 6(3)(b)*—Lex Fori

As already clarified, Art 6(3)(b) of Rome II allows a private antitrust claimant to base his claim on *lex fori* in cases where the markets in several countries have been affected. Article 6(3)(b), being an exception to the special rule of Art 6(3)(a) of Rome II, is restrictive in a number of ways. There are three main conditions that need to be satisfied by a claimant who wishes to invoke *lex fori* under Art 6(3)(b) of Rome II. First, the action must be brought before a Member State court. This requirement can be easily explained in view of the fact that Arts 101 and 102 TFEU have exterritorial application and could not be avoided merely by bringing the action before a non-EU court. Secondly, the plaintiff could rely on the *lex fori* only if the EU competition law issues were brought before the court of the defendant's domicile. In other words, the EU legislator links the application of the *lex fori* with the basis of Member States' court jurisdiction.[155] The third requirement, which needs to be satisfied by a claimant who wishes to invoke the *lex fori*, is that the market in the Member State, must be among those directly and substantially affected by the restriction of competition. This requirement seems to be consistent with the fact that under Rome II the main connecting factor that is to be used in order to identify the applicable law in competition law claims is the 'country where the market is affected.'

It should be noted though that Art 6(3)(b) of Rome II goes further and requires the market in the Member State in question to be 'directly and substantially' affected, which is a higher threshold than the one which is to be established under Art 6(3)(a) of Rome II.[156] More specifically, in order to sue a sole defendant on the basis of *lex fori*, a plaintiff must establish that the market in that Member State is among those directly and substantially affected by the restriction of competition. If the action was to be brought against multiple defendants, then Art 6(3)(b) of Rome II states that the law of the forum may be applicable only if the 'restriction of competition on which the claim against each of these defendants relies directly and substantially affects *also* the market in the Member State of that court'. The EU legislator seems to infer that in such cases the restrictions on competition would affect the markets in more than one country. This may also suggest that in a significant majority of competition law cases, where Art 6(3)(b) of Rome II would be relied upon, the anti-competitive practice or conduct in question may affect trade between Member States, which means that the claim would be based on an EU competition law infringement.[157]

In view of that, Art 6(3)(b) is meant to ensure that the application of *lex fori* would only occur in cases where the market in the Member State in question is among those 'directly and substantially' affected by the infringement of EU competition law. This raises the question of how the Member States courts should

[155] For a detailed discussion of the issue of jurisdiction, see chs 2, 3 and 4 above.
[156] See: Fitchen (n 132) 365.
[157] See Commission Guidelines (n 142) [9]–[22]. See also: Plender and Wilderspin (n 6) 627–28.

interpret the words 'directly and substantially' which are meant to indentify one single law of a Member State court to be applicable as to the assessment of damages and remedies claimed in respect of claims based on infringements of EU competition laws that had taken place in several countries. Dickinson[158] points out that the Commission had proposed the concept of 'directly and substantially' affected market to be defined as follows:

> When determining whether or not a restriction of competition affects a market directly and substantially, in particular the prices, outputs, innovation or the variety of products on that market, due regard must be given to the position and the importance of the undertakings involved on the market for the products concerned.[159]

The Commission proposal does not feature in Rome II. Nevertheless, it could be expected that the question of market in a particular Member State is among those 'directly and substantially' relevant and should involve a factual assessment on the basis of the material available of the position and the importance of the defendant's companies on the forum's market. More material would be available before a Member State court in follow-on EU competition law action than in a stand-alone action. In any case, the test should be whether there is a sufficient degree of probability that the implementation of the agreement or practice has a direct and substantial effect on the market of the Member State where the antitrust action is brought.[160]

The stronger the market position of the defendant/s in the Member State where the actions is brought, the more likely it is that an anti-competitive agreement or practice is capable of having a direct and substantial affect on the market in the Member State in question.[161] This is meant to ensure that the *lex fori* would only be applicable if the market of the forum is directly and substantially affected. This would be so even if the market in another Member State is directly and substantially affected as well.

Article 6(3)(b), nevertheless, has been criticised because '[i]ssues of directness and passing-on may potentially interact with Article 6(3)(b)'s condition precedent concerning direct and substantial effects when this is pleaded to the court.'[162] In spite of the criticism, it seems to this author that the question of whether the claimed antitrust damage has been passed-on does not arise at the stage when a Member State court determines whether the agreement or practice has a direct and substantial effect on the market for the choice of law purposes.[163] The 'direct damage' within the meaning of Rome II[164] occurs in competition cases in the country where the market is affected.[165] This would certainly be so, if the

158 Dickinson (n 94) 425.
159 Commission document SPI (2007) 42 [3.5.2007] 9, cited in Dickinson (n 94) 425.
160 Compare Commission Guidelines (n 142).
161 Ibid [45].
162 Fitchen (n 132) 368.
163 A somewhat different opinion has been expressed by Fitchen (n 132) 368–69.
164 See Recital 16 of Rome II and Art 4(1) of Rome II. See more: Fitchen (n 132) 367.
165 See Recital 21 of Rome II.

market in the Member State, where the action was brought, had been directly and substantially affected because, for example, the market in question had been foreclosed. The questions as to which heads of damages would be recoverable would only arise at the stage when such issues as the nature of harm caused, causation and the assessment of damages were dealt with by the national court after the applicable law had been identified.[166]

That said, it is not easy to find a justification as to why the court's jurisdiction needs to be based in the defendant's domicile. It is difficult to see why a claimant in an EU competition law action, who sues a defendant (domiciled in Germany or France) in England on the basis of Art 5(3) of Brussels I, cannot rely on Art 6(3)(b) of Rome II. It is unfortunate that the plaintiff could rely on the *lex fori* only if the EU competition law issues were brought before the court of the defendant's domicile, which seems to indicate that a private antitrust claimant, who wishes to base his claim on the *lex fori*, will have to follow the defendant to the Member State of his domicile. Moreover, the defendant may not necessarily be domiciled in a country where the market had been directly and substantially affected. For example, as it was already submitted,[167] it would be more difficult for a court at the defendant's domicile to consider the economic and legal context of an agreement, which was implemented and affected the plaintiff's business within the market of another Member State. One may say that the rationale behind such a rule was that jurisdiction under Art 2 of Brussels I would be international, whilst jurisdiction under Art 5(3) of Brussels I could sometimes be restricted to the local harm.[168] However, one should not forget that the forum's jurisdiction based on Art 5(3) of Brussels I could not be restricted to the local harm in cases where the claim is brought before the court at the place of the event giving rise to the antitrust damages.[169] Furthermore, Art 6(3)(b) of Rome II could not be applicable in cases where a stand-alone EU competition law action for damages was brought as a counter-claim under Art 6(3) of Brussels I in an action for enforcement of an (allegedly) anti-competitive contract brought under Art 5(1) of Brussels I.

In spite of the criticism, Art 6(3)(b) of Rome II would work reasonably well in cases where the jurisdiction against the two defendants, a foreign company and an English domiciled company, was based on Art 6(1) of Brussels I (or English traditional rules if the second defendant was not domiciled within the EU). In cases brought under Art 6(1) of Brussels I, the plaintiff the defendant would have the choice of suing both defendants in either of the Member States in which one of them is domiciled, so that a claimant may well have a choice of several forums.[170] The word 'also', in Art 6(3)(b) of Rome II, leaves no doubt that the court of the

166 See more: Komninos (n 12) 199–214.

167 See ch 2, section 2.2.1 above.

168 *SanDisk Corp v Koninklijke Philips Electronics NV* [2007] EWHC 332 (Ch); [2007] Bus LR 705 [25].

169 See more: ch 3, section 3.2.2.2.3 above. Compare Pineau (n 132) 324.

170 See more: chs 2 and 3 above. See also Fawcett and Torremans (n 28) 197.

defendant's domicile would apply *lex fori* to the assessment of damages resulting not only from the claim based on a direct and substantial restriction of competition on the market of the forum, but also on claims based on infringements of EU competition laws that had taken place in another country.[171] The wording of Art 6(3)(b) of Rome II, however, leaves no doubt that it is not meant to deal with all the cases affecting markets in several countries, but only those which fall within its ambit. If the plaintiff cannot satisfy the 'directly and substantially affected market' test, or if the jurisdiction of a Member State court was not based on the defendant's domicile, the law applicable to a non-contractual obligations arising out of restriction of competition should be determined by Art 6(3)(a) of Rome II.

5.3.2.3 The Issue of Forum Shopping: Choice of Law in Competition Law Actions

The fact that Rome II suggests that the *lex fori* may have a role to play in some EU competition law cases may suggest that the forum shopping issue needs to be discussed in the context of Art 6(3)(b) of Rome II.[172] 'Forum shopping' describes the scenario of 'a plaintiff by-passing his natural forum and bringing his action in some alien forum which would give him relief or benefits which would not be available to him in his natural forum.'[173] In their observations in respect of decentralised enforcement of EU competition law, seven Member States feared that the decentralisation could lead to forum shopping.[174] Furthermore, the risk of forum shopping has been raised by industry and lawyers as one of their main concerns.[175] The attitude towards forum shopping has generally been disapproving.[176] However, given the EU policies which are meant to encourage private antitrust enforcement, one should differentiate between a plaintiff in an EU competition law claim, who takes legitimate advantage of the applicable laws in a particular Member State and one that is 'condemned' as a forum shopper.[177]

A private antitrust claimant may be entitled to choose where to bring his EU competition law claim because in the European context there could be numerous differences in the laws of the available forums, which can lead to advantages

[171] See also Helner (n 129) 64.

[172] Compare A Bell, *Forum Shopping and Venue in Transnational Litigation* (OUP, Oxford, 2003) 39.

[173] *Chaplin* (n 120) 401 (Lord Pearson); J Fawcett, 'Forum shopping—some questions answered' (1984) 35 *Northern Ireland Law Quarterly* 141.

[174] DG COMP White Paper on the Reform of Regulation 17—Summary of the observations February 29, 2000, available at http://europa.eu.int/comm/competition/antitrust/others/wp_on_modernisation/summary_observations.html, 16.

[175] Ibid.

[176] See more AG Slater, 'Forum Non Conveniens: A View from the Shop Floor' (1988) 104 *LQR* 554, 561–62. See also M Monti, 'Competition Law Reform', speech made at the CBI Conference on Competition Law Reform London, June 12 http://ec.europa.eu/comm/competition/speeches/text/sp2000_008_en.html.

[177] Compare J Harris, 'Forum shopping in international libel' (2000) 116 *LQR* 562. See also *Berezovsky v Michaels* [2000] 1 WLR 1004 (HL).

in choosing to conduct a trial in one Member State rather than another. For example, these could include such matters as: pre-trial discovery; costs (eg the availability of contingency fees); and opt-out collective redress proceedings. Further, the availability of exemplary (or punitive) damages could often depend on *lex fori*.[178] Rome II which promotes a partial application of the *lex fori* in EU competition law seems to encourage 'forum shopping'[179] in view of the fact that, as already noted,[180] a private antitrust claimant, who intends to sue multiple defendants under Art 6(1) of Brussels I, would often have a choice of forum.[181] This appears to indicate that such a choice should not be deprecated.[182] In other words, a plaintiff in an EU competition law claim can hardly be blamed for going to another forum, if he discovers that he could recover greater compensation in this forum.[183] Hence, it has been submitted that '[t]he unavoidable consequence, even if perhaps unintended, is that [EU] law fosters (and some may even say blesses) forum shopping search of the rule which endows the claimant with the highest damages award for the breach of a given competition rule or rules.'[184]

Nonetheless, the attitude towards forum shopping in competition law claims should be disapproving in cases where the plaintiff chooses a forum which is not well placed to determine the action, or inconvenient to the defendant in order to harass him deliberately.[185] For example, a pre-emptive action may be brought before courts in a Member State that lacks significant expertise with EU competition law claims, or before courts where proceedings may take longer before a final decision is rendered. In addition, a mala fide plaintiff may act to the defendant's disadvantage by bringing an action in a court where he would pay smaller compensation in a potential counter-claim for antitrust damages.[186] This would be particularly so, where two equivalent obligations arising under the same contract must be performed in more that one Member State.[187] Therefore, it seems that the wide bases for jurisdiction taken together with the lack of a possibly for a first seised Member State court to decline jurisdiction in an EU competition law action under the Brussels I Regulation would make it more difficult to stop forum shopping in cases where the plaintiff chooses a forum which is not well placed to deal

[178] See section 5.3.3 below.

[179] Compare Bell (n 172) 39.

[180] Chs 2 and 3 above.

[181] See Schlosser Report [1979] OJ C59/71, 97.

[182] Bell (n 172) 60. See *The Atlantic Star* [1974] AC 436 (HL) 471 (Lord Simon). See also C. McLachlan, Lis Pendens *in International Litigation* (Martinus Nijhoff Publishers, Leiden/Boston, 2009) 37.

[183] Compare *Castanho v Brown & Root* [1981] AC 557 (HL).

[184] Pineau (n 132) 327–28.

[185] Fawcett (n 173) 144.

[186] Although, the defendant may decide to defend against the plaintiff's declaration of non-liability and bring his damages claim in another proceeding in a different country, this would result in extra costs.

[187] Compare: Case C-420/97 *Leathertex v Bodetex* [1999] ECR I-6779; Case C-386/05 *Color Drack v Lexx International Vertriebs* [2007] ILPr 455 [45].

with an EU competition law case.[188] This gives rise to the question how forum shopping can be stopped in the European context.

As already noted,[189] the problem of parallel proceedings and the problem of forum shopping could be dealt with if a possibility for a Member State court to deny a trial to a forum shopping plaintiff was envisaged by the EU legislator. For example, a Member State could have a possibility to decline jurisdiction in an EU competition law claim (eg non-liability declaration) brought in a Member State court when the court, which is well placed to hear and determine the action, was elsewhere. Linking the court's jurisdiction with the effects on competition within a country's territory could be an efficient way to deal with forum shopping.[190] Such a tool has been already used by the US courts when dealing with forum shopping in relation to private antitrust law claims. This can be best illustrated by the judgment of the US Supreme Court in *Empagran*,[191] in which by dismissing the action the US Supreme Court did not allow the plaintiff to bypass his natural forum and bring his antitrust action in the US Federal Courts which would give him treble damages which would not be available to him in his natural forum.[192] The English court could follow the US approach in cases not falling within the ambit of the Brussels I Regulation and decline to exercise jurisdiction because, for example, the anti-competitive conduct took place in the US and had no appreciable effect within the EU and England in particular, where multiple damages may not be available as a remedy.[193] However, the problem is that the American experience is impossible to follow under the current version of the Brussels I Regulation which precludes a court of a Member State from declining the jurisdiction conferred on it by the Regulation. This would be so, even if the jurisdiction of no other Member State was in issue or the proceedings had no connecting factors to any other Member State. Thus, these issues need to be addressed at EU level. [194]

[188] See more ch 4 above.

[189] Ch 4 above.

[190] In the European context, a similar model for allocation of cases between the NCAs has been employed within the European Competition Network. See Commission (EC), 'Cooperation within the Network of Competition Authorities' (Notice) [2004] OJ C101/43 [8].

[191] *Empagran* (n 84) 542 US 155; See also: *F Hoffmann La Roche v Empagran* 417 F 3d 1267 (US Court of Appeals, DCC); *Kruman v Christie's Int'l* 129 F Supp 2d 620 (2001). See also: C Ryngaert, 'Foreign-to-foreign claims: The US Supreme Court's Decision (2004) v The English High Court's Decision (2003) in the Vitamins case' (2004) 25 *European Competition Law Review* 611; Adolphsen (n 80); RW Beckler and MH Kirtland, 'Extraterritorial Application of US Antitrust Law: What is a "direct, substantial, and reasonably foreseeable effect" under the Foreign Trade Antitrust Improvements Act?' (2003) 38 *Texas International Law Journal* 11.

[192] This does not mean that *Empagran* (n 84) entirely and absolutely eliminated the problem of forum shopping, but it may be used as an example how the problem of forum shopping could be dealt with in some cases. Compare M Furse, *Competition Law of the EC and UK* (6th edn, OUP, Oxford, 2008) 79. See also M Furse, '*Provimi v Aventis*: damages and jurisdiction' (2003) *Competition Law Journal* 119.

[193] See ch 4 above.

[194] See ch 4 above.

5.3.3 Mandatory Provisions and Public Policy

5.3.3.1 Mandatory Provisions

Difficulties as to identifying the applicable competition law provision could arise if non-Member States' markets were affected by an antitrust infringement which was litigated in England. Would EU competition law rules be applicable if the market of a non-EU country was directly and substantially affected? Article 16 of the Rome II Regulation contains a rule giving priority to overriding mandatory provisions. The rule is similar to the provision of Art 9(2) from the Rome I Regulation. However, Rome II makes no reference to overriding mandatory provisions of the law of the other countries. More specifically, Art 16 states that:

> Nothing in this Regulation shall restrict the application of the provisions of the law of the forum in a situation where they are mandatory irrespective of the law otherwise applicable to the non-contractual obligation.

The fact that Rome II employs similar terminology as the one used by Rome I leaves no doubt that Arts 101 and 102 TFEU are to be regarded as overriding mandatory provisions within the meaning of Art 16 of Rome II as well as under Art 9(2) of Rome I. Much of what was said with regard to overriding mandatory provisions of the forum within the meaning of Rome I is equally relevant here.[195] Indeed, Arts 101 and 102 TFEU, being part of the law of each and every Member State, would be applicable in competition law cases where the agreement or practice was 'implemented' within the EU and had an appreciable effect on competition or inter-state trade within the EU.

5.3.3.2 Public Policy of the Forum

As already outlined, Arts 101 and 102 TFEU do not determine what damages or remedies could be sought by a claimant who suffered loss as a result of breach of EU competition law. Although a person who is injured by anti-competitive practice would be able to seek compensation for actual loss and loss of profit plus interest,[196] punitive antitrust damages as a remedy may be available in some Member States, but not in others where such damages may be unknown or regarded as contrary to public policy.

On the one hand, it is generally accepted by the Court of Justice that it is possible for a Member State court to award exemplary or punitive damages.[197] In England, there are instances in which the plaintiff can recover not only the compensatory loss, which will put the injured party in the same position he would have been in had he not sustained the wrong,[198] but also exemplary

[195] See section 5.2.3.
[196] *Manfredi* (n 110) [26].
[197] Ibid [93] and [99].
[198] *Livingston v Rawyards Coal Co* (1880) 5 App Cas 25, 39.

damages.[199] Punitive damage would be available in England if the infringements of EU competition law was deliberate and carried out with full knowledge of the illegality of the actions leading to an important distortion of competition, which is of exclusive benefit to the infringers.[200] If *Devenish* is to be believed, punitive damages are also known in Cyprus and in Ireland.

On the other hand, punitive (or exemplary) damages are not only unknown in some Member States (eg France,[201] Hungary[202] and Spain[203]), but they may also be contrary to public policy of the forum in some Member States (eg Germany[204] and Italy[205]). This is reflected in Recital 32 of the Rome II Regulation, which states that non-compensatory or punitive damages of an excessive nature may be regarded as being contrary to the public policy of the forum.[206] This seems to suggest that *lex fori* may still be important in antitrust damage actions brought in the European context. Indeed, as a result of not dealing with the available remedies for breach of Articles at EU level, a plaintiff should carefully choose the EU jurisdiction, in which to bring private proceedings to enforce competition law as the *lex fori* may have a role to play in this regard.[207]

Given the fact that 'punitive damages are undoubtedly one of the topics where the common law and continental European civil law seem worlds apart', an important question in the European context is whether a German or Italian court could award exemplary or punitive antitrust damages when applying English law, if applicable under the Rome II Regulation. It has been submitted that Recital 32 does not 'categorise all exemplary or punitive damages as being contrary to public policy but only "excessive" damages in those categories'.[208] However, it seems to this author that the question whether the punitive damage is excessive could only arise in a Member State where such damages are permitted under its legal system.[209] Different considerations would apply in a Member State where punitive damage is not part of the Member State's legal order which does not recognise a plaintiff's right to be punitive (ie the civil aspect of punitive damages)

199 *Rookes v Barnard* [1964] AC 1129; *Devenish* (HC) (n 114) [44] aff'd *Devenish* (CA) (n 115) [143]. See also V Wilcox, 'Punitive damages in England' in H Koziol and V Wilcox (eds), *Punitive Damages: Common Law and Civil Law Perspectives* (Springer, Vienna/New York, 2009) 7.

200 *Devenish* (HC) (n 114) [44].

201 JS Borghetti, 'Punitive damages in France' in Koziol and Wilcox (n 199) 55.

202 A Menyhard, 'Punitive damages in Hungary' in Koziol and Wilcox (n 199) 87, 91.

203 P del Olmo, 'Punitive damages in Spain' in Koziol and Wilcox (n 199) 137.

204 Punitive damages may be incompatible with fundamental principles of German law. See N Jansen and L Rademacher, 'Punitive damages in Germany' in Koziol and Wilcox (n 199) 75, 76. See also *Devenish* (HC) (n 114) [33].

205 AP Scarso, 'Punitive damages in Italy' in Koziol and Wilcox (n 199) 103, 108.

206 See Danov (n 123). See also MR Isidro, 'Punitive damages from a private international law perspective' in Koziol and Wilcox (n 199) 237.

207 Danov (n 123) 430.

208 Beaumont and Tang (n 120) 136.

209 Excessiveness a punitive damages award could be scrutinised in the US. See *BMW of N Am Inc v Gore* 517 US 559 (1996). See more BC Zipursky, 'A theory of punitive damages' (2005–2006) 84 *Texas Law Review* 105.

and regards such damages as merely punishing and deterring the defendant's conduct (ie involving a criminal law aspect only).[210] As the exemplary damages by definition are 'additional to an award which fully compensates the claimant for his loss, and which are intended to punish and deter',[211] it is difficult to see how in practice a national court that regarded an award of exemplary or punitive damages as being contrary to public policy would not categorise such damages as excessive for the purposes of the Rome II Regulation. It has been submitted by Hay that 'Recital 32 … acknowledges the aversion of many states against punitive damages and expressly authorizes the refusal to award them under the law otherwise applicable under the Regulation.'[212] Therefore, Recital 32 could be used to reduce the effect of the applicable law, entitling a Member State court not to give effect to *lex causae*, if the awarded damage would be non-compensatory and excessive under *lex fori*.[213]

Although an English court would award punitive (or exemplary) damage in an appropriate EU competition claim,[214] Recital 32 would entitle a Member State court that regarded an award of punitive damages as being contrary to public policy to deny the application of English law (ie *lex causae*) as far as it awards exemplary damages because such antitrust damage would be non-compensatory and excessive under its *lex fori*. For those purposes, a Member State court that regarded an award of punitive damages as being contrary to public policy would not refuse to apply applicable English law as to the calculation of damages, but simply decline to make any calculation and/or punitive damages awards, on the ground that it regards such damages as involving criminal law aspects and raising public policy concerns.

But, what would be the effect of Recital 32 of Rome II in England, if an English court was applying Irish law or Cypriot law, if applicable under the Rome II Regulation? A more liberal interpretation of Recital 32 may be adopted by English courts. Punitive (or exemplary) damages would not be regarded as excessive for the purposes of Rome II if the court had found that the compensatory damages were 'inadequate to punish [the defendant] for his outrageous conduct, to mark … disapproval of such conduct and deter him from repeating it …'.[215] Thus, it seems that Recital 32 would not preclude an English court to award exemplary (or punitive) damage when applying the law of Ireland or Cyprus, if there is a deliberate and conscious breach of EU competition law, resulting in tortfeasors' financial gain.[216] However, once an English court had calculated the damage by

[210] Zipursky (n 209) 106–07.

[211] *Devenish* (HC) (n 114) [14].

[212] P Hay, 'The Development of the public policy barrier to judgment recognition within the European Community' (2007) *The European Legal Forum* 289, 293.

[213] See more: Danov (n 123) 432–33.

[214] The principle of *non bis in idem* would preclude the award of exemplary damages in a case in which the defendant had already been fined by the European Commission.

[215] *Rookes* (n 199) 1228 (Lord Devlin). See more: Wilcox (n 199) 26–28.

[216] *Devenish* (HC) (n 114) [44].

applying, for example Irish law, it could decide that excessiveness makes the award contrary to English public policy. Accordingly, in cases where the 'market is, or is likely to be affected, in more than one country' and Art 6(3)(b) of Rome II is potentially relevant, a private antitrust plaintiff should carefully select where to bring an EU competition law claim, considering the type of damages that could be pleaded in the context.[217]

But can an English court award multiple damages when applying US antitrust law, if applicable under the Rome II Regulation? Should the English enquire into the excessiveness of US treble damages? The universal application under Art 3 of the Rome II Regulation and the wording of Art 6 leave no doubt that in cases, where the conduct in question had no appreciable effect on competition or interstate trade within the EU, then the antitrust laws of the country (including non-Member State laws) in which the market is affected is to be applicable. What if the market were affected within the US? Article 21 states that:

> The application of a provision of the law of any country specified by this Regulation may be refused only if such application is manifestly incompatible with the public policy (*ordre public*) of the forum.

As already discussed, Recital 32 of Rome II goes further to state that non-compensatory or punitive damages of an excessive nature may be regarded as being contrary to the public policy of the forum. The question is whether such damage awards would be compatible with the fundamental public policy interest of an English court? Should an English court enquire into the excessiveness of punitive damages awarded by the foreign court?

It has been submitted that there could be a possibility that an award of multiple damages would infringe the Protection of Trading Interests Act 1980, which may affect the availability of such damages in England.[218] Section 5 of the 1980 Act restricts enforcement of overseas judgments awarding multiple damages (ie an amount of damages arrived at by doubling, trebling or otherwise multiplying a sum assessed as compensation for the loss or damage sustained by the person in whose favour the judgment is given). On this basis, it has been submitted that, 'in England a court applying US law has no power to order the payment of triple damages—a power provided under US antitrust legislation.'[219] Therefore, it seems that the prevailing opinion[220] is that an English court should refuse to multiply the sum assessed as compensation on the ground that multiple damages would be contrary to its public policy. But why should an English court disapply provision of foreign law awarding treble damages even if the relevant anti-competitive conduct is significantly foreign insofar as that conduct causes independent foreign harm and

[217] Danov (n 123) 432.

[218] Morse (n 147) 895; Dickinson (n 94) 408.

[219] N Blackaby and C Partasides, *Redfern and Hunter on International Arbitration* (5th edn, OUP, Oxford, 2009) 529.

[220] Ibid. Morse (n 147) 895; Dickinson (n 94) 408.

that foreign harm alone gives rise to the plaintiff's claim?[221] There are good reasons suggesting that the Protection of Trading Interests Act 1980 should be revised.

First, in some cases a refusal to apply the foreign law as to the existence, the nature and the assessment of damage or remedy claimed may defeat the policy involved in following the foreign substantive law.[222] A rule precluding an English court from awarding multiple damages in such a scenario would undermine US antitrust enforcement policy. Such a rule would fly in the face of the EC/US Antitrust Cooperation Agreement.[223] Although the latter agreement was signed in the centralised enforcement era, its aim to promote the sound and effective enforcement of US and EU competition laws should be more important than ever. This would be a very important consideration in cases involving the application of US antitrust law.

Secondly, the 1980 Act seems to assume that the punitive (or exemplary) damage are always excessive within the meaning of Recital 32. This may not always be so. It has been submitted that:

> ...Victims who claim damages in essence serve the social goal of deterrence. However, starting a lawsuit entails costs, which are privately borne. This might lead to too few lawsuits being brought. Increasing the expected damages of victims by awarding punitive damages may solve this problem.[224]

If the US legislature has decided that the probability of detection of an illegal cartel is 33 per cent and compensatory damages should be tripled to provide the correct incentives,[225] an English court need not regard such damage as excessive within the meaning of Recital 32. If the EU competition law rules, which are regarded as overriding mandatory provisions within the meaning of Art 16 of Rome II, were not applicable, then it is difficult to see why English law should supplant America's own determination about how best to enforce its own antitrust laws in a case, in which the anti-competitive conduct took place in America causing anti-competitive harm there.[226] Such a deduction may be reinforced by outlining the OFT opinion that doubling damages could be an appropriate starting point in cases where an English court was considering an award of exemplary damages for breaches of competition law.[227] A liberal revision of the 1980 Act should be on the agenda, which may easily make England the most favourable private antitrust forum in Europe.

[221] Compare *Empagran* (n 84) 542 US 166.

[222] WW Cook, '"Substance" and "procedure" in the conflict of laws' (1932–1933) 42 *Yale Law Journal* 333, 344.

[223] 'Agreement between the Government of the United States of America and the Commission of the European Communities Regarding the Application of their Competition Laws' (n 89).

[224] LT Visscher, 'Economic analysis of punitive damages' in Koziol and Wilcox (n 199) 220, 224–25.

[225] Ibid 223.

[226] Compare *Empagran* (n 84) 542 US 165.

[227] Office of Fair Trading, *Response to the European Commission's Green Paper, Damages actions for breach of the EC antitrust rules* (2006) OFT 844.

5.4 Applicable Law: Competition Law Actions for Nullity of a Contract brought together with a Tortious Claim for Antitrust Damages

It has been submitted that 'there are a number of situations in which an international contract may be associated with a tort claim which has international connections.'[228] In the context of this book, the most obvious examples is where a party brings a contractual claim for invalidity of a contract that is allegedly in conflict with EU competition law together with a contingent claim for antitrust damages which is tortious in nature. It appears that the choice-of-law problems would arise if the English court had found that the contract would be invalidated by the applicable antitrust law provisions and had to deal with the contingent claim for antitrust damages. Recital 7 of Rome I states that '[t]he substantive scope and the provisions of this Regulation should be consistent with … Regulation (EC) No 864/2007 of the European Parliament and of the Council of 11 July 2007 on the law applicable to non-contractual obligations (Rome II).'[229] Article 1 of Rome II leaves no doubt that the latter Regulation is to be applied in situations involving choice of law in tort.

Indeed, Art 6(4) of Rome II clarifies that 'the law applicable under this Article may not be derogated from by an agreement pursuant to Article 14.'[230] The absolute prohibition has been criticised by some commentators.[231] Fitchen goes further to make a case for reviewing the Rome II Regulation, so that to allow the parties to make a restricted choice of law subject to requirements preventing evasion of mandatory rules.[232] However, it seems to this author that such a liberal proposal could not be supported. It would hardly seem efficient to permit a monopolist to have a choice-of-law provision that restricts, for example, the available remedies even if the monopolist was sued in the courts where a plaintiff (or plaintiffs) could recover higher damages under *lex fori* which could be applicable in the context of Art 6(3)(b) of Rome II.[233] It should be noted that Art 6(4) is not only meant to ensure that mandatory provisions are not evaded, but also to secure that monopolists (or undertakings enjoying market power) would not be allowed

[228] Nygh (n 17) 235.

[229] Regulation (EC) 864/2007 of the European Parliament and of the Council of 11 July 2007 on the law applicable to non-contractual obligations (Rome II) [2007] OJ L199/40.

[230] See also: de Boer (n 131).

[231] T Petch, 'The Rome II Regulation: an update: part 2' (2006) 21 *Journal of International Banking Law and Regulation* 509, 511; Fitchen (n 132) 344–46. Compare Pineau (n 132) 327.

[232] Fitchen (n 132) 346.

[233] RA Epstein and MS Greve, 'Introduction: The intractable problem of antitrust jurisdiction' in Epstein and Greve (n 83) 1, 24. See also Pineau (n 132) 328.

to limit their liability in antitrust law actions by relying on appropriately drafted choice-of-law clauses.

Accordingly, the law identified by the Rome I Regulation to govern the validity of an allegedly anti-competitive agreement would not be applicable to claims in tort which would be governed by the applicable law as indentified by Rome II.[234] Therefore, even if the *lex contractus* were expressly chosen by commercial parties to a contract, the English court may not give effect to the choice made by the parties as Art 6 of Rome II is set to determine the law applicable to non-contractual obligations arising out of restrictions of competition. The Rome II solution appears to be consistent with the approach advocated by Sir Otto Kahn-Freund in his 1968 Hague Lectures.[235] According to him, 'delictual liability should be determined by the law indicated by the choice-of-law rule applicable to a foreign tort and that the validity of a contract or any clause thereof should be determined by the proper law of the contract'.[236]

In other words, the *lex contractus* would only be applicable to determine the legality of the contractual obligation. This would be clearly so in cases falling within the scope of Art 9(3) of Rome I. The latter provision leaves no doubt that the foreign overriding provisions would not apply with regard to related antitrust tortious claims which could raise such issues as causation and assessment of antitrust damages. Furthermore, even where EU competition law were applied to declare an anti-competitive agreement null and void, Arts 101 and 102 TFEU do not define the issue of causation and assessment of damages which need to be addressed by the English court in the context of the tortious antitrust claim. It would make no sense if the English applied the *lex contractus* to the claim in tort after it had disregarded the choice of law as determined by Rome I, in order to determine the issue of validity, by applying the relevant overriding mandatory provisions.

5.5 Concluding Remarks

In spite of the principle of supremacy, and the fact that Arts 101 and 102 TFEU are regarded as mandatory provisions of the *forum* suggest that choice-of-law rules would be irrelevant in some EU competition law cases, the foregoing analysis demonstrates that choice-of-law rules have a role to play in antitrust claims. This would be clearly so with regard to issues on which EU competition law is silent.

[234] See *Cheshire, North & Fawcett* (n 14) 780. Compare: Briggs (n 87) 400–01 and 419; Art 14 of Rome II.

[235] See O Kahn-Freud, 'Delictual Liability and the Conflict of Laws' (1968) II Rec des cours 1 discussed in Nygh (n 17) 247–49.

[236] Nygh (n 17) 248. See also: CGJ Morse, *Torts in Private International Law* (North-Holland Publishing, Amsterdam 1978) 191; P North, 'Contract as a tort defence in the conflict of laws' in P North, *Essays in Private International Law* (Clarendon Press, Oxford, 1993) 98–108.

On the one hand, it should be admitted that the application of choice-of-law rules to some of these issues would be of academic interest. For example, the EU principle of effectiveness could make the question of the standard of proof not really practically important. The significance of the choice-of-law rules relevance to the consequences of the principle of severance of invalidity of a clause that is in conflict with EU competition law would be minimised by the fact the European legal system would most probably share common principles in this context.

On the other hand, the fact that choice-of-law rules would indicate the scope of the defendant's liability, and respectively, what a plaintiff would be entitled to recover in a private antitrust damages claim, leaves no doubt that private international law would have an important role to play in the context of private antitrust claims. Accordingly, there could be different outcomes if exemplary or punitive antitrust damages are pleaded, as they may be available in one Member State, but not in another. Indeed, the fact that often the EU legislator gives predominant role to *lex fori* in cases where the market is affected in several countries and punitive damages are pleaded indicate that a private antitrust plaintiff in Europe should carefully select where to bring an EU competition law claim, considering the law of the forum. Although, it would be unfair that different damages are awarded for the same breach of the very same rule, a different level of redress would come to no surprise in view of the fact that EU has opted for a private international solution. Indeed, the purpose of Rome II is the unification of choice-of-law, not the harmonisation of the Member States' remedies in tortious actions based on EU competition law.

6

Foreign Judgments in Relation to EU Competition Law Claims before English Courts

6.1 Introduction

It is well established that an English court will have jurisdiction to hear and determine a claim for enforcement of a judgment of a foreign court.[1] The rules on recognition and enforcement of foreign judgments apply to all judgments, including those in relation to EU competition law claims. No foreign judgment can be enforced in England until it has been recognised.[2] Enforcement will not always follow, though. Recognition alone is sufficient, for example, where a foreign court's decision is merely declaring that a contract is contrary to Arts 101 and 102 TFEU and thus void. But what are the powers of the English courts with regard to recognition and enforcement of a foreign judgment that misapplies or disregards EU competition law?

Under English law, a basic distinction can be made between recognition and enforcement under the Brussels I regime, and recognition and enforcement under the English traditional rules. Neither set of rules has been used extensively in EU antitrust cases. It should be noted, nonetheless, that proceedings with regard to recognition and enforcement of foreign judgments would give rise to few special problems in cases involving EU competition law issues. Normally, the English court would be precluded from reviewing a foreign judgment as to its substance on the basis that an adjudicating court was believed to have erred in its determination of the merits.[3]

However, specific issues in the context of recognition and enforcement of foreign judgments in relation to EU competition law claims could arise in view of the fact that Arts 101 and 102 TFEU enjoy a 'public policy' character for

[1] CPR PD 6B, para 3.1(10).

[2] CPR 74.9(2)(a).

[3] See Art 36 of the Brussels I Regulation. See the English common law approach: (a) error of fact—*Henderson v Henderson* [1843–60] All ER Rep 378 (Vice-Chancellor's Court); (b) error of law—*Castrique v Imrie* [1861–73] All ER Rep 508 (HL), *Godard v Gray* [1870] 6 LRQB 139 (Court of Queen' Bench), *Minna Craig Steamship v Chartered Mercantile Bank* [1897] 1 QB 460 (CA).

private international law purposes.[4] Public policy—being a generally recognised international principle[5]—is a ground for refusing recognition under the Brussels I Regulation and English law as well. Thus, foreign judgments would have a *res judicata* effect in England only after they had been duly recognised,[6] which suggests that the recognising court should be entitled to determine whether a foreign judgment is in conflict with its public policy, and EU competition law in particular.

It seems that after the private antitrust enforcement reform, the English court faced with a foreign judgment in relation to an EU competition law claim will primarily have to ascertain whether such a judgment is to be recognised and enforced in England. The private international law problems in such cases are to do with the ambiguous content of 'public policy' in the meaning of the Brussels Regulation and English traditional rules which could give rise to some uncertainty as to the scope of review of judgments in relation to EU competition law cases. One of the most common issues that the English court would need to determine with regard to judgments in relation to EU competition law claims is whether their recognition would be contrary to public policy if the court with original jurisdiction had misapplied or neglected Arts 101 and 102 TFEU.

Does a non-application or a wrong application of Arts 101 and 102 TFEU entitle the English court to refuse recognition of a foreign judgment in relation to an EU competition law claim? Would the answer to this question depend on whether the recognition and enforcement is sought under the Brussels I regime or under English common law? Should the long-term objective of the EU to abolish the public policy exception for all judgments in civil and commercial matters be fulfilled (at all) with regard to decisions in relation to EU competition law? The aim of this chapter is to answer those questions. To this end, the problems, which might prove particularly difficult with regard to enforcement of foreign judgments misapplying or neglecting EU competition law, will be highlighted. The main issues are to do with the scope of review and grounds for refusing recognition of such judgments under the Brussels I Regulation and English common law. In this context, the long-term objective of the European Union to abolish the *exequatur* for all judgments in civil and commercial matters,[7] and the Court of Justice's ruling

[4] See Case C-126/97 *Eco Swiss China Time v Benetton International ('Eco Swiss')* [1999] ECR I-3055 [38]; Case C-38/98 *Renault v Maxicar* [2000] ECR I-2973. See also: R Plender and M Wilderspin, *The European Private International Law of Obligations* (3rd edn, Sweet & Maxwell, London, 2009) 634 and 746. The public policy character of EU competition law is discussed in detail in section 6.2.3 below.

[5] See more: C-J Pointon, 'The EEC Convention on the recognition and enforcement of civil and commercial judgments, and its applications for English law' (1975) 2 *Legal Issues of European Integration* 1, 47–48.

[6] For the position under English common law, see P Barnett, *Res Judicata, Estoppel and Foreign Judgments: The preclusive effects of foreign judgments in private international law* (OUP, Oxford, 2001) 31 and 41. For the position under the Brussels I Regulation, see Case 42/76 *Josef de Wolf v Harry Cox* [1977] ECR 1759 [3] (judgment), 1772 (AG Mayras).

[7] See Tampere European Council 15/16 October 1999: Conclusions of the Presidency www.europarl.europa.eu/summits/tam_en.htm [34]; Commission (EC), 'Review of Council Regulation

in *Renault*,[8] should be carefully considered. The special regime for enforcement of judgments in relation to US antitrust claims and the powers of the courts under the Protection of Trading Interests Act will be briefly highlighted as well.

6.2 Powers of the English Courts under the Brussels I Regulation

The Brussels regime is based on mutual trust in the legal systems within the EU.[9] Article 33 of the Brussels I Regulation clearly stipulates that 'a judgment given in a Member State shall be recognised in the other Member States without any special procedure being required'.

6.2.1 Definition of 'Judgment' and Decisions of NCAs

A specific issue that would arise in the context of private EU antitrust law actions relates to the question of whether the decisions of NCAs are to be regarded as 'judgments' for the recognition and enforcement purposes. The issue of the recognition and enforcement of decisions taken by NCAs is left out of Regulation 1/2003.[10] The White Paper on modernisation, however, seems to indicate that an NCA decision is enforceable only within the territory on which the authority in question operates.[11] Can NCAs' decisions be recognised and enforced under Brussels I? Are decisions of NCAs within the scope of the Brussels I Regulation?

Decisions of NCAs are given in the context of administrative public proceedings in which NCAs enjoy extensive investigative and decision-making powers.[12]

(EC) No 44/2001 on Jurisdiction and the Recognition and Enforcement of Judgments in Civil and Commercial Matters' (Green Paper) COM (2009) 175 final.

[8] *Renault* (n 4).

[9] Recital 16 of the Brussels Regulation. See also: Case C-172/91 *Sonntag v Waidmann* [1993] ECR I-1963 [70].

[10] It has been submitted that 'Article 10 EC [now Art 4(3) TEU], while not requiring Member States to automatically and mutually recognise the legal force of all decisions which are adopted to implement Article 81 or 82 EC [now Arts 101 and 102 TFEU], can certainly be construed in such a way as to impose a duty on Member States to recognise the validity of foreign NCA decision on a case-by-case basis. This means that recognition would take place only when a request is made by the Member State which adopted the decision and only by the NCA of the Member State to which the request is submitted.' See S Brammer, *Co-operation between National Competition Agencies in the Enforcement of EC Competition Law* (Hart Publishing, Oxford, 2009) 428–29. Even if this interpretation was correct, the effect of such recognition would be somewhat limited as the foreign NCA would only be recognised by the local NCA being part of the same ECN.

[11] White Paper on Modernisation of the Rules implementing Articles 85 and 86 of the EC Treaty, Commission Programme 99/027 [60]. See A Komninos, *EC Private Antitrust Enforcement: Decentralised Application of EC Competition Law by National Courts* (Hart Publishing, Oxford, 2008) 77; Brammer (n 10) 426–436.

[12] Komninos (n 11) 119.

Although one could say that decisions of public authorities do not produce *res judicata* effect, it should be pointed out that decisions of public administrative authorities enjoy finality.[13] Indeed, it is well established that a *res judicata* effect is not a pre-condition for the purposes of recognition under the Brussels I Regulation, as the words '*res judicata*' have been deliberately omitted by the EU legislator from the text of the Regulation.[14] Article 1 of Brussels I seems to suggest that 'judgments given in a [Member] State in civil commercial matters by … administrative tribunals must be recognized and enforced in the other [Member] States.'[15] As already concluded, an EU competition law claim brought before Member State courts is properly regarded as a 'civil and commercial matter' for the purposes of the Brussels I Regulation.[16] Therefore, it seems that a decision of an NCA would be within the scope of the Regulation as long as it relates to a civil or commercial matter. This means that a decision (or part of a decision) of an NCA in the ECN, which imposes fines on an undertaking that has infringed Arts 101 and 102 TFEU, would not be within the scope of Brussels I.[17] However, a decision (or part of a decision) of an NCA in the ECN, which establishes an infringement of Arts 101 and 102 TFEU, should be within the scope of Brussels I.[18] The importance of such decisions in respect of antitrust proceedings before national courts was acknowledged by the EU legislator in the White Paper on damages.[19]

But are foreign NCAs' decisions to be regarded a 'judgments' for the purposes of Art 32 of the Brussels I Regulation? One of the main requirements for the recognition and enforcement purposes is that the judgment must be given by a court or tribunal of a Member State. The Court of Justice has also firmly held that to be classified as a judgment the decision must emanate from a judicial body of a Member State.[20] Are the NCAs judicial bodies? Article 35 of Regulation 1/2003 provides that Member States are to designate the competition authorities responsible for the application of Arts 101 and 102 TFEU. Article 35(2) makes clear that designated authorities may include judicial authorities.[21] Most Member States, however, have designated an administrative, rather than a judicial, body because most follow the EU scheme of having an administrative body investigating and deciding cases.[22] Clearly, the requirement for 'a decision to emanate from a judicial

[13] X Groussot and T Minssen, 'Res Judicata in the Court of Justice case-law: balancing legal certainty with legality?' (2007) 3 *European Constitutional Law Review* 385.

[14] Jenard Report [1979] OJ C59/1, 43.

[15] Jenard Report (n 14) 42. See also: Schlosser Report [1979] OJ C59/71 [23].

[16] See more: ch 1, section 1.6.1.1 above.

[17] Case 29/76 *Lufttransportunternehmen GmbH & Co KG v Organisation Européenne pour la Securité de la Navigation Aerienne (Eurocontrol)* [1976] ECR 1541 [4]–[5].

[18] *Eurocontrol* (n 17) [4].

[19] Commission (EC), 'Damages actions for breach of the EC antitrust rules' (White Paper) COM (2008) 165 final [2.3].

[20] Case C-414/92 *Solo Kleinmotoren v Boch* [1994] ECR I-2237 [17]. Compare Jenard Report (n 14) 42. See also Schlosser Report (n 15) [23].

[21] See Joined cases 209–213/84 *Ministère Public v Lucase Asjes* [1986] ECR 1425 [55]. See also: Case 172/73 *BRT v SABAM* [1974] ECR 51.

[22] Eg Bulgaria, Czech Republic, France, Italy, Romania, the UK.

body of a Member State' will not be met where the task of applying Arts 101 and 102 TFEU is entrusted to administrative authorities. For example, one may think that decisions of the OFT (being an independent government department and administrative body) would not qualify as a 'judgment of a court of competent jurisdiction'.[23] A different result for the purposes of the Brussels I Regulation can be reached with respect to NCAs' decisions adopted in countries[24] where the judicial bodies are designated as NCAs.[25] Such a different outcome could be explained by the fact that the decisions of NCAs, which are judicial bodies, may be regarded as judgments within the meaning of Art 32 of Brussels I.

A uniform result as to the recognition and enforcement of all NCAs decisions under Brussels I could be achieved if the 'judgment' in Art 32 of Brussels I was interpreted so as to include a final decision of any NCA exercising judicial functions, as long as it is a decision which is related to civil and commercial matters. This would be so, if a final decision of an NCA establishes an infringement of Arts 101 and 102 TFEU for the purposes of private antitrust enforcement. The need for such a broad interpretation can be further strengthened by pointing out that even though a decision which is made by the OFT is not to be regarded as a judgment within the meaning of Art 32 of Brussels I, a different interpretation can be made for the purposes of Brussels I if an appeal was made in respect of the OFT. For example, Sch 4 of the 2002 Act permits most decisions of the CAT to be enforceable by registration at the High Court in England and Wales (or corresponding procedure in Scotland and Northern Ireland). Through those provisions, the decision becomes enforceable in the same way as a judgment of the High Court. Decisions of the CAT could be further appealed before the Court of Appeal or Court of Session, respectively.[26] There is no doubt that in the latter case the judgment of the Court of Appeal would preclude recognition and enforcement of the foreign judgment in England. Thus, it seems that if a complaint against a decision of the OFT had been lodged, then in some cases the judgment rendered at the appeal could be regarded as a judgment. If no appeal against a decision of the OFT had been made, however, it would not be regarded as a judgment within the meaning of Brussels. The different results are due to the different constitutional positions of a court, on the one hand, and other public authorities, on the other hand. Nonetheless, it appears that this outcome could not be desirable and the issue should be addressed during the course of the Brussels I review.

[23] Compare *The Sennar (No 2)* [1985] 1 WLR 490 (HL) 499.

[24] Eg Austria and Ireland. In other countries, the task of applying Arts 81 and 82 is entrusted to quasi-judicial bodies, which are only part of the NCA from an organisational point of view (e.g. Germany).

[25] See D Cahill, JD Cooke and W Wils, (eds) *The Modernisation of EU Competition Law Enforcement: FIDE 2004 National Reports* (CUP, Cambridge, 2004). See also: C Kerse and N Khan, *EC Antitrust Procedure* (5th edn, Sweet & Maxwell, London, 2005) 260.

[26] See s 49 of the Competition Act 1998.

6.2.2 Recognition and Enforcement of Judgments under Brussels I

Judgments of the Member States' courts are eligible for registration for enforcement in England.[27] Such registration serves as a decision that the judgment is recognised for the purposes of the Brussels I Regulation.[28] Article 36 of the Regulation holds that under no circumstances may a foreign judgment be reviewed as to its substance. In other words, the accuracy of findings of law or fact made by the adjudicating court cannot be reviewed by the recognising court.[29] Reopening on the merits an EU competition law claim, which has been tried in a Member State's court, would run directly against the Regulation's aim for rapid recognition and enforcement of foreign judgments. As a result, a judgment given in a Member State would be easily recognised in England. Such '[r]ecognition gives the foreign judgment the force of *res judicata*.'[30] But, does this mean that under the Brussels I Regulation a foreign judgment in relation to an EU competition law claim would be automatically given the same effects in the recognising state as it has in the state in which it was rendered?[31]

Article 34(1) lays down an important exception to the duty of an English court to recognise a foreign judgment.[32] It provides that a judgment given by the court of a Member State shall not be recognised 'if such recognition is manifestly contrary to public policy in the state in which recognition is sought.'[33] The importance of competition policy for achieving the objectives of the EU could suggest that the public policy defence would be often pleaded where foreign judgments in relation to EU competition claims are at issue.[34] Is European public policy part of English public policy? What are the powers of the English court where a foreign judgment is allegedly based on an agreement in conflict with Arts 101 and 102 TFEU? Does the neglect or the wrong application of Arts 101 and 102 TFEU by the adjudicating court violate English public policy for the purposes of Art 34(1) of the Brussels I Regulation? These are the main questions that will be addressed in this section. Accordingly, first, the public policy character of EU competition law for the purposes of Art 34(1) will be briefly considered. Secondly, the possibility of not recognising a foreign judgment founded on contracts contrary to Arts 101 and 102 TFEU will be discussed.

[27] See CPR 74.3.

[28] See CPR 74.10.

[29] Case C-7/98 *Krombach v Bamberski* [2000] ECR I-1935 [36]. See also Jenard Report (n 14) 46.

[30] *Josef de Wolf* (n 6) 48 (AG Mayras) and [3] (Court of Justice decision). See also Barnett (n 6) 273.

[31] Compare: Case 145/86 *Hoffmann v Krieg* [1988] ECR 645 [11].

[32] *Josef de Wolf* (n 6) [3].

[33] It should be specified that the meaning of that provision is that the question is not whether a judgment is itself contrary to public policy but whether its recognition or an order for its enforcement would have that effect. See *Hoffmann* (n 31) [17] (AG Darmon).

[34] Eg *Eco Swiss* (n 4); *Renault* (n 4).

6.2.3 Public Policy Character of EU Competition Law for the Purposes of Recognition and Enforcement of Foreign Judgments in England

It is well settled that the public policy exception within the meaning of the Brussels I Regulation 'ought to operate only in exceptional cases'.[35] This is reinforced by the incorporation of the word 'manifestly' in Art 34.[36] Public policy cannot be relied upon unless recognition of a foreign judgment would constitute a breach of a rule of law regarded as essential in the legal order of the state, in which recognition is sought.[37] This entails the following questions: How is the content of English public policy defined for the purposes of Art 34(1)? Does the concept of public policy in an individual Member State cover Arts 101 and 102 TFEU?

It has been held that it is not for the Court of Justice to define the content of public policy of a Member State for the purposes of recognition and enforcement of judgments under the Brussels I Regulation.[38] The interpretation of Art 34(1), however, cannot be left exclusively to national courts. There are at least two reasons for that. First, an exclusive interpretation of this provision by the different national courts could result in the Regulation being applied in different ways. Moreover, it is well established that EU law must be observed in its entirety throughout the territory of all the Member States.[39] A fortiori, EU public policy is to be respected by each and every Member State's court. Secondly, by adopting an excessively broad interpretation of Art 34(1) the national courts could undermine the entire aim of the Regulation.[40] Therefore, there is little doubt that it would be for the Court of Justice to interpret the concept of public policy and set up the limits by reference to which the doctrine of public policy should be applied by national courts.[41] How must those limits be identified with regard to judgments in relation to EU competition law claims?

It seems that a notion of 'European public policy' that includes Arts 101 and 102 TFEU would not only ensure uniform application of the Brussels I Regulation, but also meet the demands for more coherent and uniform private enforcement of EU competition law.[42] If public policy in the meaning of Art 34(1) had covered EU competition law, then the recognising court would have the option to refuse recognition of a foreign judgment where the legitimate

[35] Jenard Report (n 14) C59/44. See also: *Hoffmann* (n 31) [10] and [21]; Case C-78/95 *Hendrickman v Magenta Druck & Verlag* [1996] ECR I-4943.

[36] 'Manifestly' does not appear in the Brussels or Lugano Conventions: L Collins (ed) *Dicey, Morris and Collins on the Conflict of Laws* (14th edn, Sweet & Maxwell, London, 2006) 661.

[37] *Krombach* (n 29) [37]. See also *Renault* (n 4).

[38] See *Krombach* (n 29) [23].

[39] Case 246/80 *Broekmeulen* [1981] ECR 2311.

[40] *Renault* (n 4) [58] (AG Alber).

[41] See *Krombach* (n 29) [22] and [23].

[42] See the position of the Dutch government in *Renault* (n 4) [46] (AG Alber). Compare the Commission's opinion in *Renault* (n 4) [48]–[53] (AG Alber).

interests in the enforcement of Arts 101 and 102 TFEU had not been addressed by a foreign court.

Some commentators, however, do not favour an autonomous interpretation of the public policy exception for the purposes of the Brussels I Regulation.[43] For example, the invention of 'European public policy' has been condemned by Briggs and Rees, who have pointed out that the notion of 'public policy is national, not supranational'.[44] In spite of the fact that the wording of Art 34(1) refers to public policy of an individual Member State, it is beyond doubt that European public policy is part of its public policy as well.[45]

It has been submitted by Advocate General Alber that the concept of 'public policy' in Art 34(1) includes principles of EU law.[46] The expressions 'public Community policy' and 'public economic policy of the Community' were also used by Advocate General Saggio when delivering his opinion in the *Eco Swiss* case.[47] Not surprisingly, the term 'European public policy' has also been used by some legal academic writers.[48] Moreover, Thoma[49] argues that the public policy exception is no longer purely national, but has changed under EU law.[50] Similarly, it has been submitted by Mills that 'although the ECJ has rejected arguments for the direct formation of an autonomous Community meaning of public policy,[51] it might be suggested that it has indirectly developed an equivalent idea.'[52]

There are sound reasons to state that Arts 101 and 102 TFEU should enjoy public policy character in England for the private international law purposes. First, such a deduction can be strengthened by making reference to Art 119 TFEU, which holds that EU and Member States' economic policies should be 'conducted in accordance with the principle of an open market economy and free competition'. Furthermore, the Protocol on the Internal Market and Competition annexed to the Treaty on European Union explicitly states that 'the internal market as set out in Art 3 of the Treaty on European Union includes a system ensuring that competition is not distorted.'[53]

[43] See A Briggs and P Rees, *Civil Jurisdiction and Judgments* (5th edn, Informa, London, 2009) 688; see also: *Dicey, Morris and Collins* (n 36) 661–662. Compare Recital 32 of the Rome II Regulation.

[44] Briggs and Rees (n 43) 688.

[45] CMV Clarkson and J Hill, *The Conflict of Laws* (3rd edn, OUP, Oxford, 2006) 258.

[46] *Renault* (n 4) [58] (AG Alber). Compare: *Hoffmann* (n 31) [16] (AG Darmon).

[47] See *Eco Swiss* (n 4) [38] (AG Saggio).

[48] Eg Clarkson and Hill (n 45). H P Meidans, 'Public policy and *ordre public* in the private international law of the EC/EU: Traditional positions of the Member States and modern trends' (2005) 30 *EL Rev* 95, 104; A Mills, *The Confluence of Public and Private International Law* (CUP, Cambridge, 2009) 194–98.

[49] The English edition of the book by I Thoma, *Die Europäisierung und die Vergemeinschaftung des nationalen ordre public* (Mohr Siebeck, Tübingen, 2007).

[50] See also Case C-394/07 *Gambazzi v Daimler Chrysler Canada Inc* [2009] ILPr 38 (Court of Justice) [46]; Briggs and Rees (n 43) 24.

[51] *Renault* (n 4) [46] (AG Alber).

[52] Mills (n 48) p 195.

[53] Compare old Art 3(1)(g) TEC. See more: J Drexl, 'Competition law as part of the European Constitution' in A von Bogdandy and J Bast (eds), *Principles of European Constitutional Law* (2nd edn, Hart Publishing and Verlag CH Beck, Oxford and Munich, 2009) 659, 662–69.

Secondly, the provisions of Regulation 17/62 provided for public enforcement of EU competition law by the Commission. The special interest in encouraging private enforcement of antitrust law was reflected in Regulation 1/2003. Moreover, as already mentioned,[54] the Commission published a Green Paper[55] and later a White Paper[56], the aims of which were to identify the appropriate incentives for private antitrust damages claims and to adopt any new legislation. At the time of writing, a Directive on damages actions is being finalised. In the Green Paper, the Commission has clearly outlined that the damages actions were set to provide special incentive for private antitrust law enforcement. Private actions, though, cannot replace public enforcement. According to the Commission, '[t]he role of the public authorities will continue to be of crucial importance in detecting anti-competitive practices such as cartels, where the special investigations powers vested in the public authorities and leniency programme are indispensable for efficient enforcement of competition law.'[57] All of the foregoing considerations indicate that Arts 101 and 102 TFEU should be regarded as a public policy matter.

In addition, the importance of Art 101 TFEU could be deduced from its sub-s 2, which stipulates that agreements concluded in breach of the prohibition contained in Art 101(1) are automatically void. The Court of Justice has held that in such cases nullity is retroactive, irrespective of whether or not any statement to that effect is made by the body responsible for deciding the matter.[58] The retroactive nullity of agreement that distorts competition reaffirms the fundamental character of Art 101 TFEU. In line with that, the English court has held that a breach of Art 101 is to be regarded as an illegal act—not only is the said agreement rendered void, but also the Commission may impose fines on all parties to the agreement.[59] In spite of the fact that Art 102 TFEU does not include a provision equivalent to Art 101(2) TFEU, which prescribes that any agreements prohibited by Art 101(1) TFEU shall be automatically void, the Court of Justice has stated that a similar consequence applies to any breach of Art 102 TFEU.[60] Moreover, under English law, traditionally the 'doctrine of restraint of trade' is based on

[54] See above, ch 1, section 1.2.

[55] Commission (EC), 'Damages actions for breach of EC antitrust rules' (Green Paper) COM (2005) 672 final. See also: N Kroes, 'Enhancing actions for damages for breach of competition rules in Europe' *Speech at the Harvard Club, New York* 22 September 2005 http://europa.eu/rapid/pressReleasesAction.do?reference=SPEECH/05/533&format=PDF&aged=1&language=EN&guiLanguage=en; N Kroes, 'The Green Paper on antitrust damages: empowering European citizens to enforce their rights' at the European Parliament Workshop on damages actions for breach of the EC antitrust rules http://ec.europa.eu/comm/competition/antitrust/actionsdamages/speech_06062006.pdf.

[56] White Paper on Damages (n 19).

[57] Commission Staff Working Paper SEC(2005) 1732 [13]. See also: White Paper on Damages (n 19).

[58] Case 48/72 *Haecht v Wilkin-Janssen* [1973] ECR 77 [25]–[27]. See also: See *Eco Swiss* (n 4) [36] (AG Saggio).

[59] *Gibbs Mew v Gemmel* [1997] ECC 97 (CA) [16] and [40].

[60] *BRT* (n 21). See more: U Bernitz, 'The sanction of voidness under Arts 82 EC and its relation to the right to damages' in A Ezrachi (ed), *Article 82 EC: Reflection on its Recent Evolution* (Hart Publishing, Oxford, 2009) 187, 188–89.

public policy.[61] This seems to indicate that English public policy will also include Arts 101 and 102 TFEU, so an English court will be entitled to refuse recognition of a foreign judgment, since it will be based on a void and illegal contract.

On top of that, another argument for the public policy character of EU competition law for the purposes of recognition and enforcement of foreign judgments in England can be derived from the Court of Justice ruling in *Eco Swiss*.[62] The *Eco Swiss* judgment was rendered in the context of an application for annulment of arbitral awards that were alleged to be contrary to public policy by virtue of the nullity of the parties' licensing agreement under EU competition law. In spite of the differences between the regimes of enforcement under the New York Convention and the Brussels I Regulation, there is no reason to suggest European public policy has different content for those purposes.[63] The analogy can be justified by the fact that the wording in the corresponding provisions of the Brussels I Regulation[64] is identical to that found in the New York Convention.[65] The fact that the Brussels Regulation[66] and the New York Convention[67] are quite different legal instruments should not be given too much weight, because Art 34 of Brussels I follows an identical provision contained in other intergovernmental instruments—the Brussels and Lugano Conventions.[68] What should be stressed is that all those instruments plainly state that it is the recognition of a foreign verdict that must be contrary to the public policy of the forum.

Nonetheless, the fact that the Brussels I Regulation is concerned with recognition and enforcement of judgments rendered by the Member States suggests that powers of the national courts to deny enforcement of a judgment will be more limited in comparison to their powers to refuse enforcement of arbitral awards. It is doubtful whether a foreign judgment, which misapplies EU competition law though enjoying public policy character, is *ipso facto*, contrary to English public policy.[69] This fact, however, does not change the public policy character of Arts 101 and 102 TFEU for the purposes of recognition and enforcement of foreign judgments in England.

Based on the foregoing considerations, there are very sound arguments favouring the view that the *Eco Swiss* ruling, that EU competition law may be regarded as

[61] *Esso Petroleum v Harper's Garage* [1968] AC 269 (HL) 298 (Lord Reid).

[62] *Eco Swiss* (n 4) [38] and [41]. See also: Meidans (n 48) 106; J-P Beraudo, 'Egregious error of law as grounds for setting aside an arbitral award' (2006) 23 *Journal of International Arbitration* 351, 361.

[63] Compare: Meidans (n 48) 105.

[64] See Art 34(1).

[65] See Art V(2)(b) of the New York Convention.

[66] The Brussels I Regulation was adopted by the Council as a supranational legal instrument on the basis of Art 65 TEC. See more: PR Beaumont, 'European Court of Justice and Jurisdiction and enforcement of judgments in civil and commercial matters' (1999) 48 *ICLQ* 223, 225–29.

[67] The New York Convention was prepared by the United Nations and agreed to as an intergovernmental instrument by a diplomatic conference.

[68] The latter is applicable within the European judicial area, which consists of the EU Member States plus Iceland, Norway and Switzerland. See also Beraudo (n 62) 357.

[69] Compare Beraudo (n 62) 361.

a matter of public policy within the meaning of the New York Convention, would be followed for the purposes of Art 34(1) of the Brussels I Regulation. It can be concluded that Arts 101 and 102 TFEU would enjoy public policy character in England for the purposes of recognition and enforcement of foreign judgments. This can be sustained by the European case law and the fact that public interest in the enforcement of EU competition law is repeatedly reflected in the special remedial system enacted within the EU and England. Such a conclusion will reflect the importance of Arts 101 and 102 TFEU and prevent parties evading their application.

Having clarified the public policy character of EU competition law, the powers of the recognising court with regard to foreign judgments misapplying Arts 101 and 102 TFEU will be examined in the following section.

6.2.4 Wrong Application or Neglect of EU Competition Law as a Public Policy Defence

The public policy character of Arts 101 and 102 TFEU means that it would be for the court addressed to verify of its own motion whether recognition would be contrary to EU competition law.[70] The Court of Justice case law,[71] however, indicates that the doctrine of public policy may not be easily invoked in proceedings for recognition and enforcement of foreign judgments with regard to EU competition law claims. Indeed, it appears that the answer to the question whether it is contrary to English public policy to recognise a judgment that misapplies Arts 101 and/or 102 TFEU requires balancing potentially conflicting requirements. On the one hand, the fundamental importance of Arts 101 and 102 TFEU in the EU legal order should always be considered.[72] On the other hand, requirements for rapid recognition and enforcement of judgments under the Brussels I Regime should be taken into account. The importance of the *res judicata* doctrine under both the EU and English legal systems should also be considered in seeking the balance. In view of that, the scenarios where EU competition law has been wrongfully applied or neglected by the court with original jurisdiction will be respectively highlighted.

6.2.4.1 EU Competition Law was Wrongfully applied by an Adjudicating Court

A public policy defence based on an alleged substantive error in the application of rules of EU competition law was inter alia raised in the *Renault* case. In this

[70] See Jenard Report (n 14) C59/44. See also: Joined Cases C-430/93 and C-432/93 *Van Schijndel and Van Veen v SPF* [1995] ECR I-4705; Joined Cases C-295/04–C-298/04 *Manfredi v Lloyd Adriaticco* [2006] 5 CMLR 17 [31].

[71] Eg *Krombach* (n 29) [37]; *Renault* (n 4).

[72] Compare *Eco Swiss* (n 4) [38] (AG Saggio). See more section 6.2.3 above.

case, the questions referred to the Court of Justice arose out of a French plaintiff's application to enforce a French judgment in Italy.[73] The French court had awarded damages for breach of the plaintiff's intellectual property rights by the defendant, an Italian company. Before the recognising court, the defendants contended that due to an error in the application of fundamental principles of EU law, the judgment should not be declared enforceable because inter alia it was contrary to public policy.[74] The Court of Justice held that under the Brussels I regime the recognising court cannot refuse recognition of a foreign judgment solely on the ground that it considers that EU law was misapplied by the court with original jurisdiction.[75] The Court of Justice went further to clarify that such an error does not constitute a manifest breach of law, so it cannot justify the Italian court refusing recognition on the basis of public policy.[76]

The *Renault* ruling was justified by the availability of appropriate mechanisms, which were set to guarantee the proper application of EU law by the adjudicating national court.[77] The possibility for making a reference under Art 267 TFEU (ex Art 234 TEC) in cases where the national court had any doubts about the interpretation of EU competition law provisions was outlined as a means guaranteeing proper interpretation and application of that law. This could be further strengthened by pointing out that Regulation 1/2003 provided a special mechanism for co-operation between the Commission and national courts with regard to any question concerning application of EU competition law.[78] For example, Art 15(2) of Regulation 1/2003 requires a copy of any written judgment in relation to Arts 101 and 102 TFEU to be forwarded to the Commission. This rule is meant to enable the Commission to detect any misapplication of EU competition law and intervene by submitting written observation to the Member State court under Art 15(3) of Regulation 1/2003.[79] Indeed, the mechanisms provided by Regulation 1/2003 are set to ensure that the court with original jurisdiction is best placed and qualified to determine whether an agreement was, or was not, in accordance with Arts 101 and 102 TFEU.

The Court of Justice also held that it would be necessary and always possible to exhaust the appeal process of the state in question. Certainly, Art 34(1) cannot be considered as such a means of appeal because it is meant to ensure that recognition of the foreign judgment is not contrary to public policy of the Member State, where recognition is sought. Article 36 explicitly states that 'under

[73] The judgment was final, so the French plaintiff applied to the Corte d'Appelo di Torino for a declaration of enforceability of that judgment in Italy under Arts 31 and 32 of the Brussels Convention (Arts 37 and 38 of the Brussels I Regulation).

[74] See Art 27(1) of the Brussels Convention and Art 34(1) of the Brussels I Regulation.

[75] *Renault* (n 4) [33].

[76] *Renault* (n 6) [34]. See also: J Hill, *International Commercial Disputes in English Courts* (3rd edn, Hart Publishing, Oxford, 2005) 422; Briggs and Rees (n 43) 688–89.

[77] *Renault* (n 4) [34]. See also ch 7, section 7.5.5.3 below.

[78] See Art 15 of Regulation 1/2003.

[79] See Brammer (n 10) 47.

no circumstances may a foreign judgment be reviewed as to its substance'. It has been submitted that Art 36 should be considered as covering even review on the ground of public policy.[80] This view was upheld by the English court which stated that the Regulation precludes the court from reviewing the conclusions of a foreign court in cases where the foreign court has 'ruled on precisely the matters that a defendant seeks to raise when challenging the judgment'[81] on the ground of public policy. This is in line with the view that the public policy exception contained in Art 34(1) should be interpreted in accordance with the general spirit of the Brussels I Regulation[82] and its aim of ensuring the rapid recognition and enforcement of judgments in other Member States.[83] Referring to the *Renault* case, Beraudo states that the 'misapplication of public policy rule, from which parties cannot derogate, does not lead necessarily to a judgment contrary to public policy as to its enforcement in another Member State.'[84] The editors of *Dicey, Morris and Collins* went further and interpreted the *Renault* ruling as holding that where the adjudicating court had misapplied EU competition law, the effect could not be regarded as serious enough to trigger the application of Art 34(1).[85]

Further support for concluding that an error in the application of Arts 101 and 102 TFEU committed by the Member State's court does not trigger Art 34(1) of Brussels I may find its basis in the doctrine of *res judicata*,[86] which has two bases.[87] First, it is justified by the fact that an individual should not be vexed twice with the same matter. The second basis refers to the public interest that there should be an end in litigation.[88] The latter normally denotes considerations of wider social and economical interests and will be of relevance for denying review over the merits of a judgment rendered by a Member State court. The fundamental importance of the principle of *res judicata* for the EU legal order and national legal systems was recently reaffirmed by the Court of Justice in *Rosmarie Kapferer v Schlank & Schick*.[89]

Thus, it can be concluded that the English court is not allowed to review a foreign judgment in which the Member State's court has applied EU competition law, even if to do so would enable it to remedy an infringement of EU law.[90] Indeed, the *Renault* ruling that recognition cannot be refused on the ground that EU law was

[80] P Kaye, *Civil Jurisdiction and Enforcement of Foreign Judgments* (Professional Books, Oxford, 1987) 1447. See also Hill (n 76) 417. Compare *Gambazzi* (n 50) [46].

[81] *Interdesco v Nullifire* [1992] 1 Lloyd's Rep 180 (QBD (Comm) 187.

[82] See Jenard Report (n 14) 42. See also: *Hoffmann* (n 31) [10].

[83] See *Solo Kleinmotoren* (n 20) [20]; Case C-267/97 *Coursier v Fortis Bank* [1999] ECR I-2543 [25]; *Krombach* (n 29) [19].

[84] Beraudo (n 62) 360–361.

[85] *Dicey, Morris and Collins* (n 36) 662. See also: A Briggs, *The Conflict of Laws* (OUP, Oxford, 2002) 123; Meidans (n 48).

[86] Compare Art 37 of the Brussels I Regulation.

[87] *Vervaeke v Smith* [1983] 1 AC 145 (HL) 161.

[88] Ibid.

[89] Case C-234/04 *Rosmarie Kapferer v Schlank & Schick* [2006] ECR I-2585 [20]. See also: Case C-224/01 *Kobler* [2003] ECR I-10239 [38]; *Josef de Wolf* (n 6) 1772 (AG Mayras). See more: Barnett (n 6) 273.

[90] *Rosmarie Kapferer* (n 89) [21]. See also *Eco Swiss* (n 4) [46]–[47].

misapplied would be followed in cases where the defendant invoked a public policy defence arguing that Arts 101 and/or 102 TFEU had been wrongfully applied. Thus, an error in application of EU competition law does not violate English public policy for the purposes of Art 34 of the Brussels I Regulation. This is a rather unfortunate outcome, in view of the fact that a Member State authority's individual administrative decision that is in conflict with EU law must be disregarded when assessing its validity.[91] Although the national courts must ensure the legal protection which individuals derive from the direct effect of EU law,[92] there is no legal basis for denying recognition of a Member State court's judgment in cases where EU competition law was misapplied by the court with original jurisdiction.

In spite of the foregoing consideration, in antitrust cases there is potential for previously unavailable evidence of illegal behaviour to come to light, given the enforcement activities of the European Commission and NCAs. In other words, in such a scenario in support of the allegation that the recognition of a foreign judgment should be refused on ground of public policy the defendant will seek to rely on new evidence that EU competition law had been manifestly disregarded by the foreign court.

6.2.4.2 New Evidence—EU Competition Law Disregarded by the Adjudicating Court

This sub-section aims to determine the course that the recognising court should adopt where the defendant sought to raise EU competition law for the first time as a defence to recognition under the Brussels I Regulation, together with new evidence to the effect that Arts 101 and 102 TFEU should have been applied by the original court.[93] There is no European or English authority directly addressing the question of whether in such a case Art 34(1) can preclude recognition/enforcement of a foreign judgment under the Brussels I Regulation. As already outlined, the national system of legal remedies taken together with Art 267 TFEU (ex Art 234 TEC) and Regulation 1/2003 provided sufficient guarantee that EU competition law would be properly applied, if it was raised before a national court. It is, however, well established that EU law does not require national courts to raise on their own motion the breach of Arts 101 and 102 TFEU, as such a duty would oblige them to abandon the passive role assigned to them by the legislation in some Member States.[94] If Arts 101 and 102 TFEU were not raised before the court with original jurisdiction, then Art 267 TFEU and mechanisms provided by

[91] Case C-224/97 *Ciola v Land Vorarlberg* [1999] ECR I-2517 [33]–[34]. See more: F Becker, 'Application of Community Law by Member States' Public Authorities: Between Autonomy and Effectiveness' (2007) 44 *CML Rev* 1035.

[92] Case C-213/89 *R v Secretary of State for Transport ex p Factortame* [1990] ECR I-2433 [19].

[93] The cases where Arts 101 and 102 TFEU have been raised, but the adjudicating court after trying the merits of the EU competition law claim has decided that it is non-applicable, will fall within the hypothesis that was examined in the preceding sub-section.

[94] *Van Schijndel* (n 70). See more: Komninos (n 11) 225–26.

Regulation 1/2003 could not be seen as a means guaranteeing coherent application of EU competition law.

Thus, the question is what the powers of an English court will be in a scenario where there is new evidence that EU competition law was disregarded by the foreign court. In such a case the EU competition law issues would be left undecided by a Member State's court, so that the EU competition law point would not be *res judicata*. At recognition stage, a national court should verify whether a foreign judgment is rendered in manifest disregard of Arts 101 and 102 TFEU and thus in conflict with English public policy. Such a review would need to be made, in order for a recognising court to be able to determine whether the public policy defence has been met.[95] A foreign judgment rendered in manifest disregard of Arts 101 and 102 TFEU could be refused recognition on the ground of public policy and may not have the force of *res judicata* in England as being in conflict with its public policy.[96]

However, in every case where an applicant raises a public policy defence arguing that the judgment is rendered in manifest disregard of EU competition law, he should present new evidence that a foreign judgment is based on an illegal agreement.[97] This is due to the fact that the application of Arts 101 and 102 TFEU is a fact-based assessment. If the said evidence was before the adjudicating court, the issue will be *res judicata*, so new evidence will always be required. The 'new evidence' requirement would be satisfied if decisive new documents, which suggest that there is an EU competition law infringement, were discovered after the foreign judgment was rendered. For example, such new evidence may be derived from the European Commission's decision or a decision of a foreign NCA[98] which was not before the foreign court. Alternatively, such new evidence may have been held back by the judgment creditor.[99] What would the powers of the English courts be in such a scenario?

As already discussed, there are two major Court of Justice cases,[100] where compatibility of a decision with EU competition rules has been raised as a public policy defence before a recognising court. Both cases, though, should be distinguished from the scenario where Arts 101 and 102 TFEU had been manifestly disregarded by a foreign court and there is new evidence for that. In the *Renault* case, the foreign court had ruled on the matter that was sought to be raised by

[95] *Gambazzi* (n 50) [46]. See also Briggs and Rees (n 43) 686.

[96] See Art 34(1) of Brussels I. See also: *Josef de Wolf* (n 6) 48 (AG Mayras) and [3] (Court of Justice decision); Barnett (n 6) 273.

[97] Although this conclusion is drawn by analogy by D Gordon, 'Fraud or new evidence as grounds for actions to set aside judgments' (1961) 77 *LQR* 358, 361, a rather out-of-date opinion, it seems to the author that similar consideration should be apply in EU competition law cases where there is new evidence indicating an EU competition law infringement.

[98] An NCA decision is enforceable only within the territory on which the authority in question operates. See White Paper on Modernisation (n 11) [60]. See also: Komninos (n 11) 77; Brammer (n 10) 427.

[99] See Art 595(2) of the French New Code of Civil Procedure.

[100] *Renault* (n 4); see in context of arbitral awards *Eco Swiss* (n 4).

the defendant when challenging the judgment on the ground of public policy.[101] Although, there is a closer match between the examined scenario (ie neither the parties nor the adjudicating court had raised Arts 101 and/or 102 TFEU) and the facts in the *Eco Swiss* case, the result in the *Eco Swiss* case might have been differently decided if the arbitrators had had the possibility to make a preliminary reference under Art 267 TFEU (ex Art 234 TEC). Having said that, the powers of the courts with regard to a foreign judgment neglecting Arts 101 and 102 TFEU will be clarified after taking into account its public policy character and relevant English case law.

It was earlier outlined[102] that under English law an agreement that is in conflict with EU competition law is void and illegal. It is well established that where an agreement is manifestly illegal, the English court will refuse to enforce it, even if the point arises for the first time on appeal.[103] The rationale behind that rule is that the courts may not be used to enforce an illegal agreement. But can the English court be used to enforce a foreign judgment based on an agreement that is illegal and void under Arts 101 and/or 102 TFEU? There are good arguments suggesting that if faced with such a question, the English court would follow the test that was put forward with regard to an application for registration of a foreign judgment in *Interdesco*.[104] Although, in the latter case, the challenge was on the basis of fraud, the same test should also apply to cases, where a foreign judgment disregarding Arts 101 and 102 TFEU was challenged on the ground of public policy. According to Collier,[105] public policy should not be treated differently from fraud because the real justification for refusing to enforce a judgment where there was fraud is that its enforcement will be contrary to public policy. This is reinforced by the fact that fraud is not listed as a separate heading in the defences available under Art 34 of the Brussels I Regulation.[106] To be precise, under the Regulation, fraud is generally considered as an instance for applying the doctrine of public policy.[107] Following this line of reasoning, the enforcement of a foreign judgment based on an illegal contract under Arts 101 and/or 102 TFEU should

[101] Ie if Arts 101 and 102 TFEU were raised before the court with original jurisdiction, then Art 267 TFEU and mechanisms provided by Regulation 1/2003 could be seen as a means guaranteeing coherent application of EU competition law.

[102] See ch 5, section 5.2.1 above.

[103] *Bank of India v Trans Continental Commodity Merchants* [1982] 1 Lloyd's Rep 427 (QBD (Comm)), 429 (Bingham J); aff'd *Bank of India v Trans Continental Commodity Merchants* [1983] 2 Lloyd's Rep 298 (CA). See also: *Holman v Johnson* [1775–1802] All ER Rep 98 (KB) 99; *Scott v Brown, Doering, McNab* [1892] 2 QB 724 (CA); *Snell v Unity Finance* [1964] 2 QB 203 (CA) 213; *Van Schijndel* (n 70) [48] (AG Jacobs).

[104] *Interdesco* (n 81); aff'd *Société d'Informatique Service Réalisation Organisation v Ampersand Software* [1994] ILPr 55 (CA).

[105] JG Collier, 'Public policy and foreign judgments—undue influence—a difficult answer to a simple problem' (1984) 43 *CLJ* 47, 49.

[106] At common law fraud is a basis for refusing to recognise a foreign judgment even if the issue of fraud was raised in the original proceedings and rejected.

[107] Schlosser Report (n 15) [192].

be regarded as another example where the doctrine of public policy can preclude enforcement of such judgment.

The public policy character of EU competition law should prevent recognition and enforcement of a judgment that is based on a contract that is prima facie anti-competitive. This will be especially true in cases involving hard-core restrictions on competition (ie price fixing or market sharing) that are implemented in the United Kingdom. This follows from ss 188–90 of the 2002 Act which impose criminal responsibility for the persons who commit a cartel offence. The English courts may not recognise a judgment based on an agreement that is manifestly illegal under EU competition law and the 2002 Act. This suggests that the *Interdesco* test should apply by analogy in cases where enforcement of a foreign judgment based on an agreement in conflict with EU competition law is sought before English courts.

Accordingly, the first aspect that the English court would need to consider in this context is whether regard to EU competition law was given by the adjudicating court.[108] Even if the foreign court had not ruled on Arts 101 and 102 TFEU and the subject-matter is not *res judicata*, the court should be very careful when deciding whether a foreign judgment based on an illegal agreement can constitute offence against English public policy. Strong reasons such as new evidence for a manifest breach of EU competition law for that should be demonstrated by the applicant.

Secondly, the English court acting under Art 34(1) is not to be viewed as an appellate jurisdiction with regard to a foreign judgment neglecting EU competition law. The court should ask itself whether a breach of its public policy still exists in view of the fact that proceedings for redress against the judgment allegedly in conflict with EU competition law can be, or could have been, lodged in the courts of the state of origin.[109] It seems to this author that in many cases where there is new evidence that the judgment is rendered in manifest disregard of EU competition law, the judgment debtor would try not only to rely on the public policy defence to deny recognition of the judgment in England, but also to reopen the final judgment before the courts at the Member State where the judgment was rendered if that was possible under national procedural law.[110] If there was a possibility of the defendant bringing new proceedings alleging a manifest infringement of EU competition law before the adjudicating court, then the foreign court would be best placed to determine whether there was an infringement of Arts 101 and 102 TFEU.[111] The foreign court could rely on Arts 15 and 16 of Regulation 1/2003, which are set to ensure coherent application of Arts 101 and 102 TFEU by national courts. Such an appeal, however, would be regarded as an extraordinary

[108] Compare opinion of AG Saggio in *Eco Swiss* (n 4) [38].

[109] Compare: *Interdesco* (n 81) 188. See also *Renault* (n 4) [33].

[110] The CPR provide for such a possibility, see CPR 52.17. See more: A Komninos, 'Effect of Commission decisions on private antitrust litigation: setting the story straight' (2007) *CMLR* 1387, 1415–16.

[111] Compare: *Interdesco* (n 81) 189. See also Briggs and Rees (n 43) 690–91.

appeal and should not to be considered as an 'ordinary appeal' within the meaning of Brussels I,[112] so that in such a scenario an English court would not be entitled to grant a stay of the recognition proceedings.[113]

Thirdly, if there was evidence that EU competition law was manifestly disregarded and there was no possibility for the defendant to bring fresh proceedings alleging a manifest infringement of EU competition law before the courts of the Member State where the judgment is rendered, then it should be considered whether in similar circumstances a challenge of an English judgment would be permitted.[114] For example, an English judgment may be set aside on the basis of new evidence that would have had a material effect upon the decision of the court.[115] If an English judgment can be set aside in these circumstances, there is no good reason why a foreign judgment should not be denied recognition in cases where there is new evidence[116] demonstrating that the foreign judgment was rendered in a manifest disregard of EU competition law and thus was based on an agreement that is in conflict with EU competition law.[117] In this context, an English court would be entitled to trigger Art 15(1) of Regulation 1/2003 and seek assistance from the Commission as to the application of EU competition law in view of the fact that this would be a case raising concerns about the coherent application of Arts 101 and 102 TFEU across the EU. Indeed, the fact that the denial of the foreign judgment's recognition would have effect only in England seems to indicate that the Commission may on the ground of Art 15(3) of Regulation 1/2003 decide to submit *amicus* observation. Such an intervention by the Commission could be justified in view of the fact that a recognition and enforcement of a judgment rendered in a manifest disregard of EU competition law would be an imminent threat to the coherent application of Arts 101 and 102 TFEU. The Commission may even go further and initiate administrative proceedings at EU level, resulting in a decision which prohibits the anti-competitive agreement or practice. It has been submitted that such '[a] Commission decision, though not constituting *res judicata* for civil proceedings, nevertheless binds its

[112] Case 43/77 *Industrial Diamond Supplies v Luigi Riva* [1977] ECR 2175.

[113] *Interdesco* (n 81) 189. In this case, the High Court judgment was made in the context of '*recours en revision*' brought in France, being the country where the judgment was given.

[114] *Interdesco* (n 81) 188.

[115] Under English law, a judgment can be set aside on the basis of new evidence. See *Re Barrell Enterprises* [1973] 1 WLR 19 (CA) 24 (Russell LJ); *Stewart v Engel* [2000] 3 All ER 518 (CA). The judge will also have a jurisdiction to vary or revoke an order under CPR 3.1(7), if the applicant was able to present before the court evidence or argument, which was not placed before the court on an earlier occasion. (But order in CPR 3.1(7) does not include judgment. See *Nelson v Clearsprings* [2006] EWCA Civ 1252.) See also N Andrews, *English Civil Procedure—Fundamentals of the New Civil Justice System* (OUP, Oxford, 2003) 960.

[116] Such evidence may be presented by a third party or the applicant himself. As far as English judgments are concerned, the Court of Appeal has an implicit jurisdiction to do what is necessary to achieve its two principal objectives of correcting wrong decisions and ensuring public confidence in the administration of justice. See *Taylor v Lawrence* [2002] 3 WLR 640 (CA).

[117] Compare the recognition and enforcement of foreign judgments, see Hill (n 76) 392.

addressees and gives rise to negative duties of deference for the national courts pursuant to Art 16(1) of Council Regulation 1/2003.'[118]

The different outcomes between the scenario where EU competition law was merely allegedly misapplied[119] and the case where new evidence for a manifest disregard of EU competition law comes into light can be justified by the public interest in the enforcement of EU competition law that is reflected by the criminal punishment envisaged for a 'cartel offence' by the 2002 Act, which must preclude recognition of a judgment based on an illegal agreement. Furthermore, such a result would be compatible with the public interest of uniform and consistent application of EU competition law as promoted by Regulation 1/2003.

6.2.5 Irreconcilability of a Foreign Judgment with a Commission or an NCA Decision

The main issues that will be addressed in this sub-section relate to the question of whether the recognising court would be entitled to refuse recognition of a judgment that is in conflict with a decision of the Commission or an NCA. Article 34(3) of Brussels I provides that a judgment given by the courts of a Member State shall be refused recognition if it conflicts with a judgment[120] given in a dispute between the same parties[121] in the state in which recognition is sought. Thus, a judgment in relation to an EU competition law claim that has been given in the state in which enforcement is sought would operate as a defence against the recognition of a foreign judgment in relation to that claim. Article 34(4) of Brussels I goes further and provides that a judgment given by the court of a Member State shall be refused recognition: 'if the judgment is irreconcilable with an earlier judgment given in another Member State or in a third state involving the same cause of action and between the same parties, provided that the earlier judgment fulfils the conditions necessary for its recognition in the Member State addressed.' Are these requirements met in the situation where a foreign judgment is contrary to a decision rendered by the Commission or the OFT?

It was earlier clarified that recognition of a foreign judgment cannot be refused on the ground of public policy where EU competition law was misapplied by an adjudicating court.[122] A different outcome, however, may be reached in cases where that very judgment is in conflict with a decision of the Commission. Such a result can be deduced from the principle of sincere cooperation as reflected

[118] Komninos (n 110) 1416. Compare White Paper on Modernisation (n 11) [102]. Art 16 of Regulation 1/2003 and its implications for the recognition and enforcement proceedings are further considered in section 6.2.5 below.

[119] See section 6.2.4.1 above.

[120] It should be determined whether those judgments entail legal consequences which are mutually exclusive. See *Hoffmann* (n 31) [22].

[121] See ch 4, section 4.2.1.1 above.

[122] Section 6.2.4.1 above.

in Art 4(3) TEU. In view of this provision, it has been held that national courts must exercise their powers to avoid the risk of judgments that are in conflict with Commission decisions.[123] The duty of national courts to avoid the risk of conflicts with the Commission decisions is upheld by the Court of Justice in two leading cases—*Delimitis*[124] and *Masterfoods.*[125] This is reinforced by Art 16 of Regulation 1/2003, which binds national courts to take every effort, in order to avoid judgments conflicting with decisions which have been (or are about to be) the subject of a Commission decision.[126] The problem, however, is that EU law contains no rule which requires the court to follow the Commission decisions which are not between the same parties and on the same subject matter.[127] That limits the effect of Regulation 1/2003.

In addition, the reading of Art 16 leaves no doubt that this provision is addressed to the court that has original jurisdiction in an EU competition law claim. One may go further and claim that it is not for the recognising court to inspect whether a decision of a Member State court is in accord with a Commission decision on the same subject-matter between the same parties. Notwithstanding, arguments suggesting that the English courts have an obligation to avoid recognising foreign judgments that run against Commission decisions related to Arts 101 and 102 TFEU can be inferred from the principle of primacy of EU law and Regulation 1/2003.[128] The case law of the Court of Justice also contains some hints as to the relation between EU competition law, on the one hand, and the national legislation and concordant judicial practices, on the other hand. It has been held that 'national legislative or judicial practices, even on the supposition that they are common to all the Member States cannot prevail in the application of the competition rules set out in the Treaty.'[129] This has been justified by the argument that such practices would be contrary to the principle of sincere cooperation as embodied in Art 4(3) of the TEU and would render the EU rules ineffective.[130] Judgments that are in conflict with the Commission decisions that are related to EU competition law 'undermin[e] legal certainty, leaving parties in doubt as to where they stand, and infring[e] the integrity of the EU legal order.'[131] Recognition of a foreign judgment, which is irreconcilable with a decision of the Commission, will create an irreconcilable inconsistency in the application of the EU's competition policy to the relevant market. There are strong arguments

[123] Case C-344/98 *Masterfoods v HB Ice Cream* [2000] ECR I-11369 [38]. See also: *Hasselblad v Orbinson* [1985] QB 475 (CA) 504; *Iberian UK v BPB Industries* [1997] EuLR 1 (ChD) 16. See more: Kerse and Khan (n 25) 298.

[124] Case C-234/89 *Delimitis* [1991] ECR I-935.

[125] *Masterfoods* (n 123) [49].

[126] *Masterfoods* (n 123) [51] and [52]; *Interpreneur Pub Company v Crehan* [2006] UKHL 38, [2006] 3 WLR 148 (HL) [64–66].

[127] *Crehan* (n 126) [70]–[71].

[128] See also: Komninos (n 110).

[129] Joined Cases 43 and 63/82 *VBVB and VBBB v Commission* [1984] ECR 19 [40].

[130] Case C-393/92 *Almelo* [1994] ECR I—1477 [40] (AG Darmon).

[131] Compare *MTV Europe v BMG Records* [1997] EuLR 100 (CA) 105.

suggesting that a foreign judgments running counter a Commission decision must not be recognised and enforced under the Brussels I Regulation on the ground of public policy. Further, a recognising court faced with a foreign judgment running counter to a Commission judgment should certainly rely on Art 15 of Regulation 1/2003 and notify the Commission as there would be an imminent threat to the coherent application of EU competition rules in the EU.

The deduction that a foreign judgment running counter to a Commission decision must be denied recognition can be reinforced by outlining that the irreconcilability of the foreign judgment with the Commission decision will be easily detected on the face of the judgment, whose recognition or enforcement is sought. For example, the conflict between such decisions can be easily spotted where a foreign judgment enforces an agreement that is declared to be void by the Commission. The irreconcilability is to be regarded as existing in cases where 'the binding authority which the decision of the national court has … conflicts with the grounds and operative part of the Commission's decision. Consequently the limits of the binding authority of the national court and the content of the Commission's decision must be examined every time.'[132]

The fact that the court's original jurisdiction did not comply with its duty that is found in Art 16 of Regulation 1/2003 suggests that a judgment that is in conflict with a Commission decision should be unsustainable in recognition or enforcement proceedings. This can be supported by recalling that on grounds of public policy the English court should deny recognition of a foreign judgment that is in conflict with Arts 101 and 102 TFEU. The authority of the Commission decisions in this context is reflected by the principle that those decisions are in principle presumed to be lawful and accordingly produce legal effects until such time as they are annulled or withdrawn.[133] Where a national court has doubts as to the validity or interpretation of a Commission decision it may refer a question to the Court of Justice for a preliminary ruling under Art 267 TFEU.[134] In view of that, it is not only the non-recognition of an irreconcilable judgment that should follow, but also such a judgment should be set aside by the Member State's courts where the judgment was rendered.[135]

In light of the foregoing, it can be concluded that the obligation to avoid a conflict[136] between decisions of a national court and the Commission would apply not only to the adjudicating court, but also to the recognising court. Moreover, Art 16 of Regulation 1/2003 and the public policy character of EU competition law leave no doubt that it will be against English public policy to recognise a decision that is contrary to a Commission decision. Thus, a fortiori, due to Art 16 of

[132] *Masterfoods* (n 123) [16] (AG Cosmas).
[133] Case C-137/92 P *Commission v BASF* [1994] ECR I-2555 [48].
[134] *Masterfoods* (n 123) [54].
[135] Compare *Noga v Abacha (No 2)* [2001] 3 All ER 513 (QBD (Comm)) [40].
[136] The issue what is conflict between Commission administrative proceedings and national civil proceedings was discussed in *Crehan* (n 126). See more: Komninos (n 110) 1397–1404.

Regulation 1/2003 the recognising court should owe a duty to take all appropriate measures to avoid recognition of a foreign judgment that conflicts with a decision of the Commission.

The conflict within the meaning of Art 16 of Regulation 1/2003, nevertheless, does not exist between a foreign judgment and a Commission decision in cases where the judgment deals with a distribution agreement between company A and distributor 1 in Germany and Austria, whilst the Commission decision deals with virtually the same contract between the same company and distributor 2 in Ireland and the United Kingdom. Nonetheless, if such a Commission decision was not before the adjudicating court, it must be viewed as highly persuasive prima facie evidence that the court with original jurisdiction misapplied EU competition law.[137] The Commission has applied Arts 101 and 102 TFEU for many years and has specialised departments that are responsible for supervising enforcement of EU competition law. Accordingly, its findings carry a degree of authority, even if such authority is not binding.[138]

If an NCA's final decision, finding an infringement of EU competition law, was regarded as a judgment for the purposes of Brussels I, then no particular difficulties would arise under Brussels I. Difficulties, however, may arise if the NCAs, which are administrative authorities, were not considered as judgments. Nevertheless, the fact that there is an OFT decision which would be enforceable in England could suggest that a recognition and enforcement of a foreign judgment, which is in conflict with an OFT decision, would lead to irreconcilable decisions having incompatible consequences on the same subject matter and between the same parties in the same jurisdiction. It is well established that public policy may be used to deal with an objection, which does not fall within the scope of other defences of recognition.[139]

Therefore, there are strong arguments suggesting that an English court should be entitled to hold that it is against English public policy to recognise a foreign decision, which is irreconcilable with an OFT decision. If such an OFT decision was not before the adjudicating court, it must be viewed as a persuasive prima facie evidence that the court with original jurisdiction misapplied EU competition law.[140] The argument that English public policy would prevent the recognition of a foreign judgment that runs against an OFT decision, however, would be weakened by the fact that Art 16 of Regulation 1/2003 says nothing about the decisions of an NCA. This issue has been addressed by the White Paper on damages, in which the Commission has proposed a rule to the effect that national courts cannot take decisions running counter to an NCA decision finding an EU competition law infringement.[141] If such a rule were adopted, then it would

[137] *Crehan* (n 126) [69]. See more section 6.2.4.2 above.

[138] Case C-128/92 *HJ Banks v British Coal* [1994] ECR I-1209 [60] (AG Van Gerven).

[139] Compare: *Hoffmann* (n 31); *Hendrickman* (n 35).

[140] *Crehan* (n 126) [69]. See more: section 6.2.4.2 above.

[141] White Paper on Damages (n 19) [2.3].

be questionable, however, whether an English court could refuse recognition on the ground of public policy of a foreign judgment which is irreconcilable with a decision of an NCA in the ECN. If such an NCA decision was not before the adjudicating court, it must be viewed as a highly persuasive prima facie evidence that the court with original jurisdiction misapplied EU competition law.[142] These difficulties seem to indicate that the foregoing problems would be better addressed if the EU legislator stated that the word 'judgment' in Art 32 of Brussels I includes NCAs' decisions finding an infringement of EU competition law.[143] Such interpretation of Art 32 of could be adopted under the current version of Brussels I if read together with Art 1 and would probably be easily approved in any country, where a judicial body has been designated as an NCA for the purposes of applying Arts 101 and 102 TFEU.[144]

6.2.6 Recognition and Enforcement of Foreign Judgments in Relation to Collective Redress Antitrust Actions[145]

There are three main issues that need to be considered in the context of recognition and enforcement of foreign class judgments in the European context. The first issue relates to the question of whether a class action settlement would be enforceable under Brussels. The second problem lies with recognition and enforcement of a class judgment that is irreconcilable with a Member State class judgment in a dispute involving the same infringement and the same defendant, but initiated on the basis of special jurisdictional rules by a different plaintiff class that is domiciled in another Member State. Finally, it needs to be considered whether the requirement for a 'fair trial and hearing' may trigger the public policy defence in relation to a class judgment issued against absent plaintiffs under the opt-out regime.

6.2.6.1 Enforcement of Class Action Settlements

Article 58 states that 'a settlement which has been approved by a court in the course of proceedings and is enforceable in the Member State in which it was concluded shall be enforceable in the State addressed'. Brussels I does not provide a definition of what would be a court settlement within the meaning of Art 58. The Court of Justice held that court settlements for these purposes are essentially contractual in nature, so that even if reached before a judge of a Member State, a court settlement may not be regarded as a judgment.[146] However, different regimes for refusing recognition and enforcement of foreign judgments

[142] *Crehan* (n 126) [69]. See more section 6.2.4.2 above.
[143] See section 6.2.1 above.
[144] See Art 35(2) of Regulation 1/2003.
[145] See more: M Danov, 'The Brussels I Regulation: cross-border collective redress proceedings and judgments' (2010) 6 *Journal of Private International Law* forthcoming.
[146] *Solo Kleinmotoren* (n 20) [17]–[18]. See also: *Landhurst Leasing Marcq* [1998] ILPr 822 [33] (CA).

and denying enforcement foreign settlements are available under the Brussels I Regulations. A declaration of enforceability of such a settlement will be refused only if enforcement of the instrument is manifestly contrary to public policy in the Member State addressed.

The question that may arise with regard to class action settlements is whether a court settlement is to be regarded as a court judgment for the purposes of Art 34(3) and (4) of Brussels I. The Court of Justice ruling that a court settlement is not to be regarded as a judgment for the purposes of Arts 32 and 34 of Brussels I appears to indicate that a foreign class judgment would not be denied recognition and enforcement, even if irreconcilable with a court settlement involving the same cause of action and between the same parties. Such a deduction would be far from precise. In England, a settlement is done by judgments recording the consent of the parties—so-called 'judgment by consent'.[147] The English Court of Appeal held that 'if a party agrees to a judgment being entered by conceding the issues, the judgment is … within Article [32]'[148] Thus, there is no doubt that the English consent judgments are to be regarded as judgments for the purposes of Art 34 the Brussels I Regulation.[149] In other words, a foreign class judgment would be denied recognition and enforcement, if irreconcilable with an English court settlement involving the same cause of action and between the same parties.

Similarly, the English court should be entitled to refuse enforcement of a foreign court settlement, which is not regarded as a court judgment for the purposes of Art 34(3) and (4) of Brussels I, as being in conflict with an English class judgment involving the same cause of action and between the same parties. This would be certainly done on the ground that it would be against its public policy to enforce a collective settlement that is irreconcilable with a class judgment rendered in England. In such a scenario, enforcement would lead to incompatible consequences in respect of the same dispute between the same parties, so non-enforcement of a foreign court settlement should follow. Thus, it seems that preclusive effects of court settlements in respect of class actions would not give rise to any particular difficulties in the European context. On this basis, one may argue that the Court of Justice ruling, read together with Arts 57 and 58, seems to suggest that the effect of the *Solo* judgment can be minimised with regard to class actions as the court settlement would be refused enforcement if it conflicts with an English class judgment.

However, private international law problems would be bound to arise in cases where an English court is asked to enforce a Member State's class judgment, involving the same cause of action and between the same parties, which is irreconcilable with a foreign court settlement that is contractual in nature within the

[147] See CPR 40.6. See more: Andrews (n 115) 551.

[148] *Landhurst* (n 146) [37].

[149] See the opinion of the AG Gulmann in *Solo Kleinmotoren* (n 20) 2245. See also: Andrews (n 115) 551; JJ Fawcett and JM Carruthers, *Cheshire, North & Fawcett Private International Law* (14th edn, OUP, Oxford, 2008) 599.

meaning of the *Solo* judgment. The public policy defence that can be triggered if the foreign court settlement were irreconcilable with an English class judgment would not be available in this context. This clearly suggests that the issue of enforcement of collective court settlements needs to be addressed in the course of revision of the Brussels I Regulation.

6.2.6.2 Recognition and Enforcement of Conflicting Class Judgments in Relation to EU Competition Law Claims

It was earlier mentioned that sub-sections 3 and 4 of Art 34 of Brussels I deal with the problem of recognition and enforcement of irreconcilable judgments. Does a judgment in relation to a collective redress action that has been given in the state in which enforcement is sought, operate as a defence against the recognition of a foreign judgment in relation to a foreign plaintiff class against the same defendant and for the same breach? Is the situation different if the irreconcilability is with an earlier Member State's class judgment in a dispute involving the same infringement and the same defendant, but initiated on the basis of special jurisdictional rules by a plaintiff class domiciled in another Member State?

As already illustrated,[150] the 'same parties' requirement contained in Art 34(3) of Brussels I will not be easily satisfied in such scenarios. For example, a class judgment rendered by the English court in respect of a cross-border antitrust infringement case should not prevent recognition and enforcement of a French class judgment in relation to collective redress proceedings resulting from the same cross-border antitrust infringement but brought by a different plaintiff class. Further, it seems that the English class judgment, though irreconcilable with the French class judgment, should be recognised in France under Brussels I. It appears that in either case, the recognising court would not be entitled to deny recognition under Art 34(3) as the 'same parties' requirement would not be met. However, recognition would lead to irreconcilable class judgments affecting the plaintiff class domiciled in France and the plaintiff class domiciled in England, having incompatible consequences in respect of the same antitrust infringement. As already mention in the context of other judgments, one way to circumvent such a result would be to hold that it is against English public policy to recognise a foreign class judgment that is irreconcilable with an English class judgment.[151] The argument that English public policy would prevent the recognition of a foreign class judgment that runs against an English class judgment, however, would be weakened by *Hoffmann*.[152] In this case, the Court of Justice held that the public policy exception in Brussels I is not applicable in cases where the issue is whether a foreign judgment is compatible with a national judgment. In such scenarios 'the

[150] See ch 4, where the 'same parties' requirement is discussed in the context of Art 27 of the Brussels I Regulation.

[151] Compare section 6.2.5, which suggests that the public policy exception may also be relevant in the context of other judgments irreconcilable with NCAs' decisions.

[152] *Hoffmann* (n 31).

issue must be resolved on the basis of the specific provision'.[153] Nevertheless, it would still be open to argue that the public policy defence would not be precluded in cases where the specific provisions are not applicable as the 'same parties' requirement has not been satisfied.

The public policy exception, however, would not prevent recognition in cases where the irreconcilability is with an earlier Member State's class judgment in a dispute involving the same antitrust infringement and the same defendant but initiated on the basis of special jurisdictional rules by a plaintiff class domiciled in another Member State. In such a scenario, the irreconcilability would not be with an English class judgment, but the inconsistency would be between two Member States' class judgments. Given the fact that Brussels I clearly states that the judgments should be 'involving the same cause of action and between the same parties', it is difficult to see how an English court would deny recognition of any of those incompatible class judgments.

In view of that, it would be more appropriate if the rules relevant to judgments in relation to collective redress actions may be modified by the working group involved in the ongoing programme of the proposed reform concerning Brussels I. Thus, a sub-section laying down special conditions for refusing recognition and enforcement of foreign judgments could be considered by the legislators. Such a provision may entitle the court to deny recognition of a foreign judgment in relation to collective redress proceedings resulting from the same infringement but brought by a different plaintiff class before another forum. This solution would not only prevent recognition of irreconcilable foreign class judgments dealing with the same subject matter and brought against the same defendant in different Member States, but also serve as an incentive for consolidating related collective redress proceedings by relying on Art 28 of Brussels I.

6.2.6.3 Opt-Out Regime Antitrust Class Judgments and the Requirement for 'Fair Trial and Hearing'

Interesting private international law issues would also arise in the context of a collective judgment rendered in an opt-out class action in one of the few EU Member States that have adopted this model for collective redress proceedings (eg Spain or Portugal). It is well established that in such cases the action may have been brought on behalf of an identifiable group of consumers. The inherent problems are to do with the binding effect of class judgments and the question of which group members are actually bound by such judgments, as a 'fair trial and hearing' defence may be raised by the absent members of the class.[154] For example, the CJC report refers to Portuguese law[155] to show that

[153] *Hoffmann* (n 31) [21].

[154] See T Eisenberg and G Miller, 'The role of opt-outs and objectors in class action litigation: theoretical and empirical issues' (2004) 57 *Vanderbilt Law Review* 1529; C Hodges, *The Reform of Class and Representative Actions in European Legal Systems* (Hart Publishing, Oxford, 2008) 120–26.

[155] See ch 4, section 4.2.1.3.1 above.

the due process notice in collective redress actions may be given 'by means of an advertisement or advertisements made public by any form of the media or by public notice, depending on whether general or geographically specific interests are at issue, without the need for personal identification of those for whom it is destined'.[156] If the English legislator adopted a similar approach, then the Service Regulation would have no role to play in deciding the adequacy of an opt-out public notice for the purposes of a later judicial estoppel. As already mentioned,[157] Art 1(2) of the Regulation indicates that it would not be used to determine the adequacy of notice made to unidentified parties who are notified through newspapers or public notices. Furthermore, the opt-out regime presupposes the existence of a large number of 'unrepresented class members' who would not opt out of the proceedings.[158] This gives rise to the question of whether there would be a breach of Art 6 ECHR in cases where the foreign court has issued a class judgment that is binding to absent/unrepresented members of the plaintiff's class who had not opted out from the foreign collective redress proceedings.

It is well established that the right to 'fair trial and hearing' is embodied in the ECHR. A breach of Art 6(1) of the ECHR could trigger the public policy exception contained in Art 34(1) of the Brussels I Regulation,[159] or the natural justice defence contained in Art 34(2), which covers the right to a fair trial.[160] It has been submitted that 'using the [public policy] defence, the courts automatically should hold that enforcement would be against public policy where there has been a breach of Article 6 standards in the judgment granting state'.[161]

There would not be a problem with Art 6 ECHR if the plaintiff class had achieved a successful outcome of the collective redress proceedings. However, private international law problems would arise if a defendant, who had successfully defended a collective redress action abroad, sought recognition of the class judgment before an English court. For example, such a judgment may be put forward as a defence in collective redress proceedings brought by the plaintiff class that has not opted in to the foreign proceedings.[162] Would the Member State

[156] Art 15(2) of Portuguese Law Law No 83/95 of 31 August, *Right of Proceeding Participation and Popular Action* See H Antunes www.globalclassactions.stanford.edu/PDF/Portugal_Legislation.pdf. See also D Fairgrieve and G Howells, 'Collective redress procedures—European Debates' (2009) 58 *ICLQ* 379.

[157] See ch 4, section 4.2.1.3.1 above.

[158] Compare V Morabito, 'Class actions instituted only for the benefit of the clients of class representative's solicitors' (2007) 29 *Sydney Law Review* 5.

[159] *Krombach* (n 29). See also: *Pordea v Times Newspaper* [2000] ILPr 763 (French Cour de Cassation). See J Fawcett, 'The impact of Article 6(1) of the ECHR on private international law' (2007) 56 *ICLQ* 1, 24–29.

[160] *Maronier v Larmer* [2002] EWCA Civ 774; [2003] QB [27].

[161] Fawcett (n 159) 44. See also: *Gambazzi* (n 50) [39]–[43] (AG Kokott).

[162] The fact that the problem may arise in the European context was acknowledged by HE Loiseau and A Johnston, who spoke at the BIICL seminar entitled 'Group Actions, including Class Actions: Cross-border Aspects' (23 June 2008). See also *Greg Currie v McDonald's* [2005] 7 CPC (6th) 60, 250 DLR (4th) 224, 195 OAC 244, 74 OR (3d) 321 (Ontario Court of Appeal).

court's judgment rendered against the absent plaintiffs under the opt-out regime be recognised under Brussels I?

It already mentioned,[163] it is not for the Court of Justice to define the content of public policy of a Member State for the purposes of recognition and enforcement of judgments under the Brussels I Regulation.[164] Therefore, it would be for the English court to determine whether to recognise a class judgment rendered in an opt-out regime by a Member State court.[165] There are two policies that should be balanced in this context. On the one hand, it is well established that a default judgment may be regarded as being in conflict with Art 34 sub-ss (1) and (2), which are intended to ensure that a judgment would not be recognised under the Brussels I Regulation if a party has not had the opportunity of defending himself before the foreign court.[166] On this basis, one could argue that the absent members of the plaintiff class may oppose recognition of a class judgment that goes against them. On the other hand, if such a class judgment were refused recognition on the basis of Art 34(1) or (2), then such a result would be unacceptable for the collective redress proceedings defendant. Indeed, such a defendant would be bound to numerous members of the plaintiff class, but if the defendant won the case then he could yet be subject to other suits brought by absent/unrepresented members of the plaintiff class who had not opted in to the collective redress proceeding, because the class judgment would have been refused recognition on the ground of the public policy defence under Art 34(1) and/or the adequacy of the public notice defence under Art 34(2). As a result, the issue would not be *res judicata* and another collective redress action may be brought in another forum by the absent/unrepresented members of the plaintiff class. This seems to be an inappropriate outcome, as different Member States would have to reopen the same issue, which might result in irreconcilable judgments.[167]

A more appropriate solution[168] would be to follow the approach adopted by the Court of Appeal in another context and hold that the recognising court 'should apply a strong presumption that the procedures of other signatories of the Human Rights Convention are compliant with Article 6'.[169] Although the *Maroneri* judgment has been criticised,[170] the European Commission's efforts

[163] See section 6.2.3 above.

[164] See *Krombach* (n 29) [23].

[165] Compare *Gambazzi* (n 50) [26]–[34].

[166] Case 166/80 *Peter Klomps v Karl Michel* [1982] 2 CMLR 773 [9].

[167] See P Rogerson, 'Issue estoppel and abuse of process in foreign judgments' (1998) *Civil Justice Quarterly* 91.

[168] A less appropriate solution would be to adopt the opt-in regime in respect of a plaintiff's class domiciled in another Member State (see ch 4, section 4.2.1.3.1 above). The latter approach would not solve all problems, because in such a case parallel proceedings would be bound to arise. In other words, such a solution would not be adequate unless accompanied by a rule allowing a Member State court to decline jurisdiction if there is another court that is more appropriate to hear and determine the collective redress action in question (see ch 4 above). See also Danov (n 145).

[169] *Maronier* (n 160) [25].

[170] Fawcett (n 159).

to encourage collective redress proceedings in Europe, taken together with the domestic policies favouring such action, may be a strong argument favouring the *Maroneri* approach with regard to collective redress actions. This would be a very strong argument in the countries where the opt-out regime is (or is about to be) adopted. On the contrary, this will be a weak argument in the Member States where the opt-in regime is adopted. Thus, the current law suggests that a class judgment rendered in an *opt-out* regime may be recognised in one Member State but not in another. This leaves no doubt that the issue of recognition and enforcement of judgments rendered in an *opt-out* regime needs to be addressed by the European legislature.

6.2.7 Recognition and Enforcement of Foreign Judgments Awarding Punitive (or Exemplary) Damages[171]

The fact that England (and several other legal systems in the EU[172]) award exemplary (or punitive) damages in certain cases suggests that the courts in these Member States would normally enforce a Member State's court judgment awarding punitive damages in EU antitrust claims. However, Recital 32 indicates that on the basis of Art 34(1) of the Brussels I Regulation, other Member State courts can deny recognition and enforcement of the part of a judgment awarding excessive punitive antitrust damages, as being contrary to their public policy to recognise and enforce it.[173]

One may argue that a court charged with the recognition of a foreign judgment under the Brussels I Regulation is not at liberty to consult Rome II's Recitals to determine public policy for the purposes of Art 34 of Brussels I. This may be strengthened by noting that to refer to Rome II at this stage seems very like reopening the merits of the earlier case to question the application of the law of the original court. However, it should be recalled that Recital 32 is meant to acknowledge that the punitive damages awards may be against public policy of some Member States.[174] If this were so for the choice of law purposes, it is difficult to see why the concept of public policy should be different for the recognition

[171] See M Danov, 'Awarding exemplary (or punitive) antitrust damages in EC competition cases with an international element—the Rome II Regulation and the Commission's White Paper on damages' (2008) 29 *ECLR* 430, 434–35.

[172] *Devenish Nutrition Ltd v Sanofi-Aventis SA* [2007] EWHC 2394 (Ch) [33].

[173] Danov (n 171). See also: P Hay, 'The development of the public policy barrier to judgment recognition within the European Community' (2007) *The European Legal Forum* 289, 293–94; MR Isidro, 'Punitive damages from a private international law perspective' in H Koziol and V Wilcox (eds), *Punitive Damages: Common Law and Civil Law Perspectives* (Springer, Vienna/New York, 2009) 237, 250.

[174] Hay (n 171) 293. See also: Commission (EC) 'The common position of the Council on the adoption of a Regulation of the European Parliament and of the Council on the law applicable to non-contractual obligations ("Rome II")' (Communication) COM (2006) 566 final; Isidro (n 173) 250; Plender and Wilderspin (n 4) 751–52.

and enforcement purposes.[175] Indeed, the irreconcilability of the part of the judgment awarding exemplary damages, with public policy of the forum, will be easily detected on the face of the judgment for which recognition or enforcement is sought. Accordingly, the recognising court would not review the Member State court's judgment with regard to its merits, but would simply refuse recognition of part of the judgment, so far as the exemplary antitrust damages being contrary to its public policy was concerned. It is the effect of the part of the judgment awarding punitive antitrust damages that would affect the essential values of the legal system which regards such damage awards as being in conflict with its public policy, so that no reopening the merits would occur at the stage where a recognising court is denying recognition of an award of punitive damages.[176]

It can be concluded that the words of Recital 32 have a wide meaning and, therefore, one may suggest that they are meant to recognise at EU level that national public policy, in respect of non-compensatory exemplary or punitive damages, should be given due regard at the recognition and enforcement stage. Thus, what the court needs to do when justifying non-recognition of judgments awarding such damages is to stress that the exemplary or punitive damage was given in addition to compensatory award and is thus against its public policy.[177] This would be a problem, as leaving the question of what damages a private antitrust plaintiff could recover to be dealt with under Brussels I and Rome II may give small and medium-sized businesses and consumers across the EU a different level of redress and protection, which would largely depend on where the action is first brought.[178]. The issue needs to be addressed at EU level.

6.2.7.1 Concluding Remarks

It can be concluded that EU competition law would enjoy public policy character in England for the purposes of recognition and enforcement of foreign verdicts. This can be sustained by the European case law and the fact that public interest in the enforcement of Arts 101 and 102 TFEU is repeatedly reflected in the special remedial system enacted within the EU and England. In view of that, the most common issue that the English court would need to determine with regard to judgments in relation to EU competition law claims is whether their enforcement under the Brussels I regulation would be contrary to public policy if the court with original jurisdiction had misapplied or neglected Arts 101 and 102 TFEU.

The analysis above suggests that an error in application of EU competition law does not violate English public policy for the purposes of Art 34 of the Brussels I Regulation. As a result, the English court is not allowed to review a foreign judgment in which the Member State's court has applied EU competition law, even

[175] Hay (n 171) 293–94.
[176] Ibid 294.
[177] Danov (n 171).
[178] See also Commission (EC) 'Consumer Collective Redress' (Green Paper) COM (2008) 794 final [22].

if to do so will enable it to remedy an infringement of EU law. Notwithstanding, recognition/enforcement should be denied in cases where there is new evidence showing that the judgment is based on an illegal agreement that is in conflict with Arts 101 and 102 TFEU. The different outcomes are due to two main reasons. First, the public interest in the enforcement of EU competition law that is reflected by the criminal punishment envisaged for a 'cartel offence' by the 2002 Act precludes recognition of a judgment, if there is new evidence that that judgment is based on an illegal agreement. Secondly, if an English judgment may be set aside on the basis of new evidence that would have had a material effect upon the decision of the court, there is no good reason why a foreign judgment must be treated more favourably.

Article 16 of Regulation 1/2003 and the public policy character of Arts 101 and 102 TFEU indicate that it will be against English public policy to recognise a foreign judgment that is contrary to a Commission decision. More difficulties and uncertainties, however, are bound to arise in regard to decisions rendered by the OFT because they do not amount to a judgment of a court of competent jurisdiction, and Art 16 does not refer to decisions of an NCA.

In view of that, it can be stated that the long-term objective of the European Union to abolish the public policy exception for all judgments in civil and commercial matters should not yet be fulfilled in relation to private enforcement of competition law. There are at least two good reasons for that. First, the Commission has outlined the risk that some of the new Member States may be unable to correctly apply EU law unless they achieve irreversible progress on their judicial reforms.[179] Secondly, in spite of the mechanisms envisaged by Regulation 1/2003, the judges in some of the new Member States lack experience in dealing with complicated antitrust laws. The problems are rooted in the fact that antitrust laws in some of those countries were adopted only in the 1990s. Although, those laws mirrored the western model, they ignored the specific features of the socialist heritage and lack the decades of experience in applying those laws.[180] Thus, the abolition of the public policy exception may be premature with regard to judgments in relation to EU competition law claims.

6.3 Powers of the English Courts at Common Law

Suppose that US and Canadian manufacturing companies concluded an anticompetitive agreement with an English company that has exclusive distributorship rights for Europe. The North American companies have formed an association for

[179] Eg Commission (EC), 'Bulgaria's progress on accompanying measures following Accession' (Report) COM (2007) 377 final; Commission (EC), 'Romania's progress on accompanying measures following Accession' (Report) COM (2007) 378 final.

[180] T Varady, 'The emergence of competition law in (former) socialist countries' *American Journal of Commercial Law* 229, 261.

the joint promotion of their exports, exchanging information on the marketing of their products in Europe and agreeing on export prices. The agreement is void under EU competition law, but is valid under the Webb Pomerene Act 1918. The US Federal Court enforces the agreement and gives a judgment ordering the English company to pay damages for non-performance of the contract. The North American companies apply for enforcement of the US judgment in England. The English company raises as a defence that enforcement infringes English public policy, which includes European public policy.[181] Judgments emanating from countries that are outside of the EU are unable to benefit from 'automatic' recognition under the Brussels Regime, so their recognition depends primarily upon rules at common law.[182] English traditional rules will be applicable for the recognition of judgments rendered by courts located outside the EU, provided that the UK has not entered into a bilateral treaty with another state pursuant to the 1920 Act[183] or the 1933 Act.[184]

England would clearly be the appropriate forum for enforcement in England, and it could not be suggested that there would be any other forum which would be suitable for determining the defences to enforcement of foreign judgments.[185] This will include the defence that enforcement of the foreign judgments based on an agreement in conflict with EU competition law is contrary to English public policy. Accordingly, the focus in this section will be on the question of whether under the doctrine of public policy, the English court should refuse recognition of a foreign judgment misapplying EU competition law. The answer will be provided through examination of relevant common law rules. The specific regime for recognition and enforcement of judgments in competition cases that is contained in the Protection of Trading Interests Act 1980, which implements special UK policy designed to prevent the enforcement of judgments awarding multiple damages, will be briefly examined as well.[186]

Before examining those rules, however, it should be stressed that English public policy with regard to EU competition law for the purposes of recognition/ enforcement at common law is the same as under the Brussels I Regulation.[187] Based on that, there is no doubt that for these purposes English public policy will include European public policy and in particular EU competition laws.

[181] See *Eco Swiss* (n 4). See section 6.2.3 above.

[182] HL Ho, 'Policies underlying the enforcement of foreign commercial judgments' (1997) 46 *ICLQ* 443.

[183] Pt II of Administration of Justice Act 1920.

[184] Foreign Judgments (Reciprocal Enforcement) Act 1933.

[185] Compare *Tasarruff Mevduati Sigorta Foun v Demirel* [2006] EWHC 3354 (Ch); [2007] ILPr 8 [56]. See also CPR PD 6B para 3.1(10).

[186] Although, the Act is drafted in terms capable of applying to a judgment of any country, it is designed for decisions of the US courts which have assumed jurisdiction under US legislation over the extra-territorial activities of a trans-national corporation. See KW Patchett, *Recognition of Commercial Judgments and Awards in the Commonwealth* (Butterworths, London, 1984) [3.24].

[187] See more section 6.2.3 above

Accordingly, public policy will be the main defence against recognition of a foreign judgment in relation to EU competition law claims at common law as well.

6.3.1 EU Competition Law was Misapplied/Neglected by the Foreign Court

When faced with an application for enforcement of a foreign judgment misapplying EU competition law at common law, the English court is not confined by the aim and narrow interpretation of the provisions of the Brussels I Regulation. As a result, at common law the English court may have broader powers for denying enforcement of a foreign judgment misapplying or neglecting EU competition law. Accordingly, in this section these powers will be examined with regard to a foreign judgment that neglects to apply, or makes an error in applying, Arts 101 and 102 TFEU.

In English law there is a 'general proposition … that when you bring an action on a foreign judgment, you cannot go into the merits, which have been tried in the foreign court.'[188] Such a result is in line with the considerations of comity and duty of the courts to put an end of litigation.[189] The recognising court could not try an alleged misapplication (or neglect) of EU competition law without going into the merits. It seems that that rule would preclude an English court from examining whether the foreign court had applied Arts 101 and 102 TFEU. Another proposition of English law, however, is that a party to an action can impeach a foreign judgment on the ground of public policy.[190] As already outlined,[191] English public policy will include EU competition law. A foreign judgment based on a contract in conflict with Arts 101 and/or 102 TFEU will be contrary to English public policy and should not be recognised in England. No action will be sustainable on such a judgment.[192] Accordingly, the English court needs to decide which of the two opposing propositions should prevail in cases where the defendant shows a 'good arguable case' case that EU competition law has been misapplied or neglected by the foreign court.

In other words, the question is: is the unique public interest in the enforcement of EU competition law sufficient to allow an English court to deny recognition of a foreign judgment which is in conflict with Arts 101 and 102 TFEU? On this point there appears to be no direct English authority. It seems that the nearest analogy is *Rousillon v Rousillon*,[193] where an action was brought for

[188] *Vadala v Lawes* [1890] 25 QBD 310 (CA) 316 (Lindley LJ). See also *Ellis v McHenry* [1870–71] 6 LRCP 228 (Court of Common Pleas) 238. The only exception to this rule is allegation of fraud (see *Syal v Heyward* [1948] 2 KB 443 (CA)).

[189] *Henderson* (n 3) 381–82; *Israel Discount Bank of New York v Hadjipateras* [1983] 3 All ER 129 (CA) 134. Compare *Adams v Cape Industries* [1990] ChD 433 (CA). See also Andrews (n 115) 952.

[190] *Hadjipateras* (n 189) 133.

[191] Section 6.2.3 above.

[192] See *Hadjipateras* (n 189) and *Vervaeke* (n 87).

[193] *Rousillon v Rousillon* [1880] 14 LRChD 351 (Ch D).

enforcing a French judgment on an agreement in restraint of trade. In this case, it was argued by the plaintiffs that even if the contract was void by the law of England as against public policy, yet, in as much as the contract was made in France, it must be good in England. Fry J held that the English court will not enforce a contract against English public policy, wherever it may have been made.[194] Enforcement of the foreign judgment, however, was refused for a different reason, which was related to the fact that the French court had had no jurisdiction.[195] Nevertheless, in *Re Macartney*,[196] Astbury J after referring to the cited statement from *Rousillon v Rousillon* explained that '[it] applies directly to the non-enforceability of foreign judgments founded on contracts contrary to public policy'.[197] Based on that there are sound arguments suggesting that at the recognition stage, an English court would be entitled to hear and determine whether a foreign judgment is in conflict with Arts 101 and 102 TFEU which enjoy a public policy character in England. This would be so, if the defendant had established a 'good arguable case' that EU competition law was misapplied or neglected by the foreign court.[198]

Such a deduction could be questioned. One may ask how a judgment rendered by a non-EU court applying the law of a foreign legal system be realistically tested for non-compliance with EU competition law. However, it should be recalled that 'recognition describes the general process by which an English court determines whether a foreign decision is entitled to legal operation or effect in England.'[199] In doing so, the English court has a discretionary power to refuse the recognition of a foreign judgment which is in conflict with English public policy[200] and in particular Arts 101 and 102 TFEU. Some important factors that may be considered in this context are whether the dispute is closely connected with England, and whether the anti-competitive agreement was implemented within the EU and England in particular.[201] If the English courts were not allowed to refuse the recognition of a foreign judgment which is in conflict with Arts 101 and 102 TFEU, then a monopolist could have avoided the application of EU competition law by including a choice of non-EU court clause and choosing the law of a non-EU legal system.[202] The court should not allow a party to take advantage of an agreement meant to distort competition and should not enforce at common law a foreign

194 Ibid 369.
195 See also: Collier (n 105) 48.
196 *Re Macartney* [1921] 1 ChD 522 (Ch D).
197 Ibid. 528. Compare Collier (n 105) 48.
198 Compare *Syal* (n 188) 448.
199 Barnett (n 6) 32.
200 Mills (n 48) 257.
201 Mills (n 48) 259.
202 See RA Epstein and MS Greve, 'Introduction: The intractable problem of antitrust jurisdiction' in Epstein and MS Greve (n 78) 1, 24; J Basedow, 'Jurisdiction and choice of law in the private enforcement of European competition law' in J Basedow (ed), *Private Enforcement of EC Competition Law* (Kluwer Law International, The Hague, 2007) 229, 236.

judgment that is based on an illegal and void agreement under EU competition laws. It will be against English public policy to enforce such a judgment.

This deduction can be strengthened by pointing out that the foreign courts could not avail themselves on the preventive and corrective mechanisms, which are set to guarantee the proper application of EU law by the Member State's courts. More specifically, the foreign court would not have the possibility for making a reference under Art 267 TFEU.[203] The mechanism for co-operation between the Commission and national courts envisaged in Regulation 1/2003 would not be applicable to proceedings taking place outside of the EU either. As already mentioned, if the applicability of prohibitions laid down under competition law were made to depend on the place where the parties litigate, the result would obviously be to give an easy means of evading those prohibitions. Such an outcome cannot be justified. It seems that English courts, where faced with a foreign judgment which seeks recognition, should check whether the legitimate interest in the enforcement of Arts 101 and 102 TFEU had been properly addressed by the adjudicating court. This is due to the extra-territorial application of EU competition laws which indicates that Arts 101 and 102 TFEU apply to an agreement or practice entered into between non-EU undertakings outside the EU, if the agreement was (or was intended to be) implemented within the EU.[204]

The English court, however, would be faced with an issue of estoppel as to the validity of the disputed contracts. The estoppel prevents parties to plead in subsequent proceedings an issue that has already been raised in the foreign proceedings.[205] It has been submitted that such estoppel would cover defences which might have been raised but were not actually raised in the foreign proceedings.[206] The possibility of raising the issue of estoppel based on a foreign judgment in relation to EU competition law claims should not be denied per se. But, as already outlined, special consideration should be given to the different national procedural rules and the lack of assistance of the Commission and Court of Justice in respect to proceedings taking place outside of the EU. Based on that it seems that the main question before an English court will be whether a foreign court misapplied or neglected the EU competition law. This question could not have been submitted and decided by the foreign court.[207] To answer that question the English court will have to review whether the judgment is in conflict with EU competition law as being part of English public policy.

[203] Compare: *Renault* (n 4), where the possibility for making reference under Art 267 TFEU was also duly outlined by the Court of Justice as another means guaranteeing proper interpretation and application of EC competition law.

[204] Joined Cases 89/85, 104/85, 114/85, 116–117/85, and 125–129/85 *Ahlstrom v Commission* [1988] ECR 5193 (*Wood Pulp* cartel case).

[205] *Carl Zeiss Stiftung v Rayner (No 2)* [1967] 1 AC 853 (HL); *Sennar* (n 23). See more: Barnett (n 6) 133–82.

[206] *Johnson v Gore Wood* [2002] 2 AC 1 (HL) 31 (Lord Bingham).

[207] Compare *Abouloff v Oppenheimer* [1882] 10 QBD 295 (CA) 302.

Further, the 'abuse of process'[208] may be raised together with the issue of estoppel. Although these issues are separate and different from each other, they may be raised as objecting to the EU competition law claim, when it is raised for the first time before the recognising court. In this context, the crucial question that should be determined by the English court is whether the plaintiff was in all the circumstances misusing or abusing the process of the court. It is, however, wrong to hold that because a matter could have been raised in earlier proceedings it should have been, so as to render raising of it in the latter proceedings necessarily abusive.[209]

Therefore, a defendant to an action seeking registration of a foreign judgment in England would be entitled to ask an English court to check whether the judgment in question is in conflict with English public policy and in particular Arts 101 and 102 TFEU. In this context, the English court would be allowed on the basis of public policy to check whether the legitimate interest in the enforcement of EU antitrust law had been addressed by the foreign court, if the defendant had established that Arts 101 and 102 TFEU was misapplied or disregarded by the foreign court, then the English court should deny recognition and enforcement of a foreign judgment as being in conflict with English public policy. If this were not the case, a well-established rule of EU law, which holds that any agreement running against Arts 101 and 102 TFEU is void, would be disregarded and undertakings enjoying market power would be allowed to avoid the application of EU competition law by litigating before non-EU courts where different laws could be applicable (or EU competition laws would be applied less restrictively). Therefore, the recognition of a foreign judgment disregarding or misapplying EU competition law should not be permitted, since its enforcement would be incompatible with English public policy.

The result at common law would be in contrast with the result that would be reached if EU competition law was wrongfully applied by a Member State's court and recognition or enforcement was sought under the Brussels I Regulation.[210] It seems that at common law, the English court will have more powers in relation to EU competition law claims. Indeed, the court will be entitled to examine whether a foreign court had properly applied EU competition law and deny recognition to a judgment based on a misapplication of EU competition law. This is due to the fact that the answer to the question whether an error of interpretation of EU competition law is capable of violating English public policy at common law is not confined by the aim and narrow interpretation of the provisions of the Brussels I Regulation. Furthermore, foreign courts could not avail themselves of the preventive and corrective mechanisms, which are set to guarantee the proper interpretation and application of EU law by the Member States' courts.

[208] An improper use of legitimate recognition and enforcement proceedings used to delay recognition/enforcement of a foreign judgment.

[209] *Gore Wood* (n 206) 31 (Lord Bingham).

[210] See section 6.2.4.1 above.

6.3.2 Irreconcilability of a Foreign Judgment with a Commission or an NCA Decision

Apart from bringing an EU competition law claim before different national courts, EU antitrust law issues could have been dealt with by the Commission and an NCA.[211] Accordingly, given those enforcement activities, there may be cases in which a foreign court gives an answer that is inconsistent with the findings of the Commission or an NCA. This gives rise to the question: would public policy preclude recognition of a foreign judgment where that judgment contradicts a decision of the Commission on the same subject matter between the same parties?

The rule of non-recognition of a foreign judgment that is inconsistent with a previous decision of a competent English *court* results from the operation of the doctrine of *res judicata*.[212] It is well established that under English traditional rules a court would not recognise a foreign judgment that is inconsistent with a previous decision of a competent English court.[213] Three requirements need to be satisfied for that purpose.[214] First, the judgment must be of a court of a competent jurisdiction, final and conclusive, and on the merits. Secondly, the foreign judgment must be on the same subject matter. Thirdly, the judgment must be between the same parties.[215] It seems that a decision of the Commission (or the OFT) would not satisfy the first requirement, which refers to 'judgment of a court of competent jurisdiction'. In this respect the situation will be similar to that under EC rules.[216] Having said that the question is whether English public policy can be used to deal with an objection that a foreign judgment is in conflict with a decision of the Commission or the OFT.

As already submitted,[217] Art 16 of Regulation 1/2003 entitles the English court to refuse recognition of a foreign judgment, even if otherwise unimpeachable, if it is inconsistent with a previous decision of the Commission on the same subject matter between the same parties.[218] As far as decisions of the Commission are concerned the result under the English traditional rules will be again similar to that under the EU rules. Thus, recognition of a foreign judgment based on an illegal agreement that is contrary to EU competition law will be contrary to English public policy.

[211] See R Nazzini, *Concurrent Proceedings in Competition Law: Procedure, Evidence and Remedies* (OUP, Oxford, 2004).

[212] See Barnett (n 6) 8–27; Hill (n 76) 397.

[213] *Vervaeke* (n 87); *ED&F Man (Sugar) v Haryanto (No 2)* [1991] 1 Lloyd's Rep 429 (CA). See also PB Carter, 'Private International Law—Decisions of British Courts during 1991' (1991) 62 *British Yearbook of International Law* 447, 461.

[214] *Sennar* (n 23) 499.

[215] See *Carl Zeiss* (n 205) 910–11, 928–29, 936–37, 944–46.

[216] *Solo Kleinmotoren* (n 20) [17]. See more section 6.2.5.

[217] See more section 6.2.5 above.

[218] *Crehan v Inntrepreneur Pub* [2004] EWCA Civ 637; [2004] EuLR 693 [98] (CA).

How about the case where the foreign judgment contradicts decisions of the OFT on the same subject matter between the same parties? As already outlined,[219] a decision of the OFT could be regarded as a judgment of a court of a competent jurisdiction, so recognition of a foreign judgment that contradicts a decision of the OFT could be refused. Moreover, even if an OFT decision was not regarded as a judgment, a decision of the OFT would be the result of an application of English public policy to the same facts. There appears to be no inherent reason why, giving every weight to the *res judicata* effect of a foreign judgment, the English court should surrender its own public policy. On the contrary, there are sound arguments (such as public interest in the enforcement of Arts 101 and 102 TFEU that is reflected by the criminal punishment envisaged for a 'cartel offence' by the 2002 Act) for holding that it is against English public policy to recognise a foreign decision based on an agreement that is declared illegal by an OFT decision. It is not certain which proposition would be adopted by the English court when faced with a foreign judgment that is in conflict with an OFT decision. It will be for the English court to rule on the incompatibility with English public policy of a foreign judgment that contradicts decisions of the OFT on the same subject matter between the same parties.

6.3.3 Recognition and Enforcement of US Antitrust Class Action Judgments

As already demonstrated, collective redress actions issued under an opt-out regime by a Member State court may be recognised in England, provided the English court applies a strong presumption that the procedures of other signatories of the Human Rights Convention are compliant with Art 6. Indeed, it is well established that the Brussels I regime is based on the principle of mutual trust between the legal systems in the EU. Should an English court recognise a US antitrust class judgment?

Although there is no English authority dealing with the question of whether a US class judgment is to be recognised and enforced in England, it has been submitted that:

> A judgment in class action proceedings in the United States cannot be recognized as against a person who was offered membership of the class, or who was even regarded by the American court as a member of that class, if he did nothing which English law sees as a submission or consent to the jurisdiction of the American court.[220]

This statement, however, should not be taken to mean that recognition of a foreign class judgment should be per se denied. It rather indicates that the true question before an English court would be whether the fact that a plaintiff did not

[219] See section 6.2.1 above.

[220] A Briggs, *Agreements on Jurisdiction and Choice of Law* (OUP, Oxford, 2008) 349–50.

opt out from the US class action proceedings would put him in a position where it could be said that he consented to jurisdiction.[221] There are good arguments suggesting that the answer to this question could be in the affirmative as far as US antitrust class action judgments are concerned. This has been recently acknowledged in a Report[222] made by the Civil Justice Council (CJC), that recommends legislative adoption of a collective opt-out regime in England which would both provide better access to justice and judicial efficiency, and result in more efficient private enforcement procedures.[223] In view of that, a denial per se of recognition of American class action judgments would undermine US antitrust enforcement policy which would fly in the face of the concept of comity which has an important role to play in the context of cross-border antitrust enforcement co-operation activities.[224]

Comity in this context is to do with the 'recognition which one nation allows within its territory to the legislative, executive or judicial acts of another nation having due regard both to international duty and convenience, and to the rights of its own citizens or of other persons who are under the protection of its laws.'[225] The importance of comity in antitrust cases can be demonstrated by a recent judgment in which the US Supreme Court held that the principles of comity would make unreasonable the application of US antitrust laws to conduct which is largely foreign, and declined to exercise jurisdiction for lack of subject matter jurisdiction.[226] Such an attitude of American courts would ensure that the US courts would not have exercised jurisdiction *in personam* unless there was a sufficient connection between the effect upon the US market and the allegedly anti-competitive conduct. The fact that such an antitrust claim would raise a question of the effect on an anti-competitive contract or practice on US public policy, which could not an issue that would be capable of fair resolution in any foreign court, would be enough to qualify the US forum as a court of competent jurisdiction.[227]

[221] Compare Briggs (n 220) 345.

[222] Civil Justice Council, 'Improving access to justice through collective actions—developing a more effective and efficient procedure for collective actions', *Final Report* www.civiljusticecouncil.gov.uk/files/Improving_Access_to_Justice_through_Collective_Actions.pdf.

[223] Ibid 88.

[224] Agreement between the Government of the United States of America and the Commission of the European Communities Regarding the Application of their Competition Laws (1991) 30 *International Legal Materials* 1491.

[225] *Morguard Investments Ltd v De Savoye* (1991) 76 DLR (4th) 256 at 269 (Supreme Court of Canada). See also: *Cheshire, North & Fawcett* (n 149) 515.

[226] *F Hoffmann-La Roche Ltd v Empagran* (2004) 542 US 155, 124 SCt 2359 (US Supreme Court). Compare the requirement for jurisdiction over the subject matter under English common law. See *A-G for Trinidad and Tobago v Eriche* [1893] AC 518, 522–23 (PC). For an opinion suggesting that the ruling in *Empagran* does not completely avoid the claims based on foreign harm, see M Furse, *Competition Law of the EC and UK* (6th edn, OUP, Oxford, 2008) 79.

[227] Compare CPR PD 6B para 3.1(6)(c). See also section 6.3.3 above.

Therefore, there are good arguments suggesting that a final US class action judgment should be recognised in England, provided that the plaintiff had been given an adequate notice for the foreign class action.[228]

6.3.4 The Protection of Trading Interests Act[229]—Special Regime

The Protection of Trading Interests Act[230] caused a significant shift in British policy relating to the control of international restrictive practices. The purpose of the 1980 Act is to nullify inter alia the extraterritorial effect in the UK of the US antitrust legislation.[231] It has been submitted that the rationale behind the Act is the conviction that US antitrust law operates in violation of public international law, as far as it has extraterritorial effect.[232] The 1980 Act raises interesting questions related to English public policy that denies recognition of foreign judgments awarding multiple damages in antitrust claims.

Section 5(2) of the 1980 Act provides that a court in the UK cannot enforce a judgment for multiple damages.[233] The effect can be easily illustrated by taking as an example the scenario that arose in *British Airways Board v Laker Airways*.[234] If Sir Freddie Laker had established his anti-trust claim in the United States against British Airways, he would have been entitled to multiple damages. Any award of multiple damages, however, would not have been enforceable in the UK due to s 5 of the 1980 Act.

Section 5 has been criticised. First, it has been submitted that it ignores even the compensatory element in an award of multiple damages.[235] Secondly, the prohibition of enforcement of a judgment awarding multiple damages does not depend on whether the applicable antitrust laws were applied extra-territorially by the foreign court.[236] For example, s 5 would prevent one US corporation enforcing in the UK a judgment in an antitrust suit against another US (or a third country) corporation,

[228] JCL Dixon, 'The *res judicata* effect of a US class action settlement' (1997) 46 *ICLQ* 134, 150–51. See also: *Currie* (n 128) [42]–[43].

[229] K Huntley, 'The Protection of Trading Interests Act 1980: Some jurisdictional aspects of enforcement of antitrust laws' (1981) 30 *ICLQ* 213; DL Jones, 'Protection of Trading Interests Act 1980' (1981) 40 *Civil Law Journal* 41; AV Lowe, 'Blocking extraterritorial jurisdiction: the British Protection of Trading Interests Act, 1980' (1981) 75 *American Journal of International Law* 257; MA Blythe, 'The extraterritorial impact of the anti-trust laws: Protecting British Trading Interests' (1983) 31 *American Journal of Comparative Law* 99; L Collins, 'Blocking and Clawback Statutes: The United Kingdom Approach' (1986) *Journal of Business Law* 372 and 452; *Cheshire, North & Fawcett* (n 149) 561–63; Hill (n 76) 399–400.

[230] 1980, c 11; in force March 20, 1980.

[231] The aim of the act was 'to reassert and reinforce the defences of the United Kingdom against attempts by other countries to enforce their economic and commercial policies unilaterally on us.' See Hansard HC vol 973 col 1533 (1979). See also *British Airways Board v Laker Airways* [1985] AC 58 (HL) 89 (Lord Diplock). See also s 5(2)b and 5(4) of the 1980 Act.

[232] *Laker Airways* (n 231).

[233] According to s 5(3), 'a judgment for multiple damages means a judgment for an amount arrived at by doubling, trebling or otherwise multiplying a sum assessed as compensation for the loss or damage sustained by the person in whose favour the judgment is given.'

[234] *Laker Airways* (n 231).

[235] Blythe (n 229) 123.

[236] *Cheshire, North & Fawcett* (n 149) 562.

which had assets and a place of business in England, even if the antitrust agreement or abusive practice, which was implemented in the US, affected the US market only.[237] Indeed, in a similar situation probably an English court would have applied Arts 101 and 102 TFEU which may also have extraterritorial application.[238]

In reply to this criticism, it has been stated that from the viewpoint of British public policy, enforcement of judgments of multiple damages is inherently objectionable.[239] However, there has been a recent shift in EU and domestic policy, suggesting that multiple damages could be among the incentives that may serve the Commission's goal to encourage private antitrust law in Europe.[240] In one of the responses to the Green Paper, it has been submitted that, 'multiplication of damages is needed from a deterrence perspective to neutralise the low probability of detection of prohibited cartels'.[241] In its response, the Office of Fair Trading[242] also considered that doubling damages at the discretion of the court may be an appropriate starting point in cases where a Member State court is considering an award of exemplary damages for breaches of competition law. However, the possibility for Member State courts to award multiple damages (eg double damages) was not addressed in the White Paper.[243]

Nevertheless, one may argue that a review of the 1980 Act should be on the agenda in the United Kingdom. Indeed, a refusal to enforce a foreign judgment awarding remedies which are considered appropriate at the place where the anti-competitive conduct took place and where the anti-competitive harm was caused may defeat the legitimate foreign policy and undermine the foreign antitrust enforcement policy.[244] It is difficult to see why an English court should be entitled to refuse recognition of an award of multiple damages in cases in which the dispute is only connected in a very limited way with England.[245]

6.4 Conclusion

It is beyond doubt that English public policy covers also European public policy. Articles 101 and 102 TFEU enjoy a public policy character for the purposes

[237] *British Airways Board v Laker Airways* [1984] QB 142 (CA) 162.

[238] Blythe (n 229) 123. *Cf Wood Pulp* (n 204).

[239] Note from the British Ambassador in Washington to the US State Department: Note No 25 (27 November 1979) cited in Blythe (n 229) 123.

[240] Commission (EC), 'Damages actions for breach of the EC antitrust rules' (Green Paper) COM (2005) 672 final. See also: Danov (n 171).

[241] Response provided by Erasmus University para.3.6, available at http://ec.europa.eu/competition/antitrust/actionsdamages/files_green_paper_comments/erasmus_university.pdf.

[242] Office of Fair Trading, *Response to the European Commission's Green Paper, Damages actions for breach of the EC antitrust rules* (2006) OFT844, paras 4.2–4.3.

[243] White Paper on Damages (n 19). At the time of writing, a Directive on damages action is being written.

[244] See ch 5, section 5.3.3 above.

[245] Mills (n 48) 259.

of recognition and enforcement of foreign judgments in England as they are fundamental provisions, which are essential for the accomplishment of the tasks entrusted to the EU and, in particular, for the functioning of the internal market. This suggests that a public policy defence can be pleaded in cases concerned with foreign judgments in relation to EU competition law claims. The powers of the English court in regard to foreign judgments misapplying EU competition laws, however, would depend on whether the recognition and enforcement is sought under the Brussels regime or under the traditional English rules.

A foreign judgment, which misapplies EU competition law though enjoying a public policy character, is not *ipso facto* contrary to English public policy under the Brussels I Regulation. It seems that where the court with original jurisdiction has ruled on Arts 101 and 102 TFEU the recognising court will be precluded from reviewing the conclusion of the foreign court. This conclusion is clearly adopted by the Court of Justice. In competition cases, however, there is the potential for previously unavailable evidence of illegal behaviour to become available at the recognition stage. Recognition should be denied by the English court in cases where the defendant brings new evidence that the judgment was rendered by another Member State court in manifest disregard of EU competition law and if there was no possibility for the defendant to bring fresh proceedings alleging a manifest breach of EU competition law before the adjudicating court. Indeed, if an English judgment may be set aside on the basis of new evidence that would have had a material effect upon the decision of the court there is no good reason why a foreign judgment must be treated more favourably. This will be of great relevance in cases involving hard-core restrictions on competition (eg price-fixing or market-sharing) that are implemented in the United Kingdom. This follows from ss 188–90 of the 2002 Act that are imposing criminal responsibility for the persons who commit a cartel offence.

The English court has wider powers in regard to foreign judgments rendered by courts from outside the EU. This is due to fact that the answer to the question whether an error of interpretation of EU competition law is capable of violating English public policy at common law is not confined by the aim and narrow interpretation of the provisions of the Brussels I Regulation. Furthermore, foreign courts could not avail themselves of the preventive and corrective mechanisms which are set to guarantee the proper interpretation and application of EU law by the Member States courts.

Furthermore, the public policy character of EU competition law indicates that it will be against English public policy to recognise a foreign judgment that is contrary to a decision of the Commission. This is so under the English traditional rules and the EU rules as well. That can be deduced from the principle of sincere cooperation (as reflected in Art 4(3) of the TEU) and Art 16 of Regulation 1/2003. A fortiori, it appears that an English court would not recognise a foreign judgment, even if it is inconsistent with a previous decision of the Commission on the same subject matter between the same parties. The conflict within the meaning of Art 16, nevertheless, does not exist between a foreign judgment and a Commission decision in cases where the judgment deals with a distribution agreement between company A and distributor 1 in Germany and Austria, whilst the Commission decision deals with virtually the same contract between the same company and distributor 2 in Ireland and the United Kingdom. Nonetheless, if such a Commission decision was not before the adjudicating court, it must be viewed as highly persuasive prima facie evidence that the court with original jurisdiction misapplied EU competition law. Recognising a foreign judgment that is in conflict with a Commission decision that is related to EU competition law would undermine legal authority, leaving parties in doubt as to where they stand, and would infringe the integrity of the EU legal order.

More difficulties, however, are bound to arise in regard to decisions rendered by the NCAs. Article 34(3) is not applicable in a case where a decision has been made by the OFT, since irreconcilability is not with a judgment. Nonetheless, recognition must be avoided because it will lead to irreconcilable decisions having incompatible consequences on the same subject matter and between the same parties in the same jurisdiction. One way to evade recognition is to hold that it is against English public policy to recognise a foreign judgment, which is irreconcilable with an OFT decision. If such an OFT decision was not before the adjudicating court, it will be viewed as persuasive prima facie evidence that EU competition law was misapplied. The alternative to the public policy exception would be to hold that the NCAs' decisions should be regarded as given by judicial bodies. This would be a strong argument in any Member State, where a judicial body has been designated as an NCA for the purposes of applying Arts 101 and 102 TFEU.

7

Arbitral Tribunals' Jurisdiction and Awards in Relation to Competition Law Claims

7.1 Introduction

Private international law will have an important role to play in arbitral proceedings involving private antitrust claims. Arbitral tribunals that are asked to deal with such a dispute will have to ascertain, first, whether they can rule on the competition law action in question. In other words, the first issue that needs to be addressed by the arbitrators is whether antitrust disputes are 'capable of settlement by arbitration'. This prerequisite is commonly referred to as the 'arbitrability of disputes'.[1] The answer to the question whether a competition law dispute is capable of settlement by arbitration would depend on the law governing the issue of arbitrability. Indeed, the arbitrability of a dispute, as a condition for arbitrators' jurisdiction, can be deduced by s 81(1)(a) of the English Arbitration Act 1996[2] and Art II(1) of the New York Convention.[3]

[1] See *Comandate Marine Corporation v Pan Australia Shipping Pty* [2006] FCAFC 192; [2008] 1 Lloyd's Rep 119 (Federal Court of Australia New South Wales District Registry) [200]. See more. G Gaja (ed), *International Commercial Arbitration: New York Convention* (Oceana Publications, Dobbs Ferry, NY, 1978–1996) vol 1 (loose-leaf) [B2]; J Hill, *International Commercial Disputes in English Courts* (3rd edn, Hart Publishing, Oxford, 2005) 652; GB Born, *International Commercial Arbitration* (2nd edn, Wolters Kluwer, The Netherlands 2009) 766-833; N Blackaby and C Partasides, *Redfern and Hunter on International Arbitration* (5th edn, OUP, Oxford, 2009) [1.64] and [2.111]–[2.125]. For Scotland, see Art 34(2)(b)(i) and Art 36(1)(b)(i) of Model Law in sch 7 of Law Reform (Miscellaneous Provisions) (Scotland) Act 1990. See also Art V(2) of the 1958 New York Convention and Art VI(2)(c) of the 1961 European Convention.

[2] See M Mustill and S Boyd, *The Law and Practice of Commercial Arbitration in England* (2nd edn, Butterworths, London, 1989) 150; Hill (n 1) 652.

[3] It has been argued that a court may refuse to enforce an agreement to arbitrate a subject matter that is non-arbitrable in domestic law under Art II(3) as well as under Art II(1). This is justified by the fact that awards rendered under such agreements could not be enforced under Art V(2) the agreement would be 'incapable of being performed'. See Exec Doc E, 90th Cong, 2d Sess, 19 (1968); G Haight, *Convention on the Recognition and Enforcement of Foreign Awards* (1958) 27–28 quoted in *Mitsubishi Motors v Soler Chrysler-Plymouth* 473 US 614; 87 L Ed 2d 444. The *Mitsubishi* case and its implications for the purposes of this thesis are discussed in more detail in section 7.3.2 below.

Secondly, the law applicable to the substance of an antitrust dispute would have an impact not only on the issue of arbitrability, as restrictions on arbitrability may also arise out of substantive competition laws[4] (eg EU competition law[5]), but also on the availability of damages that may be awarded. It is well established that even where different substantive competition laws agree about primary anti-competitive conduct that is to be forbidden, they disagree dramatically about appropriate remedies.[6] Can an arbitral tribunal based in Scotland award punitive (or exemplary) damages? Although Recital 32 of Rome II appears to indicate that non-compensatory or punitive damages of an excessive nature may be regarded as being contrary to the public policy of the forum, it is questionable whether arbitral tribunals have any forum at all. Can an arbitral tribunal based in England award multiple damages, if, say, US antitrust law governs the merits of a competition law dispute?

Thirdly, interesting questions will also arise with regard to jurisdiction of courts when called for support in relation to EU competition law arbitration proceedings and when called to review an arbitral award dealing with antitrust claims. Further attention should be paid to the question whether the special mechanisms that are set in Regulation 1/2003 to maintain a coherent application of EU competition law are applicable to proceedings before an arbitral tribunal, so that they could be available in respect of antitrust arbitral proceedings.

This chapter attempts to examine the issues that may arise before arbitral tribunals in private antitrust proceeding and to highlight the powers of national courts in support of such proceedings and control over arbitral awards in relation to antitrust law claims.

7.2 Jurisdiction of Arbitrators in Competition Law Disputes—Some Preliminary Issues

From a jurisdictional point of view, the non-arbitrability of competition law disputes may preclude the application of antitrust law by arbitral tribunals. In other words, an agreement to arbitrate an EU antitrust law dispute, which is non-arbitrable, would be unenforceable before national courts.[7] Further, an arbitral award dealing with competition law issues, which were non-arbitrable, should

[4] L Idot, 'Introductory Report' in ICC Publication No 480-3 *Competition and Arbitration Law* (ICC Publishing, ICC, 1993) 39, 53; J-P Maire and D Hahn, 'Competition regulations and evolution of concept of arbitrability' in ibid 89, 94.

[5] Eg fines and directions under Arts 23 and 24 of Regulation 1/2003 fall within the exclusive jurisdiction of the Commission, and may not be arbitrated.

[6] *F Hoffmann-La Roche Ltd v Empagran* (2004) 542 US 155, 167.

[7] ss 9 and 81(1)(a) of the 1996 Act. *ET Plus v Welter* [2005] EWHC 2115 (Comm); [2006] 1 Lloyd's Rep 251 (HC). See Art II(1) New York Convention. *Cf* dissenting opinion in *Mitsubishi* (n 3). See also *American Safety Equipment Corp v JP Maguire & Co* 391 F2d 821 (CA2 1968) 826–27.

be set aside by the court at the seat of arbitration[8] and/or refused recognition and enforcement by the national courts.[9] Therefore, the questions of whether the competition law issues are arbitrable, and what law governs arbitrability of antitrust law issues, are not purely academic, but, on the contrary, very practical ones which are of huge importance. Before focusing on the arbitrability of competition law disputes, however, a preliminary issue that is to do with the question whether the invalidity of a main contract invalidates an arbitration clause needs to be addressed.[10]

It is well settled that arbitration exists only through the will of the parties, who can tailor it to their liking and according to their needs. The arbitration agreement, however, could be incorporated in a contract, which is void due to Art 101 TFEU. It is well established that nullity under Art 101(2) is retroactive, irrespective of whether or not any statement to that effect is made by the body responsible for deciding the matter.[11] In spite of the fact that Art 102 TFEU does not include a provision equivalent to Art 101(2), which prescribes that any agreements prohibited by Art 101(1) shall be automatically void, the Court of Justice of the EU has stated that a similar consequence applies to any breach of Art 102 TFEU.[12] This leads to the question of whether the invalidity of a main contract will also invalidate an arbitration clause. One possible answer is that if the main contract is void, then the agreement to arbitrate is also invalid, so arbitrators cannot have jurisdiction on the basis of that arbitration clause. According to Idot,[13] if that solution was adopted, then the arbitrator could have been in a situation where he would have to declare that he had no jurisdiction to hear and determine a competition law dispute after he had already determined that the main contract was void as being in conflict with Arts 101 and/or 102 TFEU.

A more satisfactory outcome is produced through the 'doctrine of separability'. Under this doctrine, an arbitration clause is treated as an agreement that is separate from the main contract, so that if the contract is void, the arbitration clause will remain valid and bind the parties to resolve their dispute by arbitration.[14] The doctrine is widely implemented in Europe.[15] Examples of its legislative acceptance can be discovered in s 7 of the 1996 Act, s 16(1) of the Model Law that is implemented in Scotland, and Art 1053 of the Netherlands Arbitration Act. It should

[8] Compare s 81(1)(a) of the 1996 Act; Hill (n 1) 652. For Scotland, Art 34(2)(b)(i) of Model Law in sch 7 of the Law Reform (Miscellaneous Provisions) (Scotland) Act 1990 will have the same effect.

[9] s 103(3) of the 1996 Act. See also Art V(2)(a) of the New York Convention.

[10] The question of whether the invalidity of a main contract invalidates a choice of court agreement was discussed in ch 2, section 2.2.7 above.

[11] Case 48/72 *Haecht v Wilkin-Janssen* [1973] ECR 77 [25]–[27].

[12] Case 172/73 *BRT v SABAM* [1974] ECR 51.

[13] Idot (n 4) 54. See also *Gosset v Carapelli* [1963] *Revue Critique de Droit International Privé* 615 (Cour de Cassation (7 May 1963)).

[14] T Varady, JJ Barcelo and AT von Mehren, *International Commercial Arbitration: A Transnational Perspective* (2nd edition, American Casebook Series, Thomson West, 2002) 154.

[15] See s 16(1) of UNCITRAL Model Law. See also the decision of the German Bundesgerichtshof of February 27, 1970 *BGHZ* 253, 315, and the decision of the French Cour de Cassation in *Gosset* (n 13).

be noted that as far as England is concerned, an arbitration clause contained in a written contract is regarded as a distinct agreement and could be affected only by a claim directly affecting the validity of the arbitration agreement.[16] As a result, an allegation that the contract, under which the arbitration is brought, is itself void (due to Arts 101 and 102 TFEU) does not preclude an arbitral tribunal from hearing and determining an EU competition law dispute.

The implications of the doctrine of separability for the jurisdiction of arbitral tribunals in antitrust claims could be illustrated by the decision of the German Bundesgerichtshof in *Fruchtsäfte*. In this case, the court dealt with the question whether an arbitration agreement in a contract of restraint of competition is an independent obligation separate from the rest of the contract. It was held that the invalidity of the main contract did not invalidate the arbitration clause, since the parties would in any case have reached an agreement to arbitrate even if they had known that their contract was null and void.[17] The main practical advantage in the present context is that separability ensures that a dispute over validity of a contract with regard to Arts 101 and 102 will be settled by arbitration as being the dispute settlement mechanism that is chosen by the parties. Indeed, there is no doubt that the courts in most European jurisdictions including England and Scotland, would regard an arbitration clause as an agreement independent from the other terms of the main contract. As a result, the arbitral tribunals will be entitled to determine whether an agreement is or is not in conflict with EU competition law. This though is subject to the arbitrability of such disputes.

7.3 Arbitrability of Competition Law Issues

Private antitrust enforcement before arbitral tribunals can take different forms. It may be limited to an action for nullity of a contract that is in conflict with Arts 101 and 102 TFEU. The arbitrators may not only be requested to apply civil sanctions of nullity to a contractual relationship, but also be asked to award compensatory (or even punitive) competition law damages. Which of those claims are arbitrable? Generally, it is for the national legislator to determine which matters may or may not be resolved by arbitration. The Member States are free to do that in accordance with their political, social and economic policy.[18] Therefore,

[16] *Premium Nafta Products Ltd v Fili Shipping* [2007] UKHL 40, [2008] 1 Lloyd's Rep 254 (HL) [17]. See also: *Harbour Assurance v Kansa General International Insurance* [1993] QB 701 (CA); *Fiona Trust Holding Corp v Privalov* [2007] EWCA Civ 20; [2007] Bus LR 686; *Redfern and Hunter on International Arbitration* (n 1) [2.89]–[2.100].

[17] BGH, *Fruchtsafte*, 29 February 1969, GP, 1970, II 139, quoted in A Redfern and M Hunter, *Law and Practice of International Commercial Arbitration* (3rd edn, Sweet & Maxwell, London, 1999) 150–51.

[18] *Redfern and Hunter on International Arbitration* (n 1) [2.114].

in order to answer to determine the issue of arbitrability in any antitrust dispute involving arbitration, the English court and arbitral tribunals based in England will first have to ascertain the applicable law to arbitrability.

Which law should determine arbitrability of competition law claims under the English Arbitration Act 1996? The answer to this question is far from certain, as the issue of arbitrability could arise in several related, but quite distinct legal contexts. For example, in England, there are four stages at which the question of arbitrability of an antitrust law issue may arise.[19] This could happen in the course of: arbitration proceedings, court proceedings related to s 9 of the 1996 Act,[20] setting aside proceedings,[21] or recognition and enforcement proceedings.[22]

7.3.1 Law Applicable to Arbitrability under the 1996 Act[23]

There is nothing in the English legislation to indicate the system of law by reference to which the question of arbitrability is to be tested. Moreover, there is no English authority directly on this point.[24] The question of the law applicable to arbitrability has been widely discussed by commentators.[25]

There are strong arguments suggesting that, as a matter of English law, the arbitrability should be governed by the law of the seat of arbitration. First, such a solution would overlap with the law governing an arbitration agreement in cases where the parties had not furnished any express indication in this respect. The Court of Appeal recently held that 'an agreement to arbitrate will normally have a closer and more real connection with the place where the parties have chosen to arbitrate than with the place of the law of the underlying contract in cases where the parties have deliberately chosen to arbitrate in one place disputes which have arisen under a contract governed by the law of another place.'[26]

[19] J Beechy 'Arbitrability of Anti-trust/Competition Law Issues—Common Law' (1996) 12 *Arbitration International* 179, 182.

[20] See ss 9 and 81(1)(a) of the 1996 Act.

[21] See Art 81(1)(a) of the 1996 Act; for Scotland, Art 34(2)(b)(i) of Model Law in sch 7 of Law Reform (Miscellaneous Provisions) (Scotland) Act 1990.

[22] See ss 103(3) of the Act 1996. For Scotland, Art 36(1)(b)(i) of Model Law in sch 7 of Law Reform (Miscellaneous Provisions) (Scotland) Act 1990. See also Art V(2) of New York Convention.

[23] M Danov, 'The law governing arbitrability under the Arbitration Act 1996' (2008) *Lloyd's Maritime and Commercial Law Quarterly* 536.

[24] Hill (n 1) 652.

[25] See: B Hanotiau, 'What Law Governs the Issue of Arbitrability' (1996) 12 *Arbitration International* 391; M Blessing, 'The law applicable to the arbitration clause and arbitrability' in AJ van den Berg (ed), *Improving the efficiency of arbitration agreements and awards: 40 Years of Application of the New York Convention* (ICCA Congress Series No 9, Kluwer Law International, The Hague, 1999) 168; H Arfazadeh, 'Arbitrability under the New York Convention: the *lex fori* revisited' (2001) 17 *Arbitration International* 73; L Collins and others, *Dicey, Morris and Collins on the Conflict of Laws* (14th edn, Sweet & Maxwell, London, 2006) 719–20; Hill (n 1) 652; Danov (n 23) 536–45.

[26] *C v D* [2007] EWCA Civ 1282; [2008] 1 Lloyd's Rep 239 (CA) [26]. See also: Dicey, Morris and Collins (n 25) 720; A Arzandeh and J Hill, 'Ascertaining the proper law of an arbitration clause under English law' (2009) 5 *Journal of Private International Law* 425. Compare *Sumitomo Heavy Industries v Oil and Natural Gas Commission* [1994] 1 Lloyd's Rep 45 (QBD (Comm)) 57.

Secondly, by choosing a country in which to arbitrate, the parties create a close connection between the arbitration and that country. It would be reasonable to assume from their choice that they attach importance to the relevant laws of that country.[27] It seems that the fact that the parties have agreed to that specific place for arbitration is a very strong pointer that implicitly they must have chosen the laws of that place to govern the arbitrability. Moreover, the arbitrability admittedly is a matter of procedure (being linked with the compulsory jurisdiction of courts or other public authorities[28]), as opposed to being a matter of substantive law. Accordingly, arbitrability, being a matter of procedure, should be 'governed by the law of the country in which the arbitration is held, on the ground that it is the country most closely connected with the proceedings'.[29] It is well established that the parties, when contracting to arbitrate in a particular place, consented to having the procedural matters governed by the law of that place.[30]

The deduction could be supported by the 1996 Act,[31] which indicates that the court proceedings will not be stayed in England with regard to the subject matter of the dispute that is non-arbitrable.[32] As a result, an arbitration agreement with regard to disputes that are not arbitrable will become unenforceable. In other words, if antitrust claims were non-arbitrable under English law, then arbitration in England could only continue after the non-arbitrable issues had been determined by the competent court. If arbitration went forward and an arbitral award determined the issues which were non-arbitrable under English law, then this award would be easily set aside.[33]

Thirdly, the importance of the law of the seat of arbitration in all matters ancillary to arbitration can be strengthened by the recent report on the application of the Brussels I Regulation in the Member States.[34] Although, the report in question appears to employ the term 'place of arbitration', which could give rise to some uncertainty in cases where the seat of arbitration is in one Member State, while the place of hearings is in another Member State,[35] there is little doubt that the

[27] *Union of India v McDonnell Douglas* [1993] 2 Lloyd's Rep 48 (QBD (Comm)) 50. See also *Bank Mellat v Helleniki Techniki* [1984] QB 291 (CA) 301 (Kerr LJ).

[28] See Danov (n 23). See also Hill (n 4) 652, Arfazadeh (n 25) 80.

[29] *James Miller v Whitworth Street Estates* [1970] 1 Lloyd's Rep 269; [1970] AC 583 (HL) 607, 609, 612 and 616.

[30] *Channel Tunnel Group v Balfour Beauty Construction* [1993] 1 Lloyd's Rep 291; [1993] AC 334 (HL) 357–58. See also *McDonnell Douglas* (n 27).

[31] See more, Danov (n 23).

[32] For Scotland, Art 1(5) of Model Law in sch 7 of Law Reform (Miscellaneous Provisions) (Scotland) Act 1990 will have the same effect. See also FP Davidson, *International Commercial Arbitration: Scotland and the UNCITRAL Model Law* (W.Green/Sweet & Maxwell, Edinburgh, 1991) 24.

[33] See ss 81(1)(a) and 103(3) of the 1996 Act. See also: Art 34(2)(b)(i) of Model Law in sch 7 of Law Reform (Miscellaneous Provisions) (Scotland) Act 1990 will have the same effect. Danov (n 23) 541–42.

[34] Study JLS/C4/2005/03, B Hess, T Pfeiffer and P Schlosser, *Report on the Application of Regulation Brussels I in the Member States* (Final Version—September 2007) [132] http://ec.europa.eu/civiljustice/news/docs/study_application_brussels_1_en.pdf.

[35] Art 16 of the LCIA Arbitration Rules 1998. See also: G Petrochilos, *Procedural Law in International Arbitration* (OUP, Oxford, 2004) 24; Hill (n 1) 673; Commission (EC), 'Review of Council Regulation

authors of the report have acknowledged the importance of the court at the seat of arbitration. Such an approach is in line with the jurisprudence in England, where the court in *Bank Mellat* held that:

> A particular feature of English law … is the relationship between the courts and arbitrations, which is well known to be considerably closer than in most civil law jurisdictions, as well as in the US.[36]

Therefore, the law of the seat of arbitration must be considered, if the arbitrability is raised before an arbitral tribunal that has its seat of arbitration in England. Further, law of the seat of arbitration would also have an important role to play in cases where the issue of arbitrability is raised in the course of court proceedings related to s 9 of the 1996 Act[37] or setting aside proceedings. Although s 103(3), read together with Art V(2) of the New York Convention, suggests that the law of the court at the place of recognition and enforcement of an award is important when this stage is considered, an English court may also apply the law of the seat of arbitration in cases where the matter is arbitrable under English law and no setting aside application has been brought before the foreign court.[38]

7.3.2 Arbitrability of Competition Law Claims under English Law

In practice, arbitrability of competition law disputes is rarely explicitly authorised[39] or prohibited[40] by the Member States' national arbitration laws. A scrutiny of arbitration laws shows that there are two types of test that are applied in the legislation of the Western European countries. Under the first test, an issue will be arbitrable where parties are free to dispose of their rights where such rights may be litigated.[41] According to the second test, any claim involving an economic interest will be arbitrable.[42] Restrictions on arbitrability, however, may exist in other legal instruments. For example, in France, Art 2060 of the Civil Code excludes from arbitration 'all matters in the realm of public policy'.[43]

(EC) No 44/2001 on jurisdiction and the recognition and enforcement of judgments in civil and commercial matters' (Green Paper) COM (2009) 175 final.

36 *Bank Mellat* (n 27) 301 (Kerr LJ).

37 Or court proceedings related to Art II of the NYC.

38 See more: Danov (n 23).

39 Eg s 1(3) of the Swedish Arbitration Act of 1999, where it is stated that 'arbitrators may rule on the civil law effects of competition law', though their authority is expressly limited to effects *inter partes.*

40 Eg Art 11(1) of the Lithuanian Law on Commercial Arbitration explicitly states that disputes connected with competition may not be submitted to arbitration.

41 Eg Art 2(1) of Spanish Arbitration Act 2003; Art 806 of Italian Code of Civil Procedure, Art 1(1) of Portuguese Arbitration Law, Art 1676 of Belgium Code Judiciar 19 May 1998; and Art 1020 of Netherlands Arbitration Act (Code of Civil Procedure).

42 Eg Art 1030 of German ZPO; and Art 177 of Swiss Code on Private International Law.

43 For that purpose the debate about arbitrability of competition law in French Law has been obscured to a great extent by the question of whether the invalidity of the submission to arbitration

The lack of specific national rules related to arbitrability of competition law claims gave rise to wide discussions all over Europe as to whether such claims are arbitrable in principle.[44] For example, even before Regulation 1/2003, which is meant to enhance private antitrust enforcement in Europe, the interaction between the competition law and arbitration had been examined by the Member State courts in France,[45] Germany,[46] Italy,[47] Switzerland[48] and Sweden.[49] The review of the case law shows that the problem was more difficult to be solved under the laws of the countries where matters of public policy[50] were deemed to be non-arbitrable. For example, due to the public policy character of competition law there were some difficulties in establishing whether those disputes were arbitrable in France. Nevertheless, ultimately the arbitrability of antitrust issues was favoured by the Paris Cour D'Appel and French Cour de Cassation.[51]

Under English law there are very few restrictions on the types of dispute which are arbitrable.[52] The test that has been suggested is that 'any dispute or claim concerning legal rights which can be subject to an enforceable award, is capable of being settled by arbitration.[53] The Court of Justice ruling in the *Eco Swiss* case[54] can be regarded as implicitly confirming the arbitrability of Arts 101(1) and (2)

results from the fact that the dispute concerned matters of public policy, or from the fact that public policy had been breached.

[44] Eg ICC Publication No 480-3 (n 4); Some important papers, which are concerned with the Arbitration and Reform in the EC Competition law, were submitted in the Florence Annual EU Competition Law and Policy Workshops (2001)—see C-D Ehlermann and I Atanasiu (eds) *European Competition Law Annual 2001: Effective Private Enforcement of EC Antitrust Law* (Hart Publishing, Oxford, 2003); D Waelbroeck, D Slater and G Even-Shoshan, 'Comparative Report: Study on the conditions of claims for damages in cases of infringement of EC competition law', 133, available at http://ec.europa.eu/comm/competition/cartels/studies/comparative_report_clean_en.pdf.

[45] Paris Cour d'Appel, 20/6/1989 *SPD v DPF* [1989] Rev Arb. 280, note Idot; CA Paris, 19/5/1993 *Labinal v Mors* [1993] Rev Arb 645; CA Paris, 19/5/1993 *Velcros* [1994] Rev Arb 164.

[46] BGH, *Zimcofot*, judgment of 20 May 1966, WuW/E BGH 810; 17 WuW, 220; *cf* the interpretation of German law by the US Federal Court in *Mitsubishi* (n 3) (473 US 661); See more L von Zumbusch, 'Arbitrability of antitrust claims under US, German and EEC law: the "international transaction" criterion and public policy' (1987) 22 *Texas International Law Journal* 291, 305.

[47] *Coveme SpA (Italy) v Compagnie Francaise des Isolants SA (France)* (1993) *Yearbook of Commercial Arbitration* 422 (Corte di Appello, Bologna).

[48] Decision of the Chambre de Recours of the Vaud Cantonal Tribunal dated 28 October 1975, *Ampalgas v Sofia; G SA v V SpA* [1996] ECC 1 (Bundesgericht [Swiss Federal Supreme Court]) 28 April 1992; See more: M Blessing, 'Mandatory Rules of Law *versus* Party Autonomy in International Arbitration' (1997) 14 *Journal of International Arbitration* 23.

[49] Decision T 4366-02, *Dirland Telecom SA v Viking Telecom AB (Publ)*, Decision of the Court of Appeal for Western Sweden of 29 December 2003, discussed in G Blanke, 'Decision T 4366-02, *Dirland Telecom SA v Viking Telecom AB (Publ)*, Decision of the Court of Appeal for Western Sweden of 29 December 2003' (2005) 26 ECLR 432, 434–35.

[50] EU competition law can be a matter of public policy for the purposes of the New York Convention. See Case C-126/97 *Eco Swiss China Time v Benetton International ('Eco Swiss')* [1999] ECR I-3055. See more, section 7.5.5.1 below.

[51] *Labinal* (n 45); *Velcros* (n 45).

[52] Hill (n 1) 652.

[53] Mustill and Boyd (n 2) 149.

[54] *Eco Swiss* (n 50). The *Eco Swiss* case and its implications for the purposes of this book are discussed in more detail in section 7.5.5.1 below.

and 102 TFEU. In this case, the Court of Justice was asked whether arbitrators are under an obligation to raise questions of EU law of their own motion not only where the national legal order requires them to do so, but also where it merely gives them discretion to do so.[55] The Court of Justice did not answer that question (although the Advocate General had suggested a negative answer).[56] The Court, however, stated that an award that disregards Art 101 TFEU must be refused enforcement, on the ground of public policy.[57] In other words, if an arbitral tribunal failed to apply EU competition law, then the award could be subject to challenge before national courts. As a result, after the *Eco Swiss* case, arbitrators are bound to consider competition law issues, in order to 'render an enforceable award'.[58] Indeed, the general arbitrability of EU competition law has been recently confirmed by the English High Court in the *ET Plus* case.[59] In this case, the Court held that 'there is no realistic doubt that such "competition" or "anti-trust" claims are arbitrable'.[60]

Moreover, it has been held by the English Court that the question of arbitrability in English law must be determined by considerations similar to those deployed by the US Supreme Court in the *Mitsubishi* case.[61] In this case, a Puerto Rican corporation entered into distribution and sales agreements with a Swiss corporation which manufactured automobiles in Japan. This automobile manufacturer was the product of a joint venture between the Swiss corporation and a Japanese corporation. The sales agreement contained a clause providing for arbitration by the Japan Commercial Arbitration Association. Subsequently, disputes arose from a slackening of the sales of the automobiles. The Japanese manufacturer brought an action against the Puerto Rican corporation in the US District Court for the District of Puerto Rico, seeking an order to compel arbitration. The District Court ordered arbitration of all the issues raised in in the complaint, and the federal antitrust issues raised in the counter-claim by the Puerto Rico corporation. Indeed, it was clearly held that antitrust claims are arbitrable and must be submitted to arbitration. The US Court went further and outlined that there is no reason to assume that international arbitration would not provide an adequate mechanism for awarding damages in antitrust claims.[62]

Accordingly, if the US approach were followed in England, then all competition law claims including actions for antitrust damages would be arbitrable under English law. Indeed, if competition law claims are arbitrable in principle, there is no reason to suggest that arbitrators will not be competent to hear and determine a competition law damages claim, provided the parties' arbitration agreement was

[55] Joined Cases C-430/93 and C-431/93 *Van Schijndel and Van Veen v SPF* [1995] ECR I-4705.
[56] *Eco Swiss* (n 50) [26] (AG Saggio).
[57] *Eco Swiss* (n 50) [37].
[58] See eg ICC r 35; LCIA r 32.2.
[59] See *ET Plus* (n 7).
[60] Ibid [51].
[61] *Westacre Investments v Jugoimport-SPDR* [1999] QB 740 (QBD (Comm)) 768–69; aff'd *Westacre Investments v Jugoimport-SPDR* [2000] QB 288 (CA). See also Beechy (n 19) 188.
[62] *Mitsubishi* (n 3) [635] and [636].

sufficiently wide to encompass its determination. Are antitrust damages claims, which are tortious in nature, covered by a standard arbitration clause?

It has been established that broad language referring 'all claims' or 'all disputes' to arbitration includes tort claims. That will be so, as long as there is a 'sufficiently close connection between that claim and the [contract] to bring the claim within the arbitration clause, even though framed technically in tort'.[63] The test of 'sufficiently close connection'[64] would be satisfied if the claimant could show that the resolution of the contractual issue is necessary for a decision on the tortious claim, or, that the contractual and tortious disputes are so closely knitted together on the facts that an agreement to arbitrate on one can properly be construed as covering the other.[65] It seems that a competition law damages claim can easily satisfy this test, since the question whether the contract distorts competition would be significant for the damages claim. Such a deduction can be further strengthened by a recent judgment in which Lord Hoffmann held that:

> [T]he construction of an arbitration clause should start from the assumption that the parties, as rational businessmen, are likely to have intended any dispute arising out of the relationship into which they have entered or purported to enter to be decided by the same tribunal.[66]

In the *ET Plus* case,[67] it was held that there is no basis for the conclusion that a clause would cover contractual claims between parties regarding non-performance of the contract but not closely connected tortious claims relying on the same facts. The High Court had no doubt to conclude that tortious claims arising out of a breach of EU competition law fell within the arbitration clause and must be determined by the arbitral tribunal.[68] Although, the High Court ruling was in the context of an application for a stay of legal proceedings with regard to arbitration that was already proceeding abroad, it seems that the same would be true if a principal claim for invalidity of a contract that is in conflict with competition laws was brought together with an antitrust damages claim.[69] It seems that most of the more common forms of arbitration clause are sufficiently wide to give an arbitrator jurisdiction over EU antitrust tort claims.[70]

Therefore, it is beyond doubt that an arbitral tribunal based in England would have jurisdiction to apply Arts 101 and 102 TFEU. Furthermore, arbitrators will be entitled to rule over closely knitted tortious claims for damages arising out of a

[63] *Woolf v Collis Removal Service* [1948] 1 KB 11 (CA) 18.

[64] *The Playa Larga* [1983] 2 Lloyd's Rep 171 (CA) 183; *The 'Angelic Grace'* [1995] 1 Lloyd's Rep 87 (CA) 89.

[65] *Playa Larga* (n 64) 183; *Angelic Grace* (n 64) 89. Compare: *Dalimpex v Andrzej Janicki* [2000] ILPr 180 (Superior Court of Justice, Ontario) [40].

[66] *Fili Shipping* (n 16) [13].

[67] See *ET Plus* (n 7).

[68] Ibid [41] and [51].

[69] See Maire and Hahn (n 4) 96. See also: Idot (n 4) 54.

[70] See Mustill and Boyd (n 2) 117. See also: *Redfern and Hunter on International Arbitration* (n 1) [2.56].

breach of EU competition law claims for damages. This would be so, if the parties' arbitration agreement was sufficiently wide to encompass determination of EU competition law claims.[71] Such approach of English law should be welcomed and would be in line with the common law approach to claims for antitrust damages.

However, this does not mean that an arbitral tribunal based in England would have jurisdiction to deal with each and every competition law dispute as restrictions on arbitrability may stem from the substantive law applicable to the merits of a dispute. For example, under Regulation 17/62, the arbitrators had no *power* to apply Art 101(3) TFEU, which was to be exclusively applied by the Commission.[72] Although, it has been argued that even under the old system an 'arbitrator could, in theory, interpret [an agreement] in such a way that [Art 101(3) TFEU] conditions are no longer fulfilled by [it]',[73] it was, nonetheless, clear that the Commission's monopoly on the application of Art 101(3) TFEU would preclude the arbitral tribunals from granting an exemption. This meant that non-arbitrability of Art 101(3) was decided at EU level. This was so, even if the competition law issues were regarded as arbitrable under the law of a particular Member State. In other words, in view of the principle of supremacy, the arbitrators were precluded from exercising jurisdiction in a case, where the application of Art 101(3) was an issue.[74] Therefore, a stay of proceedings had to be granted in cases where Art 101(3) was an issue. Hence, unless a block exemption regulation (due to its direct effect) applied[75] or an individual exemption was granted, arbitral tribunals that had to assess restrictive provisions faced difficulties. The repeal of Regulation 17/62 gives rise to the question concerning the scope of an arbitrator's jurisdiction with regard to Art 101 TFEU after Regulation 1/2003 came into force. An arbitral tribunal could not (and should not) address the issue of arbitrability under applicable substantive law (and Art 101(3) TFEU in particular) unless it had been determined what competition laws are applicable to the merits of the parties' dispute.

But, does the fact that Arts 101 and 102 TFEU are regarded as overriding mandatory provisions in England and enjoy public policy character suggest that an arbitral tribunal based in England should always apply them and is an arbitral tribunal based in England always bound to apply EU competition law[76]? Can the parties choose another antitrust law to determine the validity of contract? What if there is a conflict between the law applicable to the merits of the dispute and mandatory rules of English law?

[71] *Playa Larga* (n 64) 183. See also: RB von Mehren, 'The *Eco Swiss* case and International Arbitration' (2003) 19 *Arbitration International* 465, 469.

[72] Mustill and Boyd (n 2) 149; P Roth (ed), *Bellamy and Child: European Community Law of Competition* (5th edn, Sweet & Maxwell, London, 2001) 815. See also: Sir N Phillips, 'The Situation in England' in ICC Publication No 480–3 (n 4) 303; R Nazzini, *Concurrent Proceedings in Competition Law: Procedure, Evidence and Remedies* (OUP, Oxford, 2004) 327.

[73] W Brown, 'Commercial Arbitration and the European Economic Community' (1985) 2 *Journal of International Arbitration* 21, 28.

[74] See Mustill and Boyd (n 2) 149.

[75] CM Schmitthoff, 'Arbitration and EEC Law' (1987) 24 *CML Rev* 143, 147.

[76] Compare ch 5, section 5.2.3.2 above.

7.4 The Law Applicable to the Substance of a Competition Law Dispute

The English Arbitration Act 1996 has endorsed the principle of freedom of choice and party autonomy.[77] Article 46(1) states that:

> The arbitral tribunal shall decide the dispute—
> (a) in accordance with the law chosen by the parties as applicable to the substance of the dispute, or
> (b) if the parties so agree, in accordance with such other considerations as are agreed by them or determined by the tribunal.

Therefore, the parties may select the laws of a country as applicable to the substance to their dispute. The parties may also agree under Art 46(1)(b) that their dispute is to be decided in accordance with such other considerations as *lex mercatoria* or equity.[78] But, what if there is a dispute as to the validity of a contract (or of any term of a contract) that is alleged to be void and illegal as distorting competition? The 1996 Act does not address the question of how to treat the mandatory rules of the forum.[79] Although, the wording of the provisions indicates that there is no limit to the parties' freedom to choose competition laws governing the validity of their agreement, it has been submitted that an arbitrator sitting in England has a duty to apply English competition law which has direct effect and forms part of the *lex fori*.[80] Such an approach would appear to work reasonably well in cases where the parties have expressly or implicitly[81] chosen their dispute to be governed by English law. Indeed, an award that takes account of the mandatory rules of the forum, which enjoy public policy character, would not be set aside by the court at the seat of arbitration.[82] The proposition that an arbitral tribunal based in England should have a duty to apply Arts 101 and 102 TFEU could have certainly been justified if the (allegedly) anti-competitive contract had been implemented in England, but it is difficult to understand why arbitrators should do so in cases where the only connection of the antitrust dispute with the European Union (and England in particular) was the seat of arbitration. Such a duty would have been theoretically reinforced if the view that the place of

[77] See more: Hill (n 1) 686–97.

[78] Hill (n 1) 689–90.

[79] Compare Arts 3(4) and 9 of Rome I.

[80] M Mustil and S Boyd, *Commercial Arbitration Companion Volume* (2nd edn, LexisNexis Butterworths, London, 2001) 80. See also: SI Dempegiotis, 'EC competition law and international arbitration in the light of EC Regulation 1/2003' (2008) 25 *Journal of International Arbitration* 365, 382–83.

[81] In England, there is a presumption that by choosing England as the seat of arbitration, the parties have impliedly chosen their dispute to be governed by English law. See: *Hamlyn & Co v Talisker Distillery* [1894] AC 202; *Compagnie Tunisienne de Navigation SA v Compagnie d'Armement Maritime SA* [1971] AC 572; *Egon Oldendorff v Libera Corp* [1995] 2 Lloyd's Rep 64. See also: DR Thomas, 'Arbitration agreements as a signpost of the proper law' (1984) *Lloyd's Maritime and Commercial Law Quarterly* 141; Hill (n 1) 687.

[82] See section 7.5.5 below.

the seat of arbitration was the forum of arbitration were adopted with regard to international commercial arbitration in England.[83] However, this is questionable in view of the fact that international arbitration is regarded by its very nature as being separate from national systems of law.[84] Similarly, in the context of an antitrust dispute, the US Federal Court held that an 'international arbitral tribunal owes no prior allegiance to the legal norms of particular states'.[85]

Accordingly, it has been submitted that 'in international situations the arbitrator takes the place of all the courts which might have had jurisdiction to determine the dispute in the absence of arbitration agreement.'[86] The international spread of assets in companies involved in antitrust infringements taken together with the wide bases for jurisdiction under Brussels I and Member States' exorbitant rules may suggest that this would be often a difficult task because not all foreign nations have similar competition laws.[87] In addition, most antitrust laws are often regarded as mandatory provisions of the forum and enjoy extraterritorial effect. This may suggest that it will be quite common for an arbitral tribunal to be required to consider the issue of legality of an allegedly anti-competitive contract by being asked to apply (sometimes contradictory) competition laws of several countries. Which mandatory provisions should be applied by an arbitral tribunal in such cases in view of the fact that anti-competitive agreements and/or practices may potentially affect the market in several countries?

It has been argued that in cases where the parties have chosen the law of a country to govern their dispute regarding compatibility of their contract with competition law, 'it will be concluded from the outset that the arbitrator will have to apply the mandatory rules of that law.'[88] This opinion seems to be consistent with the principle of 'party autonomy', and views arbitration as a consensual process.[89] However, if the arbitrators recognised and gave unlimited effect to any choice of law made by the parties, then evasion of EU competition law would be the result. For example, a French producer of gadgets and an English distributor of the same product may choose the law of New York as applicable to their agreement that is (allegedly) in conflict with Arts 101 and/or 102 TFEU and performed in England. If the arbitrator had to apply the mandatory rules of the chosen law, then it would not be EU competition law, but US Federal antitrust law which would determine the validity of the agreement in question (or of any term of it).

[83] P Nygh, *Autonomy in International Contracts* (OUP, Oxford, 1999) 226–28. Petrochilos (n 35) 22–24.

[84] *SA Coppee Lavalin NV v Ken-Ren Chemicals & Fertilizers Ltd* [1995] 1 AC 38 (HL) 52 (Lord Mustill).

[85] *Mitsubishi* (n 3) (473 US 628).

[86] Hill (n 1) 695. See also Dempegiotis (n 80) 383.

[87] Compare *Empagran* (n 6) (542 US 167).

[88] Y Derains, 'Public policy and the law applicable to the dispute in international arbitration' in P Sanders (ed), *International Council for Commercial Arbitration—Comparative Arbitration Practice and Public Policy in Arbitration* (TMC Asser Institute, The Hague, 1986) 227, 244 quoted in Nygh (n 83) 230.

[89] Compare: *Coppee Lavalin* (n 84) 51.

In view of the foregoing, a better solution would be if the arbitral tribunals were entitled to make a conflict-of-laws analysis, in order to decide which set of overriding mandatory provisions should apply in competition cases. Such a conflict-of-laws analysis would allow the arbitral tribunals 'to give effect to mandatory provisions claiming application if those rules are enacted by a State having a close relationship with the contract.'[90] Such an approach would also take account of the 'fact that currently approximately 100 countries have enacted their own cartel laws and can therefore—unlike in the past—also prevent restraints of trade effectively.'[91] It would also allow an arbitral tribunal to apply the mandatory rules of the forum which is sufficiently closely connected with the substance of the dispute.[92] As a result, the arbitrators would render an award that is enforceable. It is well established that an award that is not consistent with EU competition law can be denied recognition and enforcement on the ground of public policy.[93] Moreover, the conflict-of-laws analysis will be consistent with s 46(3) of the 1996 Act, which states that 'to the extent that there is no such choice or agreement, the tribunal shall apply the law determined by the conflict of laws rules which it considers applicable.'

The application of conflict-of-laws analysis would also result in EU competition law being applicable to the issue of validity of a contract (or of any term of a contract) that is alleged to be void and illegal as distorting competition in cases where all the relevant elements are connected with the EU irrespective of the law chosen by the parties. But what if Art 101(3) TFEU was raised at issue? Is this provision arbitrable as a matter of EU law?

7.4.1 The Relationship between the Law Applicable to the Substance of Competition Law Dispute and the Issues of Arbitrability

As already clarified, restrictions on arbitrability may stem from the applicable substantive competition laws.[94] Once an arbitral tribunal has determined the law applicable to the merits of an antitrust law dispute, the issue of arbitrability as a matter of substance would need to be addressed. Under Regulation 17/62, it was well settled that arbitrator were not entitled to apply Art 101(3) TFEU, as the Commission had exclusive jurisdiction in this respect.[95] Has this changed after the repeal of Regulation 17/62?

[90] O Lando, 'The *Lex Mercatoria* in international commercial arbitration' (1985) 34 *ICLQ* 747, 767–68. See also: Nygh (n 83) 231–32; Hill (n 1) 696.

[91] J Adolphsen, 'The conflict of laws in cartel matters in a globalised world: alternatives to the effects doctrine' (2005) *Journal of International Private Law* 156, 160.

[92] A Mills, *The Confluence of Public and Private International Law* (CUP, Cambridge, 2009) 290.

[93] See section 7.5.5 below.

[94] See also: Idot (n 4) 53; Maire and Hahn (n 4) 94.

[95] Mustil and Boyd, *Companion Volume* (n 80) 82.

Regulation 1/2003 entitles national courts to apply Art 101(3), but does not mention arbitral tribunals. The DG Comp Staff Working Paper goes further and defines private enforcement as 'enforcement by means of legal action brought by the victim of anti-competitive behaviour before a *court*'[96] (emphasis added). Does this definition suppose that the national courts have exclusive jurisdiction to apply Art 101(3) TFEU in private antitrust enforcement proceedings? Before discussing the arguments pro and contra arbitrability of Art 101(3), the evolution of the Commission's attitude towards the application of EU competition law in arbitration proceedings during the years of centralised antitrust enforcement must receive due regard.

7.4.1.1 Commission's Attitude towards Arbitrating Antitrust Law Disputes under the Old Regime

At one time, the Commission regarded arbitration as a means that could be used by cartel members in order to escape EU competition rules.[97] The confidentiality of arbitral proceedings was the main cause for the Commission's mistrust towards application of EU competition law in arbitration proceedings. This was disclosed by Jacques Werner,[98] who wrote about his discussions with officials from the DG Comp.[99] Commentators also have stated that the confidentiality of arbitration and public mission of competition law are contradictory.[100]

A more positive attitude towards arbitration has subsequently been shown by the Commission.[101] The Commission had also begun to use arbitration proceedings as a tool for monitoring and enforcing certain exemption decisions

[96] See Commission Staff Working Paper SEC 2005 [2]. The omission of arbitration in the Green Paper is criticised in Dechert's *Comment on EU Damages Green Paper*, see LLP http://ec.europa.eu/comm/competition/antitrust/others/actions_for_damages/133.pdf.

[97] A McClellan, 'Commercial Arbitration and European Community Law' (1989) 5 *Arbitration International* 68, 70; L Idot, 'Arbitration and the Reform of Regulation 17/62' in Ehlermann and Atanasiu (n 44) 305; M Bowsher, 'Arbitration and Competition' in T Ward and K Smith (eds), *Competition Litigation in the UK* (Sweet & Maxwell, London, 2005) 398, 410–11. The negative attitude of the Commission towards arbitration in general can be illustrated by its decisions in IV/30.437 *Rockwell/Iveco* [1983] OJ L224/19 and IV/93 *EMO* [1979] OJ L11/16. See also: Commission Regulation (EEC) 2349/84 of 23 July 1984 on the application of Article 85(3) of the Treaty to certain categories of patent licensing agreements (the old Patent Licence Block Exemption Regulation) [1984] OJ L219/15 Art 9(1); Commission Regulation (EEC) 556/89 of 30 November 1988 on the application of Article 85(3) of the Treaty to certain categories of know-how licensing agreements (the old Know-How Block Exemption Regulation) [1989] L61/1 Art 7(1).

[98] The former Vice-Chairman of the ICC Commission on the Law and Practices Relating to Competition.

[99] J Werner, 'Application of Competition Laws by Arbitrators: The Step Too Far' (1995) 12 *Journal of International Arbitration* 21, 23.

[100] Eg HG Gharavi, 'The proper scope of arbitration in European Community Competition Law' (1996) 11 *Tulane European and Civil Law Forum* 185, 202–03.

[101] M Dolmans and J Grierson, 'Arbitration and the Modernisation of EC Antitrust Law: New Opportunities and New Responsibilities' (2003) 14 *ICC International Court of Arbitration Bulletin* 37, 38; Bowsher (n 97) 411. See also: Commission Regulation 1400/2002 on the application of Article 81(3) of the Treaty to categories of vertical agreements and concerted practices in the motor vehicle sector [2002] OJ L203/30 Recital 11.

under the old Regulation 17/62.[102] Furthermore, in EU antitrust and merger control proceedings, arbitral tribunals have adjudicated on the correct implementation or non-implementation of behavioural commitments.[103] It is expected that the Commission could extend this approach also to 'commitment decisions'[104] issued under Regulation 1/2003.[105] Indeed, Ehlermann suggests that in future, the Commission will have to take a more positive approach towards arbitration, as that is important for the success of the enhanced private enforcement of EU competition law.[106]

7.4.1.2 Arbitrability of Art 101(3) TFEU under the New Regime

The key question is to do with the scope of arbitrability of EU competition law issues after the enforcement reform was implemented within the EU. On the one hand, if the silence of Regulation 1/2003 on the issue of arbitrability is regarded as not changing the situation in relation to the application of Art 101(3) in arbitral proceedings, then it will be EU law that is determining arbitrability (ie the principle of supremacy). On the other hand, if the absence of an EU rule governing the issue of arbitrability is interpreted as leaving it for the domestic legal system of each Member State to determine that question, then it will be English law that determines arbitrability (ie the principle of procedural autonomy subject to the principles of effectiveness and equivalence), which will mean that Arts 101 (as a whole) and 102 TFEU would be arbitrable in England.

7.4.1.2.1 Arguments Contra Arbitrability of Art 101(3) TFEU

Not surprisingly, the fact that the issue of arbitration was left out of Regulation 1/2003 resulted in opposing opinions, which were expressed by the commentators, in regard to the scope of arbitrators' jurisdiction with regard to EU competition law claims. According to one view, it would not be reasonable to infer that

[102] Eg IV/30.566 *UIP* [1989] OJ L226/25 [33]; See also: G Blanke, 'The Role of EC Competition Law in International Arbitration: *A Plaidoir*' (2005) 16 *European Business Law Review* 169, 170. See also Case No IV/M.235 *Elf Aquitain—Thyssein/Minol* available in the CELEX database, Document No 392M0235 [13]. See more M Blessing, *Arbitrating Antitrust and Merger Control issues* (Bär & Karrer, Zürich, and Helbing & Lichtenhahn, Basel/Geneva/Munich, 2003) http://www.baerkarrer.ch/upload/publications/4_3_14.pdf.

[103] To date, the use of international arbitration in the context of behavioural commitments is more common than in structural commitments. See C Nisser and G Blanke, 'Reflections on the role of the European Commission as Amicus Curiae in International Arbitration Proceeding' (2006) 27 *European Competition Law Review* 174, 175. See also: G. Blanke, 'International arbitration in EC merger control: a 'supranational' lesson to be learnt' (2006) 27 *European Competition Law Review* 324; G Blanke, 'The use of arbitration in EC merger control: latest developments' (2007) 28 *European Competition Law Review* 673; DA Hofmann and OM Kunz, 'Arbitration clauses proposed by the EU Commission in antitrust and merger procedures—current approach and deficiencies' in T Zuberbuhler and C Oetiker (eds) *Practical Aspects of Arbitrating EC Competition Law* (Schulthess, Basel, 2007) 149–186.

[104] Dolmans and Grierson (n 101) 39. See Art 9 of Regulation 1/2003.

[105] See Nisser and Blanke (n 103).

[106] Ehlermann and Atanasiu (n 44) 303; For a contrary view, however, see R di Brozolo, 'Antitrust: A paradigm of the relations between mandatory rules and arbitration—a fresh look at the "second look"' (2004) *International Arbitration Law Review* 33.

the Commission merely missed the arbitration point.[107] This is reinforced by the fact that the White Paper's gap was identified by Professor Idot[108] and Professor Edward,[109] who was a judge and member of the Court of Justice at that time. Both of them criticised the absence of arbitration in a reform that was meant to encourage private antitrust enforcement. Indeed, the fact that Art 6 of the Regulation refers to national courts but does not mention arbitral tribunals may be regarded as a conscious act, resulting in limitation of arbitrators' jurisdiction with regard to EU competition law claims. Based on that, Maud Piers claims that: 'it is reasonable to conclude from this omission that arbitrators have no power to rule on Article 101(3) exemption petitions.'[110] That deduction may be strengthened by the definition of private enforcement, which was given by the Commission Staff Working Paper. According to it, private enforcement is 'enforcement by means of legal action brought by the victim of anti-competitive behaviour before a *court*' (emphasis added).[111] Thus, non-inclusion of arbitration in Regulation 1/2003 may be interpreted as implicitly precluding arbitrability of Art 101(3).

Possibly inadequate economic knowledge of arbitrators has been raised inter alia as an additional argument against arbitrability of EU competition law issues. For example, it has been claimed that antitrust law claims raise questions that are generally beyond the grasp of the arbitrators, who do not have a sound knowledge of economics.[112] This argument has been justified by limited experience of arbitrators in dealing with Art 101 in general and potentially complicated economic issues that arise in this respect. This argument can be further strengthened in view of the strong economics-based approach with regard to EU competition law enforcement that has been developed during the years of centralised enforcement of Art 101(3) TFEU.[113] The Commission has set a conceptual framework that is meant to improve legal certainty and to facilitate proper economic analysis for antitrust law enforcement purposes. A solid market definition methodology and market structure analysis are at the heart of this framework.[114]

[107] AP Komninos, 'Arbitration and the Modernisation of European Competition Law Enforcement' (2001) 24 *World Competition* 211, 218.

[108] L Idot, 'A French point of view on the radical decentralisation of the implementation of Article 81(1) and (3)' in Claus-Dieter Ehlermann and Isabella Atanasiu (eds), *European Competition Law Annual 2000: The Modernisation of EU Competition Law* (Hart Publishing, Oxford, 2001).

[109] D Edward, 'The Modernisation of EC Antitrust Policy. Issues for Courts and Judges' in Ehlermann and Atanasiu (n 108).

[110] M Piers, 'How EU law affects arbitration and the treatment of consumer disputes: the Belgian example' (Nov 2004–Jan 2005) *Dispute Resolution Journal* 76, 80.

[111] See Commission Staff Working Paper SEC 2005 [2].

[112] Gharavi (n 100) 203–04; See also Werner (n 99) 23; A Riley, 'The Antitrust Modernisation: The Commission does very nicely—Thank you! Part II between the idea and the reality: Decentralisation under Regulation 1' (2003) 24 *European Competition Law Review* 657, 667.

[113] Eg Commission (EC), 'Definition of relevant market for the purposes of Community competition law' (Notice) [1997] OJ C372/5 [17] and [24]. See also S Bishop and M Walker, *The Economics of EC Competition Law: Concepts, Application and Measurement* (2nd edn, Sweet & Maxwell, London, 2002).

[114] D Hildebrand, 'The European School in EC competition law' (2002) 23 *World Competition* 3.

The question of how the Commission would monitor the application of Art 101(3) in arbitral proceedings has been raised.[115] Accordingly, it has been submitted that uniform interpretation and application of EU law is not as well protected in commercial arbitration as it is in national courts, since arbitrators are deprived of the Court of Justice and the Commission assistance.[116] Regulation 1/2003 introduced mechanisms that aim to meet concerns on the consistency of enforcement of EU competition law.[117] The Commission published a number of notices[118] which are addressed to the national competition authorities and national courts and aim to ensure efficient and uniform application of the EU competition rules. The fact that none of the measures in Regulation 1/2003 refers to arbitration may be used to suggest that Art 101(3) should not be arbitrable at all. Accordingly, there appear to be some strong reasons indicating that Art 101(3) should not be arbitrable as a matter of EU law.

The Draft Regulation[119] has given further room for opposing arbitrability of Art 101(3) TFEU. The main arguments for that lay in the text itself. Under Art 6 of the Draft, 'national courts before which the prohibition in Article [101 (1) TFEU] is invoked shall also have jurisdiction to apply Article [101](3)'. This has been interpreted as limiting arbitrators' jurisdiction in regard to Art 101(3) TFEU, since it refers only to national courts. This has been justified by the word 'also', which seems to have been limiting the reform's benefits to the national authorities and national courts covered.[120] This argument has been weakened by the fact that the word 'also' from the Draft Regulation was omitted from the final text of Regulation 1/2003 which states that 'national courts shall have the power to apply Articles [101 and 102 TFEU]'.

7.4.1.2.2 Arguments Pro Arbitrability of Art 101(3) TFEU

There appear to be more academic opinions favouring arbitrability of Art 101 as a whole.[121] Komninos and Idot have claimed that an express provision should have been included, if EU law intended to preclude arbitrators from applying Art 101(3).[122] Such a view is in accord with the common law jurisprudence as outlined in *Mitsubishi*.[123] Nazzini[124] finds another justification of why Regulation

[115] Edward (n 109).

[116] Case 102/81 *Nordsee v Reederei Mond* [1982] ECR 1095. See also: Gharavi (n 100) 204; Hill (n 1) 699. Compare Komninos (n 107) 223–24.

[117] Eg Arts 13, 15 and 16 of Regulation 1/2003.

[118] Commission (EC), 'Co-operation between the Commission and the courts of the EU Member States in the application of Articles 81 and 82 EC' (Notice) [2004] OJ C101/54–64; Commission (EC), 'Co-operation within the Network of Competition Authorities' (Notice) [2004] OJ C101/43–53.

[119] Commission (EC), 'Proposal for a Council Regulation on the implementation of the rules on competition laid down in Articles 81 and 82 of the Treaty' COM (2000) 582.

[120] See more detailed discussion of the Draft provision in Idot (n 97) 317; Komninos (n 107) 221.

[121] Komninos (n 107) 221; Idot (n 97) 316; Dempegiotis (n 80).

[122] Komninos (n 107) 221; Idot (n 97) 316.

[123] *Mitsubishi* (n 3) (473 US 628).

[124] Nazzini (n 72) 335. See the definition of 'the authorities of the Member States' that is given in *BRT* (n 12) [18]–[20].

1/2003 does not refer to arbitration. According to him, the Regulation is aimed at national institutions that are public authorities under EU law, whilst arbitral tribunals are not an authority or court of the Member States. This is indeed what the Court of Justice held in the *Nordsee* case.[125] The statement was subsequently reaffirmed in the *Eco Swiss* case.[126] Thus, the prevailing view is that Regulation 1/2003 does not preclude arbitrability of Art 101(3) TFEU.

Such a deduction can be further reinforced by main aims of the decentralisation reforms which were to synchronise the enforcement of Art 101(3) with that of Art 101(1) and (2) and to lighten the workload of the Commission.[127] More specifically, one of the consequences of the decentralisation reform was to give Art 101(3) direct effect.[128] This can be deduced if the old case law[129] is read in the context of the repealed Regulation 17/62 and the purpose of the current Regulation 1/2003. Before Regulation 17/62 was adopted, the Court of Justice had held clearly that 'in accordance with the text of Article [101](2), which referring to agreements or decisions "prohibited pursuant to this Article" seems to regard Articles [101](1) and (3) as forming an indivisible whole.'[130] This is unconditionally confirmed by Regulation 1/2003. Indeed, before the entry into force of Regulation 17/62, the authorities of the Member States applied the nullifying provisions only in respect of agreements and decisions which had been held to fall under Art 101(1) and had not qualified for exemption under Art 101(3) TFEU.[131] It seems that the repeal of Regulation 17/62 results in restoring the unitary application of Art 101 TFEU by the same authority or court in the course of the same proceedings. Accordingly, the compatibility of the agreement with Art 101(1) and the declaration of inapplicability of the prohibition under Art 101(3) TFEU are to be given by the same body (eg national court or arbitral tribunal).

Therefore, it can be concluded that the direct effect of Art 101 TFEU as a whole follows not only from Regulation 1/2003, but also from the Treaty on the Functioning of the European Union. This could be supported by the opinion of the Advocate General in the *Bosch* case.[132] According to him, it would have been contrary to the most elementary considerations of justice to allow the application of Art 101(1), which is sanctioned with automatic nullity, without allowing the undertaking concerned to avail themselves of the provisions of Art 101(3). Thus, the only obstacle to arbitrability of Art 101(3) was Regulation

[125] *Nordsee* (n 116) [10].

[126] *Eco Swiss* (n 50) [34]. See also: *Nordsee* (n 116) [11]–[12].

[127] Commission (EC), 'Modernisation of the Rules Implementing Articles 81 and 82 of the EC Treaty', Commission Programme No 99/027 (White Paper) COM (1999) 101, OJ [1999] C 132/1 [69] and [73]. The logic of the reform as an argument indicating that Art 81(3) EC is arbitrable is also outlined by Idot (n 97) 317. See also Komninos (n 107) 219–22.

[128] C-D Ehlermann, 'The Modernisation of EC Antitrust Policy: A Legal and Cultural Revolution', (2000) 37 *CML Rev* 537; Komninos (n 107) 222–23; Idot (n 97) 316; Nazzini (n 72) 335.

[129] Case 13/62 *Bosch v Van Rijn* [1962] ECR 45.

[130] Ibid 52.

[131] Ibid.

[132] Ibid 66 (AG Lagrange).

17/62 that gave to the Commission a monopoly to issue an exemption under that provision. The repeal of Regulation 17/62 and the doctrine of direct effect give another good reason for the application of Art 101 TFEU as a whole in arbitral proceedings.[133] To render an enforceable award, after the *Eco Swiss* case, the arbitral tribunals must not only safeguard the prohibition of Art 101(1), but also apply Art 101(3) that creates legal rights that must be safeguarded by the arbitrators.[134]

The arbitrability of Art 101(3) can be further sustained and backed up by some practical considerations.[135] The main one is that if the arbitrators were prevented from applying Art 101(3), then in a dispute over the validity of a contract that includes an arbitration clause it would not be easy to find an effective and appropriate mechanism for determining the antitrust law issues.[136] Under Regulation 1/2003, it would not be possible to submit such cases to either the Commission or an NCA. It is true that it would be still open to turn to the national courts. It should be recalled, however, that after Regulation 17/62 had been repealed, it would not be possible to get issued a separate decision of exemption or declaration of applicability of Art 101(3).[137] Indeed, after the reform, Art 101 TFEU is an indivisible whole and it must be applied as such. In this respect, the existing arbitration agreement and established arbitrability of Art 101(1) and (2) would affect the court's jurisdiction.[138] The difficulties can be illustrated by a simple example, where a defence under Art 101(2) is lodged by a licensee with regard to a claim for payment of royalties that is made by a licensor. In such a case, it would be open to the licensor to claim that their agreement satisfies the conditions of Art 101(3) and is enforceable.[139] Thus, the arbitrators must have a power to judge whether those conditions are satisfied.

Moreover, the submission that arbitrators lack the ability to rule on complicated antitrust issues can be opposed by outlining that arbitrators in deciding cases have always been facing complex legal and economic policy-connected problems.[140] Moreover, Art 6 of Regulation 1/2003 explicitly empowers national judges, who are also the only legal practitioners to apply Art 101(3) TFEU. That

[133] See also Nazzini (n 72) 335.

[134] Compare: *BRT* (n 12) [16]; Case C-282/95 *P Guerin Automobiles v Commission* [1997] ECR I-1503 [39]; Case C-453/99 *Courage v Crehan* [2001] ECR I-6297 [23].

[135] Some practical considerations are also outlined by Komninos to favour arbitrability of Art 101(3) TFEU. See Komninos (n 107) 222–23. See also Nazzini (n 72) 335–37.

[136] Idot (n 97) 317.

[137] See more: A Komninos, *EC Private Antitrust Enforcement: Decentralised Application of EC Competition Law by National Courts* (Hart Publishing, Oxford, 2008) 86–87. According to Komninos, '[t]o speak of a competence to apply Article [101(3)] no longer makes sense.' See Komninos (n 136) 86.

[138] See s 9 of the 1996 Act. For Scotland, see Art 8 of Model Law in sch 7 of Law Reform (Miscellaneous Provisions) (Scotland) Act 1990.

[139] Art 1 of Regulation 1/2003.

[140] Eg investment disputes for an alleged unlawful expropriation—ICSID Case No ARB/03/16 *ADC v The Republic of Hungary;* ICSID Case No ARB/04/15 *Telenor Mobile Communications v The Republic of Hungary.*

was adopted despite the fact that the judges' ability to deal with difficult antitrust law issues had been questioned.[141] For that reason, it has been argued that if judges are competent to apply Art 101 as a whole, it is difficult to give any compelling reason why arbitrators cannot adjudicate such competition law issues.[142] Arguments favouring arbitrators' ability to deal with competition law issues can also emerge from the American experience, where the arbitrability of antitrust law issues is well settled.[143]

In addition, international arbitrators frequently are drawn from the legal as well as the business community. In cases where the dispute has an important EU competition law component, the parties and their counsellors with whose assistance they have agreed to settle their dispute can be expected to select arbitrators accordingly.[144] In addition, arbitrators may always appoint economic or legal advisers to assist them.[145] Professor Lowenfeld goes further and describes as a 'myth' the submission that complicated issues such as those arising under antitrust laws could not be dealt with by arbitrators.[146]

Furthermore, it seems that the increased flexibility of the arbitral procedure could well suit an EU competition law dispute. It has been submitted in this context that arbitral tribunals avail themselves of much more extensive powers of discovery than some national courts in Europe.[147] Although the mechanisms that aim to meet concerns on the consistency of enforcement of EU competition law contained in Regulation 1/2003[148] and the subsequently published Commission's notices[149] make no reference to arbitration, it would be for the national courts to support and supervise the application of EU competition law by arbitral tribunals.[150] Thus, it seems that the problem is more to do with identification of the mechanisms in Regulation 1/2003 that are applicable in arbitral proceedings and the appropriate mechanisms need to be identified.[151]

It can be concluded that there is nothing in EU law and in particular Regulation 1/2003 to preclude arbitrability of Arts 101 (as a whole) and 102 TFEU. The silence of the Regulation taken together with the rationale of the reform and the principle of procedural autonomy suggest that the question of arbitrability of

[141] See more HM Gilliams, 'Modernisation: from policy to practice' (2003) 28 *EL Rev* 451, 457.

[142] Komninos (n 107) 223; Idot (n 97) 315–17. See also Nazzini (n 72) 336.

[143] See C Jones, *Private Enforcement of Antitrust Law in the EU, UK and USA* (OUP, Oxford, 1999) 85. See also *Mitsubishi* (n 3) (473 US 635–37).

[144] *Mitsubishi* (n 3); Dolmans and Grierson (n 101) 49.

[145] Eg ss 37 of the 1996 Act. See also Dolmans and Grierson (n 101) 49.

[146] AF Lowenfeld, 'The *Mitsubishi* case: another view' (1986) 2 *Arbitration International* 178, 182.

[147] See Komninos (n 107) 222; Panel Discussion Three in Ehlermann and Atanasiu (n 44) 297. See also ss 34(2)(d) and 42 of the 1996 Act.

[148] Eg Arts 13, 15 and 16 of Regulation 1/2003.

[149] Commission (EC) 'Co-operation between the Commission and the courts of the EU Member States in the application of Articles 81 and 82 EC' (Notice) [2004] OJ C101/54–64; Commission (EC) 'Co-operation within the Network of Competition Authorities (Notice) [2004] OJ C101/43–53.

[150] This is due to the public policy character of EU competition law. See more section 7.5.5 below.

[151] For a detailed discussion of the available mechanisms for maintaining uniform and efficient private EU competition law enforcement, see sections 7.5 and 7.6 below.

EU competition law claims is left for the domestic legal system of each Member State.[152] The principle of national procedural autonomy is subject to the principles of effectiveness and equivalence. Accordingly, when determining the question of arbitrability, the Member States must not make 'practically impossible or excessively difficult the exercise of rights conferred by EU law'.[153] It seems though that even if explicitly adopted by a Member State, the non-arbitrability of EU competition law claims would not have such an effect because what could not be settled by arbitration may still be decided in national courts. If, however, competition law issues were not arbitrable, then the arbitral tribunals would have to stay proceedings and refer the question to national courts. Inevitably, this will result in delay and parties will incur higher costs, but parties should have been aware of that when selecting the seat of arbitration. Based on that, it can be concluded that it will be for English law to determine the arbitrability of Art 101 and as a matter of English law Arts 101 (as a whole) and 102 TFEU are arbitrable.

7.4.2 The Law Applicable to the Substance of a Competition Law Dispute and the Assessment of Antitrust Damage

As already mentioned, if the arbitration clause is broad enough, an arbitral tribunal may have jurisdiction over a claim for invalidity of a contract that is brought together with a contingent tortious claim for antitrust damages. The question is what law would govern the assessment of competition law damages. It seems that in the context of the assessment of damages, the EU is moving towards non-binding guidance for the courts.[154] Such guidelines may well be used by arbitral tribunals as well. However, even though it is out of doubt that a person who is injured by a contract liable to restrict or distort competition would be able to seek compensatory damages, punitive antitrust damages may be available in some national legal orders,[155] but not in others. There is no doubt that a tribunal sitting in England and applying English law would be entitled to award punitive antitrust damages for a breach of Arts 101 and/or 102 TFEU.[156] But what if an arbitral tribunal based in England applied US Federal antitrust law to invalidate

[152] Case C-261/95 *Palmisani* [1995] ECR I-4025 [27]; *Courage* (n 134) [29]. See also: Mustill and Boyd (n 2) 149–150; Nazzini (n 72) 334.

[153] Joined Cases C-295/04 to C-298/04 *Vincenzo Manfredi v Lloyd Adriatico Assicuriazioni* [2006] 5 CMLR 17 [62]. For the principle of effectiveness, which could be used to limit Member States' procedural autonomy see more: F Becker, 'Application of Community law by Member States' public authorities: between autonomy and effectiveness' (2007) 44 *CML Rev* 1035.

[154] Oxera and multi-jurisdictional team of lawyers led by Dr A Komninos, 'Quantifying antitrust damages: towards non-binding guidance for courts—Study prepared for the European Commission' http://ec.europa.eu/competition/antitrust/actionsdamages/quantification_study.pdf.

[155] Under English law, exemplary or punitive damages are available in stand-alone antitrust actions. See *Devenish Nutrition Ltd v Sanofi-Aventis SA* [2007] EWHC 2394; [2008] 2 WLR 637 (Ch) [18]; aff'd [2008] EWCA Civ 1086; [2009] 3 WLR 198 (CA).

[156] DStJ Sutton, J Gill and M Gearing, *Russell on Arbitration* (23rd edn, Sweet & Maxwell, London, 2007) [6–104].

a contract which was closely connected with the US? Can arbitrators sitting in England go further and apply US law awarding treble damages?[157] It was demonstrated that in private antitrust proceedings before national courts, Recital 32 of the Rome II Regulation could be used to reduce the effect of the applicable law, entitling the court not to give effect to *lex causae,* if the awarded damage would be non-compensatory and excessive under *lex fori.*[158]

On the one hand, arbitral tribunals do not a have a forum.[159] This may suggest that a tribunal sitting in England and applying US antitrust law may be entitled to award treble-damages if the arbitration clause is widely drafted,[160] because this remedy, being a chief tool in the US antitrust enforcement scheme, can be sought outside American courts.[161] Although the arbitrators do not have a forum, they should render an enforceable award.[162] However, as already outlined, an award of multiple damages could infringe the Protection of Trading Interests Act 1980 and be against English public policy,[163] so that such an award may be set aside by the English court to the extent it is contrary to English public policy.[164] In support of that it can be claimed that '[i]f an award is set aside by the courts of the seat the award will generally cease to be enforceable in other countries under the New York Convention.'[165] This could be a very strong argument against the possibility for arbitrators sitting in England to award treble antitrust damages.

On the other hand, it is well established that even if the courts of the seat of arbitration had set aside an arbitral award, the court of the country where the recognition and enforcement is sought would not be obliged to follow the decision of the court at the seat of arbitration.[166] Indeed, Art V(1)(e) of the NYC gives discretion to the recognising court on whether to deny recognition and enforcement of an award that has been set aside by the court at the seat of arbitration. An important consideration in the latter context would be the ground on which the arbitral award was set aside by the foreign court. If the award was set aside on

157 *Redfern and Hunter on International Arbitration* (n 1) 528–31.

158 M Danov, 'Awarding exemplary (or punitive) antitrust damages in EC competition cases with an international element—the Rome II Regulation and the Commission's White Paper on damages' (2008) 29 *European Competition Law Review* 430, 432.

159 See: Nygh (n 83) 226–28; Hill (n 1) 695; P. Landolt, *Modernised EC Competition Law in International Arbitration* (Kluwer Law International, The Hague, 2006) 128.

160 *Russell on Arbitration* (n 156) [6-104]; *Redfern and Hunter on International Arbitration* (n 1) [9.45].

161 *Mitsubishi* (n 3) (473 US 635).

162 Eg see Art 32(2) of the London Court of International Arbitration Rules; Art 35 of the ICC Rules of Arbitration.

163 See ch 5, section 5.3.3 above. See also: CGJ Morse, 'Torts in private international law: a new statutory framework' (1996) 45 *ICLQ* 888, 895; A Dickinson, *The Rome II Regulation: The Law Applicable to Non-contractual Obligations* (OUP, Oxford, 2008) 408.

164 *Russell on Arbitration* (n 156) [6-106].

165 Hill (n 1) 696. See also: *Russell on Arbitration* (n 156) [6-106].

166 Eg *Pabalk Ticaret v Norsolor* (1985) 24 *International Legal Materials* 360–65; *Chromalloy Aeroservices, A Division of Chromalloy Gas Turbine Corp (US) v The Arab Republic of Egypt* 939 F Supp 907 DDC (1996). See also: Nygh (n 83) 228–29; T Varady, JJ Barcelo and AT von Mehren, *International Commercial Arbitration* (3rd edn, Thomson West, Minnesota, 2006) 857–74; Petrochilos (n 35) 309–13.

the ground that treble damages are against English public policy, it is difficult to see why an American court should refuse recognition of enforcement of the award which had taken account of the fact that treble damages are an important element of the US enforcement regime.

Furthermore, despite the fact that an arbitral award of treble damages may not enforceable on the public policy ground under the New York Convention in some countries,[167] one should note that the question of the assessment of antitrust damages and available remedies before an arbitral tribunal would arise after the antitrust breach had been established by the arbitrators applying US antitrust law. At this stage the arbitrators may well infer where the recognition and enforcement of an arbitral award would be sought. Therefore, it seems that an arbitral tribunal sitting in England would have the power to award treble damages if it were clear from the facts that the losing party had assets in the US and the award would, most probably, be enforced there. This would clearly be so in cases where the parties' arbitration agreement was sufficiently wide to encompass the determination of antitrust claims under US federal law.[168]

7.5 Jurisdiction of English Courts in Proceedings Ancillary to Arbitration in Relation to EU Competition Law Claims

It has been submitted that the lack of special institutional support by the Commission and the Court of Justice would result in imperfect, inefficient and non-uniform enforcement of EU competition law in arbitral proceedings.[169] The lack of such support has been raised as an argument against arbitrability of Arts 101 and/or 102 TFEU.[170] Although, in the light of the foregoing arguments, the lack or the existence of special institutional support will not affect the arbitrability of EU competition law claims, the purpose of this section is to consider the availability of appropriate mechanisms that may ensure that arbitral tribunals may be regarded as an alternative forum for private EU competition law enforcement. In this context, the important role that is to be played by national courts in proceedings ancillary to arbitration in relation to Arts 101 and/or 102 TFEU claims should be emphasised.

It is well established that despite an arbitration agreement and the fact that an arbitral tribunal has jurisdiction, the English courts may have jurisdiction with

[167] *Redfern and Hunter on International Arbitration* (n 1) [9.49].
[168] Ibid [9.45].
[169] Compare the claims made by Gharavi (n 100) 204; JH Dalhuisen, 'The Arbitrability of Competition Issues' (1995) 11 *Arbitration International* 151, 158; Hill (n 1) 698–99.
[170] See Gharavi (n 100) 204.

regard to some ancillary matters under CPR 62.2.[171] An 'arbitration claim'[172] for these purposes normally has to be commenced in the High Court.[173] Although that form of assistance by the courts with regard to arbitration proceedings is irrespective of the peculiarities of EU competition law, it will be of importance to its uniform and efficient private enforcement.[174]

Accordingly in this section, first, the court support as regards ordering provisional measures, taking evidence and making reference to the Court of Justice will be examined below. Secondly, the powers of the English court to set aside domestic awards in relation to an EU competition law claim and recognition of foreign awards concerned with such claims[175] will be examined. The public policy character of Arts 101 and 102 TFEU for those purposes will be duly outlined as well.

7.5.1 Support by the Court as Regards Provisional Measures

For example, in EU competition law claims, damages could arise out of loss of business opportunities.[176] Such heads of the claim seem to be difficult to prove and quantify.[177] An injunction preserving the status quo and restraining illegal conduct and/or practice that is in conflict with EU competition law until the arbitral tribunal can make its final award crucial in this scenario. The importance of such an order can be illustrated by way of a simple example. An English distributor may sell a particular product under a distributorship agreement concluded with a non-EU manufacturer. Subsequently, the distributor may find out that the agreement is in breach of EU competition law, since it restricts his ability to determine the sale price and aims at driving him out of business, as a take-over of his distributorship network is contemplated by the manufacture through another distributor. Based on that, the distributor may make an EU competition law claim before the arbitral tribunal and seek an injunction that should restrain the foreign manufacturer from imposing any condition intended to distort competition. He may go further, and

[171] ss 2(3), 43, 44 of the 1996 Act. See also CPR 62.2. For Scotland, see Art 27 of the Model Law in sch 7 of Law Reform (Miscellaneous Provisions) (Scotland) Act 1990. See also: *Sokana Industries v Freyere* [1994] 2 Lloyd's Rep 57. See more Hill (n 1) 678. See also Petrochilos (n 35) 91–93 and 100–07.

[172] '[A]ny application to the court under the Arbitration Act' is to be regarded as an arbitration claim under CPR 62.2(1)(a).

[173] High Court and County Courts (Allocation of Arbitration Proceedings) Order 1996 (SI 1996/3215); High Court and County Courts (Allocation of Arbitration Proceedings) (Amendment) Order 1999 (SI 1999/1010). The general rule is that a claim form should be served on a respondent personally within the jurisdiction. If the claim form cannot be served in England, then the court permission for service out of jurisdiction may be sought. The CPR 62.5 lists the types of applications, which may be served abroad. See also *Sumitomo Heavy Industry* (n 26).

[174] See A Komninos, 'Assistance to Arbitral Tribunals in the Application of EC Competition Law' in Ehlermann and Atanasiu (n 44) 363–85.

[175] A claim to enforce a New York Convention award would not be considered as an arbitration claim, so it is dealt with after an application is made under CPR 62.18. See also CPR 62.2.

[176] *Manfredi* (n 153) [100].

[177] *Redfern and Hunter on International Arbitration* (n 1) [7.46].

seek a 'freezing' order[178] restraining the defendants from disposing of any property in England and preventing him from defeating any ultimate judgment by removing his assets from the jurisdiction. What are the powers of the arbitral tribunal with regard to making such orders or awards in EU competition law claims?

The trend goes to arbitral tribunals granting provisional measures themselves.[179] This is reflected in s 39(1) of the 1996 Act, which provides that an arbitral tribunal may order on a provisional basis any relief they would have the power to grant on a final award. Such provisional orders would be subject to adjustment as necessary when the arbitrators make their final award.[180] Section 48 details the remedies that may be given by the arbitrators on the merits. More specifically, s 48(5)(a) states that 'the tribunal has the same powers as the court to order a party to do or refrain from doing anything'. Thus, it seems that s 39 read together with s 48 would cover a provisional order restraining a foreign manufacturer from imposing conditions intended to distort competition.

There is, however, no clarity with regard to the powers of an arbitral tribunal to make a freezing order under s 39. One view seems to allow that the parties could agree under s 39(1) to give arbitrators power to make on a provisional basis such an order.[181] According to another opinion,[182] however, s 39(1) would confer no power on arbitrators to make a freezing order, even with the parties' agreement. This claim is supported by the fact that s 39(1) only relates to a power to order on a provisional basis the relief which an arbitral tribunal can grant in a final award under s 48(5)(a). Further, a freezing order cannot be made under s 48(5)(a) because this provision is confined to final awards and substantive remedies on the merits.[183] Therefore, there are strong arguments suggesting that an arbitral tribunal based in England cannot make a 'freezing' order under ss 39 and/or 48 of the 1996 Act.

Accordingly, an application for a freezing order for the purposes and in relation to arbitral proceedings must be made to a national court under s 44(2)(e). Section 2(3) provides that powers conferred on courts by s 44 apply even if the seat of arbitration is outside England or no seat has been designated or determined.

[178] CPR 25(1)(f); *Channel Tunnel* (n 30); *Fourie v Le Roux* [2007] UKHL 1; [2007] 1 WLR 320 (HL). See also N Andrews, *English Civil Procedure: Fundamental of the New Civil Justice System* (OUP, Oxford, 2003) 423–53.

[179] Eg Art 17 of the UNCITRAL Model Law on International Commercial Arbitration. Art 17 of the Model Law is adopted in sch 7 of the Law Reform (Miscellaneous Provisions) (Scotland) Act 1990. However, there might be competition cases in which a party may need to obtain if the provisionsal measures from the courts. See more Gaillard and Savage (eds), *Fouchard, Gaillard, Goldman on International Commercial Arbitration* (Kluwer Law, The Hague/Boston/London, 1999) 720–28.

[180] See s 39(3) of the 1996 Act.

[181] *Russell on Arbitration* (n 156) [5-077 and 5-085]. See also Departmental Advisory Committee on Arbitration Law, *Report on the Arbitration Bill February 1996 & Supplementary report of Arbitration Act January 1997* (Department of Trade and Industry, London, 1997) [203].

[182] Mustil and Boyd, *Companion Volume* (n 80) 330–31. See also Report on the Arbitration Bill (n 181) [201].

[183] *Kastner v Jason* [2004] EWCA Civ 1599; [2005] 1 Lloyd's Rep 397 [16] (CA). See also Mustil and Boyd (n 2) 315; *Russell on Arbitration* (n 156) [5-077].

This seems to be in accord with Art 31 of the Brussels Regulation, which entitles the English court to grant provisional measures in the European context, to support of arbitration proceedings taking place outside of England.[184] Hill has pointed out the difficulties in defining the relationship between s 44 of the 1996 Act and Art 31 of the Brussels I Regulation as interpreted by the Court of Justice in *Van Uden Maritime*.[185] It has been submitted that:

> Even if the Court of Justice's view on provisional measures in support of arbitration proceedings is accepted as correct, this part of the judgment is not easy to interpret. However, its implications would appear to be, first, that in cases where the defendant is domiciled in a member state, the English courts' powers under section 44 of the 1996 Act are limited to granting measures which can be regarded as 'provisional' as that term is understood by the Court and, secondly, the grant of provisional measures under section 44 is conditional on the existence of a real connecting link between the subject-matter of the measures sought and the territorial jurisdiction of the English court.[186]

In other words, a provisional measure would only be granted under Art 31 of Brussels I if the sought measure is 'intended to preserve a factual or legal situation so as to safeguard rights'[187] and/or there was 'a real connecting link between the subject-matter of the measures sought and territorial jurisdiction of the [English] court.'[188] If a provisional measure could not be granted under Art 31 of Brussels I, then a provisional measure may still be granted by the English court if the applicant, who wishes to apply for interim relief, could show why an English court is the 'natural forum' to grant the relief sought. According to Lord Mustill, in cases where the seat of arbitration is located in a foreign country, the court of that country is 'the natural forum for the source of interim relief'.[189]

In any case, if the seat of arbitration is England, then the English court would certainly be the natural to grant a provisional measure under s 44 of the 1996 Act. In the *Lauritzencool* case,[190] a plaintiff applied under s 44(2)(e) for an interim injunction to preserve the status quo. The court proceedings were ancillary to an arbitration, where an alleged breach of Art 101 TFEU was also an issue. The test for an interim injunction as put forward in *American Cyanamid v Ethicon*[191] refers to the question whether a plaintiff could be adequately compensated in damages should the uncertainties be resolved in his favour. Applying this test

184 Case C-391/95 *Van Uden Maritime v Firma Deco-Line* [1998] ECR I-7091 [25] and [33]. CPR 6.19.

185 Hill (n 1) 336, 678 and 679.

186 Hill (n 1) 336.

187 *Van Uden Maritime* (n 184) [37]. See also Case C-261/90 *Reichert and Dresdner Bank*, Case C-261/90, [1992] ECR I-2149.

188 *Van Uden Maritime* (n 184) [40].

189 *Channel Tunnel* (n 30) 368. Compare *Spiliada Maritime Corp v Cansulex* [1987] AC 460 (HL) 476.

190 *Lauritzencool v Lady Navigation* [2004] EWHC 2607 (Comm); [2005] 1 260 (QBD (Comm)); aff'd [2005] EWCA Civ 579; [2005] 2 Lloyd's Rep 63 (CA).

191 *American Cyanamid v Ethicon* [1975] AC 396 (HL) 406 and 408. See also *Bath and North East Somerset v Mowlem* [2004] EWCA Civ 115; [2004] BLR 153 (CA) [11].

in the *Lauritzencool* case, the court concluded that the questions which arose in the arbitration were serious issues to be tried, and held that damages would not be adequate to compensate the plaintiff for the loss unless an injunction was granted.[192] By contrast, damages would be an adequate remedy for the defendants if the injunction was wrongfully granted.[193] Thus, the court granted an injunction to preserve the status quo in support of arbitration proceedings.

In the light of the foregoing, it can be concluded that in most cases under English law the arbitrators may themselves order the appropriate provisional measures. Where that is not possible, the support of the court may be sought. However, interim relief measures are discretionary and require a consideration of a number of issues, so every case would have to be assessed individually.

7.5.2 Support by the Court as Regards Taking Evidence

Discovery of certain documents that are necessary to establish the facts of a case may be of huge importance in EU competition law claims. By the repeal of s 12(6) of the 1950 Act, the disclosure questions have been taken from the court and have been given to the arbitral tribunal.[194] This is recognised by ss 33 and 34 of the 1996 Act. More specifically, s 34(2)(d) explicitly states that disclosure is a matter for the arbitral tribunal. If the tribunal does decide to make an order under s 34(2)(d), it must be careful to set out clearly what a respondent party must do.[195] In a case where the parties are reluctant to co-operate, then an arbitrator can go through a peremptory order under s 41. If the party fails to comply with that order, then the English court could intervene under s 42 and make an order requiring a party to comply with the peremptory order made by the tribunal. It should be noted that s 42 does not provide the court with jurisdiction to order a discovery, but merely to order that a party complies with the arbitrator's order.[196]

Nevertheless, some difficulties may be encountered by arbitral tribunals when arbitrators are trying to take and preserve evidence with regard to EU competition law arbitral proceedings. This is due to the fact that, for example, an arbitral tribunal does not possess a power to compel the attendance of relevant witnesses.[197] Furthermore, an arbitration agreement is concerned just with the relationships between the parties. This will prevent an arbitral tribunal from issuing orders to third parties.[198] It is therefore sometimes necessary to apply to the court for an

[192] *Lauritzencool* (HC) (n 190) [58].

[193] Ibid [59].

[194] *BNP Paribas v Deloitte and Touche* [2003] EWHC 2874, [2004] 1 Lloyd's Rep 233 [13] (QBD (Comm)).

[195] *Morris v Redland Bricks* [1970] AC 652 (HL) 664–67 (Lord Upjohn). See also DM Cato, *Arbitration Practice and Procedure: interlocutory and hearing problems* (2nd edn, LLP, London, 1997) 974.

[196] Cato (n 195) 686.

[197] Compare s 43(2) of the 1996 Act. See more: *Redfern and Hunter on International Arbitration* (n 1) [5.10]–[5.13].

[198] See *Fouchard, Gaillard, Goldman* (n 179) 727.

order to produce evidence,[199] since EU competition law claims often involve third parties.[200] The court of the country where the seat of arbitration is located would be the natural forum that should provide assistance in obtaining evidence from the third parties in antitrust claims.[201]

The 1996 Act provides for assistance by the English court in obtaining third party evidence at the request of a party to arbitral proceedings, if arbitration hearings are held in England. Section 43(1) states that the same court procedures as are available in relation to legal proceedings can be used to secure the attendance before the tribunal of a witness in order to give oral testimony or to produce documents or other material evidence. The court has a discretionary power to order a witness to produce evidence on the basis of Art 43 in support of foreign arbitral proceedings. This follows from s 2(3), which specifies that s 43 applies at the discretion of the English courts even if the seat of arbitration is outside England and Wales.[202] It is well settled that the courts of the place of arbitration—and not the arbitrators themselves—may request the assistance of English courts.[203] Section 43(3), however, limits the application of s 43(1) by providing that these court procedures may only be used if the witness is in the UK and the arbitral proceedings are being conducted in England or Wales. Court intervention may also be necessary if the evidence is situated in a third country. It seems that the limitation in s 43(3) could be significant in regard to EU competition cases where the witnesses and evidence are in different jurisdictions. This would be a concern if the court at the place of the witnesses' domicile does not have a power to order a witness to produce evidence in support of arbitral proceedings in England.

The witness summons to produce documents under s 43 must make clear to the witness what is required of him. Accordingly, the documents to be produced must be identified with sufficient certainty to leave no real doubt in the mind of the witness about what he is required to do.[204] In this context, it should be outlined that the witness may face penal sanctions if he fails to comply with the witness summons. It seems that s 43(1) may well be relied on in cases where the proof of an EU competition law infringement requires specific documents to be present by a number of third parties.[205]

199 Ibid.

200 Eg trade associations, other competitors.

201 See more TH Webster, 'Obtaining evidence from third parties in international arbitration' (2001) 17 *Arbitration International* 143–63.

202 The UNCITRAL Model Law, however, does not provide such assistance. (See Art 27, but read it together with Art 1(2).) See more Webster (n 190) 146.

203 See in particular M Rubino-Sammartano, *International Arbitration Law and Practice* (Kluwer Law, The Hague/London/Boston, 2001) 399.

204 *Tajik Aluminium Plant v Hydro Aluminium* [2005] EWCA Civ 1218; [2006] Lloyd's Rep 155 (CA) [28].

205 This could be of use when the alleged breach of competition law involves collusive behaviour by a party to the arbitration and third parties.

It should be pointed out, however, that s 43 does not give the court a power to order a disclosure from a third party in respect of arbitration proceedings.[206] An 'order for disclosure made against a third party' must be distinguished from 'witness summons to produce documents' under s 43(1), which can be ordered by the court.[207] An order for disclosure normally directs the person to whom it is addressed to carry out a reasonable search for documents in his possession falling within classes which are often broadly described and to list them for the information of the parties to the proceedings. By contrast, under the witness summons to produce documents, the person is obliged to bring the documents to which the summons refers to court, not simply to list them or make them available for inspection.

It appears that arbitrators may well be dependent on the assistance of the English courts with regard to taking evidence in EU competition law claims, especially in a case where evidence from third parties must be collected. Notwithstanding, the 1996 Act sets appropriate mechanisms which may well be used by parties and arbitral tribunals to obtain assistance in taking evidence. Therefore, it can be concluded that as far as interim relief and taking of evidence are concerned, arbitral tribunals with the assistance of the English court can be an appropriate and efficient alternative forum of private antitrust enforcement.

7.5.3 Reference to the Court of Justice through the English Courts

The preliminary reference procedure of Art 267 TFEU (ex Art 234 TEC) entitles the Member State court or tribunal to request the Court of Justice to give ruling on interpretation of EU competition law, which is necessary to enable that court or tribunal to give its judgment. This mechanism is set to preserve the EU character of the law established by the Treaties and 'has the object of ensuring that in all circumstances this law is the same in all States of the [EU].'[208] It is expected that this procedure will be used more often by national courts applying Art 101(3), at least initially.[209] The question of whether an arbitration tribunal, whose award depends on the validity of a contract under EU law, is authorised to make a preliminary reference to the Court of Justice arose in the *Nordsee* case. In this case, the Court of Justice held that an arbitral tribunal is not a 'court or tribunal of a Member State' within the meaning of Art 267 TFEU.[210] The *Nordsee*

[206] *BNP Paribas* (n 194) [12]. See also *Tajik Aluminium Plant* (n 204) [26].

[207] *Tajik Aluminium Plant* (n 204) [24].

[208] Case 166/73 *Rheinmuhlen* [1974] ECR 33, 38.

[209] D Edward, 'Reform of Article 234 Procedure: The Limits of the Possible', in O'Keeffe and Bavasso (eds), *Liber Amicorum in Honour of Lord Slynn of Hadley, Judicial Review in European Union Law* (Kluwer Law, The Hague/London/Boston, 2000) vol 1.

[210] *Nordsee* (n 116) [10]–[12]; *Eco Swiss* (n 50) [34]. See also Case C-54/96 *Dorsh Consult* [1997] ECR I-496; [1998] 2 CMLR 237 [23]; Case C-516/99 *Schmid* [2002] ECR I-4573; [2004] 3 CMLR 12 [34]. On the Art 234 EC debate in view of the court's increasing workload, see Edward (n 209); see also Komninos (n 174) 368.

ruling was recently confirmed by the Court of Justice.[211] Nevertheless, *Nordsee* has been criticised as denying the possibility for arbitrators to receive a preliminary ruling with regard to some important EU competition law cases that may be brought before the arbitral tribunals.[212] Indeed, some commentators claimed that this position should have been abandoned, since it could lead to inconsistent application of EU competition law.[213] Is it really so?

In the *Nordsee* case, it was held that:

> [I]f questions of [EU] law are raised in an arbitration resorted to by agreement the ordinary courts may be called upon to examine them either in the context of their collaboration with arbitration tribunals, in particular in order to assist them in certain procedural matters or to interpret the law applicable, or in the course of review of arbitration award.[214]

Thus, the Court of Justice has contemplated the possibility for making a reference to the Court of Justice through national courts. Under English law, ordinary courts may often be called upon to intervene in arbitration proceedings. More specifically, the preliminary question on EU law could be brought by arbitral tribunals before the Court of Justice indirectly through the English courts at three stages. First, this may happen while the arbitration is still going on in the form of a request by the arbitrator for assistance under s 45 of the 1996 Act. Secondly, a preliminary reference could be made through s 69 that provides a mechanism for a party to appeal to the court on a question of law arising out of an award. Finally, EU law may be raised when setting aside or at the stage recognition and enforcement of an arbitral award is sought before the English court. In this section the scope for arbitral tribunals to request indirect preliminary reference to the Court of Justice through English courts will be discussed, and the appropriate rules will be considered below.

Under s 45 of the 1996 Act, a party to arbitration proceedings may apply to the court to determine any question of law. There are three conditions that must be satisfied by the applicant.[215] First of all, the question of law must arise out of arbitration proceedings. The term 'question of law' in the meaning of s 45 is defined by s 82(1) as the law of England and Wales.[216] It is beyond doubt that EU competition law is an integral part of English law.[217] Secondly, the question

[211] Case C-125/04 *Denuit v Transorient* [2005] ECR I-923 [12]–[13].

[212] D Marugg and SB Kaimakliotis, 'Parallel Proceedings' in Zuberbuhler and Oetiker (n 103) 71, 75.

[213] G Bebr, 'Arbitration tribunals and Article 177 of the EEC Treaty' (1985) 22 *CML Rev* 489, 504; Gharavi (n 100) 201. See also: F-B Weigand, 'Evading EC Competition Law by Resorting to Arbitration?' (1993) 9 *Arbitration International* 249, 253.

[214] *Nordsee* (n 116) [14]. Nazzini interprets the *Nordsee* ruling as launching a 'second look doctrine' as adopted by the US Supreme Court in *Mitsubishi* (n 3) (473 US 638). See Nazzini (n 72) 331. See also Komninos (n 174) 374; Dempegiotis (n 80) 387.

[215] *Taylor Woodrow Holding v Barnes & Eliott* [2006] EWHC 1693 (TCC) [54].

[216] Cato (n 195) 1128.

[217] Case 26/62 *Van Gend en Loos* [1963] ECR 1, 12. See Komninos (n 174) 375. Compare Liebscher, 'European Public Policy after *Eco Swiss*' (1999) 10 *American Review of International Arbitration* 81, 86.

of law must substantially affect the rights of the parties. It seems that this would be easily satisfied where the requirements of Art 267 TFEU are met.[218] Thirdly, the agreement of all parties to arbitration would be required. If not all parties agree about that, then the permission of the arbitral tribunal will be required. The English court would have discretion as to whether the question of law is to be determined once the above-mentioned conditions have been satisfied. This follows from the word 'may' in the first line of s 45.[219] Moreover, it has been held that 'the judge has to consider the application on its merits. If he is not satisfied that the question of law proposed for determination ought to be determined at that stage he should refuse the application.'[220] The inability of arbitrators to make a reference to the Court of Justice must be among the factors that are to be taken into account by English courts when deciding whether to make an application for such a preliminary reference.[221]

A preliminary reference may also be made to the Court of Justice through the English court under s 69 of the 1996 Act, which provides a mechanism for an appeal on substance from an award to be made to the court.[222] Section 69(3), however, confers judicial discretion to refuse leave to appeal from an arbitrator's award in the face of objection by any of the parties.[223] In view of that, the applicant must identify a question of law which the arbitral tribunal has wrongly decided.[224] The court must decide 'any question of law arising from an award' on the basis of findings of fact that are made by the arbitral tribunal.[225] Moreover, for a permission to be given the point of law should be capable of a serious argument.[226] A strong prima facie case that the arbitrators have misinterpreted or misapplied Art 101 TFEU would clearly constitute an error of law and would allow such questions to be appealed under s 69. Alternatively, the applicant must show that 'the question is one of general public importance and the tribunal is at least open to serious doubt'.[227] The latter requirement may be easily satisfied in cases where there is prima facie evidence from one side that the award is based on an agreement that is in conflict with Art 101 TFEU. Once the case is before the court, then the requirements that are put forward by Art 267 TFEU must be also satisfied before a preliminary application is made through s 69 procedure. A very good

[218] See Komninos (n 174) 374. See also O Chukwumerije, 'Judicial Supervision of Commercial Arbitration: The English Arbitration Act of 1996' (1999) 15 *Arbitration International* 171, 181.

[219] *Taylor Woodrow* (n 215) [56].

[220] *Babanaft International v Avant Petroleum* [1982] 1 WLR 871 (CA) 882.

[221] Compare A Arnull, 'Reference to the European Court' (1990) 15 *EL Rev* 375, 377.

[222] Hill (n 1) 698.

[223] See *Pioneer Shipping v BTP Tioxide* [1982] AC 724 (HL); *Antanios Compania Naviera v Salen Rederierna* [1985] AC 191 (HL); See also C Lewis, 'Leave to appeal under the Arbitration Act 1979' (1982) *Lloyd's Maritime and Commercial Law Quarterly* 271; DR Thomas, 'The Antanios: The Nema guidelines reconsidered' (1985) *JBL* 200.

[224] See s 69(3)(c)(i) of the 1996 Act. *Surefire Systems v Guardian ECL* [2005] EWHC 1860; [2005] BLR 534 (TCC) [32].

[225] *The 'Baleares'* [1993] 1 Lloyd's Rep 215 (CA) 228 (Lord Steyn).

[226] *Bulk Oil v Sun International* [1984] 1 WLR 147 (CA) 154 (Ackner LJ).

[227] See s 69(3)(c)(ii) of the 1996 Act. See also *The 'Kerman'* [1982] 1 Lloyd's Rep 62, 66–67.

example of a case that reached the Court of Justice through appeal on the point of law mechanism is *Bulk Oil v Sun International*.[228] In this case the court clearly stated that '[a]s an arbitrator cannot refer any question to Luxembourg, there would first have to be an appeal from the award.'[229] Accordingly, an appeal on a substance from an award that applies EU competition law may allow the English court to make a preliminary reference if a question of law within the meaning of s 69 is raised and the requirements of Art 267 TFEU are satisfied.

Finally, as the Court of Justice contemplated in the *Nordsee* case,[230] the English courts may be called to review an arbitration award during the setting aside proceedings and enforcement proceeding. Accordingly, the court may ask for a preliminary ruling on any question on the interpretation of EU competition law that arose in the course of the arbitral proceedings. An example for a case that reached the Court of Justice through Art 267 TFEU is *Eco Swiss*.[231] In this case, the Dutch Supreme Court referred to the Court of Justice for a preliminary ruling five questions on the interpretation of Art 101 which arose in proceedings brought by Benetton in relation to enforcement of an arbitration award ordering it to pay damages to Eco Swiss for breach of a licensing agreement. The possibility of a preliminary reference to the Court of Justice through national courts does exist in other Member States as well.[232]

The above analysis shows that in appropriate circumstances, the question of EU competition law may reach the Court of Justice despite the fact that the parties have chosen to resolve their EU competition law dispute by arbitration. In light of that it seems that it would be for national courts, in their ancillary functions to arbitration proceedings, to ensure the observance of EU competition law. This can be further sustained by outlining the powers of courts with regard to arbitral awards in relation to antitrust claims.

7.5.4 Multi-Party Arbitral Proceedings in Relation to EU Competition Law Claims

It is well established that the consensual nature of arbitration may result in arbitral tribunals' inability to join third parties in arbitration or consolidate arbitral

[228] *Bulk Oil* (n 226). The reference to the ECJ was made by the Commercial Court in London, but the dispute between the parties had originally been determined in an English arbitration procedure. See more GIF Leigh and S Velik, 'Leave to appeal from arbitrator's award on point of EEC Law' (1984) 9 *EL Rev* 128.

[229] *Bulk Oil* (n 226) 151.

[230] *Nordsee* (n 116) [14].

[231] *Eco Swiss* (n 50).

[232] Eg Art 1050 of the German ZPO expressly provides that 'the arbitral tribunal or a party with the approval of an arbitral tribunal may request from a court assistance in taking evidence or performance of other judicial acts, which the arbitral tribunal is not empowered to carry out.' It has been submitted that an application to German courts with a request for preliminary reference to the ECJ could well be made on grounds of Art 1050 GAA. See more: Komninos (n 174) 375. But compare Art 5 of UNCITRAL Model Law.

proceedings without parties' consent.[233] However, multi-party disputes are quite common in competition law cases. In this section, the problems related to arbitration involving multiple plaintiffs and/or multiple plaintiffs will be examined.

7.5.4.1 Multiple Defendants

A party to an arbitration agreement may wish to bring an antitrust claim against the subsidiary (who implements a cartel agreement that is entered into by its parent or implements abusive practice in England) and the parent company that neither signed nor consented to the arbitration agreement. The need to bring an antitrust claim against the parent company also may arise because the subsidiary may not have many assets. In addition, the participation of the parent company would allow the arbitrators to make disclosure orders under s 34(2)(d) to both respondent parties. This would be very important in view of the fact that discovery of certain documents that are necessary to establish the facts of a case may be of huge importance in EU competition law claims. However, the parent company would have no incentives to join or to be joined in the arbitral proceedings.[234] Is a parent company bound by an arbitration agreement which is signed or consented to by its subsidiary?[235]

By using the concept of the 'group of companies', an arbitral tribunal may find that a parent company is bound by an arbitration agreement concluded by its subsidiary. According to this doctrine, 'a group of companies constitutes one and the same economic reality [*une realité économique unique*] of which the arbitral tribunal should take account when it rules on its own jurisdiction'.[236] However, it has been submitted that a single economic unit would not be enough for an arbitral tribunal to establish that a parent would be bound by an agreement to arbitrate; the existence of implied consent (or conduct amounting to such consent) would be required.[237] Further difficulties would arise out of the fact that the doctrine of 'group companies' forms no part of English law.[238]

Nevertheless, the doctrine of 'single economic unit', which has a role to play in private antitrust proceedings,[239] may lead to a different result in EU competition

[233] *Sun Life Assurance Company of Canada and others v Lincoln National Life Insurance Co* [2004] EWCA Civ 1660; [2005] 1 Lloyd's Rep 606 (CA) [68].

[234] See also Mustill and Boyd (n 2) 142–43.

[235] It has been submitted that the term 'piercing the corporate veil' should be distinguished from 'extension of an arbitration clause to non-signatory'. See B Hanotiau, 'Multiple parties and multiple contracts in international arbitration' in Permanent Court of Arbitration, *Multiple Party Actions in International Arbitration* (OUP, Oxford 2009) 35, 40.

[236] ICC Award No 4131 *Dow Chemical France (France), Dow Chemical Company (USA), Dow Chemical AG (Switzerland), Dow Chemical Europe (Switzerland) v Isover Saint Gobain (France)* (1984) 9 *ICCA Yearbook* 131, 136 (Interim Award (23 September 1982)).

[237] P Mayer, 'Extension of the arbitration clause to non-signatories' in *Multiple Party Actions in International Arbitration* (n 235) 189, 198; Hanotiau (n 235) 38.

[238] *Peterson Farms Inc v C & M Farming Ltd* [2004] EWHC 121 (Comm); 2004 1 Lloyd's Rep 603 [59]. See also J Leadley and L Williams, 'Peterson Farms: There is no Group of Companies Doctrine in English Law' (2004) 7 *International Arbitration Law Review* 111.

[239] *Provimi v Aventis Animal Nutrition* [2003] EWHC 961 (Comm); [2003] ECC 29.

law cases. In such cases, a parent company and its subsidiary, notwithstanding their legal status, form a single economic unit.[240] This would certainly be an important factor that needs to be considered by the arbitral tribunal when deciding on its jurisdiction over the parent company in EU competition law claims brought against the subsidiary and its parent. The fact that in such cases 'the subsidiaries do not enjoy real autonomy in determining their cause of action in the market, but carry out instructions issued to them by the parent company controlling them'[241] should be considered sufficient to justify the parent company being bound to arbitrate the Arts 101 and/or 102 TFEU claims arising out of the contract. Accordingly, in EU competition law cases, the parent company could be bound by an arbitration agreement which was signed (or consented to) by its subsidiary.

7.5.4.2 Collective Redress Proceedings before Arbitration Tribunals: a Case for Reform

As already seen, the class actions (or representative/group proceedings) have been widely discussed in the European[242] and domestic[243] contexts. But what if a party to an arbitration agreement wanted to initiate collective redress proceedings against a company which abuses its dominant position by tying purchases, by imposing an obligation on its customers to obtain all or most of their supplies exclusively from it? Does a standard arbitration clause, which states that all disputes arising out of the contract are to be resolved by arbitration, preclude the party from bringing collective redress antitrust proceedings in national courts? What if the action was brought by consumers?

If a claimant brings a collective redress proceeding before the court, the defendant would have no incentives to concur to this procedure.[244] There is no reason for a defendant, who allegedly acts in breach of EU competition law, to be willing to join court proceedings in view of the fact that the rationale for promoting collective redress proceedings is to make 'possible litigation that would not be in the courts at all if individual actions were required'.[245] Shall the court stay the legal proceedings and compel arbitration on the basis of s 9 of the 1996 Act and Art II of the New York Convention?

240 *Provimi* (n 239) [31]. See also Case C-73/95 *Viho v Commission* [1996] ECR I-5457.

241 *Viho* (n 240) [16].

242 Commission (EC), 'Damages actions for breach of the EC antitrust rules' (White Paper) COM (2008) 165 final; Commission (EC), 'Consumer Collective Redress' (Green Paper) COM (2008) 794 final.

243 Office of Fair Trading, 'Private actions in competition law: effective redress for consumers and business—Recommendations from the Office of Fair Trading', OFT916 resp; Civil Justice Council Final Report, 'Improving access to justice through collective actions—developing a more effective and efficient procedure for collective actions', < www.civiljusticecouncil.gov.uk/files/Improving_Access_to_Justice_through_Collective_Actions.pdf.

244 Compare Mustill and Boyd (n 2) 142.

245 KW Dam, 'Class actions: efficiency, compensation, deterrence, and conflict of interest' (1975) 4 *Journal of Legal Studies* 47, 49. See also C Hodges, 'From class actions to collective redress: a resolution in approach to compensation' (2009) *Civil Justice Quarterly* 41.

One may argue that a national court should not compel arbitration if a party to an arbitration agreement brought a follow-on collective redress action (or opted-in to such an action) after a national competition authority or the Commission had already declared an antitrust infringement. In such cases, there would be a principal tortious claim for damages, and no contractual claims as the EU competition law infringement would have been clearly established by a public authority. In view of that, the court may decide that follow-on collective tortious claims that are to do with remoteness and assessment of antitrust damages are not within the scope of a standard arbitration clause, so that a stay of legal proceedings should not be granted.[246] However, it should be recalled that in such a scenario the tortious claim would be closely knitted to a contractual EU competition law claim as to whether the whole contract or only part of it had been invalidated as being in conflict with EU competition law. Thus, the answer to the question of whether the court should stay its proceedings could depend on whether the collective redress actions were brought on behalf of commercial companies or consumers.

It has been submitted by Hill[247] that an arbitration agreement would normally be unenforceable against a consumer by virtue of the Unfair Terms in Consumer Contracts Regulations 1999.[248] The latter rules clearly state that terms which have the effect of excluding the consumer's right to take legal action by requiring the consumer to take disputes to arbitration are regarded as unfair and should be legally ineffective.[249] This deduction can be sustained not only in respect of claims for a pecuniary remedy which does not exceed the amount specified by the legislator,[250] but also with regard to claims exceeding that amount, unless there are legal provisions explicitly providing for class actions arbitrations in England.[251] Therefore, court proceedings should not be stayed and no arbitration should be compelled in cases where a collective redress action was brought by a consumer, who is party to an arbitration agreement. In such cases, the arbitration clause would be regarded as an unfair term with the meaning of the 1999 Regulations.

However, an English court should stay legal proceedings and refer the matter to arbitration in cases where the claimants (eg distributors or licensees or wholesalers) are not consumers, who are parties to arbitration agreements and want to bring a collective redress action against a dominant undertaking seeking civil sanctions of nullity of a contractual relationship, together with antitrust damages. But is there a possibility of class arbitrations[252] taking place in England?

[246] Compare *Provimi* (n 239) where the scope of jurisdictional clauses under Art 23 of the Brussels I Regulation was discussed by the High Court.

[247] J Hill, *Cross-border Consumer Contracts* (OUP, Oxford, 2008) 212–14. See also Joined Cases C-240/98 to C-244/98 *Oceano Grupo Editorial v Salvant Editors* [2000] ECR I-4941.

[248] Unfair Terms in Consumer Contracts Regulations 1999 SI 1999/2083.

[249] Hill (n 247) 212–13.

[250] s 91(1) of the 1996 Act. See also Unfair Arbitration Agreements (Specified Amount) Order 1999 SI 1999/2167.

[251] Compare s 35 of the 1996 Act; Hill (n 247) 214.

[252] *Redfern and Hunter on International Arbitration* (n 1) [2.197]–[2.203].

Under the 1996 Act an arbitral tribunal does not have the power to order arbitration proceedings to be consolidated with other arbitration proceedings unless the parties agree to confer such power to the tribunal.[253] This is a rather unfortunate solution, as there is no means to consolidate arbitrations arising from different, but related and similar contracts (ie a 'network of agreements'[254]) which may affect trade between Member States, for example, due to the network effects of these agreements on the market in question. In view of that, it is not clear how the European and domestic policy favouring collective redress actions can be implemented by parties to arbitration agreements.

It has been submitted that 'parties to an LCIA arbitration could be subject to a consolidation or a class arbitration order even over the objection of one of the two parties….' [255] Strong[256] seems to argue that class arbitration could theoretically take place in England under Art 22.1(h) of the LCIA Rules, which allows 'upon the application of a party, one or more third persons to be joined in the arbitration as a party provided any such third person and the applicant have consented thereto in writing.' Although Art 22.1(h) will be of relevance even where the other party to arbitration proceedings is objecting against the joinder of the third party, its effect could be limited in view of the fact that an application from one of the original parties to arbitral proceedings and consent from the third party would always be required.[257]

Furthermore, the prevailing opinion seems to be that '[t]here is no provision in the LCIA Rules that deals with the question of the consolidation of two otherwise distinct arbitrations ….'[258] In addition, an important issue which may need to be considered in the context of collective redress action is whether the scope of the arbitration clause is broad enough to include a possibility of class action at all. Whilst it may be argued that the assumption of one-stop arbitration as laid down in *Fili Shipping*[259] would mean that the arbitration clause could be interpreted broadly, it should be noted that 'parties agree to arbitrate with particular claimants or respondents, not with the whole world.'[260]

[253] s 35 of the 1996 Act. See also: *Abu Dhabi Gas Liquefaction v Eastern Bechtel Corp* [1982] 2 Lloyd's Rep 425; *The Eastern Saga* [1984] 2 Lloyd's Rep 66.

[254] See Case 23/67 *Brasserie de Haecht v Wilkin-Janssens (No 1)* [1967] ECR 407. See more: J Goyder and A Albors-Llorens, *Goyder's EC Competition Law* (5th edn, OUP, Oxford, 2009) 102–03.

[255] S. I. Strong, 'The sounds of silence: Are U.S. arbitrators creating internationally enforceable awards when ordering class arbitration in cases of contractual silence or ambiguity' (2009) *Michigan Journal of International Law* 1017, 1081. Strong though seems to admit that a subsequent class arbitration award could be refused recognition and enforcement on the ground of Art V(1)(d) if the arbitral proceedings were consolidated despite the objection of one of the parties. (See Strong (n 255) 1081.)

[256] Strong (n 255) 1081–1082.

[257] See more: A Winstanley, 'Multiple parties, multiple problems: a view from the London Court of International Arbitration' in *Multiple Party Actions in International Arbitration* (n 235) 213, 217–18; P Turner and R Mohtashami, *A Guide to the LCIA Arbitration Rules* (OUP, Oxford, 2009) 148–51.

[258] Turner and Mohtashami (n 257) 151. See also: Winstanley (n 257) 218–19.

[259] *Fili Shipping* (n 16) [13].

[260] WW Park, *Arbitration of International Business Disputes: Studies in Law and Practice* (OUP, Oxford, 2006) 111.

Therefore, it seems that the answer to the question how the European and domestic policy favouring collective redress actions can be implemented by parties to arbitration agreements under the current legislation is far from certain. There seem to be strong arguments suggesting that the issue of class arbitrations should be addressed by the English legislature in view of the current reform that is meant to foster collective redress proceedings in England. The case for legislative reform in England can be further strengthened by the fact that there are appropriate judicial review mechanisms that are available under the 1996 Act in respect of arbitral awards rendered in England and abroad, which would ensure that EU competition law had been properly applied by arbitral tribunals. In doing that, a lot can be gained by the US experience, where class arbitrations have been taking place in some states for years.[261]

7.5.5 Review of Arbitration Awards in Relation to EU Competition Law Claims

It is well established that EU law must be observed in its entirety throughout the territory of all the Member States.[262] The control of its application in arbitration proceedings is left to national systems of law.[263] Although s 69 of the 1996 Act provides for an appeal on a point of law,[264] the opportunities to appeal an arbitral award to national courts on points of law are severely limited in other Member States. Such prospects are wholly excluded in most of them.[265] Moreover, s 69 is applicable only with regard to awards rendered in England. Based on that, it has been submitted that such limitations on a national court's right to control arbitration would have an adverse effect on the unified application of EU competition law.[266]

An arbitral award, however, is opened for review by a national court if the 'unruly horse of public policy comes out'.[267] In spite of the fact that 'public policy'

[261] Eg *Green Tree Financial Corp v Bazzle* 539 US 444 (2003); California Code of Civil Procedure s 1281.3. See also: Park (n 260) 110–11; EP Tuchmann, 'The administration of class action arbitrations' in *Multiple Party Actions in International Arbitration* (n 235) 325; R Chernick, 'Class-wide arbitration in California in *Multiple Party Actions in International Arbitration* (n 235) 337; Strong (n 255).

[262] Case 246/80 *Broekmeulen* [1981] ECR 2311.

[263] *Nordsee* (n 116) [14].

[264] See more section 7.5.3 above.

[265] Hill (n 1) 698–99; P Berger, 'The Modern Trend towards Exclusion of Recourse against Transnational Arbitral Awards: A European Perspective' (1989) 12 *Fordham International Law Journal* 605. See also: Gharavi (n 100) 200–01.

[266] C Baudenbacher and I Higgins, 'Decentralisation of EC competition law enforcement and arbitration' (2002) 8 *Columbia Journal of European Law* 1, 6.

[267] It was held by Chief Justice Hobart over 300 years ago that the '[p]ublic policy is an unruly horse'. Referring to this quotation, however, Lord Denning added: 'with a good man in a saddle, the unruly horse can be kept in control. It can jump over obstacles. It can leap the fences put up by fictions and come down on the side of justice.' See *Enderby Town FC v The FA* [1971] Ch 591 (CA) 606. See also T D de Groot, 'The Impact of the *Benetton* Decision on International Commercial Arbitration' (2003) 20 *Journal of International Arbitration* 365.

is an ambiguous and complex legal concept, it is contained in all laws[268] and its violation can lead to 'an appeal through the back door'.[269] Under English law it is well established that consideration of public policy 'should be approached with extreme caution'.[270] It has to be shown that there is some element of illegality, or that the enforcement of the award would be clearly injurious to the public good or, possibly, that enforcement would be wholly offensive to public policy.[271] Having outlined that, in this sub-section first the public policy character of Arts 101 and 102 TFEU will be briefly introduced. After that, the implications of the public policy character of EU competition rules will be examined in regard to setting aside proceedings (domestic awards) and recognition and enforcement proceedings (foreign awards) brought before national courts.

7.5.5.1 Public Policy Character of EU Competition Law for the Purposes of Judicial Review of Arbitration Awards

The major case where the incompatibility of an award with national public policy was invoked is *Eco Swiss*.[272] In its decision the Court of Justice held that the EU competition law rules may be regarded as a matter of public policy within the meaning of the New York Convention.[273] This is justified by the importance of Arts 101 and 102 TFEU[274] entailing public interest in the enforcement of EU competition law legislation. Based on the public policy character of EU competition law provisions, it can be argued that the judicial control over the arbitral awards in relation to Arts 101 and/or 102 TFEU would provide national courts with an efficient tool, which will contribute to uniform application of EU competition law. The fact that Arts 101 and 102 TFEU enjoy public policy character would broaden the scope of the courts' review with regard to arbitral awards in relation

268 That is reflected in the UNCITRAL Model Law as well. See more: Berger (n 265) 638–43.

269 Berger (n 265) 638.

270 *Deutsche Schachtbau- und Tiefbohrgesllschaft v Ras Al-Khaimah National Oil* [1990] 1 AC 295 (HL) 316.

271 Ibid.

272 *Eco Swiss* (n 50). See also Case C-393/92 *Almelo v NV Energiebedrijf Ijsselmij* [1994] ECR I-1477 [23]. See more M Furse and L D'Arcy, '*Eco Swiss China Time Ltd v Benetton:* EC Competition Law and Arbitration' (1999) 20 *European Competition Law Review* 392, 394.

273 *Eco Swiss* (n 50) [39]. See also: MC van Leyenhorst and IPM van den Nieuwendijk, 'Characterisation of competition law as public policy' in Zuberbuhler and Oetiker (n 103) 25, 33–36; N Hukkinen, 'Application of competition law *ex officio*' in Zuberbuhler and Oetiker (n 103) 43–57. The questions as to whether Art 81 is to be regarded as a matter of public policy for the purposes of the Brussels Regulation and what are the powers of the English courts in respect of foreign judgements misapplying EU competition law were discussed in ch 6 above.

274 Ibid [36]. Art 119 TFEU states that EU and Member States' economic policies should be 'conducted in accordance with the principle of an open market economy and free competition.' The Protocol on the Internal Market and Competition annexed to the Treaty on European Union goes further to state that 'the internal market as set out in Article 3 of the Treaty on European Union includes a system ensuring that competition is not distorted'. See more: J Drexl, 'Competition law as part of the European Constitution' in A von Bogdandy and J Bast (eds), *Principles of European Constitutional Law* (2nd edn, Hart Publishing and Verlag CH Beck, Oxford and Munich, 2009) 659, 662–69. See also old Art 3(1)(g) TEC.

to EU competition law claims, which is the cost for letting EU competition law disputes go to arbitration.[275]

Accordingly, it seems that compliance of an arbitral award with the EU competition rules may be scrutinised at two stages by the Member States' courts. First, such control may be exercised in setting aside proceedings. Many jurisdictions—including England[276] and Scotland[277]—provide that an award may be challenged on the ground that it is contrary to public policy. Secondly, Art V(2) of the New York Convention[278] states that the recognition and enforcement of an award may be refused, if this would be contrary to public policy. The powers of English courts with regard to arbitral awards in relation to Arts 101 and/or 102 TFEU will be examined below.

7.5.5.2 Setting Aside Proceedings of Arbitral Awards in Relation to EU Competition Law Claims

An application for setting aside of an arbitral award on a ground of public policy may be served out of the jurisdiction with the permission of the court if the award was made in England.[279] As already outlined, the public policy character of Arts 101 and 102 TFEU indicates that national courts should have higher scrutiny over arbitral awards in relation to EU competition law claims. As a result, the national courts can set aside an arbitration award that is contrary to Arts 101 and 102 TFEU as being in conflict with public policy.[280] Section 68(2)(g) explicitly allows a party to arbitration to apply to the court and challenge an award on the ground that it is contrary to English public policy. There is little doubt that European public policy forms a part of English public policy, so that an award that is in conflict with EU competition law will be contrary to English public policy.[281]

The proposition that an English court can set aside an award based on a contract that is contrary to Arts 101 and/or 102 TFEU and thus void and illegal as a matter of English law[282] may be further strengthened by the judgment in the *Taylor* case.[283] In this case, the award was based on a contract for a sale of Irish

[275] Compare W Park, 'National Law and Commercial Justice: safeguarding procedural integrity in international arbitration' (1989) 63 *Tulane Law Review* 647, 669. Nazzini even goes further and speaks about endorsement of 'second look doctrine', which emerged after *Mitsubishi* (n 3), by the ECJ. See Nazzini (n 72) 352–53.

[276] s 68(2)(g) of the 1996 Act. See also Dempegiotis (n 80) 390–91.

[277] Art 34(2)(b)(ii) of the Model Law in sch 7 of Law Reform (Miscellaneous Provisions) (Scotland) Act 1990.

[278] Art 103(3) of the 1996 Act, which implements the New York Convention provision in England. For Scotland see Art 36(1)(b)(ii) of Model Law in sch 7 of Law Reform (Miscellaneous Provisions) (Scotland) Act 1990.

[279] CPR 62.5(1)(a). An award is deemed made in England if the seat of arbitration was in England. See s 53 of the 1996 Act.

[280] *Eco Swiss* (n 50) [39].

[281] See CMV Clarkson and J Hill, *The Conflict of Laws* (3rd edn, OUP, Oxford, 2006) 260. See more: arguments about the public policy character of EC competition law in Sch 6, section 6.2.1 above.

[282] *Gibbs Mew v Gemmell* [1998] EuLR 588 [40] (CA).

[283] *Taylor v Barnett* [1953] 1 Lloyd's Rep 181 (CA).

stewed steak at two shillings and four pence per pound, which was in excess of the price authorised by the Maximum Price Order. It was clearly pointed out that the court will set aside an arbitrator's award if it seeks to give effect to a contract which is illegal or contrary to public policy.[284] Denning LJ reasoned that 'an arbitrator has no jurisdiction or authority to award damages on an illegal contract. It is obvious that the Court would not itself enforce such an award. Equally, it should not allow it to stand.'[285] Lord Phillips interpreted this ruling by stating that the court refused to enforce the award because the arbitrator would have no jurisdiction to make an award on an illegal contract, as the arbitration agreement would be void.[286] A different opinion, however, was expressed by the Court of Appeal in the *Harbour Assurance* case,[287] where all three judges held that the *Taylor* ruling was not based on jurisdiction, but on misconduct by the arbitrator, who failed to take into account the illegality of the contract.[288] Thus, it seems clear that under English law the court may not give effect to an award that is contrary to EU competition law. However, this would not be because the arbitral tribunal would have no jurisdiction to rule over an illegal contract, but because such an award would be in conflict with English public policy.

Further, it has been submitted by Lord Phillips[289] that the English court would not review an arbitral award if the arbitrators had failed to properly give effect to English competition law. This submission was based on an old judgment rendered in *Birtley v Windy Nook*[290] (the UK at that time was not part of the EU and EU competition law was not an issue at all). In this case, the court held that there is nothing on the face of the award to indicate that it is an unreasonable restraint of trade, against the interest of the parties or the public. According to the court, the judge is not entitled to look behind the award and become in effect an appeal tribunal for arbitral proceedings. It is for the parties to put forward their competition law related claims and take the appropriate steps for that purpose before the arbitral tribunal.[291] The *Birtley* case, however, should be distinguished, because in its judgment the court held inter alia that there was no rule in the contract that could possibly distort competition.[292] Although the court was 'not entitled to look behind the award', the judge did check the contract, which the award was based on, and held obiter that the contract was not in restraint of trade. It seems that if there were an anti-competitive clause in the contract, a different result might have been reached by the court. Moreover, when EU competition law is at stake,

[284] Ibid 184 (Singleton LJ).
[285] Ibid 187 (Denning LJ).
[286] Phillips (n 72) 307.
[287] *Harbour Assurance* (n 16).
[288] *Harbour Assurance* (n 16) 712–13 (Gibson LJ); 718 (Leggatt LJ); 725–26 (Hoffmann LJ). See also: *Soleimany v Soleimany* [1999] QB 785 (CA) 799.
[289] Phillips (n 72) 307.
[290] *Birtley and District Co-Operative Society v Windy Nook and District Industrial Co-Operative Society (No 2)* [1960] 2 QB 1.
[291] Ibid 14.
[292] Ibid 11.

the English court will have jurisdiction to set aside an award that is based on a contract that is in conflict with Arts 101 and/or 102 TFEU as these provisions express English public policy. This would be in accord with the ruling in the *Taylor* case, where it was held that an award based on an illegal contract cannot stand.[293]

In view of the above, it is beyond doubt that EU competition law is part of public policy for the purposes of setting aside proceedings conducted by English courts. Therefore, the English court would set aside under Art 68(2)(g) an award based on a contract that was in conflict with Arts 101 and 102 TFEU as being void and illegal. An award that is set aside may not be recognized under the New York Convention[294].

7.5.5.3 Recognition and Enforcement of Arbitral Awards in Relation to EU Competition Law Claims

The enforcement of a foreign arbitral award in England will be governed by the public policy rules of the *lex fori*.[295] Under s 103 of the 1996 Act, enforcement of a Convention award 'shall not be refused' except in certain limited cases, and enforcement 'may also be refused' if it would be contrary to public policy to enforce the award. The doctrine of public policy is regarded as a guardian of the fundamental policies of the forum.[296] After the *Eco Swiss* case, there is no doubt that due to the fact that EU competition law provisions express the fundamental economic system of the EU[297], Arts 101 and 102 TFEU are to be regarded as a matter of public policy for the purposes of the New York Convention.[298] Accordingly, arbitral awards would risk not being enforced by a Member State's court (and in particular the English court) on public policy grounds, if it failed to properly address Arts 101 and 102 TFEU.

However, problems may arise though because the *Eco Swiss* case did not clearly address the issue of the scope of judicial review of arbitral awards in relation to EU competition law claims. Does such a review involve broad examination of whether an arbitrator properly applied EU competition law (ie review of the merits)?[299] The difficulties can be easily demonstrated by the Paris Cour D'Appel decision in *Thales v Euromissile*.[300] In this case, Euromissile was awarded damages on the

[293] *Taylor* (n 283) 187 (Denning LJ).

[294] See Art 5(1)(e) of the New York Convention.

[295] s 2(2)(b). See *Soleimany* (n 288) 798–800. See also Art V(2)(b).

[296] JDM Lew, *Applicable Law in International Commercial Arbitration: a Study in Commercial Arbitration Awards* (Oceana Publications, Dobbs Ferry, New York, 1978) 532 [403].

[297] See Art 119 TFEU and the Protocol on the Internal Market and Competition annexed to the Treaty on European Union. See more: Drexl (n 274) 662–69. Compare old Arts 2 and 3 TEC.

[298] *Eco Swiss* (n 50) [36] and [39].

[299] Compare: Park (n 275) 669.

[300] *Thales v Euromissile* (Cour d'Appel (Paris) 18 November 2004) discussed by T Thomasi, 'The Paris Court Of Appeal Looks at a request for the annulment of an award for breach of EC competition law: a first application in France of the principles laid down by the ECJ in *Eco Swiss*' (2005) *International Arbitration Law Review* 55; A Komninos, 'Paris Court of Appeal refuses to set aside

basis of a licensing agreement that stipulated that Euromissile held for 20 years the exclusive right to produce the missile. A dispute arose when Thales decided to produce the missiles itself through a subsidiary. The dispute was brought before the International Chamber of Commerce and an award for about £70 million in damages was rendered in favour of Euromissile. Thales applied to the Paris Court of Appeal to set an award aside on the ground that the licensing agreement was incompatible with the EU competition law rules and, thus, null and void. Thales' competition law argument was based on the excessive duration of the exclusivity and on the market-sharing elements therein. The French Court considered that the applicant's arguments and the evidence produced did not reveal a 'flagrant, real and concrete'[301] violation of EU competition law, and dismissed Thales' application. Based on that decision, Komninos argues that 'an arbitrator's failure to apply EU competition law will result in the annulment or non-recognition/non-enforcement of an arbitral award on public policy grounds only in exceptional cases involving hard-core restrictions.'[302] But if a market-sharing agreement is not enough justification for the French court to check whether an arbitral award is not based on a contract that is void under Arts 101 and/or 102 TFEU, then it is difficult to see what will be.

Referring to the judgment of the French court, Komninos argues that 'a foreign arbitral award should be denied recognition/enforcement only in the most extreme circumstances, where there is a clear and very serious violation of competition law and this is upheld by the arbitral tribunal.'[303] Such a conclusion is not in accord with the Court of Justice judgments in the *Eco Swiss* case[304] and the *Nordsee* case.[305] The reading of these cases suggests that the fact that special institutional support[306] is not always available to arbitral awards applying EU law and the public policy character of Arts 101 and 102 TFEU have justified the higher scrutiny by the national courts over arbitral awards, where arbitrators failed to address the questions of EU competition law. The Court of Justice has clearly put forward that 'every [EU law] provision should be given a uniform interpretation, irrespective of the circumstances in which it is to be applied.'[307] In the *Eco Swiss* case, the Court of Justice held that questions concerning the interpretation of EU competition law are open to examination by national courts at

arbitral award for public policy violation' (2004) 17 *White & Case International Dispute Resolution Newsletter* 2; J Gaffney and S Wade, 'Characterization of competition law as public policy and the enforcement of arbitral awards' in Zuberbuhler and Oetiker (n 103) 123, 137–38; E Stylopoulos, 'Powers and duties of arbitrators in the application of competition law: an EC approach in the light of recent developments' (2009) 30 *European Competition Law Review* 118, 120.

301 Translation by Thomasi (n 300).

302 See Komninos (n 300).

303 A Komninos, 'Dutch court refuses to enforce US arbitral awards on public policy grounds for violation of EU competition law' (2006) 19 *White & Case International Dispute Resolution Newsletter* 5, 7.

304 *Eco Swiss* (n 50) [36]–[40].

305 See *Nordsee* (n 116) [14].

306 Eg Art 267 TFEU and Art 15 of Regulation 1/2003.

307 *Eco Swiss* (n 50) [40]. See also Case C-88/91 *Federconsorzi* [1992] ECR I-4035 [7].

the award-enforcement stage. This seems to indicate that, at recognition stage, a Member State court should be entitled to verify whether a foreign arbitral award is rendered in conflict with Arts 101 and 102 TFEU and thus in conflict with EU public policy. Such a review would need to be made, in order for a recognising court to be able to determine whether the public policy defence has been met.[308]

Nonetheless, it has been submitted that 'a form of merits review' would go well beyond any review called for under Art V of the New York Convention.[309] Beraudo[310] goes further and states that an award which misapplies the public policy regulations of EU law would not be *ipso facto* contrary to public policy. This claim is based on the Court of Justice ruling in *Renault v Maxicar*,[311] which was rendered under the Brussels Convention. A distinction, however, must be made between recognition and enforcement of judgments under the Brussels I Regulation[312] and recognition and enforcement of foreign arbitration awards. In the *Renault* case, the Court of Justice has emphasised the availability of appropriate mechanisms, which are set to guarantee the proper application of EU competition law by the court with original jurisdiction.[313] Furthermore, it has been submitted that even under the Brussels I Regulation, which is based on the principle of mutual trust between the legal systems within the EU, 'a court is obviously entitled to conduct so much of a review as is necessary to determine whether any of the substantive defences to recognitions is made out ....'[314]

Thus, the *Eco Swiss* ruling suggests that an increased level of scrutiny is to be applied by national courts with regard to arbitral awards in relation to EU competition law claims.[315] This, however, does not mean that national courts are always allowed to intervene on the ground of public policy against an arbitral award that is allegedly based on an agreement that distorts competition. An arbitration award applying Arts 101 and/or 102 TFEU is not to be regarded as a sort of assessment under Art 1 of Regulation 1/2003 that is delegated by the parties to an arbitral tribunal. A review of an arbitral award must be made by a national court only if there is prima facie evidence from one side that the award is in conflict with EU competition law.[316] In such cases, a Member State court should consider the evidence supporting the statement that the contract is or is not in conflict with EU antitrust law, in order to determine whether the public policy defence is met.

[308] Compare a recent Court of Justice rendered in the context of Brussels I, C-394/07 *Gambazzi v Daimler Chrysler Canada Inc* [2009] ILPr 38 (ECJ) [46]. See also A Briggs and P Rees, *Civil Jurisdiction and Judgments* (5th edn, Informa, London, 2009) 686.

[309] Beechy (n 19) 186.

[310] JP Beraudo, 'Egregious error of law as a ground for setting aside an arbitral award' (2006) 23 *Journal of International Arbitration* 351, 361.

[311] Case 38/98 *Renault v Maxicar* [2000] ECR I-2973.

[312] See more ch 6.

[313] *Renault* (n 311) [33]. See ch 6, section 6.2.4.1 above.

[314] Briggs and Rees (n 308) 686.

[315] Y Bruland and Y Quintin, 'European Community Law and Arbitration: National Versus Community Public Policy' (2001) 18 *Journal of International Arbitration* 533, 545.

[316] Compare: *Soleimany* (n 288) 800. See also: *Westacre* (CA) (n 61).

The judgment of the Dutch courts in *Marketing Displays International v VR Van Raalte Reclame*[317] is a good example of how the *Eco Swiss* principles must be applied with regard to arbitral awards disregarding EU competition law. In this case, the Hague Court of Appeal upheld a lower court's refusal to recognise and enforce three US arbitral awards because they were considered incompatible with Art 101 TFEU and their enforcement would have been against Dutch and European public policy. The dispute arose out of a licensing agreement, which granted an exclusive licence to Van Raatle for the territory of Belgium, the Netherlands, and Luxembourg. The agreement provided for a grant-back clause with respect to improvements made by Van Raatle on the licensed technologies. The Block Exemption Regulation that was applicable at that time did not allow for such clauses.[318] The dispute as to payment arose before the arbitral tribunal in the US. Three awards were rendered in favour of Marketing Displays, which sought their enforcement before the Dutch Court. Enforcement was refused because the agreement was in breach of Art 101(1) due to its market-sharing elements. Furthermore, the agreement could not have benefited from an exemption under Art 101(3) TFEU. The decision of the Dutch court is a welcome development in the relationship between international commercial arbitration and EU competition law as it meets the expectations of an effective control by the national courts over arbitral awards in relation to EU competition law claims, and would ensure coherence and uniformity of Arts 101 and 102 TFEU.

More difficulties arise in cases where even though the arbitrators had considered Arts 101 and 102 TFEU and held that the contract did not distort competition, the misapplication of Arts 101 and 102 TFEU by the arbitrators was raised before the national court in the course of recognition and enforcement proceedings. In such a scenario there would be tension between the public interest that the awards of arbitrators should be respected, on the one hand, and the public interest that contracts contradicting EU competition law should not be enforced as being illegal, on the other hand.[319] It seems that the illegality of contracts in conflict with Arts 101 and/or 102 allows an English court to inquire into the applicability of EU competition law with regard to the underlying contract even if the arbitral tribunal has dealt with it, provided there is prima facie evidence from one side that the arbitral tribunal misapplied EU antitrust law provisions. It is well established under English law that 'in an appropriate case [the court] may inquire into an issue of illegality even if an arbitrator had jurisdiction and found that there was no illegality.'[320] Accordingly, if an arbitrator had made an error in law when deciding that an agreement is not in conflict with Arts 101 and/or 102 TFEU, then the award would be based on an illegal contract and such awards should stand under the English

[317] Case 04/694 and 04/695, *Marketing Displays International v VR Van Raalte Reclame,* judgment of 24 March 2005 discussed in Komninos (n 303); Gaffney and Wade (n 300) 138–39.

[318] Regulation 240/1996 on technology transfers.

[319] Compare *Soleimany* (n 288) 800.

[320] *Soleimany* (n 288) 803. See also *Westacre* (CA) (n 61) 310–11.

law. Such approach allows the English courts to ensure that the legitimate interest in the enforcement of EU competition law has been addressed and is in accord with the interest of uniform and effective private antitrust enforcement.

It can be concluded that an award, whether domestic or foreign, will not be enforced by an English court if its enforcement would be contrary to EU competition law. As a result, the compliance of an arbitral award with EU antitrust law provisions could be scrutinised by the English courts in setting aside arbitral proceedings (domestic awards) and enforcement proceedings (foreign awards). This is due to the public policy character of Arts 101 and 102 TFEU, which is based on the fundamental principles of a legal, social and economic system in the EU.

In addition to this, there are some special mechanisms under Regulation 1/2003, which have a role to play in the maintenance of a more coherent application of EU competition law and will be examined in the following section.

7.6 Coherent and Uniform Application of EU Competition Law by Arbitrators

Regulation 1/2003 envisages special mechanisms that are set to maintain coherent and uniform application of EU competition law by national courts.[321] To this end Art 15 enables national courts to ask the Commission to transmit to them information which is in its possession, or its opinion on questions concerning the application of EU competition law. Article 16 provides safeguards for consistent application of EU competition rules in cases, where there are parallel or consecutive proceedings before the Commission and national courts. Although, those mechanisms are explicitly addressed to national courts only, they may have a role to play in respect of arbitration proceedings, where the application of competition law is an issue. Accordingly, in this section, first, the possibility for arbitral tribunals to seek assistance from the Commission will be examined. Secondly, Art 16 of Regulation 1/2003 and its application to arbitral proceeding will be discussed.

7.6.1 Article 15 and its Relevance with Regard to Arbitral Proceedings

An important mechanism at the disposal of national courts dealing with EU competition law issues is the option to seek the Commission's assistance.[322] Arbitrators

[321] See more: Komninos (n 137) 90–139; S Brammer, *Co-operation between National Competition Agencies in the Enforcement of EC Competition Law* (Hart Publishing, Oxford, 2009) 85–103.

[322] See Art 15(1) of Regulation 1/2003; Commission Notice on the Co-operation Between the Commission and the Courts of the EU Member States in the Application of Arts 81 and 82 EC *Official*

also may need information of a procedural nature from the Commission,[323] or may wish to consult the Commission on points of law where application of EU competition law causes them particular difficulties. Further, arbitral tribunals may want to obtain factual data (statistics, market studies and economic analyses), which might be contained in past or current merger or antitrust files. Can an arbitrator rely on Art 15(1) of Regulation 1/2003 and/or the Commission Notice,[324] if he needs to seek the support of the Commission in EU competition law cases?

According to Nazzini, the co-operation between arbitral tribunals and the Commission would be 'limited and based on mutually agreed practices rather than on any legislative provision'.[325] This statement has been justified by the submission that Art 15(1) of Regulation 1/2003 and the Commission Notice do not apply to arbitration. Nonetheless, it has been submitted that the 'soft law'[326] nature of the Commission Notice means that its mechanism could be used by arbitral tribunals.[327] It seems that arbitrators could seek the Commission's assistance in EU competition cases, and there is nothing to preclude arbitrators from seeking such assistance.[328] That said, it should be noted that, for the period from 1 May 2004 to 29 April 2009, the Commission provided its opinion to national courts in 18 cases only.[329] Furthermore, despite the fact that arbitrators may ask for assistance from the Commission, arbitrators are not bound to do so. An award misapplying EU competition law, though, will not be enforced by the national courts,[330] so that arbitrators aiming to render an enforceable award may wish to seek assistance from the Commission.

Another question could be whether the Commission should always provide assistance to arbitrators in EU competition law cases. The fact that arbitral tribunals are not mentioned in Art 15 of Regulation 1/2003 suggests that arbitrators are not entitled to receive assistance from the Commission. It seems that the discretion of the Commission when deciding whether to provide such assistance would

Journal [2004] OJ C101/54; Joined Cases C-174/98 P and C-189/98 P *Kingdom of the Netherlands and Gerard van der Wal v Commission* [2000] ECR I-1 [20]–[24]. See also Case C-234/89 *Stergios Delimitis v Henninger Brau* [1991] ECR I-935, 991. For implications of Art 4(3) of the Treaty on European Union, see PJ Slot, 'The Enforcement of EC Competition Law in Arbitral Proceedings' (1996) *Legal Issues of Economic Integration* 101, 105. See also: the Commission's *Explanatory Memorandum; XXX*th *Report on Competition Policy—2000* (Brussels, 2001) [57]; Dempegiotis (n 80).

[323] Eg whether a certain case is pending before the Commission.

[324] Commission (EC), 'Co-operation between the Commission and the courts of the EU Member States in the application of Articles 81 and 82 EC' (Notice) [2004] OJ C101/54.

[325] Nazzini (n 72) 336.

[326] See KC Wellens and GM Borchardt, 'Soft law in European Community law' (1989) 14 *EL Rev* 267.

[327] Komninos (n 107) 229. See also Slot (n 322) 105.

[328] See M Blessing, 'Introduction to Arbitration—Swiss and International Perspectives' in S Berti, *International Arbitration in Switzerland: An Introduction to and a Commentary of Article 176–194 of the Swiss Private International Law Statute* (Kluwer Law International, The Hague, 2000) 235; Komninos (n 174) 381–82; Nisser and Blanke (n 103) 181; Dempegiotis (n 80) 388–89.

[329] See Commission (EC), 'The functioning of Regulation 1/2003' (Report) COM (2009) 2006 final [35].

[330] See more section 7.5.5 above.

ensure that support will be sought only if it is really necessary. If the Commission were bound to provide assistance in arbitral proceedings, then it could have been used as a 'cheap' legal and economic adviser. Therefore, it will be entirely in the hands of the Commission whether to assist or not.

Most recently, a 'Draft Best Practice Note on the European Commission Acting as *Amicus Curiae* in International Arbitration Proceedings' was submitted for consideration to the ICC Task Force for Arbitrating Competition Law Issues.[331] However, one should not rely too much on the possibility of the Commission intervening in arbitral proceedings, in view of the fact that during the first five year of operation of Regulation 1/2003 the Commission submitted *amicus* observation in only two cases before Member State courts in which there was an imminent threat to the coherent application of EU competition rules.[332]

Thus, instead of relying on this possibility of seeking assistance from the Commission or submission of *amicus* observation by the Commission, the parties to disputes which may involve application of EU competition law issues and their lawyers should rather be very careful to select experienced arbitrators.[333]

7.6.2 Article 16 and its Relevance with Regard to Arbitral Proceedings

As already mentioned,[334] Art 16 of Regulation 1/2003 and the Commission Notice on co-operation addressed the problem of parallel proceedings between Member State courts and the Commission by adopting and developing the Court of Justice practice.[335] However, Art 16 of Regulation 1/2003 deals neither with parallel proceedings involving NCAs[336] nor with parallel proceedings involving arbitral tribunals. Although Art 16 does not refer to arbitration proceedings, commentators seem to agree that it should be applicable by analogy in arbitral proceedings in relation to EU competition law claims.[337] Accordingly, in this section, Art 16

[331] See summary of its major aspects: Nisser and Blanke (n 103).

[332] See 'The functioning of Regulation 1/2003' (Report) (n 329) [35]. See also Art 15(3) of Regulation 1/2003. See more on the possibility for the Commission to intervene in national court proceedings in S Brammer, *Co-operation between National Competition Agencies in the Enforcement of EC Competition Law* (Hart Publishing, Oxford, 2009) 46–48.

[333] Nazzini (n 72) 336–37; Nisser and Blanke (n 103) 179.

[334] See ch 6, section 6.2.5 above.

[335] *Delimitis* (n 322) [43]–[55] and [47]. See also: Case C-344/98 *Masterfoods v HB Ice Cream* [2000] ECR I-11369; A Arnull, *The European Union and its Court of Justice,* (OUP, Oxford, 1999) 411; Commission (EC), 'Co-operation between the Commission and the courts of the EU Member States in the application of Articles 81 and 82' (Notice) [2004] OJ C101/54 [11].

[336] As for the parallel proceedings between NCAs and Member State courts, which may result in irreconcilable decision, see chs 4 and 6 above.

[337] Komninos (n 107) 231–32; R Nazzini, 'International Arbitration and Public Enforcement of Competition Law' (2004) 25 *European Competition Law Review* 153, 161. See also: Nazzini (n 72) 352; Stylopoulos (n 300) 123.

will be examined as another means of guaranteeing that arbitration awards would not be irreconcilable with decisions of the Commission and of NCAs.

It has been held by the Court of Justice that where the Commission has already decided on a case, the Commission's decision cannot be invalidated by a national court.[338] Will an on-going arbitration be affected by parallel proceedings initiated by the Commission (or an NCA) and related to the same EU competition law infringement? In a recent case, the English court assumed that if the Commission decided to investigate an alleged breach of EU competition law, then an arbitral tribunal must stay the arbitration proceedings, since otherwise there would be a substantial overlap between the matters which fall to be determined in these two proceedings. The Court went further and pointed out that if an arbitration award is inconsistent with a later Commission decision, that award could be set aside.[339] Indeed, as already clarified,[340] the public policy character of EU competition law would prevent enforcement of an arbitral award that is in conflict with Arts 101 and/or 102 TFEU. Therefore, Art 16 of Regulation 1/2003 and the public policy character of EU competition law leave no doubt that it will be against English public policy if an arbitral award that is contrary to a Commission decision was allowed to stand on the ground of public policy.[341] This can be further reinforced by pointing out that the House of Lords recently held that under Art 16 the national courts are bound to avoid conflicting judgments with regard to 'agreements, decisions or practices' that are subject of a Commission decision.[342]

In other words, Art 16 of Regulation 1/2003 indicates that the court at the seat of arbitration should owe a duty to take all appropriate measures to set aside a domestic arbitral award that runs against a decision of the Commission and thus is in conflict with English public policy. In England, a party may challenge a domestic award under s 68(2)(g) of the 1996 Act.[343] Furthermore, Art 16 of Regulation 1/2003 also suggests that an English court should owe a duty to take all appropriate measures to deny recognition and enforcement of a foreign arbitral award that runs against a decision of the Commission and thus is in conflict with English public policy. Thus, such a foreign award should not be recognised under s 103(3) of the 1996 Act.[344] Thus, an arbitral award that runs counter to a Commission decision that will be rendered would be unenforceable after such a decision is ultimately adopted.

But how about arbitral awards that are in conflict with the OFT decision that is rendered with regard to the same EU competition law infringement? The problem of parallel antitrust proceedings taking place before an NCA and another Member

[338] Case 314/85 *Foto-Frost v Haptzollamt Lubeck-Ort* [1987] ECR 4199 [12]–[20].
[339] *Lauritzencool* (HC) (n 190). Compare Dalhuisen (n 169) 151.
[340] See more: section 7.5.5 above.
[341] Compare ch 6, sections 6.2.4 and 6.2.5 above.
[342] *Innterpreneur Pub Company v Crehan* [2006] UKHL 38 [64]–[66].
[343] See more: section 7.5.5.1 above.
[344] See more: section 7.5.5.2 above.

State's court has not been explicitly addressed by Art 16 of Regulation 1/2003. However, the EU legislators seem to be considering adoption of a rule to the effect that a Member State court cannot take decisions running counter to a final decision of an NCA in the ECN finding an infringement of Arts 101 and 102 TFEU.[345] That said, the fact that there was an OFT decision which was enforceable in England would suggest that an arbitral award which was in conflict with the OFT decision should not be allowed to stand on the ground of public policy. If such an award was not set aside, or if its recognition and enforcement were not denied, then there would be irreconcilable decisions having incompatible consequences on the same subject matter and between the same parties in the same jurisdiction. Indeed, the final decision of the OFT finding an infringement of Arts 101 and 102 TFEU could be seen as a strong prima facie evidence that the arbitral tribunal had manifestly disregarded EU competition law, and thus the arbitral award is against English public policy.[346]

Based on that, it can be concluded that an arbitrator must try to avoid rendering an award that may be in conflict with a Commission or an NCA decision, in order to fulfil his duty to 'make every effort to make sure that the award is enforceable at law'.[347] Indeed, an arbitral tribunal must be very careful when rendering an award on an agreement which may subsequently be the subject of a decision by an NCA or a decision by the Commission. Arbitrators should not render an arbitral award that could run counter to a contemplated NCA decision or a contemplated Commission decision, which is made in the context of the same EU competition law infringement. This would be so, despite the fact that Art 16 of the Regulation does not refer to arbitration or NCA decisions. As already mentioned, the English court would have the opportunity to review the award in setting aside proceedings (if rendered in England) or recognition and enforcement proceedings (if the seat of arbitration was outside England and Wales). Therefore, an English court would be bound not to uphold an arbitration award that was contrary to a decision of the OFT or a decision by the Commission.[348]

7.6.3 Concluding Remarks—Arbitration and the Mechanisms under Regulation 1/2003

In any event, it can be concluded that the lack of special institutional support by the Commission and the Court of Justice could not be an argument against arbitrability of EU competition laws in England. Indeed, the public policy character of Arts 101 and 102 TFEU and the provisions of the 1996 Act indicate that an arbitral award which misapplies EU competition would be set aside by the English courts.

[345] White Paper on Damages actions (n 8) [2.3].

[346] Compare ch 6, section 6.2.5 above.

[347] Eg Art 32(2) of the London Court of International Arbitration Rules; Art 35 of the ICC Rules of Arbitration. See also Stylopoulos (n 300) 119.

[348] Nazzini (n 72) 352–53.

In this context, the courts may also seek assistance by the Court of Justice and the Commission which would ensure the consistent application of EU antitrust law in the EU. Hence, the arbitral tribunals must be very careful to avoid rendering awards which conflict with those taken or envisaged by the Commission or an NCA applying EU competition law with regard to the same infringement. This is due to the fact that the consistent application of Arts 101 and 102 TFEU by arbitrators will be further scrutinised in setting aside procedures and/or recognition and enforcement procedure. In other words, it appears that the English courts would have a last say and should determine whether EU antitrust law claims have been properly addressed by the arbitral tribunal applying Arts 101 and 102 TFEU, since enforcement of arbitral awards in England is through them and the court must deny enforcement of an award that is in conflict with EU competition law.

7.7 Conclusion

In the absence of an express EU law provision precluding arbitrability of Arts 101 and 102 TFEU, there are very strong arguments supporting the view that due to the principle of procedural autonomy the question of arbitrability of EU competition law provisions is left to be determined by the individual Member States subject to principles of effectiveness and equivalence. A reference to the national legal systems plainly disclosed that the ability to arbitrate competition law is no longer seriously challenged in the majority of the Member States.

Under English law there are very few restrictions on the types of dispute which are arbitrable. The general arbitrability of EU competition law has been recently confirmed by the English High Court. Moreover, in another judgment it has been held that the question of arbitrability in English law must be determined by considerations similar to those deployed by the US Supreme Court in the *Mitsubishi* case. In this case it was clearly held that antitrust claims are arbitrable. The US Court went further and outlined that there is no reason to assume that international arbitration would not provide an adequate mechanism for awarding damages (including punitive damages) in antitrust claims. This leaves no doubt that an arbitral tribunal based in England has jurisdiction to apply EU competition law. Furthermore, arbitrators are entitled to rule over claims for damages arising out of a breach of Arts 101 and/or 102 TFEU, provided the parties' arbitration agreement was sufficiently wide to encompass the determination of antitrust damages claims as well. Furthermore, an arbitral tribunal sitting in England would have the power to apply US antitrust law and award triple damages, provided the competition law disputes was closely connected with the US.

In spite of the arbitration agreement and the fact that the arbitrator has jurisdiction, the English courts might be called for support with regard to arbitral proceedings. Indeed, there may well be competition cases, where arbitrators called to apply EU competition law would need assistance from English courts, in order to take interim measures, collect evidence and make preliminary reference to the Court of Justice. Although that form of assistance applies irrespective of the peculiarities of EU competition law, it will be of importance to the uniform and efficient private antitrust enforcement.

Because of the public policy character of Arts 101 and 102 TFEU, and for the purposes of enforcing an arbitration award, the English courts would be entitled to review an award in an action for setting aside a domestic award or recognition and enforcement of a foreign award in relation to EU competition law claims in order to determine whether the public policy defence is met. The illegality of contracts in conflict with Arts 101 and 102 would allow the English court to inquire into the applicability of EU competition law with regard to the underlying contract even if the arbitral tribunal had dealt with it. The test that is to be applied by the English courts in this respect is whether there is prima facie evidence from one side that the award is based on a contract that is in conflict with Arts 101 and/or 102 TFEU. Therefore, it should be outlined that national courts would have a last say and should determine whether claims under EU competition law have been properly addressed by the arbitral tribunal.

8

Conclusion

8.1 Concluding Remarks

The current private antitrust enforcement regime appears to assume that private international law should be relevant to cross-border private EU competition law actions. As English traditional rules can satisfactorily allocate jurisdiction in cross-border private EU competition law actions brought against a defendant who is not domiciled in a Member State, it would seem that no reform is needed. Although the English common law doctrines of *forum conveniens* and *forum non-conveniens* are more complicated than the Brussels I rules, they seem to be better suited not only for allocating jurisdiction to courts which have a close connection with the substance of a private dispute arising under EU competition law, but also when dealing with the problems of parallel antitrust proceedings and forum shopping.

Under English common law rules, it is not simply a question of finding the basis of jurisdiction in respect of a foreign defendant, it also has to be determined whether the English court will exercise its discretionary powers to stay the action. This could provide sufficient guarantee that an English court would not accept jurisdiction over an antitrust dispute unless it was well placed to hear and determine an EU competition law claim/s. Furthermore, the English court will have wider powers in regard to foreign judgments rendered by courts from outside the EU, as the answer to the question of whether an error of interpretation of EU competition law is capable of violating English public policy at common law is not confined by the aim and narrow interpretation of the provisions of the Brussels I Regulation. This outcome is satisfactory in view of the fact that foreign courts could not avail themselves of the preventive and corrective mechanisms which are provided to guarantee the proper interpretation and application of EU law by the Member States' courts, and it would certainly provide for coherent and uniform application of EU competition law within the EU.

However, problems may arise in cases where jurisdiction is derived from the Brussels I Regulation, which would be the majority of cases that would arise in the European context. The architects of the decentralisation reform have largely ignored the question of how the post-2003 policy of the European Union, favouring private law enforcement of EU competition law, can be implemented the current private international regime. A thorough analysis of the EU private international law framework in the context of private EU competition law claims appears to indicate that the European civil justice system is not well suited to those purposes. More specifically, complicated jurisdictional issues arise with regard to the allocation of EU competition law-related claims brought between parties to a contract that is allegedly void due to a conflict with Arts 101 and 102 TFEU. It is also questionable how the multiple proceedings and the problem of forum shopping before the Member States' courts will be avoided if private EU competition law claims are brought under the Brussels I Regulation. Moreover, problems would arise in view of the fact that such issues as the available remedies for breach and assessment of antitrust damages are not dealt with at EU level, which suggests that Rome II is to be employed in order to determine the scope of the defendant's liability and what a plaintiff would be entitled to recover. The fact that punitive damages may be available in some Member States, but not in others, indicates that different courts could award different amount of damages with regard to the very same type of breach of the very same EU competition law provision. The problems would be exacerbated by the *Renault* ruling, which indicates that despite the fact that EU competition law rules enjoy public policy character for the purposes of recognition and enforcement of foreign judgments, a Member State court would not necessarily refuse recognition and enforcement of a Member State judgment that misapplies Arts 101 and 102 TFEU. Furthermore, given the enforcement activities of the European Commission and NCAs, potentially difficult problems will arise in competition law cases as previously unavailable evidence of illegal behaviour may come to light at the recognition and enforcement stage. The question of whether the recognising court will be allowed to deny recognition of a foreign judgment, in which the court with original jurisdiction had misapplied and/or disregarded EU competition law, is bound to arise in the context of private antitrust enforcement.

8.2 Reforming the Brussels I Framework

The foregoing chapters indicate that some provisions of the Brussels I Regulation are not well suited to allocating jurisdiction in EU competition law claims, and deal with the challenge of parallel antitrust proceedings. It may be left to the courts to struggle with the problem of applying the rules relevant to jurisdiction and judgments in relation to EU competition law claims. This approach would allow the national courts to use their right to refer to the Court of Justice for preliminary rulings. The advantage of this solution is that more flexible solutions, compatible with the interests of business, could be created through legal practice. There are, however, two main drawbacks that are inherent to such an approach. First, it will be difficult for the courts to deal with the problems that are due to the failings of the Brussels I Regulation, which contains provisions requiring legislative modifications. Secondly, if the jurisdictional problems were left to be solved by the courts, then the price of promoting private antitrust enforcement would have to be paid by the private litigants. Such a solution, however, would not be in line with the Commission policy seeking incentives for increasing the number of private EU competition law claims.

This indicates that another approach to addressing these problematic issues is due at EU level. The deduction that such a reform is needed is strengthened by the recently published Green Paper.[1] One option to deal with the private international law problems in relation to EU competition law claims is to use the current Brussels I framework, after making some amendments. In this context, the EU rules relevant to jurisdiction and judgments in relation to EU competition law claims may be modified by the working group involved in the ongoing programme of proposed reform concerning the Brussels I Regulation. This working group may come up with an agenda for a reform of EU jurisdiction and judgments rules that inter alia could be set to encourage private antitrust enforcement in Europe. However, a major drawback of this solution is that in many cases the provisions proposed by such a working group could be the result of compromises. In view of that, a legislative modification may be made to tackle some of the problems indicated in the foregoing chapters. Other problematic issues may be left to be dealt with by the courts. Such an attitude will result in more flexible solutions, which will avoid frequent revisions of the Brussels I Regulation that will call for certainty with regard to jurisdiction in commercial law disputes. Thus, on the basis of the identified problems in the foregoing chapters, some proposals, which promise to facilitate private antitrust law enforcement in Europe and reduce its cost, will be suggested below.

8.2.1 Amending Jurisdictional Rules

Whilst a claim for breach of EU competition law brought by a third party against parties to a contract that allegedly distorts competition is to be characterised as tortious for jurisdictional purposes,[2] difficulties are bound to arise with regard to characterisation of the nature of the EU competition law claims brought by contracting parties. Those problems are likely to arise particularly sharply where an antitrust damages claim is brought by a contracting party together with a claim seeking nullity of an agreement that is alleged to be in conflict with EU competition law. The current law suggests that the English court will have jurisdiction under Art 5(1) of Brussels I with regard to an EU competition law claim seeking nullity of a contract that is in conflict with Arts 101 and 102 TFEU. There is, however, some uncertainty concerning the jurisdiction of English courts under the Brussels I Regulation in cases where a claim for EU competition law damages is made by a contracting party. This is a problem, because the dispute about how the

[1] Commission (EC), 'Review of Regulation 44/2001' (Green Paper) COM (2009) 175 final.
[2] See ch 2.

principle of severance of illegal provisions from otherwise lawful agreements is to affect the parties' contract would be contractual in nature,[3] whereas the question of causation and quantum in a private antitrust damages claim would be tortious in nature.[4] There are two solutions that may be considered by the working group set to modify the Brussels I Regulation. Both of them would entitle the same court to apply civil sanctions of nullity to a contractual relationship, and rule on an antitrust damages claim.

The first one is to include a sub-s (d) in Art 5(1). The new sub-section may to the effect that 'Article 5(1) shall cover a claim framed technically in tort provided that there is a sufficiently close connection between that claim and the contract.' Such a provision would mean that Art 5(1) would channel all EU competition law claims brought by a contracting party.[5] This solution would be in line with what can currently be done with regard to consumer claims brought under s 4 of Chapter II of Brussels. More specifically, Art 15 could be interpreted as allocating jurisdiction in an action based on contract and tort as long as the tortious claims are closely related to the claim which is based on a contract concluded by a consumer. The rationale is for Arts 15 and 16 of Brussels I to enable the consumer to bring all claims arising out of a contract before the same court 'in order to avoid, in so far as possible, creating a situation in which a number of courts had jurisdiction in respect of one and the same contract.'[6] In other words, the Court of Justice seems to endorse the one-stop adjudication doctrine in respect of claims arising out of consumer contracts. Similar solutions may be adopted with regard to tort-based EU competition law claims brought by a contracting party.

Alternatively, another option may be even more preferable for the working group. According to it, another sentence or a new sub-s (b) may be added in Art 5(3) of Brussels I. The text would state that 'a tortious claim brought by a contracting party shall be regarded as covered by Article 5(3) of Brussels I, notwithstanding the existence of an incidental contractual issue over the validity of the contract.' Such a solution would not only be in accord with the common law approach, but will also avoid the need for determining which contractual obligation is alleged to be in breach of EU competition law. If that solution were adopted, then it would be left to the court to resolve the complex jurisdictional issues that are likely to arise in respect of locating the place of the event giving rise to damages and the place where the damage occurred for the purposes of

[3] R Whish *Competition Law* (6th edn, OUP, Oxford, 2008) 313. See also: A Komninos, *EC Private Antitrust Enforcement: Decentralised Application of EC Competition Law by National Courts* (Hart Publishing, Oxford, 2008) 156–57; U Bernitz, 'The sanction of voidness under Article 82 EC' in A Ezrachi (ed), *Article 82 EC: Reflections on its Recent Evolution* (Hart Publishing, Oxford, 2009) 187, 190–91. See more ch 5.

[4] See more ch 5.

[5] *Kalfelis* (n 37) [31] (AG Darmon). See also the opinion of AG Darmon in Case C-89/91 *Shearson Lehman Hutton* [1993] ILPr 199, 217.

[6] Case C-180/06 *Ilsinger v Martin Dreschers (acting as administrator in the insolvency of Schlank & Schick GmbH* [2009] ECR I-0000, 14 May 2009 [44].

allocating jurisdiction in EU competition law claims.[7] The court will be free to regard the place where the agreement is implemented (or intended to be implemented) as the place of the event giving rise to damage for the purposes of allocating jurisdiction in EU competition law claims under Art 5(3) of Brussels I. The analysis shows that the place where the agreement is implemented (being the place of the event giving rise to antitrust damage) will often overlap with the place where the harmful event directly produced its effects (being the place where the antitrust damage occurred).

However, if the first approach (being more in line with the civil law doctrine) were adopted and Art 5(1) had channelled all EU competition law claims brought by a contracting party, then the working group would have to look into the definitions provided in Art 5(1)(b) which might give rise to further difficulties in antitrust cases. First of all, it must be made clear in the recital of the modified Brussels I Regulation that Art 5(1)(b) shall apply in cases where obligations are complex and distribution agreements may be given as a particular example. Such a solution would be in line with the Services Directive.[8] Moreover, it will maximise the effect of the changes made by the Brussels I Regulation, avoiding complicated legal analyses that were made with regard to distribution agreements under the Brussels Convention. It will further prevent allocation of jurisdiction to courts that have little connection with the dispute. This is a necessity, in view of the lack of any provision in the Brussels I Regulation that entitles a national court to decline jurisdiction. Secondly, a welcome development could also be an addition to Art 5(1)(b) that specifies that the place of performance of the obligation in question shall be in the case of the technology transfer agreements in a Member State where, under the licence the rights over specific processes, formulae or manufacturing technology (patent or non-patent) are exercised. Such a provision would make Art 5(1) more relevant for a licensee who wishes to bring an antitrust claim in his home state under a contract that is contrary to EU competition law. Moreover, the proposed text would confer jurisdiction on courts that have a close connection with the substance of the competition law dispute and indeed the relevant market in EU competition law claims in relation to technology transfer agreements.

It was seen that the existing jurisdictional rules in Arts 2, 5 and 6 of Brussels I give wide bases for jurisdiction of Member States' courts in EU competition law cases. Articles 27 and 28 of Brussels I would not be capable of putting an end to the multiplicity of courts able to hear antitrust claims related to one and the same contract. There are two main concerns that might be addressed by the working group in this respect.

First, it would be advisable for it to be clarified that all NCAs should be regarded as 'courts' for the purposes of Arts 27 and 28 of Brussels I, as long as

[7] See ch 3.

[8] Directive 2006/123/EC on services in the internal market OJ [2006] L376/36.

they are bodies exercising judicial functions in civil and commercial matters. Therefore, it would seem that proceedings in which NCAs seek to determine whether an undertaking (or undertakings) has committed an infringement of Arts 101 and 102 TFEU should be within the scope of Brussels I. This would serve to avoid the risk of irreconcilable decisions being rendered on the same antitrust issue in two different Member States by different bodies (an NCA and a court) that are responsible for EU competition law enforcement.

However, this would not solve all problems, as the wide bases for jurisdiction with regard to EU competition law claims under the Brussels I Regulation indicate that, in the context of such disputes, the claimant often would have a choice between two or more forums, in which to proceed against the defendant. This may result in parallel proceedings and may also provide for a considerable scope for forum shopping in the European context. Accordingly, another major concern is to do with the fact that the Brussels I Regulation does not deal satisfactorily with the problem of parallel proceedings and forum shopping.[9] One way to avoid parallel proceedings and to stop forum shopping is to have a special basis for jurisdiction which requires a substantial connection with the forum in antitrust law claims. The problem with this solution is that EU competition law claims may arise in many contexts (eg they can be brought by third parties, or by contracting parties as main claims or counter-claims; often they involve more than two parties and infringements in several Member States) and not surprisingly this is not the method adopted in the EU. Articles 27 and 28 are designed to deal with the multiplicity of law suits before the Member States' courts. The assumption, however, is that the court first seised is always more appropriate.[10] However, it may often be the case that the court first seised is not well placed to hear and determine an EU competition law case because an anti-competitive agreement or practice, which has been implemented in a number of Member States, does not affect the market in the Member State where the action is brought. It is unfortunate that jurisdiction in such cases would depend on the issue of who is faster in lodging his claim.

A more satisfactory result could be reached if the court first seised was entitled to decline jurisdiction in cases where agreement or practice has no substantial direct (actual or foreseeable) effects on competition within the Member State.[11] The advantages of an approach which links the court's jurisdiction with the effects on competition within a country's territory could be demonstrated by the US Supreme Court ruling in the *Empagran* case.[12] The problem is that the American

[9] See ch 4 and ch 5, section 5.4.2.

[10] See ch 4.

[11] Compare the European approach in respect of allocation of cases between the NCAs. See Commission (EC), 'Cooperation within the Network of Competition Authorities' (Notice) OJ [2004] C101/43 [8].

[12] See *F Hoffmann-La Roche Ltd v Empagran* (2004) 542 US 155, 167; 124 SCt 2359 (Sup Ct (US)). Although the *Empagran* case did not entirely and absolutely eliminate the problem of forum shopping, it may be used as an example of how the problem of forum shopping could be dealt with in some cases.

experience is impossible to follow in the European context, because the Brussels I Regulation precludes a court of a Member State from declining the jurisdiction conferred on it by the Regulation.

However, the principle of mutual trust between the legal systems within the EU may suggest that the time is ripe for a change in the attitude. A provision which would allow a Member State to decline jurisdiction in a case where an allegedly anti-competitive agreement or practice has no substantial direct (actual or foreseeable) effects on competition within the Member State *if and only if* there is another Member State court well placed to hear and determine the case, could (and should) be considered by the EU legislator. In other words, a Member State court could be allowed to decline jurisdiction: (1) if it is a court which is not well placed to hear and determine an EU competition law case; and (2) if there is another Member State court (or even an NCA, assuming that a broader interpretation of court was adopted) that is well placed to deal with the case in question. Such a provision would ensure that a Member State court which is well placed to deal with a case would not be allowed to decline jurisdiction even if it is alleged that there is another Member State court which is better placed to hear and determine the EU antitrust claims. Thus, this would be a mechanism which is meant to guarantee that each EU competition law case would be allocated to a forum which is well placed to deal with it.[13] This is indeed something that is already done in Europe in the context of allocation of EU competition cases between NCAs (which are bodies exercising judicial functions as well) in the ECN. Such a provision would not confer a broad discretionary power and would be a welcome move towards tackling the problems of parallel proceedings and forum shopping in EU competition law claims brought under the Brussels I Regulation. Moreover, such a rule would be an important addition to an instrument that is set to allocate jurisdiction between 27 Member States and lays down such wide bases for jurisdiction in those courts.

8.2.2 Proposals with Regard to Recognition and Enforcement of Foreign Judgments

Another specific issue that could potentially arise in the context of recognition and enforcement of foreign judgments in relation to EU competition law claims relates to the question of whether the decisions of NCAs are to be regarded as 'judgments' for recognition and enforcement purposes. There are strong arguments to the effect that Arts 1 and 32 of Brussels I should be interpreted as suggesting that a decision (or part of a decision) of an NCA in the ECN, which

[13] This is indeed something that is already done in Europe in the context of allocation of EU competition cases between NCAs (which are bodies exercising judicial functions as well) in the ECN. See Commission (EC) 'Cooperation within the Network of Competition Authorities' (Notice) OJ [2004] C101/43 [8]. See more: Brammer (n 2) 155–61.

establishes an infringement of Arts 101 and 102 TFEU, should be within the scope of Brussels I as being related to a civil or commercial matter. Nevertheless, it may still be a welcome development if the revised version of Regulation 44/2001 explicitly provided that 'judgment' in Art 32 of Brussels I would include a final decision of any NCA exercising judicial functions, as long as it is a decision which is related to civil and commercial matters. Alternatively, the problem might be left to be dealt with by the courts that may interpret Art 32 broadly in the context of Art 1 of Brussels I.

Although, EU competition law enjoys a public policy character, a foreign judgment, which misapplies EU competition law though enjoying a public policy character, is not *ipso facto* contrary to English public policy under the Brussels I Regulation.[14] Indeed, in antitrust cases where the court with original jurisdiction has ruled on EU competition law, the recognising court will be precluded from reviewing the conclusion of the foreign court. In other words, the ruling of the Court of Justice in *Renault*[15] leaves no doubt that the English court should not refuse recognition and enforcement of a foreign judgment in which EU competition law had been misapplied by another Member State court. However, it could be argued that there is a distinction between the case where the original court had wrongfully applied Arts 101 and 102 TFEU and the scenario where the original court had not applied EU competition law at all. Different considerations would apply in cases where the defendant proves that there is new evidence which proves that EU competition law has been manifestly disregarded by the court with original jurisdiction. Such evidence may well come to light after a decision from the European Commission or NCAs has been rendered. In such cases, recognition could be denied if: (1) there was evidence that EU competition law was manifestly disregarded; (2) there was no possibility for the defendant to bring fresh proceedings alleging a manifest infringement of EU competition law before the courts of the Member State where the judgment is rendered; and (3) in similar circumstances a challenge of an English judgment would be permitted. If an English judgment may be set aside on the basis of new evidence that would have had a material effect upon the decision of the court, there is no good reason why a foreign judgment should be treated more favourably.

The long-term objective of the European Union to abolish the public policy exception for all judgments in civil and commercial matters should not yet be fulfilled in relation to private enforcement of competition law (unless private parties were allowed to make an appeal against a Member State court's judgment on a point of EU law before the Court of First Instance). There are at least two good reasons for that. First, there is a risk that some of the new Member States may be unable to correctly apply EU law unless they achieve irreversible progress on their judicial reforms. Secondly, in spite of the mechanisms envisaged by Regulation

[14] See ch 6.
[15] *Renault* (n 4).

1/2003, the judges in some of the new Member States lack experience in dealing with complicated antitrust laws. Although antitrust acts in those states have mirrored the western model, they ignored the specific features of the socialist heritage and lack the decades of experience in applying those rules.

Under current law there are very strong arguments suggesting that due to the public policy character of EU competition law it will be against English public policy to recognise a foreign judgment that is contrary to a decision of the Commission. This is so under the English traditional rules and the EU rules as well. That can be deduced from Art 4(3) TEU and Art 16 of Regulation 1/2003. The English court should not recognise a foreign judgment, if it is inconsistent with a previous decision of the Commission on the same subject matter between the same parties. If such a Commission decision was not before the adjudicating court, it should be viewed as a highly persuasive prima facie evidence that the court with original jurisdiction misapplied EU competition law. Recognising a foreign judgment that is in conflict with a Commission decision that is related to EU competition law would undermine legal authority, leaving parties in doubt as to where they stand, and would infringe the integrity of the EU legal order. It can be proposed that a revision of the Commission Notice on co-operation with national courts addresses the issue of recognition and enforcement of foreign judgments in relation to antitrust claims that are in conflict with a Commission decision on the same subject matter and between the same parties.

Unfortunately, in the Green Paper there is no indication that special jurisdictional bases for competition law actions in the successor to Regulation 44/2001 are on the agenda. Another possibility for a reform is setting up a new EU law on civil procedure with regard to EU competition law claims only. Before discussing this possibility, some proposals as to how the available and applicable remedies should be identified in the context of breach of EU competition law claims.

8.3 Addressing the Issue of Available Antitrust Damages and their Assessment at EU level

A recent study has presented the various methods and models which can be used in quantifying the antitrust damage.[16] In the absence of unified practice throughout the EU, different Member States could employ different methodology as to quantification of antitrust damages. Although it seems that in the context of assessment of damages the EU is moving towards non-binding guidance for the courts, the question of what remedies would be available in tort-based

[16] Oxera and multi-jurisdictional team of lawyers led by Dr A Komninos, 'Quantifying antitrust damages: towards non-binding guidance for courts—Study prepared for the European Commission' http://ec.europa.eu/competition/antitrust/actionsdamages/quantification_study.pdf.

EU competition law actions is left to be dealt with by domestic legal orders of individual Member States.

Traditionally, the common law makes a distinction between rights, which are to be governed by *lex causae*, and their enforcement, which is to be governed by *lex fori*. Although Art 15(c) of Rome II declares that *lex causae* governs 'the assessment of damages or remedy claimed', Recital 32 of Rome II read together with Art 6(3)(b) of Rome II indicates that the law of the forum may continue to play an important role with regard to the issue of available remedies because exemplary (or punitive) damage may be available in some Member States. Indeed, it was demonstrated that there could be different outcomes if exemplary or punitive antitrust damages are pleaded, as they may be available in one Member State but not in another. Thus, if the issue of available remedies was left to be dealt with by domestic law, which is to be identified by reference to Rome II, antitrust claimants from different Member States may be awarded different amount of damages for the very same breach of EU competition law. Thus, a non-binding guidance for courts may not be enough to provide for coherent and uniform application of EU competition law throughout the EU.

This leaves no doubt that the EU legislator should carefully consider whether the issues regarding the available remedies and assessment of antitrust damages should be dealt with under Rome II (as it is currently) or rather should provide for more uniformity at EU level. A reform can be enacted through the private antitrust enforcement initiative.[17] Such legislation might limit the effect of Recital 32 by providing for a right for private antitrust claimants to be punitive, so that an award of punitive damages would not be contrary to public policy per se.

8.4 Is there a Need for a Special Regulation dealing with EU Competition Law Claims?

Although it is justifiable to employ private international law when allocating jurisdiction and identifying the applicable law in cross-border private EU competition law actions brought against defendants who are not domiciled in a Member State, it might be questioned whether the EU should use the current EU private international law framework with regard to EU competition law brought in the European context. Given the fact that in the Green Paper there is no indication that special jurisdictional bases for competition law actions in the successor to Regulation 44/2001 are on anyone's agenda, another possibility for a reform may be setting up a new EU law on civil procedure with regard to EU competition law claims

[17] The European Community certainly has competence to do that. See more: F Rizzuto, 'Does the European Community have legal competence to harmonise national procedural rules governing private actions for damages for infringements of European Community antitrust rules' (2009) *Global Competition Litigation Review* 29.

only. Indeed, such a way forward might be justifiable in view of the fact that Arts 101 and 102 TFEU, forming part of each Member State's legal order, are at the heart of an EU competition law claim, so that the use of private international law in cross-border private antitrust proceedings may be questioned. Should the EU use the private international law in claims that are directly based on substantive EU competition law rules which are harmonised at EU level? It has been submitted that '[t]he purpose of [Brussels I, Rome I and Rome II] is clearly the unification of private international law, not the harmonisation of the substantive laws of the Member States, on which it may be more difficult to reach agreement.'[18] Therefore, the EU legislator may wish to consider whether the EU should use the current EU private international law framework in respect of EU competition law claims, or rather set up a Special Regulation dealing with antitrust proceedings arising in the European context.

A Special Regulation could provide for allocation of cases which would ensure that a well-placed court would be entitled to deal with an EU competition law claim—something which is not done under the current version of Brussels I. This is particularly important in view of the fact that an EU competition law infringement would normally affect (small and medium-sized) businesses and consumers in several countries, who may bring parallel antitrust proceedings in different Member States. This would contribute to a closer judicial cooperation by Member States courts in private claims based on breach of Arts 101 and 102 TFEU which would improve the daily life of consumers and businesses throughout the EU. Furthermore, avoiding such parallel proceedings would further promote the coherent and uniform application of EU competition law rules. A Special Regulation could also try to avoid the possibility for the different Member State courts to award different amount of damages with regard to the very same type of breach of the very same EU competition law provision.[19]

Such a Special Regulation could (and probably should) go a step further and guarantee the abolition of the exequatur with regard to judgments in relation to Arts 101 and 102 TFEU by envisaging a possibility for the parties to make an appeal on a point of EU competition law before the Court of First Instance. This would provide for uniform application of EU law throughout the EU by generating a growing body of EU case law in the field of private EU antitrust law enforcement.

[18] A Mills, *The Confluence of Public and Private International Law* (CUP, Cambridge, 2009) 185. See also Council of the European Union, 'The Hague Programme: strengthening freedom, security and justice in the European Union' http://ec.europa.eu/justice_home/doc_centre/doc/hague_programme_en.pdf 31.

[19] The analysis above clearly suggests that leaving the questions of where a private antitrust plaintiff can litigate, and what damages he could recover, to be dealt with under Brussels I and Rome II may give (small and medium-sized) businesses and consumers across the EU a different level of redress and protection which would largely depend on where the action is first brought. See also: Commission (EC), 'Consumer Collective Redress' (Green Paper) COM (2008) 794 final [22].

There appears to be a need for an empirical study, targeted at policy makers, to establish whether there is a case for changing the civil justice framework in Europe with regard to claims based on Arts 101 and 102 TFEU. To this end the following questions need to be addressed at EU level: should the private international law framework be used to implement the post-2003 policy of the European Union favouring private enforcement of EU competition law? Should there be a special Regulation dealing with private EU competition law actions? Should there be a possibility for an appeal to be made by private parties on a point of EU competition law before the Court of First Instance?

It seems to this author that research is needed and can be motivated by several factors. First, the fact that there are 27 Member States with different legal, political and businesses heritages may require a more direct mechanism that would guarantee uniform and coherent application of the EU competition law provisions. Indeed, the report on the functioning of Regulation 1/2003 seems to suggest that the current mechanisms are not efficient in this respect.[20] Secondly, there is the need for the EU to further encourage private enforcement of EU law.[21] Thirdly, the fact that Brussels I and Art 6(3)(b) of Rome II read together with Recital 32 of Rome II suggest that a private antitrust law claimant in Europe could be awarded different amount of damages for the very same breach of Arts 101 and 102 TFEU, depending on whether, for example, the action is brought in England (where punitive antitrust damages are available) or Germany (where they are not available).

[20] See Commission (EC), 'The functioning of Regulation 1/2003' (Report) COM (2009) 206 final.

[21] See Commission (EC), 'Damages Actions for Breach of the EC Antitrust Rules' (White Paper) COM (2008) 165 final.

INDEX